THE MODERN PRESIDENCY

FIFTH EDITION

James P. Pfiffner
George Mason University

THOMSON
WADSWORTH

Australia • Brazil • Canada • Mexico • Singapore • Spain
United Kingdom • United States

THOMSON
✳ ™
WADSWORTH

The Modern Presidency, Fifth Edition
James P. Pfiffner

Publisher: Michael Rosenberg
Editorial Assistant: Megan Garvey
Marketing Manager: Karin Sandberg
Marketing Assistant: Teresa Jessen
Marketing Communications Manager:
  Brian Chaffee
Project Manager, Editorial Production:
  Christy Krueger
Creative Director: Rob Hugel
Art Director: Maria Epes
Print Buyer: Nora Massuda

Permissions Editor: Roberta Broyer
Production Service: ICC Macmillan Inc./
  Charu Khanna
Photo Researcher: Laura Molmud
Copy Editor: Richard Camp
Cover Designer: Sue Hart
Cover Image: Michael Melford/Getty Images
Cover Printer: Thomson West
Compositor: ICC Macmillan Inc.
Printer: Thomson West

Library of Congress Control Number:
2006938704

ISBN-13: 978-0-495-18994-7
ISBN-10: 0-495-18994-4

Thomson Higher Education
10 Davis Drive
Belmont, CA 94002-3098
USA

For more information about our products,
contact us at:
Thomson Learning Academic Resource Center
1-800-423-0563
For permission to use material from this text
or product, submit a request online at
http://www.thomsonrights.com.
Any additional questions about permissions
can be submitted by e-mail to
thomsonrights@thomson.com.

For E. John Pfiffner:
godfather, uncle, artist, friend
and for Morgan Meehan Pfiffner, my son

CONTENTS

Preface

In 1933, Franklin Roosevelt had only a few aides to help him draft and shepherd into law his famous "100 Days" legislative agenda. In 2007, there were more than 400 people in the White House Office, 1,850 in the Executive Office of the President (which includes the White House Office), with a total of almost 5,000 serving the president and the White House more broadly. In the 1930s, there were fewer than 150 presidential appointees to manage the executive branch. In 2007, there were more than 600 (plus 3,000 more political appointees). In the 1930s and 1940s, the aides to the president were most often generalists. In the 1990s, the presidency comprised a plethora of complex bureaucracies filled with specialists.

This book was written to try to explain how the presidency got from there to here. As an introduction to the presidency, it does not attempt to describe or explain all aspects of the office. Rather, its purpose is to focus on the transformation of the presidency from a small group of advisers to a large collection of bureaucracies supporting the president. Thus, the emphasis is not so much on the president as a person but on all of the supporting people and institutions, what some have called the "presidential branch," to distinguish it from the rest of the executive branch over which the president presides. But the executive branch is a hierarchy accountable to the president, who plays the executive role in the constitutional separation of powers system.

In analyzing the transformation of the modern presidency, the book considers the changes in the nomination/election process as the citizenry has become more involved through primary elections. The president's relationship to the public has also been transformed through sophisticated presidential use of modern communications technology. When the president speaks publicly, the words are instantaneously broadcast throughout the world.

The book is based on the premise that organization, advisers, and institutions make a difference. If the presidency is well organized, the president is more likely to be successful. Poor administration can lead to blunders or disaster. A separate chapter is devoted to organizing the White House staff and the crucial role of the chief of staff in the modern presidency. Essential jobs for the president, such as making political appointments or liaison with Congress, began with the president designating one person to be the primary adviser. But these seedlings of organization have now grown into well-established bureaucratic units that are central to the operation of the presidency in the twenty-first century. The book traces the institutionalization of White House functions in the Executive Office of the President and explains the gradual replacement of cabinet secretaries by White House staffers as the primary advisers to the president.

Over the decades of the 20th century, the pendulum of constitutional power vis-à-vis Congress has swung back and forth. After the "Imperial Presidency" of the Johnson and Nixon years, Congress reasserted its own institutional prerogatives in the 1970s. The Reagan and George H. W. Bush administrations began a reassertion of presidential primacy. With the takeover of Congress by the Republicans in 1995, Congress began to push its own priorities, culminating in the impeachment of President Clinton in 1998. But when President George W. Bush took office, with the Republican Congress willing to do his bidding, presidential domination of the policy process reappeared. President Bush and his administration, especially after 9/11, self-consciously asserted presidential prerogatives through the commander-in-chief power, signing statements, and political control of the executive branch. Two chapters deal with presidential relations with Congress and examine more and less effective ways to promote the president's agenda in the domestic and national security arenas. Case studies present concrete, historical examples of presidential action in dealing with Congress and national security crises.

Finally, the problems of abuse of power and presidential reputation are considered. The modern presidency has seen disturbing instances of over-reaching by presidents; Watergate, Iran-Contra, and President Clinton's impeachment are three examples of crises in the presidency that were internally generated. That is, they did not originate from external "enemies" of the president but rather from inside the presidency itself. The final chapter examines these controversies as well as the question of presidential reputation and how it often fluctuates with changing historical circumstances.

This book has benefited from the generosity of others. I would like to thank Don Reisman, who originally proposed the idea to me, for his enthusiasm and encouragement. Thanks also to Ron Geisler, executive clerk to the president from 1982 to 1994, and his staff for helping me to understand the operation of the presidency, particularly the appointments process. Tim Saunders succeeded his former boss, Ron Geisler, as executive clerk to the president and generously continued to provide me with authoritative data on the presidency and the White House.

For helpful advice on this and earlier editions of this book, I would like to thank several colleagues: James Carter, Robert Cleary, Timothy Conlan, Christopher Deering, Robert Dudley, George Edwards, Hugh Heclo, Gary

Jacobson, Scott Keeter, Sam Kernell, Bruce Oppenheimer, Priscilla Regan, Barbara Sinclair, Colleen Shogan, and Katie Dunn Tenpas. The fourth edition of this book was reviewed by John D. Lees of Oakland University and Joseph K. Unekis of Kansas State University, and I would like to thank them for their insightful comments. I am grateful to Thomas Mann, Director of Governmental Studies at the Brookings Institution, who found an office for me as a Guest Scholar while I was on leave from George Mason and working on this book. Brookings was a congenial place for me to work; and my colleagues there provided helpful advice and intellectual stimulation: Sarah Binder, Chris Foreman, Jacob Hacker, Stephen Hess, Pietro Nivola, Bob Katzman, John Kingdon, Allen Schick, Kent Weaver, Joe White, Margaret Weir, as well as Tom Mann. Fellow Guest Scholars Bruce Oppenheimer and John E. Owens spent some time helping me understand the dynamics of Congress, which I appreciate. For helpful suggestions on the fifth edition, I would particularly like to thank Lara M. Brown for her insights on many dimensions of the presidency. Gerald Pomper and Richard Hardaway gave me useful advice on the Electoral College, for which I thank them.

My colleagues in the School of Public Policy at George Mason University have been personally helpful and professionally supportive of my work. For help or advice during my writing, I would like to thank Jason Hartke, Jerry Mayer, Don Kash, Cathy Rudder, and Sue Tolchin. Dean Kingsley Haynes and Senior Associate Dean James Finkelstein have provided a dynamic scholarly environment that has enriched scholarship at SPP.

Finally, I would like to express my appreciation for the love and support from my wife, Deb, throughout the writing of the several editions this book. I am also grateful for the careful attention of our children, Megan Cyr, Katherine Courtney, and Morgan Meehan, who made sure that I did not become too lonely when I was writing in my office.

James P. Pfiffner

About the Author

James P. Pfiffner is University Professor in the School of Public Policy at George Mason University. He has also taught at the University of California, Riverside and California State University, Fullerton. His major areas of expertise are the presidency, American national government, and public management. He has lectured on these topics at universities in Europe and throughout the United States, as well as at the Federal Executive Institute, the National War College, the U.S. Military Academy, and at the State, Justice, and Defense Departments. In addition to *The Modern Presidency*, he has written or edited ten other books on the presidency, including *The Strategic Presidency: Hitting the Ground Running* (2nd edition, 1996), and *The Character Factor: How We Judge America's Presidents* (2004). He has published more than eighty articles and book chapters on the presidency, American government, and public management.

He is an elected member of the National Academy of Public Administration, and he has been a panel member or on project staffs of the National Commission on the Public Service (the Volcker Commission), the Center for Strategic and International Studies, the National Academy of Sciences, and the Center for the Study of the Presidency. His professional experience includes service in the director's office of the U.S. Office of Personnel Management (1980–81) and being a Guest Scholar at the Brookings Institution. In 1990 he received the Distinguished Faculty Award at George Mason University, and in 1999 he received the College of Arts and Sciences Scholarship Award. While serving with the 25th Infantry Division (1/8 Artillery) in 1970, he received the Army Commendation Medal (with "V" device) for Valor in Vietnam and Cambodia.

President George Walker Bush at the inauguration for his second term in office on January 20, 2005. (© Brian Snyder/Reuters/CORBIS)

THE PRESIDENCY: ORIGINS AND POWERS

The American presidency underwent an amazing transformation in the last half of the twentieth century. Presidency scholars distinguish between the "traditional presidency," from 1788 to 1933, and the "modern presidency," from 1933 to the present.[1] The metamorphosis began with the presidency of Franklin Roosevelt and his presiding over major historical developments in the United States and the rest of the world through four elections.[2] The Roosevelt era marked the transformation of the presidency from a small, personalized office to a collection of specialized bureaucracies with hundreds of professional staffers. This book examines the major elements of the modern presidency, with special attention to the causes and consequences of the transformation from the traditional to the modern presidency.

Three broad themes will be explored. Chapters 1 and 2 examine the changing relationship between the president and the American people. The presidency is now much more closely linked to the people through their right to vote in primary elections. But even more striking is the familiarity people feel with the chief executive because they see the president on television virtually every day of the year. Chapters 3, 4, and 5 trace the growth of the presidency, its institutionalization, and its increasing control of the executive branch. Finally, Chapters 6, 7, and 8 explore the limits on presidential power inherent in the separation-of-powers system and examine how the balance between the two branches of government has shifted over the course of the modern presidency.

Franklin Roosevelt's twelve years in office saw the Great Depression challenge the newly industrialized nation and threaten the viability of a capitalist economy that had become one of the most powerful in the world. After weathering the Depression, the U.S. economy was jolted into high production by the demands to mobilize for World War II. When the war ended, the United States assumed world economic leadership, helped design Japan's postwar recovery, and with the Marshall Plan, invested huge amounts of capital to rebuild Europe. The United States came out of the war as leader of the victorious allies and sole possessor of the awful power of the atomic bomb.

The experience of the Great Depression led the U.S. public to demand a more positive governmental approach to the economy, and the Employment Act of 1946 embodied those expectations. The country modified the laissez-faire doctrine of minimal entanglement of government policy with the economy and determined to smooth out the economic cycles of boom and bust. The National Security Act of 1947 created a unified Department of Defense, a Joint Chiefs of Staff, and the Central Intelligence Agency. The national security policy institutions that would deal with the coming Cold War, as well as several hot wars, were in place by 1950 and would not be significantly changed until the post-9/11 era. The domination of the world by the two superpowers and the aspirations of the emerging lesser-developed nations transformed international relations. At the same time, communications technology made possible instantaneous worldwide communication and provided the ability to reach mass audiences through radio and television.

These historic changes in international relations and technology were reflected in the office of the presidency. Just as the world would never be the same after the Great Depression, World War II, and the advent of modern communications, neither would the presidency. As the office adapted to the new realities of the mid-twentieth century, the capacity of the presidency to lead a much larger national government had to be enhanced. But the changes of the 1930s and 1940s merely laid the groundwork for the full development of the modern presidency. Since then, the institutional capacity of the office has been transformed beyond the dreams of Franklin Roosevelt.

The Framers' deliberations over the nature of the presidency demonstrated their desire not only to avoid the dangers of executive tyranny (such as King George III) but also to moderate the potential for legislative extremism (such as inflating the money supply). They created an executive office that balanced legislative power but that was, because of the Electoral College, removed from the people. One of the primary dynamics of American history over two centuries has been the creation of more direct links between the president and the public, beginning with the transformation of the presidential selection process.

The nominating system has been changed from a process dominated by political parties to one driven by primary elections. The proliferation of primaries led to the development of candidate-centered election organizations that raise their own money and conduct their own campaigns. Political parties, which used to dominate presidential politics, are now clearly subordinate to presidents and presidential candidates. But the rise of the candidate-centered organization and the relative decline of political parties has made the process of governing much more difficult. Presidents must knit together their own governing coalitions rather than depend on traditional party coalitions.[3] Presidential elections have been democratized over the past two centuries, with a much broader definition of citizenship than the Framers envisioned. But presidential election outcomes still depend on the constitutional constraints of the Electoral College, as was evident in the presidential election of 2000. Modern presidents have also made deliberate use of modern communications technology to appeal directly to voters and to circumvent the traditional intervening filters of reporters and opinion leaders. The democratization of the presidency and the development of White House capacity to exploit the new communications technologies are explored in Chapter 2.

As the size and complexity of the government grew, so did the dependence of the president on a more professional White House staff. The White House staff has done more than grow in size from a few informal, generalist aides to FDR to the highly specialized and bureaucratized White House Office of more than 400 staffers in the twenty-first century. The White House staff now has the capacity, in terms of expertise and power, to initiate policy in all areas of presidential concern. It even has the capacity to carry out presidential priorities, which has been valuable at times but also can lead to trouble for the president.

The transformation of the White House can be illustrated by comparing the contemporary White House bureaucracy with FDR's White House. According to Joseph Alsop:

> There literally was no White House staff of the modern type, with policymaking functions. Two extremely pleasant, unassuming, and efficient men, Steve Early and Marvin McIntyre, handled the president's day-to-day schedule and routine, the donkey-work of his press relations, and such like. There was a secretarial camarilla of highly competent and dedicated ladies who were led by "Missy" LeHand.... There were also lesser figures to handle travel arrangements, the enormous flow of correspondence, and the like. But that was that; and national policy was strictly a problem for the president, his advisers of the moment (who had constant access to the president's office but no office of their own in the White House), and his chosen chiefs of departments and agencies.[4]

The growth in White House staff since FDR has been both a boon and a bane to presidents. Presidents now have the ability to do things in the White House that used to be done in other agencies of the executive branch (e.g., foreign policy, trade policy, and legal advice) or by political parties (e.g., personnel recruitment or public liaison).

The White House staff is now so large that it needs a formal, hierarchical organization. The argument of Chapter 3 is that ever since the growth of the White House staff under Richard Nixon, the president has needed a chief of staff to organize the White House. But the corollary to that lesson is that a chief of staff who attempts to control too much (e.g., Sherman Adams, H. R. Haldeman, Donald Regan, or John Sununu) will lead to major problems, if not disaster.

While the large White House staff gives presidents a depth of policy and political advice that was not available before, it does not assure the quality of that advice. A large staff also creates the danger that White House aides will go off on their own, doing what they imagine is in the president's best interest. Without careful monitoring, this extended White House staff can lead to disaster, as it did in the Watergate and Iran-Contra affairs.

The increase in governmental programs and the large number of agencies created during the New Deal resulted in a fragmented system that FDR tried to rein in through the proposals of the Brownlow Committee. The long-term result of the Brownlow proposals was an increasingly centralized capacity to control the executive branch from the White House, a trend that increased in momentum after 1960.

The offices and procedures that presidents created in the 1950s and 1960s soon became institutionalized. Elements of this include an elaborate and more centralized national security apparatus, an enhanced office of communications, a large legal counsel's office, a professionalized Office of Presidential Personnel, a legislative liaison capacity, and others. This growth in capacity has occurred because presidents do not want to depend on the rest of the executive branch for advice. They want immediate responses from people they trust implicitly, and they want the capacity available in the White House, not in cabinet departments.

But this capacity has set the presidency apart from the rest of the executive branch, over which the president presides as chief executive officer. Scholar Nelson Polsby argues that the single most important development during the modern presidency has been "the transformation of the American presidency from a position of leadership of the executive branch to the centerpiece of what can now sensibly be called a separate and distinct branch of government—the presidential branch."[5] In this new manifestation of the presidency, the presidential branch "sits *across* the table from the executive branch at budgetary hearings, and ... imperfectly attempts to coordinate both the executive and legislative branches in its own behalf."[6]

This "presidential branch" includes the White House Office and the Executive Office of the President (EOP). Chapter 4 examines these units in general and traces the development of several subunits in the EOP. The original purpose of these offices was to coordinate executive branch policy and provide expert advice to the president. But as the offices became institutionalized, presidents came to depend on them as tools to control the expanding executive branch. Once an office was created to perform certain important functions, the performance of those functions persisted across presidential administrations. Regardless of changes in name, the offices have grown in staff resources and importance, and contemporary presidents are not free *not* to have these functions performed. They are essential to the operation of the contemporary presidency. This increased EOP capacity has given presidents the opportunity to shape the national agenda and initiate policies as never before, but it has also created a large bureaucracy that must be policed so that it is doing what the president wants and no more.

The cabinet, from Washington's time on, has traditionally been the primary advisory body to the president. Chapter 5 analyzes the president's cabinet and how its influence has declined in recent decades. While different presidents have used their cabinets to a greater or lesser extent, all presidents have called cabinet meetings to ask advice and to communicate with their top appointees. Cabinet secretaries, being the top line officers of the government, are legally in charge of their departments and have broad leeway in carrying out the priorities of their presidents' administrations. But in the 1960s and 1970s, presidents began to centralize policy control in the White House and relegated cabinet secretaries to a distinctly subordinate role as compared with the previous 150 years of the Republic. While the relationship of some cabinet secretaries to their presidents has enabled them to maintain their traditional relative independence, most cabinet secretaries now must accept the fact that they will enjoy little access to the president and that White House staffers will probably have more influence over policy in their areas of jurisdiction than they have.

The cabinet as a deliberative body has lost its role as primary adviser to the president, but cabinet secretaries still play important roles in the presidency. Each administration also depends on the quality of the hundreds of presidential appointees in the subcabinet. Chapter 5 examines the recruitment of these appointees and their often uneasy relationship with the career civil servants who implement the laws and carry out the president's directives.

To deal with the economic crisis of the Great Depression, Franklin Roosevelt used his first one hundred days in office to push through Congress a series of laws that began the New Deal. This presidential leadership and congressional cooperation in major policy changes was unprecedented in scope and volume. The president would henceforth be the country's chief legislator. In contrast to the traditional presidency, each president now has an annual legislative agenda and a professional legislative liaison team in the White House. Chapter 6 examines how this operation grew from a one-person specialty in the late 1940s to a fully professionalized office in recent decades, and more generally examines the relationship between the president and Congress. While the president can take some actions independently, most of the major policy initiatives of any administration require congressional action. After examining the constitutional and political fundamentals of this relationship, the chapter looks at what presidents can do to maximize their chances of winning congressional approval of their legislative proposals. Most of the time during the second half of the twentieth century, interbranch relations endured the frustrations of divided government, that is, when one political party holds the presidency and the other controls one or both houses of Congress. The conclusion of the chapter is that, despite presidential domination of the executive branch, and often of the national agenda, Congress still plays a major balancing constitutional role.

The constitutional designation of the president as commander in chief of the armed forces has made the president the primary national leader in national security policy throughout the history of the Republic. The president's national security role was enhanced by the Cold War and the National Security Council

(NSC) staff in the White House. The role of Congress, never preeminent in foreign policy, was further reduced by the president's new capacity. The president's power, however, was balanced by Congress's authority to declare war.

Chapter 7 examines the war power in the modern presidency and the shift of power toward the president, to the point where President George H.W. Bush argued that he did not need congressional approval to initiate war in the Persian Gulf, and his son, George W. Bush claimed even more expansive presidential power based on the commander-in-chief clause of the Constitution. In addition to increasing claims to constitutional powers, the presidency has had, beginning in the 1960s, the capacity in the White House NSC staff to coordinate and dominate national security policy making, sometimes to the partial exclusion of the State and Defense Departments. The domination of the war power by the president, however, has not precluded active congressional intervention in other areas of defense and foreign policy.

In Chapter 8, the book turns to the potential for corruption and abuse of power in the White House. The Framers were acutely aware of the dangers of the corrupting temptations of power; they anticipated Lord Acton's axiom that power corrupts. Since those holding governmental power are not angels, the Framers designed a government in which each branch would have the motive and necessary means to resist any undue concentration of power in another branch. There have been instances of corruption at high levels in the U.S. government. This chapter examines the two most dangerous scandals: the Watergate incidents that led to President Nixon's resignation and the Iran-Contra affair of the Reagan administration. The consequences of each of these scandals were mitigated by the countervailing actions of the Congress in its investigations of the executive branch. The impeachment of President Clinton by the House of Representatives and his trial in the Senate are then examined.

The negative consequences of these incidents on the reputations of the presidents involved leads into a discussion of the public approval and historical reputations of the modern presidents. In some cases, contemporary public approval and historical reputation are in general agreement. In other cases, presidential reputations undergo reevaluation several decades after their terms in office. The historical reputations of Presidents Truman and Eisenhower have each improved markedly in recent decades. The reasons for these vagaries of presidential reputation are explored.

The book ends with the observation that, encouraged by the overpromising of presidential candidates, voters have come to hold high expectations of how effective presidents can be in solving very complex social, economic, and national security problems facing the country. When these high expectations are not met, as is frequently the case, citizens can easily become cynical. If citizens would have more realistic expectations and presidential candidates would moderate their promises, we might have a better appreciation of the possibilities of presidential leadership in a limited government of separated powers.

ORIGINS OF THE PRESIDENCY

The Framers' ideas about executive power were heavily influenced by the colonial experience and their familiarity with European history. The lessons they drew from this experience led them to distrust executive power, at least when it was unchecked. They suspected that any chief executive, if unfettered, would likely degenerate into tyranny.

The experience under King George III and his colonial governors was not a happy one for the colonists, who finally revolted against British control. Many of the royal governors abused their powers and gave short shrift to the colonial assemblies who represented the new settlers. The British monarch did not endear himself to the colonists when he imposed oppressive taxes, one of which led to the Boston Tea Party. The Declaration of Independence states: "The history of the present King of Great Britain is a history of repeated injuries and usurpations, all having in direct object the establishment of an absolute Tyranny over these States."

This experience might have led the Framers to create a constitution that severely restrained executive power and gave most governmental powers to a legislative body. The reason that this did not happen was their experience during the Articles of Confederation period. Neither the performance of the Continental Congress nor of the state assemblies was entirely satisfactory in the judgment of the Framers.

Because of the fear of executive tyranny, many states had dominant legislatures and weak executives who were chosen by the legislatures for one-year terms and who were often constrained by an executive council. This led to inefficient state governments that occasionally abused their powers and threatened property rights or inflated the money supply.

But perhaps more important in the Framers' minds was the immediate experience with the weak central government under the Articles of Confederation. The national government was run by the Continental Congress but had no independent executive. Each state had between three and five delegates to the one-house legislature, who could exercise one vote per state. The powers of the central government were restricted to those that were clearly national, including the authority to conduct war, make foreign policy, negotiate treaties, create a postal service, and regulate money. But the ability to make foreign policy was put at risk when Great Britain threatened to negotiate the end of the Revolutionary War with each state, independently, rather than with the central government.

The power to regulate money was limited by the central government's inability to impose taxes on the states; it could merely assess charges against the states but could not force payment. The national debt was increasing and the economy was doing poorly, but the states often refused to recognize each other's currency and imposed tariffs on goods coming into one state from the others. These were serious problems that the central government did not have the authority or power to solve. Contributing to all of these difficulties was the lack of an independent executive to take vigorous action to address any of the problems.

Thus, when delegates from five states met in Annapolis to deal with the problem of trade among the states, they decided to propose a broader convention, and the Continental Congress decided to call a convention in May 1787 in Philadelphia. When the Framers met in that Constitutional Convention, they brought with them a shared ambivalence about executive power, but most were convinced that the governing structure of the states had to have a stronger executive than either the separate states or the central government had up to that point. Some Framers were suspicious of an executive with too much power, and all were leery of popular opinion in the states, which was still very hostile to executive power because of the colonial experience. They knew they wanted an executive office that would provide more coherent leadership than they had under the Articles of Confederation, but they did not want to create an executive structure that would degenerate into a tyranny.

Deciding how to select the chief executive was one of the most complex challenges faced by the Framers in the summer of 1787. The method was deliberated at the Constitutional Convention on twenty-two different days and was the subject of thirty separate votes.[7] The initial Virginia Plan that was favored by the large states provided for an executive, but not a strong one. The executive could be one or several persons and would be chosen by the legislature. James Madison had come to favor a stronger executive to offset potential abuse by the legislature. According to Madison, "the legislative department is everywhere extending the sphere of its activity and drawing all powers into its impetuous vortex. ... Executive powers had been usurped."[8] Alexander Hamilton even favored an elected president who would be a virtual monarch with lifetime tenure and the title of "His Excellency."

The level of power of a chief executive would depend on several factors, including the number (single or plural), how chosen (by the legislature or popular election), length of term, re-eligibility for office, and of course the formal powers granted to the office by the Constitution. James Wilson of Pennsylvania favored a strong executive for reasons of efficiency and effectiveness: "a single magistrate" would provide the "most energy, dispatch, and responsibility to the office."[9] But the first reaction of the convention to his proposal was not enthusiasm but a "considerable pause." George Mason, however, feared that if a single person were given the executive power, he would abuse it. "If strong and extensive powers are vested in the Executive, and that Executive consists only of one person; the Government will of course degenerate into a Monarchy."[10] Edmund Randolf of Virginia saw Wilson's plan as "the Foetus of Monarchy."[11] But after a heated debate, a single executive was decided upon on August 6.

For most of the convention the assumption was that the chief executive would be chosen by the legislature, as was contemplated in the Virginia Plan drafted by James Madison. When the convention adjourned on July 25, 1787, the chief executive was to be chosen by the legislature, but the term of office was not set nor was the question of re-eligibility. The Committee of Detail reported on August 6 this formula:

> The Executive Power of the United States shall be vested in a single Person. His Stile shall be, "The President of the United States of America;" and his Title shall be,

"His Excellency". He shall be elected by Ballot by the Legislature. He shall hold his Office during the term of seven Years; but shall not be elected a second Time.[12]

But there were objections that a president chosen by the legislature would be too beholden to it and thus not independent enough. For this reason, James Wilson and Gouverneur Morris both argued for election by the people.[13]

The problem with selection by the people was not the Framers' distrust of this method's democratic nature (though the Framers were not trying to create a democracy). From their perspective, there were two problems with direct popular election of the president. The first was the probability that most citizens would not be personally familiar with all of the most qualified potential candidates. This was George Mason's concern; Mason favored the idea of popular election of the president but thought it impractical.[14] "He conceived it would be as unnatural to refer the choice of a proper character for chief Magistrate to the people, as it would, to refer a trail of colours to a blind man. The extent of the Country renders it impossible that the people can have the requisite capacity to judge of the respective pretensions of the Candidates."[15]

But the more important problem was the disadvantage some states would face if the vote were based only on population. The ratio of population of the largest state, Virginia, to the smallest in population, Delaware, was about ten to one.[16] In addition to the problem with the small states, the slave states had smaller populations, and with a direct election they would not be able to count the slave population as they had calculated their representation in Congress (counting three-fifths of the slave population).

Thus the proposal to base the election of the president on the ratio of votes that was established in the Connecticut Compromise for representation in Congress was attractive. It reassured the small states, because the ratio of influence in the vote would not be the ten to one it was between largest and smallest but rather four to one. In addition, the slave states' representation would reflect three-fifths of their slave populations. Madison put it this way: "The people at large was in his opinion the fittest in itself" for choosing the president.

> There was one difficulty however of a serious nature attending an immediate choice by the people. The right of suffrage was much more diffusive in the Northern than the Southern States; and the latter could have no influence in the election on the score of the Negroes. The Substitution of electors obviated this difficulty and seemed on the whole to be liable to the fewest objections.[17]

Thus the Brearley Committee on Unfinished Parts worked for four days and reported back to the Convention on September 4 with a plan for an electoral college. Under its plan, the selection of president would be removed from the legislature and given, in effect, to an independent "ad hoc Congress" convened solely for the purpose of selecting the president.[18] Electors would be chosen by state legislatures, but they could not be members of the national government and would not meet together because of the danger of plots and cabals. The ratio of the states to the membership of the college was exactly the same as their representation in the legislature, with the number of electors equaling the number of representatives and senators to which each state was entitled. Any changes in population among the states would be reflected in changes in their congressional representation.

Each elector could vote for two persons for president, one of whom could not be an inhabitant of the same state as the elector, and the winner had to receive a majority of all electors appointed. In the contingency that no candidate received a majority, the choice would devolve on the House of Representatives (changed from the Senate in the original Brearley Committee plan), which would choose the president from among the top five persons (changed to three by the Twelfth Amendment) receiving electoral votes. In a concession to the small states, the state delegations in the House would cast only one vote per state.

The electoral college mechanism for choosing the president was a masterpiece of political improvisation and compromise rather than a formula based on any coherent political theory. For those who favored state control or democracy, the plan provided that state legislatures could decide how the electors would be chosen. (Most began with state legislative selection and soon changed to voting by citizens in the states.) The small states were guaranteed at least three votes, but the large states would have more because of their larger delegations to the House. For those who distrusted too much democracy, the electors would be men of good judgment and character. But most importantly for the immediate compromise, all assumed that the universally acclaimed George Washington would be the first president of the Republic. The deliberations about the office of the presidency were greatly facilitated by this assumption. The Framers were thus willing to give the presidency powers that they might have hesitated to grant to the office had they not known that Washington would be its first occupant.

It is important to remember that it was not predetermined or implied in the political theory of the Framers that the president would be chosen by the people. If the convention decision of late August held, the Congress would have chosen the president, considerably weakening the office. The term of office or eligibility for reelection was not settled until the end of the convention. The options considered by the Framers included terms of office of two, three, seven, ten, fifteen, and twenty years, as well as the life term favored by Hamilton, and there were more than sixty votes taken on this issue.[19] If Congress had ended up with the power to select the president, the term of office would likely have been longer. But once it was clear that Congress would not control selection, the Framers settled on a four-year term with eligibility for reelection. The current arrangements for selecting the president have taken on an aura of fixedness that was not at all certain until the closing days of the Constitutional Convention.

This outline is a far cry from the twentieth-century vision of democracy in the United States. Since the founding, the franchise has been extended to include

- African Americans (Fifteenth Amendment, 1870)
- Women (Nineteenth Amendment, 1920)
- Citizens of the District of Columbia (Twenty-third Amendment, 1961)
- Citizens who are eighteen years of age (Twenty-sixth Amendment, 1971)

In addition, property and literacy tests for voting have been prohibited. Senators are now popularly elected (Seventeenth Amendment, 1913), and all states have decided to have presidential electors selected in popular elections. The formal and legal links of the president to the people have been supplemented by even more far-reaching changes in presidential behavior, as we will see in the next chapter.

POWERS OF THE PRESIDENT

Article II of the Constitution is brief and vague when compared with the many enumerated powers granted to Congress in Article I. The presidential Article begins: "The executive Power shall be vested in a President of the United States of America." But it is not clear whether the "executive Power" is a separate grant of power or merely a designation of the president as head of the executive branch.[20] The president derives much of his power from the execution of the laws (Section 3: "he shall take Care that the Laws be faithfully executed"), since the implementation of most laws necessarily entails a certain amount of discretion.

The commander-in-chief power is a broad grant of power and enables the president to direct the armed forces of the United States at his or her discretion. This power is affected by the power of Congress to declare war, provide for armies and navies, and set rules for their operation. The war power in important cases is, in effect, exercised by the president, as described in Chapter 7. The president has exclusive power to receive ambassadors, which implies the discretion to recognize foreign nations. But his power to appoint ambassadors to those nations is shared by the Senate, which has to confirm those nominations. The president has the power to negotiate treaties, but the Senate also shares this power by its power to ratify (by a two-thirds majority) or reject them.

The president has the authority to appoint officers of the United States, though the Senate shares the power by its confirmation duty. This power to name the political appointees who head all of the agencies of the executive branch is a significant one, allowing the president to effectively control the executive branch when he chooses, though the power levers of Congress are also significant. The appointment of judges, modified by the Senate's confirmation power, is a powerful tool. The power to appoint judges with lifetime tenure, given the low probability of the Senate to reject judicial appointments, allows the president to cast a long shadow over the interpretation of the laws. The president is also given the judicial power of granting pardons, reprieves, and amnesties. This pardon power is most often used to right individual wrongs or mitigate harshness in the judicial system, though it can have a significant political impact. For instance, Presidents Lincoln and Johnson pardoned anti-Union Southerners after the Civil War; Presidents Ford and Carter pardoned draft evaders of the Vietnam era; and President George H.W. Bush pardoned five participants in the Iran-Contra affair.

The president also has the legislative power to veto legislation, though a veto can be overridden by a two-thirds majority of each house. The president can recommend legislation to Congress, give state of the union addresses, and call Congress into special session. But these minimal formal legislative powers have been enhanced by historical development and political circumstance so that the modern president is considered the "chief legislator," a development analyzed in Chapter 6.

Presidents also have at their disposal a range of unilateral tools that can be used to accomplish their policy goals. Among these are executive orders, executive agreements, memoranda, proclamations, and reorganization plans. These tools flow from the president's authority as head of the executive branch and often allow them to avoid potential political opposition in Congress. Executive orders allow presidents to direct certain actions or policies within the executive branch and can even be used to create new agencies, as President Bush did in 2003 in establishing the Office of Faith-Based and Community Initiatives within the White House Office. President Clinton issued a proclamation that set aside about 2 million acres of wilderness in Utah as a national monument. Executive agreements (discussed in Chapter 7) allow presidents to commit the United States to agreements with other nations without going through the treaty-ratification process in the Senate. The use of unilateral tools of presidential power has increased in recent decades, especially when presidents face a Congress that is unwilling or unable to legislate on certain policy issues. [21]

Presidential scholar Richard Neustadt has observed that the separation-of-powers system is not so much a clear division of powers among the branches as it is a system of separate institutions sharing power.[22] Thus, most of the powers granted in the Constitution are not given exclusively to one branch but are divided among the branches and maintained in a shifting balance, depending on the political and historical circumstances. The congressional power of the purse (to appropriate money) can be affected by a presidential veto and by the power of the executive to actually spend the money (i.e., make contracts and write checks). The congressional war power is affected by the president's commander-in-chief power to deploy troops and order them into hostilities. Each branch's interpretation of its constitutional powers can be affected by the judicial power to interpret the law and the implied power of judicial review, that is, to declare actions of the other two branches unconstitutional.

Thus, the Framers designed a system of shared powers within a system that is purposefully biased against change. With each branch jealously guarding its prerogatives and powers (ambition must be made to counteract ambition), no one branch can move too far on its own. Thus, an overwhelming consensus must be achieved before both Congress and the president (with the acquiescence of the judiciary) can move together to make major changes in policy or direction of the country. This delicate balance of "parchment barriers" has held up amazingly well over the two centuries of U.S. history. The relative strength of the branches has shifted over the years, sometimes significantly, but the same questions of where the balance ought to lie are debated today in as strikingly similar terms as the debates of the constitutional era.

The real power of the presidency, however, is not so much a matter of formal constitutional powers, though these provide the framework within which presidents operate. The real power of presidents has been affected by the legitimacy provided by the shift to popular voting for president (despite the technical reality of the Electoral College). But historical circumstance and presidential personality have provided the opportunity for presidents to become powerful and have an impact on the history of the country. Those presidents who have been considered powerful and often great have governed the country during times of crisis or major historical change, for example, Washington, Lincoln, Wilson, and Franklin Roosevelt. Some presidents, by force of their personality and political will, have had important impacts on the direction of the country, for example, Andrew Jackson, Theodore Roosevelt, and Ronald Reagan. In addition, the apparatus of the institutional presidency, described in subsequent chapters, gives modern presidents added levers of control.

PRESIDENTIAL POWER

The term "presidential power," in contrast to the specification of formal, constitutional powers of the president, connotes the range of authority presidents have asserted, especially as opposed to the powers of Congress. Over the two centuries of the Republic, domination of national policy making has ebbed and flowed between the president and Congress, the policy-making branches. Congress tended to dominate in the first century, and presidential power gradually accumulated during the twentieth century. As Thomas Jefferson observed in 1789: "The TYRANNY of the legislature is really the danger most to be feared, and will continue to be so for many years to come. The tyranny of the executive power will come in its turn, but at a more distant period."[23] That "more distant period" occurred with the rise of executive power in the twentieth century, particularly during times of war, when presidents were given unusual deference and leeway to act as they thought best for the protection of the nation. Congress has generally been hesitant to thwart executive plans, because public opinion favors quick, determined action during times of crisis and is likely to approve of strong presidential action.

In domestic issues, Congress usually dominated the policy-making process, with a few major exceptions. In the early 1930s, President Franklin Roosevelt pushed through Congress his New Deal legislation that expanded the federal government considerably. The second exception to the rule of congressional dominance in domestic policy was Lyndon Johnson's Great Society set of initiatives of 1964 and 1965, which was second only to Roosevelt's 100 Days in the scope of domestic policy legislation. Ronald Reagan also had considerable success with his initial tax cuts and domestic policy cutbacks (see Chapter 6 for details of these periods of presidential assertion). But in foreign affairs and national security, presidents dominated policy making. The heightened presidential power during World Wars I and II was extended during the Cold War, when the Communist threat and the precarious nuclear balance allowed presidents to act more assertively in national security matters.

Twentieth-century presidential assertiveness came to a high point during the "imperial presidencies" of Lyndon Johnson and Richard Nixon. Johnson misled the country and secretly escalated the War in Vietnam in 1965. He did not want to jeopardize his Great Society Program, so he dissembled about his intentions in Vietnam.[24] Richard Nixon continued to pursue the war and resisted congressional efforts to end it. Nixon also confronted Congress on a number of issues, including war powers, control of spending (impoundment of funds), executive privilege, and the Watergate abuses of power (all discussed later in this book). Nixon's assertion of executive powers and his unwillingness to be limited by Congress or even the law, resulted in impeachment proceedings followed by his resignation in 1974.

After President Nixon's exceptional assertions of presidential power, Congress reacted in the early 1970s with a spate of laws intended to reassert congressional constitutional prerogatives. The measures included the Impoundment Control Act; the Case Act, requiring the president to report executive agreements to Congress; the Hughs-Ryan Amendment, requiring presidential "findings" for covert CIA actions to be reported to Congress; and the War Powers Resolution. The Ford and Carter presidencies acted in accord with these laws, but President Reagan began to reassert presidential powers in various ways, both legislative and executive. His administration overstepped the bounds of law during the Iran-Contra Affair, when it funneled funds from Iranian payments for arms to the Contras in Nicaragua, which was explicitly forbidden in law (see Chapter 8 for details).

At the end of the Cold War, defense spending was cut during the G.H.W. Bush and Clinton administrations. Both presidents used their executive powers fully, but they did not fundamentally challenge congressional constitutional powers in unusual ways, though both asserted the power of the president to take military action without congressional assent.

But in the twenty-first century, President George W. Bush began to assert executive power in unprecedented ways. At the beginning of his administration, he and Vice President Cheney felt that previous presidents had let Congress impinge on executive prerogatives under the Constitution and that presidential powers had to be reasserted. After the attacks of 9/11, they saw the necessity of secret presidential action and strong assertions of presidential power. Congress was controlled by Republicans and was willing to give the administration what it wanted in terms of policy; consequently, it was unwilling to challenge presidential assertions of power. The American public was traumatized by the 9/11 atrocities and was willing to let President Bush (with historically high public approval ratings for several years after 9/11) have his way, since he argued that his actions were necessary to defend the country.

Vice President Cheney, because of his previous government experience, was a dominating force in the Bush administration, particularly on national security issues. Thus, his judgments played an important role in the administration's attempt to "restore presidential power," and President Bush agreed with him. Cheney, who had served as chief of staff to President Ford, felt that Congress overreacted to Vietnam and Watergate and hobbled presidential power in unconstitutional ways. As he said, "The feeling I had [during the Ford years], and I think it's been borne out by history, that in the aftermath, especially of Vietnam and Watergate, that the balance shifted, if you will, that, in fact, the presidency was weakened, that there were congressional efforts to rein in and to place limits on presidential authority. . . . The Iran-Contra controversy to some extent was an effort by the majority to criminalize what was really a policy difference in terms of how we dealt, for example, with the situation in Nicaragua."[25] Cheney argued that congressional agreement was not necessary for the president to initiate war. When talking about the 1991 Gulf War, he asserted, "It was my view that Congress would be with us if we were successful and against us if we weren't successful and it wouldn't matter, even if they had voted for it in advance. . . . I firmly believe to this day even if the Congress had voted no we had no option but to proceed."[26]

By 2006, Cheney believed that the Bush administration had been at least partly successful in its efforts to reassert presidential prerogatives: "The president of the United States needs to have his constitutional power unimpaired. I do think that, to some extent now, we've been able to restore the legitimate authority of the presidency."[27] One White House aide articulated the administration's stance on presidential power: "The powers of the presidency have been eroded and usurped to the breaking point. We are engaged in a new kind of war that cannot be fought by old methods. It can only be directed by a strong executive who alone is not subject to the conflicting pressures that legislators or judges face. The public understands and supports that unpleasant reality, whatever the media and intellectuals say."[28] Those "conflicting pressures," of course, represent the separation-of-powers system and checks and balances created by the Constitution.

Cheney's views of presidential power fit well with President Bush's view of his personal power as president. He expressed his personal approach to leadership in 2005 when he rejected calls for Defense Secretary Donald Rumsfeld's resignation: "I listen to all voices, but mine is the final decision. . . . But I'm the decider, and I decide what is best."[29] During deliberations about the war in Afghanistan, when Bob Woodward asked if he explained his decisions to his staff President Bush replied: Of course not. I'm the commander—see, I don't need to explain—I do not need to explain why I say things. That's the interesting thing about being the president. Maybe somebody needs to explain to me why they say something, but I don't feel like I owe anybody an explanation."[30]

President Bush seemed to adopt a version of the "plebiscitary presidency," that is, once the president is elected, Congress or the laws do not constrain him, at least with respect to national security. The only check is impeachment or the election of a different president. Election gives the president the right to make the fundamental decisions about U.S. policy. President Bush put it this way, "We had an accountability moment, and that's called the 2004 elections."[31]

President Bush's stance toward his administration's action, such as the NSA warrantless wire tapping, suspending the Geneva Conventions, and imprisoning citizens indefinitely without a trial, seemed to echo Richard Nixon's attitude toward the rule of law. When former President Nixon was interviewed by

David Frost in 1977, one exchange went like this: David Frost mentioned "wiretappings, burglaries or so-called black bag jobs, mail openings and infiltration against antiwar groups and others,"—actions that were "clearly illegal." Then he asked Nixon if the president "can decide that it's in the best interests of the nation or something, and do something illegal." Nixon replied: "Well, when the president does it that means that it is not illegal." Frost: "By definition." Nixon: "Exactly. Exactly. If the president, for example, approves something because of the national security, or in this case because of a threat to internal peace and order of significant magnitude, then the president's decision in that instance is one that enables those who carry it out, to carry it out without violating a law. Otherwise they're in an impossible position."[32] Bush appointee, acting Assistant Attorney General Steven Bradbury in the Office of Legal Counsel in the Justice Department, echoed Nixon's stance in testifying before the Senate. He was asked by Senator Leahy (D-Vt.) if President Bush was right or wrong in his expansive interpretation of presidential war power. Bradbury replied: "The president is always right."[33]

President Bush's extraordinary assertions of presidential power involved his secret order to the National Security Agency to wiretap U.S. citizens without a warrant (as required by law), the authority to suspend the Geneva Conventions with respect to the treatment of war detainees, and the authority to detain citizens indefinitely without trial. Each of these issues will be examined in Chapter 7. As the pendulum of power has swung between the president and Congress over the course of two centuries, it swung decisively toward the executive during George W. Bush's administration after the beginning of the twenty-first century.

NOTES

1. See Fred I. Greenstein, "Nine Presidents in Search of a Modern Presidency," in Greenstein, ed., *Leadership in the Modern Presidency* (Cambridge, MA: Harvard University Press, 1988), pp. 296–352. See also John Hart, *The Presidential Branch* (New York: Pergamon Press, 1987); Malcolm Shaw, ed., *The Modern Presidency: From Roosevelt to Reagan* (New York: Harper & Row, 1987). Lewis L. Gould's insightful analysis places the beginning of the modern presidency at Theodore Roosevelt, see *The Modern American Presidency* (Lawrence, KS: University Press of Kansas, 2003). Some scholars have also argued that we have entered an era of the "postmodern presidency." See, for example, Richard Rose, *The Postmodern President*, 2nd ed. (Chatham, NJ: Chatham House, 1991); and Ryan Barrileaux, *The Post-Modern Presidency: the Office after Ronald Reagan* (New York: Praeger, 1988).

2. Fred I. Greenstein, "Change and Continuity in the Modern Presidency," *The New American Political System* (Washington, DC: American Enterprise Institute, 1978), pp. 451–481.

3. Lester G. Seligman and Cary R. Covington, *The Coalitional Presidency* (Chicago: Dorsey Press, 1989).

4. Joseph Alsop, *FDR: 1882–1945, A Centenary Remembrance* (New York: Washington Square Press, 1982), pp. 92–93.

5. Nelson Polsby, "Congress, National Security, and the Rise of the Presidential Branch," in Howard Shuman and Walter Thomas, eds., *The Constitution and National Security* (Washington, DC: NDU Press, 1990), p. 202.

6. Nelson Polsby, "Some Landmarks in Modern Presidential-Congressional Relations," in Anthony King, ed., *Both Ends of the Avenue* (Washington, DC: American Enterprise Institute Press, 1983), p. 20.

7. Shlomo Slonim, "Designing the Electoral College," in Thomas E. Cronin, ed. *Inventing the American Presidency* (Lawrence, KS: University Press of Kansas, 1989), pp. 33–60.

8. Federalist no. 48.

9. Max Farrand, ed., *The Records of the Federal Convention of 1787* (New Haven, CT: Yale University Press, 1966), vol. 1, p. 65.

10. Farrand, ed., *The Records of the Federal Convention of 1787* (New Haven, CT: Yale University Press, 1966), vol. 1, p. 113.

11. Farrand, ed., *The Records of the Federal Convention of 1787* (New Haven, CT: Yale University Press, 1966), vol. 1, p. 66.

12. Farrand, ed., *The Records of the Federal Convention of 1787* (New Haven, CT: Yale University Press, 1966), vol. 2, p. 171.

13. Slonim, "Designing the Electoral College," pp. 48, 49.

14. Farrand, *The Records of the Federal Convention of 1787* (June 1, 1787), vol. 2, p. 66.

15. Farrand, *The Records of the Federal Convention of 1787*, vol. 2, p. 31 (July 17, 1787). Note the nature of the analogy; a blind man is not a good judge of colors not because he is incapable of solid reasoning but rather because he cannot perceive the appropriate information. Mason's objection was a practical one, not a judgment in principle that the people were easily deceived or led astray. See James P. Pfiffner and Jason Hartke, "The Electoral College and the Framers' Distrust of Democracy," *White House Studies*, vol. 3, no. 3, 2003.

16. Richard J. Ellis, ed., *Founding the American Presidency* (Lanham, MD: Rowman and Littlefield, 1999), p. 113.

17. Farrand, *The Records of the Federal Convention of 1787*, vol. 2, pp. 56–57.

18. Slonim, "Designing the Electoral College," p. 50.

19. Thomas E. Cronin, "Presidential Term, Tenure, and Reeligibility," in Cronin, ed., *Inventing the American Presidency* (Lawrence, KS: University of Kansas Press, 1989), p. 65.

20. See the analysis by Edward S. Corwin, *The President: Office and Powers* (New York: New York University Press, 1957), pp. 3–5.

21. See William G. Howell, *Power Without Persuasion* (Princeton, NJ: Princeton University Press, 2003); Phillip J. Cooper, *By Order of the President* (Lawrence: University Press of Kansas, 2002); Kenneth Mayer, *With the Stroke of a Pen* (Princeton University Press, 2001); David E. Lewis, *Presidents and the Politics of Agency Design* (Stanford University Press, 2002).

22. Richard Neustadt, *Presidential Power and the Modern Presidents* (New York: Free Press, 1990).

23. Jefferson letter to Madison, March 15, 1789, quoted in Arthur Schlesinger, *The Imperial Presidency* (Boston: Houghton Mifflin, 1973), p. 377.

24. For an analysis of Johnson's lying about Vietnam, see James P. Pfiffner, *The Character Factor: How We Judge America's Presidents* (College Station, TX: Texas A&M University Press, 2004).

25. Kenneth T. Walsh, "The Cheney Factor," *U.S. News & World Report* (January 23, 2006), p. 48.

26. Bob Woodward, "Cheney Upholds Power of the Presidency," *Washington Post* (January 20, 2005), p. A7.

27. Susan Page, "Congress Pushing Back against Bush's Expansion of Presidential Authority," *USA Today* (July 6, 2006), from Web site.

28. Quoted in Jim Hoagland, "Two Leaders' Power Failures," *Washington Post* (March 9, 2006), p. A19.

29. White House Web site, "President Bush Nominates Rob Portman as OMB Director and Susan Schwab for USTR," (April 18, 2006), end of Q&A session.

30. Woodward, *Bush at War*, pp. 145–146.

31. Quote in Jim VandeHei and Michael A. Fletcher, "Bush Says Election Ratified Iraq Policy," *Washington Post* (January 16, 2005), p. A1. The "plebiscitary presidency" idea is articulated by Arthur Schlesinger, Jr., in *The Imperial Presidency* (Boston: Houghton Mifflin, 1973), p. 376. "The President, instead of being accountable every day to Congress and public opinion, would be accountable every four years to the electorate. Between elections, the President would be accountable only through impeachment and would govern, as much as he could, by decree." See also, Theodore Lowi, *The Personal President* (Ithaca, NY: Cornell University Press, 1985).

32. Excerpt of the Frost interview televised on May 19 1977, in "United States V. Nixon (1974)," published at http://www.landmarkcases.org/nixon/nixonview.html

33. Quoted by Sidney Blumenthal, "The Emperor's New Veto," Salon.com (July 20, 2006).

THE PRESIDENT AND THE PUBLIC

CHAPTER **2**

The relationship between the president and the American public has changed dramatically since the time of the Framers. The Constitution created a republican government; citizens would not govern themselves directly, but rather they would elect representatives to exercise governing power. The Framers were careful not to make links to the people too direct because they were afraid of mob rule and tyranny of the majority. Thus, members of the House of Representatives were the only directly elected public officials in the national government. Judges were appointed for life terms; senators were selected by state legislatures; and the president was chosen by the Electoral College.

Senators are now directly elected by the people of the states (Seventeenth Amendment, 1913), and the electors of the president are also selected by voters in the states. This chapter traces the democratization of the presidency in the United States in two major areas: first, the changes in nomination and election processes, from the congressional "King Caucus" in the early nineteenth century, to the party convention-dominated process over the next century, and finally to the primary-dominated process of the late twentieth century; and second, the effect of these democratizing developments on the conduct of the presidency. Emphasis is on the recent developments of the modern era.

The development of political parties early in the eighteenth century gave citizen partisans a greater say in who would be nominated for the presidency. The development of primary elections in the twentieth century, especially the proliferation of primaries after 1968, brought the nomination process under much closer control by rank-and-file voters and took control away from political party elites.

This democratizing trend also weakened political parties and gave way to the growth of a much more personal (rather than party) candidate. Prospective presidential candidates now had to raise their own money and put together their own campaign organizations. Appeals had to be made to the public for support rather than to a small group of party leaders. This increased the importance of television as a medium of political appeal, further weakening the strength of political parties.

These changes in nominating and electing procedures had important impacts on the conduct of the presidency. Presidents could no longer count on automatic and sustained support from their partisans in Congress or from the coalitions that traditionally supported their political parties.[1] They felt the need to carry into the White House some of the strategies used in their campaigns for nomination and election. The White House thus has developed the institutionalized capacity to reach out to the American public in unprecedented ways and to use sophisticated modern communications technologies.

We will then examine presidential elections, with the emphasis on how the president has come to be seen as the national leader elected by all of the people, that is, a national voting constituency. The perception of the legitimacy of the presidency residing in popular selection will be contrasted with the constitutional reality of the Electoral College and an analysis of the election of 2000.

Finally, we will look at the effect of these democratizing developments on the conduct of the presidency. The weakening of political parties, combined with advances in modern communications technology, has led presidents to fight for their policy agendas more by direct appeal to the public than by the traditional tactic of bargaining among Washington elites. The tactic of direct appeal for popular support has been termed "going public" by presidential scholars, and this more active presidential outreach to the public will be examined.

As with other functions of the modern presidency, the carrying out of these appeals to the public has been established in the White House and institutionalized in the Office of Communications. Along with communications technology, the science of public opinion polling has also had a great impact on the presidency, with White House staffers devoting many hours to obtaining favorable media coverage for the president and keeping public approval ratings high. The positive and negative aspects of the sometimes obsessive concern with public opinion ratings and other aspects of the "permanent campaign" will be considered at the end of the chapter.

NOMINATING THE PRESIDENT

The Framers provided no formal system for deciding the finalists from whom the electors would choose when they cast their ballots for president. All expected that Washington would be elected first, and they did not foresee the emergence of political parties. They must have assumed that since electors would be men of public affairs, they would be familiar with those most qualified to be president and the field would be narrowed to a manageable number of candidates.

Opposing political factions, however, soon developed into incipient parties, and Congress split along partisan lines, with the Federalists being opposed by the Republicans. In 1796, the Federalist John Adams was elected president, but his supporters among the electors could not agree on his running mate, so his opponent for the presidency, Thomas Jefferson, the runner-up in electoral votes, became vice president.

In 1800, the members of each of the parties in Congress met in caucus to decide who would be the presidential candidate representing their party. Though congressional caucuses were never formalized as nominating mechanisms, they continued to select presidential nominees for the first two decades of the nineteenth century. But as the Federalist Party declined and political power began to be decentralized, the caucuses began to lose power and legitimacy. In addition, "King Caucus," as it was disparagingly known, was finally discredited by the 1824 election, in which Andrew Jackson received the most popular votes, but because he did not receive a majority of the electoral votes, the selection of president was left up to the House of Representatives. When Speaker of the House Henry Clay threw his support behind John Quincy Adams, who had come in second to Jackson, Adams was elected president and then appointed Clay secretary of state.

With the congressional caucus discredited and state-based electors too dispersed to coalesce effectively around a single candidate, the developing political parties began to organize nominating conventions. Beginning in the 1830s, national nominating conventions began to develop as an increasingly formalized mechanism for nominating the person to run for president from each of the parties. Each state's delegation was based on the number of electors to which it was entitled, but the delegates from each state were chosen by the political party leaders in the states, with little participation from voters. The convention system developed throughout the nineteenth century as party leaders met to formulate a coherent platform for their candidate to run on and to strike bargains among the various factions of the party.

But the domination of the conventions by the political bosses in the various states led to criticisms that the citizenry was being relegated in selecting the president from among the two candidates chosen by the party bosses and did not have a chance to participate in selecting the candidates. As early as 1878, a petition of 9 million signatures declared that "The convention is a small body. Its members vote secretly, and are not held accountable for what they do. . . ."[2] The petition went on to demand that Congress create primary elections in which voters could choose the nominees of their parties.

This pressure for reform was intensified by the progressive movement at the end of the century. By 1912, primaries were being held in twelve states, with 33 percent of Democratic and 42 percent of Republican delegates chosen by primary. The number of states holding primaries remained between twelve and twenty for the next half century, and the number of delegates chosen by the primary method was generally between 35 and 45 percent for the two parties.[3]

But primaries in this period never caught on as the most important path to the nomination for the major presidential candidates. The initial enthusiasm for primaries fell off after World War I, in part because they were expensive and turnout by voters was relatively low. But more importantly they were a direct threat to party leaders, who could not control their outcomes. Leading contenders for presidential nominations could ignore them and depend on their reputations with the party leaders to ensure their nomination at the national conventions. Only those candidates who were long shots found the primaries essential to demonstrate that they could win votes. Front-runners felt no need to risk running in them, and only underdogs depended on primaries alone.

In 1952, for example, Senator Estes Kefauver won twelve of thirteen primaries he entered, but Adlai Stevenson, who chose not to run in the primaries, was nominated by the Democratic Party. Dwight Eisenhower entered primaries the same year, not because he was an underdog, but to demonstrate that as a popular general who had never been a partisan politician he could also win votes. In 1960, John Kennedy entered the West Virginia primary and was able to defeat Hubert Humphrey, demonstrating that a Catholic could win in a Protestant state. Humphrey summed up the professional politician's attitude toward primaries in 1960: "[A]ny man who goes into a primary isn't *fit* to be president. You have to be crazy to go into a primary. A primary, now, is worse than the torture of the rack. It's all right to enter a primary by accident or because you don't know any better, but by forethought. . . ."[4]

But all of this changed after 1968. Forty-three states had instituted primary elections by 2000, and a much larger percentage of the delegates to the national conventions were chosen by states holding primary elections: 86 percent of the Democrats and 93 percent of the Republicans.[5] This revolution in the nomination process came about as a result of a series of reforms that changed the Democratic Party and swept the Republicans along with them.

The opening shot was the traumatic Democratic convention in Chicago in 1968 in which police and antiwar demonstrators clashed violently. The Democratic Party was so torn apart by the war in Vietnam that Lyndon Johnson chose not to run for reelection after Eugene McCarthy won almost 42 percent of the vote in the New Hampshire primary against Johnson's 49 percent write-in vote. Vice President Hubert Humphrey was the party establishment's pick to succeed Johnson, but McCarthy and George McGovern were challenging Humphrey from the left in the primaries. Humphrey chose not to run in the primaries, but with the support of the party regulars he was able to control the convention and beat back the antiwar insurgents to win the nomination.

Hostility toward the war, along with the frustration of not being able to break the control of the party regulars, incited the Democratic insurgents to demand a reexamination of the nomination process. Senator George McGovern was named to head the commission that came up with a number of proposals to reform the process. The reforms that were proposed and adopted by the Democrats included the elimination of party leaders being included ex officio as convention delegates; the requirement of written notice of times and places of caucus meetings; and the establishment of quotas for women, young people (under thirty), and African Americans. This was a triumph of the amateurs over the party professionals. Later, reform commissions would modify some of these requirements, loosening the quotas and allowing more elected officials as automatic delegates, but the thrust of the reforms transformed the nominating system. Party caucuses had to be open to any member of the party who wanted to participate in them, so the party professionals would no longer be able to dominate the selection process.

The effect of these reforms can be seen in the changed demographics of delegates to national party conventions over the years. In 1968, the percentage of women delegates was 13 percent for the Democrats and 16 percent for Republicans. By 1996, the numbers had changed to 57 percent and 39 percent, respectively. In 1968, only 5 percent of the Democratic delegates were African Americans. By 1996, their representation had increased to 21 percent in the Democratic convention and 2 percent in the Republican convention.[6]

As a result of these national party reforms, many more states replaced caucus conventions with primary elections as a means of choosing delegates to the national party conventions. Since state legislatures decide on state elections, the Republican Party had no choice but to go along with changes in state laws that were often taken by Democratic-controlled legislatures.

With forty states choosing convention delegates through primary elections rather than caucuses, the nomination system was transformed. Party professionals no longer dominated the selection process. The process was much more open to "outsiders," and the Democrats chose two nonregular party candidates in 1972 and 1976: George McGovern and Jimmy Carter.

The domination of the nominating process by primary elections rather than by party professionals in caucuses and conventions has magnified the importance of early contests, particularly the New Hampshire primary. By state law, it must be the first in the nation. When other states moved up their elections, New Hampshire moved its up even earlier, maintaining its importance as the first electoral contest that candidates face. The earlier Iowa caucuses occasionally play an important role, as they did for Jimmy Carter in 1976 and for Gary Hart in 1984, but the New Hampshire contest is the make-or-break test for many candidacies.

The crucial difference is not only who wins or comes in second or third, but also who performs better or worse than expected by the media commentators who establish and magnify the conventional wisdom. This was the case when antiwar candidate Eugene McCarthy received 41.9 percent of the vote in 1968, a result that helped convince Lyndon Johnson to withdraw from the race. Many people remember that McCarthy won the primary, but in fact President Johnson received 49.6 percent as a write-in candidate. In 1979, Senator Edward Kennedy challenged President Carter and showed that Carter was vulnerable; Ronald Reagan then beat Carter in the general election. In 1992, conservative Patrick Buchanan challenged incumbent George H.W. Bush and

The effect of early presidential primaries often has more to do with whether candidates measure up to expectations than with the actual number or percentage of the votes cast for a candidate. This cartoon is about the Iowa caucuses, but it could be about any early primary. (Toles © 1996 The Buffalo News. Reprinted with permission of Universal Press Syndicate. All rights reserved.)

won 36 percent of the Republican votes. The challenge highlighted Bush's vulnerability, and he went on to lose to Bill Clinton in the general election.

The irony is that in a nation of almost 195 million voters, New Hampshire is a relatively small state (in population), and it is not representative of the rest of the nation, with very few African Americans or other Hispanics and a political culture that is generally more conservative than most of the nation. Yet the news coverage of the early contests is so crucial to candidate visibility that it can ignite the candidacy of a long shot or ruin the hopes of a front-runner. A New Hampshire victory can generate momentum that will carry a candidate into the multiple primaries over the next several weeks and is hard to stop.

The preeminent position of New Hampshire as the presidential primary bellwether may have been undercut in 1996. Conservative fundamentalist Pat Buchanan actually beat front-runner Robert Dole 27.2 percent to 26.2 percent, even though Buchanan had little chance to win the nomination and Dole easily outdistanced him in subsequent primaries. In the 2000 Republican primary, Vietnam war hero John McCain beat George W. Bush 48.5 to 30.4 percent; Bush came back in the South Carolina primary and went on to win the nomination easily.

But more importantly, independent actions by a number of states had the result of "front-loading" the primary selection process, giving the New Hampshire outcomes less time to influence the process. In the 1980s, candidates were not determined until mid- to late spring. But with more states moving their primary election dates to earlier in the spring, the 1996 nominees were known by mid-March. In 2000, New York, New Jersey, and California moved their elections to the first Tuesday in March, and half of both parties' delegates were chosen by that date and two-thirds by a week later.[7]

This increasing front-loading of primaries is seen by many as a problem for several reasons. Front-loading favors those candidates who are already well known and who can raise the most money to saturate the air waves with their ads early in the process. (Though in 1996, Senator Phil Gramm, who had raised $24 million, and Steven Forbes, who invested $30 million of his own money, proved that money cannot buy the nomination.) With so many delegates committed by mid-March, there is less chance for dark horse candidates to attract contributions and press attention.

Thus, there have been several proposals to reform the process by spreading primary elections more evenly over the spring months. This would allow voters more time to evaluate candidates and use their performance in victory and defeat to help them choose the strongest candidates. One possibility proposed by the National Association of Secretaries of State would involve primaries in four regions of the country: the East, South, Midwest, and West. The rotating primaries would be scheduled for March, April, May, and June, and each region would have its chance to hold its primaries first, in March, every sixteen years. Such a system is appealing to good-government reformers, but it would have to gain support from both political parties and all of the fifty state legislatures before it could be implemented.[8]

PRESIDENTIAL ELECTIONS

It was the intention of the Framers that the electors would be people of public affairs who would exercise independent judgment in deciding for whom to cast their ballots for president. Electors would probably be personally familiar with most candidates and would be able to judge the character of the nominees as well as their stands on policy issues. But with the development of political parties and the growth of the country, the procedures for elections began to change.

During the first half of the nineteenth century, property qualifications for voting were gradually eliminated, resulting in virtually universal white-male suffrage. States also exercised their right to determine how electors would be chosen, and by 1832 all states provided for choosing electors by votes of citizens rather than by selection by state legislatures. States also adopted the "unit rule," by which all of the electoral votes from each state would be cast for whichever candidate won a plurality of the popular vote. This winner-take-all practice increases the stakes for any candidate who has a chance to come in first in voting in any given state and helps the large states in particular, where the most electoral votes are at stake. But there is a compensating bias in favor of very small states, all of which have a minimum of three electoral votes.

PROBLEMATIC ELECTIONS

The constitutional electoral arrangement as designed by the Framers allows for the possibility that a candidate who does not receive the most popular votes (those cast by individual citizens on Election Day) will end up winning the presidency. This can happen in three different ways:

1. If there are several "faithless electors" (when an elector does not vote for the candidate to whom he or she was pledged)
2. If no candidate wins a majority in the Electoral College, and the House of Representatives selects the winner (who does not have to be the winner in the popular election)
3. If a candidate wins a majority of electoral votes without winning the majority of the popular votes

The problem of the "faithless elector" has not been a serious problem so far. Virtually all electors consider themselves morally bound to cast their ballots for the candidate to whom they are pledged, and there have been only fourteen (of nearly 20,000 electoral votes cast) faithless electors in our history.[9] Many states have passed laws that are intended to bind electors to vote for their declared candidates, but the constitutionality of such laws has not been tested and would be in serious doubt. But in an election as close as the one in 2000, several defecting electors could change the outcome.

The second condition is a real possibility; the Constitution provides that if no candidate wins a majority of electoral votes, the president is determined by a vote in the House of Representatives. The House, with one vote per state delegation and provided two-thirds of the states are present, selects the president from the top three electoral vote winners (before 1804, the top five). The vote of a majority of all of the states is necessary to elect the president. The House has selected the president twice in our history. In 1800, all Republican electors cast their ballots for Thomas Jefferson and Aaron Burr, creating a tie with neither having a majority. Thus, the election was thrown into the House, despite the general understanding that Jefferson was the presidential candidate. The House was still controlled by the lame-duck Federalists, who had been voted out of office but who would not be replaced until March 1801, giving the choice of president to the party that had lost the election. On the first ballot there were actually more votes of individual representatives for Burr than for Jefferson, but each state has only one vote, and eight states voted for Jefferson and only six for Burr. The vote in two state delegations was tied, giving Jefferson a plurality but not a majority of all the states. It was not until the thirty-sixth ballot that some

Federalists were convinced to cast blank ballots, allowing Jefferson to be elected president and Burr vice president.

This unexpected circumstance led Congress to pass the Twelfth Amendment to the Constitution providing for separate ballots for president and vice president and also providing that the House would select (by majority of all states, with one vote per state) from among the top three rather than the top five candidates if there were no majority in the Electoral College vote. The vice president would be chosen by the Senate (by majority of all senators, one vote per senator) from the top two electoral vote-getters for vice president.

In 1824, the winner of the popular vote was Andrew Jackson, who won ninety-nine electoral votes (and a plurality of the popular votes cast) compared to eighty-four votes for John Quincy Adams, forty-one for William Crawford, and thirty-seven for Henry Clay. In accord with the Constitution and the Twelfth Amendment, the House decided among the top three candidates. Speaker of the House Henry Clay threw his support behind Adams, who was elected president, to the outrage of Jackson. Adams subsequently appointed Clay to be secretary of state, in what many assumed to be a prearranged deal.

The next election in which the winner of the popular votes was not chosen president was the 1876 contest, after which the nation did not know who would be president until March 2, 1877. Two separate slates of electors were sent to Congress from Florida, Louisiana, and South Carolina. Because both houses of Congress could not agree on which slates to accept as the legitimate ones, a special commission was created to make the decision. The commission consisted of five Representatives, five Senators, and five members of the Supreme Court. The partisan split was seven Democrats and seven Republicans, with the independent Chief Justice David Davis intended to chair the commission. When Illinois appointed Davis to be Senator from Illinois, he was replaced by Republican Justice Joseph Philo Bradley, who voted with the other Republicans to award all of the twenty disputed electoral votes to the Republican candidate. This decision gave Rutherford Hayes the 185 to 184 victory in the electoral vote count and the majority he needed to win the presidency. Democrat Samuel Tilden won 4,300,590 million popular votes to 4,036,298 cast for Hayes. Thus the runner-up in the popular vote became president with 264,292 fewer votes than his opponent. Democrats agreed not to further challenge the presidential vote in exchange for an agreement by Hayes to end Reconstruction and remove the carpetbag Republican governments from the southern states. This delivery of political power in the South to the Democrats led to the disenfranchisement of African Americans in the South over the next several decades and the creation of the "solid south" for the Democratic Party.

The only election, until 2000, in which a candidate who did not win a plurality of the popular vote was directly elected president by the Electoral College occurred in 1888. Democrat Grover Cleveland, the incumbent president, ran about one percentage point ahead of his Republican opponent, Benjamin Harrison. Harrison, however, won slim majorities of the popular vote in Indiana and New York, allowing him to capture all of their electoral votes, and a majority of all electoral votes, thereby winning the election despite coming in second in the popular vote count.[10] Cleveland won a plurality by about 95,000 popular votes but received only 168 electoral votes compared with Harrison's 233. Thus there were three elections in the nineteenth century in which the runner-up in the popular vote became president because of the electoral vote provisions of the Constitution. There have been a number of close calls in the twentieth century (e.g., 1948, 1960, 1968, and 1976), though the odds are against the runner-up in the popular election becoming president.[11] But the unexpected happened in the presidential election of 2000.

THE 2000 ELECTION

Challenger George W. Bush and incumbent Vice President Al Gore ran so close a race that it culminated in a disputed election that was not decided until the Supreme Court ended the legal battles on December 12, 2000, thirty-six days after Election Day. On the night of the election, November 7, it was clearly a tight race in the Electoral College, with the outcome depending on who won Florida's twenty-five electoral votes. If Gore won Florida, he would have a solid electoral victory; if Bush took Florida, he would win by a narrow margin, with two electoral votes deciding the outcome.

On election night, it appeared that Al Gore would win in Florida, but as more returns were reported, it appeared that Bush would be the winner by a narrow margin. Vice President Gore even called Bush in the middle of the night to concede, but within a few hours it became clear that the race in Florida was too close to call.

In the final vote count, Gore clearly won the total national popular vote; he outpolled Bush by 50,996,116, to 50,456,159, winning by a margin of 539,947 votes. But the electoral vote count was a different story. The initial Florida returns showed Bush with 1,784 more votes than Gore. Florida law requires an automatic machine recount in such close races, and the next day's machine recount reduced Bush's margin to 327. With nearly 6 million votes cast in Florida, the difference between the two candidates was statistically insignificant and smaller than the margin of error that any vote counting system could guarantee. Yet who would become president hinged on the relatively insignificant number of votes that divided the two candidates.

There were a number of problems with the vote count in Florida that might have made a difference much greater than the several hundred votes that divided the two candidates. One problem was the design of the ballot in Palm Beach County. The "butterfly ballot" was designed so that the names of the candidates would appear in large type in adjacent columns, with the hole to punch between the two columns, rather than in the usual one column, with one name over the other. The design evidently confused a number of voters who intended to vote for Gore but punched the hole for Buchanan because it was near the Democratic Party designation and was the next possible hole to punch after the Republican candidates. The conclusion that a number of voters who intended to vote for Gore ended up punching the Buchanan hole can be inferred from the relatively large number of votes Buchanan received in the heavily

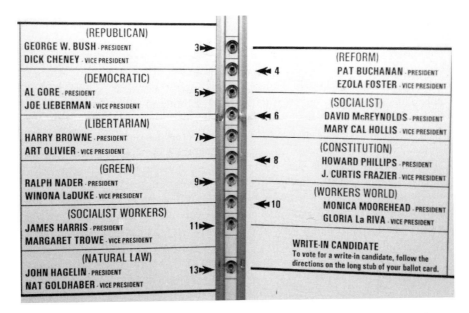

The "butterfly ballot" in Palm Beach County, Florida, was specifically designed for the 2000 election to accommodate large print for the candidates' names. But it had the effect of confusing some voters who punched the hole corresponding to Pat Buchanan when they wanted to vote for Al Gore. (AP Images)

pro-Gore Palm Beach County (3,400), more than in any other of Florida's sixty-seven counties.[12]

Other problems occurred when some voters punched more than one hole for the presidential candidates, in effect voting for more than one person (an overvote). Although one might make a reasonable argument that the above situations occurred to the detriment of the Gore candidacy, there was no practical remedy for the problem, since a reelection was not feasible and would result in serious legal problems. Voter mistakes in marking a ballot cannot be easily cured after the fact.

On the other hand, mistakes in counting the ballots after they had been marked may also have occurred, as the machine recount indicated. One problem with the punch card ballot is that the punching stylus must remove the small, perforated piece of the ballot card (the chad) associated with the candidate so that when the ballot passes through the machine, light can pass through the opening and register the vote. But if the voting machine has become clogged with chads, it is possible to push the stylus but be unable to remove the chad entirely. Thus, an attempt to vote for a candidate might not be registered by the machine (an undervote). A voter's attempt to cast a ballot might also be ignored by the machine if the voter not only punched the hole for the candidate but also wrote in the name of the same candidate (an overvote). The voter's intent would be clear, but the ballot would be invalid and not counted by the machine.

Although the Democrats could not do anything about the voter mistakes that had occurred, there were potentially enough undervotes and overvotes to change the outcome by the several hundred votes needed by Gore to overtake Bush. So Gore sought hand recounts of the ballots in four of the counties where it seemed most likely that he could pick up enough votes to reverse the outcome. Thus began the long legal battle that culminated in the Supreme Court decision that decided the race in favor of Bush.

The complex set of suits and countersuits centered around the election laws of Florida and who had the legal right to interpret them. The Florida Supreme Court ordered the Florida secretary of state, who administered the state elections, to extend the statutory deadline for counties to report their votes in order to allow the hand recounts to be completed. After the U.S. Supreme Court vacated that verdict and remanded the case for reconsideration, the Florida Supreme Court ordered hand recounts of ballots of all Florida counties, not just those challenged by Gore. It set no standard for how the ballots were to be evaluated other than the Florida law that provided that the intent of the voter should prevail.

The U.S. Supreme Court decided to hear the challenge of the Republicans, who argued that the Florida Supreme Court was misinterpreting Florida election law by setting aside the deadlines for counties to report the vote count and ordering that there be a statewide manual recount of ballots. By a 5 to 4 majority, the Court decided that the Florida Supreme Court's decision violated the equal protection clause of the Fourteenth Amendment because it did not specify the criteria by which all ballots should be judged. Different jurisdictions within the state might use different criteria to count the ballots and thus not treat all votes equally. The Court further argued that there was not enough time to establish specific standards and recount the ballots before the deadline for reporting the state's electoral votes to the Congress.

The Bush margin, when the U.S. Supreme Court stopped the recounts, was 537, and it remained the official count for the state of Florida; thus Florida's 25 electoral votes were cast for George W. Bush. Once Florida's election was determined, Bush's electoral votes totaled 271, one more than the majority of 270 (out of 538) needed to win the presidency. Al Gore, however, received credit for only 266 electoral votes because one elector from the District of Columbia cast a blank ballot to protest the lack of congressional representation for the District. Thus the faithless-elector issue was raised again. If the blank ballot had instead been cast for Gore as it was pledged, or if it was counted as a vote and two Bush electors had defected to Gore, the electoral vote total for Bush would have been 269, one vote short of a majority, and the House would have had to decide the election.[13]

A plausible argument can be made that more voters in Florida intended to vote for Gore than for Bush in 2000 (e.g., mistaken Buchanan votes, undervotes, overvotes), but there was no practical remedy for voter mistakes, and the hand recounts were stopped by the courts. One could also argue that the Florida secretary of state acted within her discretion in enforcing the statutory deadlines and that the Florida Supreme Court, in reversing her decisions, made a reasonable interpretation of state law. Finally, one could argue that the U.S. Supreme Court should not have interfered with the Florida court's interpretation of Florida law, or that it was right to intervene in order to end the dispute. But the bottom line is that those institutions and individuals who had the legal authority to do so, made the final decisions that went into effect. Whether these people made reasonable decisions will continue to be a matter of dispute.

ELECTORAL COLLEGE REFORM?

The outcome of the 2000 election raised again the question of whether our method of choosing the president should be reformed. The Electoral College system is "flawed" from the perspective of those who think that the candidate who wins the most popular votes should be elected president—or at least that the runner-up in the popular election should not be elected. This perspective, it can be argued, is consistent with evolving democratic values in the United States over the past two centuries.

But first it must be recognized that the United States is not, nor was it meant to be, a pure democracy, even if it were possible in a large nation-state of almost 300 million citizens. Nor was it contemplated that the United States government would operate under a general principle of majority rule, though majority rule is often used in decision making within governmental institutions. The governmental system was designed by the Framers to be a republic, with representatives of the people chosen to govern.

Nevertheless, since the founding of the Republic, the nature of our polity has changed in important ways, and the Constitution has been amended to reflect some of those changes. With respect to the selection of the president, the original expectations of the Framers have been modified a number of times. The states individually have made the most important decisions by deciding to place the right to select presidential electors with the citizens of the states.

Perhaps the most compelling argument that the president should be elected by direct popular vote is based on the premise that the president and vice president are the only national officials who represent the people as a whole and that the choice of the people is best approximated by the candidate who wins the most votes. In addition, with the Electoral College, the votes for the losing candidate in each state are "wasted" in the sense that they are not cumulated with the other votes for that candidate and cannot help him or her win. This argument is buttressed by the opening declaration in the Preamble to the Constitution: "We the People." The Framers intentionally required that the Constitution be ratified by special conventions called in the separate states and not by the legislatures of the states. The import of their decision is that "the people" created the Constitution, not the states. It is not too far a stretch to argue that the choice of the people ought to determine the winners of the only national elective offices in the government.

The legitimacy of the popular election of the president among the populace is buttressed by the probability that many, if not most, citizens who go to the polls to vote for president think that they are voting for president rather than a slate of electors. Some state ballots specify that the presidential vote is for a slate of electors, and some even list the individual electors, but many do not. At least this perception held until November 8, 2000.

One of the effects of the Electoral College system is that the ballots cast by all of the voters do not carry the same weight. That is, the ratio of electoral votes to population varies from state to state, benefiting the smallest states. For example the ratio of electoral votes to population in Wyoming (with 509,000 people and 3 electoral votes) is 1 to 170,000 and in California (with 36,132,000 people and 55 electoral votes) is 1 to 657,000. Thus a vote in Wyoming is several times more influential in selecting electors than a vote in California.

But small states are not necessarily the winners in the Electoral College scheme. Because most states have chosen to award all of their electors to the winner of the plurality of the votes in the state (the unit rule, or winner-take-all), the largest prizes in electoral votes are in the most populous states. Thus inhabitants of the large states benefit from candidates courting their votes. But in any given election, whether a large state will be courted depends on whether it is "in play" in the sense that either candidate might win the plurality of its votes. For instance, in the 2000 election George W. Bush did not spend much time campaigning in New York because he had conceded that a majority of New York voters would probably vote for Al Gore. For the same reason, Gore did not have a large incentive to spend much time in New York, except occasionally to shore up the party faithful. After his nomination, Al Gore did not even campaign in California, visiting the state only once, because he calculated that a majority of its votes were his anyway.[14] Similarly, Gore did not campaign much in Texas, since Bush had the state sewed up.

But the abstract inequalities of voter weight in the Electoral College system do not constitute the major problem with the system. As long as the winner of the popular vote also wins the electoral vote, the major purpose of a democratic election has been fulfilled. But this is not always the case, and the most important objection to the Electoral College design is that the runner-up in the popular vote can end up being elected president.

Over the years there have been many proposals to reform the Electoral College system, some proposing relatively minor changes, some proposing a constitutional amendment to provide for the direct popular election of the president:

The *automatic plan* would eliminate the problem of the faithless elector by automatically casting each state's electoral votes in favor of the candidate who won the plurality of popular votes in the state. There would be no individual electors to cast ballots and thus no opportunity for a vote to be cast in an unexpected direction. It would take a constitutional amendment to make such a change.

The *district plan* would give one electoral vote to the candidate who won a plurality of votes in each congressional district within a state. The extra two electoral votes would be granted to the candidate who won the most popular votes in the state as a whole (as only Maine and Nebraska do now).

The *proportional plan* would divide the electoral vote in proportion to the popular vote in each state.

The *national bonus plan* would grant a bonus of 102 electoral votes (two for each state plus the District of Columbia) to the candidate who wins the most popular votes, providing the winner has at least 40 percent of the vote. This approach would virtually eliminate the possibility that the runner-up in the popular vote would become president while at the same time preserving the distribution of electoral votes by states (though in a diluted form).

The *direct popular election of the president plan* would make the winner of the most votes nationwide the president. If neither candidate wins 40 percent of the vote, a runoff election would be held between the top two vote-getting candidates.[15]

By far the most basic and important proposal to change the Electoral College system is the proposal to amend the Constitution to provide for the direct popular election of the president. A version of this plan that was considered by Congress from 1966 to 1979, and after hearings in Congress, the proposed constitutional amendment was passed by the House in 1969 by 339 to 70. Hearings in the Senate were held over the next ten years, and in 1979 the Senate voted 51 to 48 in favor of the proposal, well short of the two-thirds majority necessary to send a proposed constitutional amendment to the states for ratification.

The defense of the Electoral College system of electing the president is not based on the intent of the Framers, because the system has changed in fundamental ways, including the development of political parties, the inclusion of a vice-presidential candidate on the team ticket, the lack of discretion of electors, the unit rule (winner-take-all) adopted by the states, and the advent of national vote-counting technology.

The strongest constitutional argument against direct popular election is that it would undermine the federal nature of our government. By guaranteeing a specific number of electoral votes to each state, the Electoral College system ensures that presidential candidates must appeal to coalitions of voters that are widely distributed throughout the country. If the federal requirement were not there, candidates might appeal to regional clusters of voters whose votes could be aggregated across states and regions. This could potentially be divisive and lead to discord. This argument for the Electoral College depends in great part on the fact that states have individually adopted the unit rule of counting all of their electoral votes as a block.

Proponents of direct popular vote argue that federalism is indeed an important component of the constitutional system, but that the Electoral College system is not crucial to its maintenance. Certainly the electoral votes of small states do not attract active campaigning by major party candidates, who tend to go where large blocks of electoral votes are. More importantly, larger states will only be contested if there is a reasonable chance of their blocks of votes going either way. With direct popular election, all votes would count for candidates, who would be less likely to write off many states merely because they could not win the plurality in that state. Those who favor direct popular vote also argue that federalism is well protected by members of the House and Senate as well as by the legislatures and governors of the states.

Defenders of the Electoral College system also argue that it is one of the key bulwarks of the two-party system in the United States and that direct popular voting for president would lead to the splintering of the two-party system and a proliferation of minor parties. They argue that minor political factions would have an incentive to run candidates for president with the goal of forcing a runoff election and extract concessions in return for their support. The hope of these minor parties would be to attract enough votes, along with other splinter parties, to prevent either of the two-party candidates from winning 40 percent of the vote and thus force a runoff. This might encourage single-issue pressure groups to enter the race merely in order to broker a winner.

Proponents of direct popular vote argue that, in addition to our political culture, the real structural basis for our two-party system is single-member districts (plurality wins, or "first past the post") for representation in Congress. It is difficult to build a viable political party if there is little chance of electing government officials. Proportional representation systems for parliamentary elections encourage smaller parties to form because they can realistically win public office. In a presidential election, the probability of winning enough popular votes to force a runoff, even in conjunction with other minor parties, is low. The present system does not prevent minor party candidates from qualifying for inclusion on ballots in many states. Nor does it prevent significant third-party candidates from running, such as Theodore Roosevelt or Ross Perot.[16]

In a popular election system, even if one minor party were able to win a significant portion of the vote and there were a runoff election, how could the leaders of that party force their supporters to vote for the person with whom the candidate made a deal? In the present system, however, electors are chosen by the party (or candidate) on the basis of loyalty. If Ross Perot had been able to win sufficient popular votes to produce a majority for another candidate in the Electoral College, he would have had much more leverage in convincing a few loyalists on his slate of electors to vote for his choice than he would have had in persuading all his supporters in a runoff election. Thus a third party forcing concessions on one of the major parties is more likely in the Electoral College system than in a popular election with a runoff provision.

Another argument of critics of the direct popular vote plan is that it would lead to endless recounts and challenges. The reasoning is that if the election were close or the 40 percent threshold were in doubt, challenges and contests would not be limited to one or a few states but would be undertaken throughout the country, and "a recount of every ballot box in the country could be necessary."[17] In the election of 2000, some commentators raised the specter of chaos when they suggested that if we had direct popular elections, the problems we saw in Florida would happen throughout the whole country.

But one of the attractions of direct popular election is that recounts would be *less* likely. In order to undertake a recount, there has to be the reasonable possibility that enough incorrect or fraudulent votes can be found to change the election outcome. It is intuitively evident that the fewer the total votes involved, the more likely it is that a close contest may result in a small number of votes deciding the election. Thus in the present system a few votes in one state may be able to make the difference in swinging a large block of electoral votes and possibly decide the election. This is what happened in Florida in the 2000 presidential election; the election was so close that the swing of a few hundred votes might realistically have changed the election outcome. Thus a recount had a plausible possibility of changing the election outcome.

In Florida, Al Gore had to find several hundred votes in order to change the outcome. If the election had been by popular vote, George Bush would have had to find more than 500,000 votes, a daunting task. Even in 1960 when Richard Nixon's supporters were working on challenges in Illinois, they would have had to find about 9,000 votes to change the outcome. And if they had finally won Illinois, they would have had to find about 40,000 votes in Texas. Since winning both of these states through recounts was unlikely, Nixon's supporters gave up. It would have been even harder to find more than 100,000 votes throughout the country, if the popular vote determined the outcome. Thus the argument of those supporting direct popular voting for president is that recounts and challenges would be less, not more, likely because the number of votes needed to change a national outcome would be much larger than the number needed to change the outcome in one state that controlled a large or deciding block of electoral votes. It is true, however, that if the national vote were close enough to force a recount, it might be very difficult to administer.

In 2006, a novel campaign for electoral reform for a "Fair Vote" was launched by a group of reformers. Recognizing the difficulty of amending the Constitution, the group proposed an ingenious plan for individual state action, thus avoiding the need to amend the Constitution. The Fair Vote plan calls for individual states to commit themselves to an interstate compact to cast their electoral votes for the winner of the nation-wide popular vote. If the compact was agreed to by states representing at least 270 electoral votes (a majority), those states could determine that the winner of the popular vote would win the election. The interstate compact would not bind any individual state until the magic 270 electoral vote total of agreeing states had signed on to the agreement.

For reformers, the proposal had the advantages of not requiring an amendment to the Constitution and of not taking effect until enough states to make it work had signed on. The potential weaknesses of the proposal included the difficulty of attracting sufficient state endorsements and its enforceability. Few individual states had strong incentives to sign on, and the problem of the "faithless elector" still remained. That is, although many states have passed laws requiring electors to cast their ballots for the winner of the popular vote in the state, the constitutionality of enforcing such requirements has not been definitively settled.

THIRD-PARTY PRESIDENTIAL CANDIDATES

The electoral system discourages third-party attempts to win the presidency. With votes aggregated by state, all but two of which (Maine and Nebraska use a district system) allocate their electoral votes by the unit rule (winner-take-all), potential third parties cannot hope to win any electoral votes unless they capture more votes in a state than either of the two major-party candidates. This is difficult to do. The most serious third-party attempt was made by Theodore Roosevelt, who ran again on the Progressive "Bull Moose" Party ticket in 1912 and captured 27.4 percent of the popular vote and 88 electoral votes to Woodrow Wilson's 41.9 percent of the vote and 435 electoral votes.[18] The Progressive Robert LaFollette, in 1924, won 16.6 percent of the popular vote and 13 electoral votes. In 1948, the Democratic Party was split when Strom Thurmond led southern Democrats, who opposed Harry Truman's stand on civil rights for African Americans, to form the Dixicrat Party, winning 2.4 percent of the popular vote and 39 electoral votes. That same year, Henry A. Wallace defected from the left of the Democratic Party and ran as a socialist, winning 2.4 percent of the popular vote, but no electoral votes because his candidacy was not regionally based.

The next serious third-party attempt was made by segregationist George Wallace, governor of Alabama, who was able to capture 12.8 percent of the popular vote and 46 electoral votes. Wallace's success in capturing so many electoral votes was due to the concentration of his racist and states' rights appeal in the South, allowing him to win several states. The next significant third-party candidate was John Anderson, a Republican member of Congress from Illinois, who in 1980 wanted to provide a moderate alternative to Ronald Reagan. He ran as an independent, but had to mount ten lawsuits to get his name on the ballot in various states; he was successful in all ten suits and got his name on all fifty state ballots.[19] Anderson's support was national, rather than regional, and he won 6.6 percent of the popular vote but no electoral votes.

The final vote for third-party candidates is usually below their early support because of the "wasted vote" argument. If it seems certain that they will not capture the presidency, and that a vote for them will not affect the outcome, their supporters cast their ballots for their second choice, one of the two major candidates, who have a better chance of winning. Thus, Wallace's final popular vote of 13.4 percent was significantly less than his peak of support in the polls of 21 percent in September 1968. In June 1980, John Anderson reached a high point of 24 percent in the polls, but he captured only one-fourth of that in the general election.[20]

In the spring and summer of 1992, it seemed a third-party candidate had a serious chance to win a significant number of votes; some thought he even had a chance to win the presidency. In February 1992, Texas billionaire Ross Perot announced on a TV talk show that he would run for president if his name was placed on the ballot in all fifty states. Among voters, disaffection with the two major parties was running high, and there was a feeling in the country that "politics as usual" was not solving the major problems facing the nation: a huge national debt and deficits above $300 billion, a sluggish economy with high unemployment, a decaying infrastructure, and a growing underclass. When Perot set up a telephone headquarters, he received six thousand calls the first day, and the spontaneous outpouring of support encouraged his candidacy.[21] He promised to confront the budget deficits and end the partisan fighting between the president and Congress.

His candidacy was taken seriously because of his widespread national support and the fact that he could match the spending of the Democrats and Republicans—even outspend them—because of his personal wealth. He promised a "first class" campaign and said he was willing to spend $100 or $200 million on it. In June 1992, he hired campaign professionals Ed Rollins, who had run Reagan's 1984 reelection campaign, and Hamilton Jordan, who had engineered Jimmy Carter's out-of-nowhere campaign in 1976. With 36 percent support in national polls, he was ahead of both President Bush and probable Democratic challenger Bill Clinton.[22]

In July, however, Perot dropped out of the race only to reenter the contest later in the fall. The final vote count gave Perot 19 percent of the popular vote, making him the most serious third-party candidate since Theodore Roosevelt. Because his appeal was national rather than regional, however, Perot did not win any electoral votes despite having almost one-fifth of the popular vote. The Perot candidacy—especially the suddenness of his appearance as a serious presidential candidate—demonstrates the weakness of political parties and the vulnerability of the political system to antigovernment and antiestablishment appeals.

The Perot candidacy was reminiscent of the 1923 draft movement enjoyed by Henry Ford. He had the broad-based support of those who felt that he would bring businesslike efficiency to the government. Ford formally pulled out after he won the Michigan primary in 1924. There is an enduring streak in American political culture that yearns for a nonpolitician to take over the government and run it on a businesslike basis, someone who would eschew the petty politics of traditional politicians. The problem is that our government of separated powers and the U.S. electoral system are not like businesses. The more serious a candidate becomes, the more bargaining and coalition-building is necessary—and things begin to look like politics as usual.

After his surprisingly strong showing in the 1992 elections, Ross Perot did his best to remain in the public eye. In the fall of 1993 he campaigned against ratification of the North American Free Trade Agreement (NAFTA) but came out second in a debate with Vice President Gore on the topic. Perot decided to institutionalize his political movement, United We Stand America, by establishing the "Reform Party" in 1995. Over the next year his supporters succeeded in qualifying the party for the ballot in all fifty states.

After criticizing public financing of presidential elections and spending more than $60 million of his own money in 1992, Perot decided to accept $29 million in public funds for his 1996 race. Despite Perot's trenchant criticism of the abuses of campaign financing and other problems with the two-party system, he was not able to capture the imagination of most voters. Four years after his first presidential campaign, he still was unwilling to be specific about the type of campaign finance system he would support or where the budget would have to be cut to bring it into balance. In the fall election he won 8 percent of the vote (and no electoral votes), respectable for a third-party attempt but nowhere near the 19 percent he shocked the country with in 1992.

The irony of third-party politics in presidential elections is that Ross Perot won 19 percent of the vote in 1992 but probably did not affect the result, yet Ralph Nader won only 2.7 percent of the vote nationally in 2000 and determined the outcome. Nader led the Green Party challenge to the two-party system and appealed to those concerned with the environment and troubled by economic globalization. Despite arguments by Democrats that he might help George W. Bush win the election, Nader campaigned vigorously throughout the country and denounced the two major parties.

As it turned out, Nader's 2.8 million votes nationally did not prevent Gore from winning a popular vote plurality of 540,000. But Nader's count in Florida of 97,500 votes dwarfed the minuscule number of votes (537) that separated Bush from Gore in that state. Exit polls indicated that 47 percent of Nader voters would have voted for Gore if Nader had not run (21 percent would have voted for Bush and 12 percent would not have voted). Thus the third-party candidacy of Ralph Nader cost Al Gore the presidency in 2000.[23]

THE GENERAL ELECTION

Once candidates have run the gauntlet of the primary elections and have been nominated by the national party conventions, they must face the general electorate in campaigning for the presidency. But the characteristics of the general electorate—all voters who will vote in the presidential election—are not the same as the people who vote in primary elections. The American electorate tends to fall into the center of the political spectrum. Most voters do not consider themselves strong Republicans or strong Democrats, but they do have a preference for one or the other party, and an increasing number of voters consider themselves independents, with no, or very weak, preferences between the two major parties.

Thus, the candidates that the two parties choose as their standard-bearers are most often in the middle of the political spectrum, and they tend to move more toward the middle (ideologically) after the primaries and as the general election approaches. This is a rational strategy for presidential candidates hoping to capture a majority of the votes in most recent elections.

In 1960, Richard Nixon, the sitting vice president, won the Republican nomination, and John F. Kennedy, a young senator from Massachusetts, was the challenger for the Democrats. Nixon emphasized the experience in foreign affairs he had gained in the Eisenhower administration, and Kennedy promised to "get the country moving again" after what Democrats considered the complacency of the Eisenhower years. Kennedy emphasized a strong defense and argued that there was a "missile gap," with the Soviet Union enjoying a distinct advantage (this later turned out not to be true). Both candidates were fiscal conservatives, but Kennedy was clearly more liberal on civil rights and other domestic issues. The campaign was about competence and character, and there was not a sharp ideological difference between the two candidates. This was reflected in the outcome of the election, one of the closest in our history, with Kennedy winning by 114,673, merely 0.3 percent of the popular vote.[24]

In 1968, Hubert Humphrey was the sitting vice president, and although he might have wanted to distance himself from his administration's policy in Vietnam, Lyndon Johnson would not allow it. Richard Nixon had come back again to capture the Republican nomination, and he said he had a plan to end the war. Even though there were differences about domestic priorities between the old-time liberal Humphrey and the fiscally conservative Nixon, the campaign brought them both to the center of the political spectrum. The result was another close election, with Nixon winning 43.2 percent of the vote against Hubert Humphrey's 42.7 percent (third-party candidate George Wallace took most of the rest of the votes).

In 1976, Jimmy Carter ran against the incumbent Gerald Ford, who had replaced Spiro Agnew as Nixon's vice president, and against the Nixon administration and Watergate. Carter projected an air of competence, being a businessman, nuclear engineer, and former naval officer, and he promised honesty in government. There were differences in political values between Carter and Ford, but their fiscal conservativism put both of them close to the middle of the American political spectrum. Again, it was a close election, with Carter receiving 50.1 percent of the vote to Ford's 48.0 percent.

With this rational tendency for political parties to put up presidential candidates who are in the middle of the political spectrum, how can we explain the Republicans' choice of Barry Goldwater in 1964 and the Democrats' choice of George McGovern in 1972? Goldwater was clearly on the right wing of the Republican Party in the 1960s. He was much more "hawkish" on Vietnam than was Lyndon Johnson, who was running as the "peace" candidate in the campaign. Goldwater promised "a choice, not an echo," emphasizing that he was not a clone of the Democratic candidate and that there was a clear ideological difference between him and the Democratic nominee. Johnson placed himself in the middle of the political spectrum and won a resounding victory in 1964, becoming president in his own right (61.0 percent to 38.5 percent).

George McGovern challenged Richard Nixon in 1972 from the left wing of the Democratic Party. The former World War II bomber pilot had built his national reputation as an antiwar candidate, and he was more liberal on economic and social issues than most voters. The electorate clearly recognized this and gave Richard Nixon an overwhelming victory in the 1972 election (60.7 percent to 37.5 percent).

How can we explain this seeming irrationality on the part of the two political parties? Goldwater was decisively to the right of the political spectrum, and McGovern was clearly to the left; each lost in a landslide. Why didn't the Republicans in 1964 and the Democrats in 1972 nominate more viable candidates?

The explanation lies in the differing levels of political activism of the general electorate and those who participate in the nomination process. The people who determine the outcome of nominations tend to be political activists who are firmly committed to political ideals. In the Democratic Party, these people are most often on the left of the spectrum; in the Republican Party, they are on the right. Goldwater and McGovern were able to activate and energize the "true believers" on their respective ends of the political spectrum to capture the nomination of their parties. The truly committed backers of such candidates are very effective in helping them win nominations. They go to caucus meetings to select national-convention delegates committed to their candidate, or they work to get out the vote for primary elections. Thus, in the fight for the nomination, they have certain advantages over their more moderate opponents.

But once the nominations are over and the candidates must appeal to the general electorate, the strategic situation is different. Most voters are not firmly committed to one end of the political spectrum. In addition, many more voters turn out to vote in the general election than in primary elections. As a result, if the winners of nominations do not move quickly toward the middle of the political spectrum, they will likely lose the election. The problem is that candidates who are very liberal or conservative may not want to move to the middle of the spectrum, or might not be able to convince voters that they are indeed moderate, after the nomination campaign.

The 1980 election contest between moderate Jimmy Carter and conservative Ronald Reagan might have turned out differently, but Reagan was able to change his image with the voters and appear much more mainstream than he had in his earlier campaigns. In addition, Carter was saddled with the hostage situation in Iran and had dropped in voter estimation. Reagan won convincingly with 50.7 percent to Carter's 41 percent of the vote, with independent John Anderson winning most of the rest of the votes. In 1988, both George H. W. Bush and Michael Dukakis held very similar policy views, and Dukakis declared that the campaign was about competence rather than ideology. But in the campaign, Bush was able to tar Dukakis with the label of "liberal" and was able to win the election quite soundly, 53.4 percent to 45.6 percent.

In 1992, Bill Clinton carefully presented himself as a moderate Democrat after winning the nomination. After the Republican convention had made appeals to the conservative wing of the party, President Bush distanced himself from the tone of the convention and moved toward the center of the political spectrum. But with an ailing economy and no obvious foreign threat to highlight Bush's foreign-policy experience, Clinton was able to win 43 percent of the popular vote to Bush's 38 percent, with Perot winning 19 percent.

In 1996, President Clinton benefited from the bimodal nature of the primary electorate. As a sitting president, he began reelection planning early and preempted challengers from the left of the Democratic Party (especially Jesse Jackson) by adroit political maneuvering and by raising huge sums for his campaign war chest. Thus, as the first Democratic president to run for reelection without a challenger in the primaries since 1964, he was able to position himself in the middle of the political spectrum, because the liberal wing of the party had no alternative candidate to vote for in the primaries. In addition, Clinton used the millions he and the Democratic Party raised to begin running TV ads in the summer of 1995; the ads were designed to establish Clinton's image as a moderate who would appeal to the broad middle of the American electorate.

Bob Dole was not so lucky. Even though he was the front-runner and had raised the most money, he had to run to his right so as not to alienate the conservative wing of the Republican Party, particularly the well-financed and effectively organized Christian Coalition. Conservative Republican voters did have alternative candidates on Dole's right, particularly Pat Buchanan, who had beat Dole in the New Hampshire primary. Thus, Dole had to run to his right in the primaries and then scramble back to the center once he had the nomination sewed up. The outcome of the 1996 race did not hinge on the ideological differences between Dole and Clinton, both of whom were in the middle of the spectrum. But the above calculations were important in the ways the two candidates presented themselves to voters early in the election year.

President Clinton won reelection in 1996 because of a number of factors, none of which was evident immediately after the huge Republican victories in the 1994 congressional elections. In early 1995, President Clinton and the Democrats were discouraged after losing both houses of Congress to the Republicans; the House was controlled by Republicans for the first time in forty years.

But Bill Clinton was fortunate because the Republicans overplayed their hand, thinking they had received a mandate to move the country in a sharply conservative direction. When they tried to implement their program by passing a budget that was balanced by cutting sharply in areas such as the environment and education, President Clinton was able to present himself as the protector of programs that Americans liked, especially Medicare. Clinton's public approval ratings rose and stayed up, while Newt Gingrich and the Republicans were seen as too extreme. (See the case study in Chapter 6 for the details of this turnaround.)

Thus, Bill Clinton went into the 1996 election year much stronger politically than he had been after the 1994 elections. He was able to position himself in the middle of the political spectrum by arguing that he was in favor of family values and personal responsibility. He was also able to argue that he could moderate the extreme policies of the conservatives in Congress led by Gingrich. In November, Clinton won with 49.2 percent of the vote against Dole's 40.7 percent. Ross Perot captured 8.4 percent of the popular vote, less than half of his 19 percent in 1992.

The campaign for the 2000 election was run from the center of the political spectrum. Al Gore was the incumbent vice president in a moderate, "New Democrat" administration. Though he had a pro-environment record, he was a moderate on military issues, being a Vietnam veteran and having voted for the 1991 Gulf War. His primary opponent, former Senator Bill Bradley, did not push him to the left in the primaries. George W. Bush had accumulated many Republican endorsements and raised a large war chest of campaign funds going into the New Hampshire primary. But when he was decisively defeated by Senator John McCain (48 to 30 percent), he moved sharply to the right in order to defeat McCain in the South Carolina primary, after which he was able to move back toward the center. In the campaign, Bush favored a large tax cut and a strong defense, echoing Ronald Reagan. But he presented himself as a "compassionate conservative" and stressed his concern for education, traditionally a Democratic issue. Bush's advocacy for more defense spending was moderated in public perceptions by his reluctance to champion an aggressive foreign policy.

So both candidates were in the middle of the political spectrum, with Nader on the left (winning 2.8 million votes) and Pat Buchanan on the right (winning 448,000 votes). In a strategic decision, Gore decided to distance himself from Bill Clinton because of the negative character associations that Clinton's impeachment might raise with the electorate. But in disassociating himself from Clinton personally, he also chose not to emphasize the Clinton administration's record of a balanced budget, high employment, and a booming economy. Rather, he focused his appeal on his personal qualifications and the promise of his future performance. George W. Bush benefited from early low expectations when he performed quite well in the presidential debates, and he reassured independents that he was a moderate rather than an extreme conservative. The result was that Gore, who many Democrats thought should have won handily, was able to win only a half million more votes than Bush, and he lost in the Electoral College.[25]

In dramatic contrast to 2000, the 2004 campaign was one of the most polarizing in American history, primarily because of the war in Iraq. President Bush ran on his war record and argued that the United States had to "stay the course" and assist the Iraqi people in establishing a democratic government. Democrats generally opposed the war because they thought the president had misled the country about WMD in Iraq, and they were doubtful that U.S. military action would lead to a stable government in Iraq. The Democrats nominated the decorated Vietnam War veteran John Kerry, in part because his military service contrasted sharply with President Bush, who had spent several years in the Texas National Guard instead of going to Vietnam. But President Bush was able to frame the campaign as a referendum on protecting the country from terrorist attack, convincing enough voters that he would do a better job protecting the country than would John Kerry.

Also, in contrast to the turnout of 54.3 percent for the 2000 election, almost 17 million more citizens voted in 2004, for a total turnout of almost 60 percent of the voting-age population voted. Even the vote of 18- to 21-year-olds jumped from 42 to 51 percent. Because feelings were so high, each party concentrated on turning out its own partisans. The Democrats were quite successful in increasing turnout, but the Republicans did even better, which explained the popular (two-party) vote outcome of 51.2 percent (62 million) for Bush and 48.8 percent (59 million) for Kerry. But the key to winning the presidency was Ohio, which Bush won by almost 120,000 votes. If about 60,000 voters had voted for Kerry instead of Bush in Ohio, with its 20 electoral votes at stake, there would have been an ironic repeat of the 2000 election: Bush would have won the popular vote and Kerry would have won the electoral vote and the presidency.

On May 1, 2003, President Bush used the setting of the aircraft carrier Abraham Lincoln off the California coast to announce the end of major combat activities in Iraq. (© Brooks Kraft/CORBIS)

ELECTORAL TRENDS

The election of 1932 and the popularity of Franklin Roosevelt in the 1930s produced the "New Deal Coalition," which endured into the 1960s. This electoral coalition included the "Solid South," blue-collar workers, Catholics, Jews, and others who favored the activist government programs of the New Deal. These political preferences translated into relatively stable party allegiances, with most voters identifying themselves with the Democratic Party and a minority with the Republicans. A smaller group considered themselves "independents." Party identification was reasonably stable over people's lives and over the middle decades of the twentieth century. It was relatively easy to predict a person's vote by their party identification. The Democratic advantage did not mean that Democrats always won the presidency, because special circumstances or an attractive Republican candidate could cause Democrats to desert their party and independents to vote heavily for the Republican. One example of this was the popularity of General Dwight Eisenhower, who was elected to the presidency in 1952 and 1956.

But the stable party allegiances that characterized the 1930s, 1940s, and 1950s began to break down in the 1960s. The beginning of the breakup of the

Democrats' large margin of preference was marked by arch-conservative Barry Goldwater's unsuccessful presidential campaign in 1964. Even though Goldwater lost in a landslide, his conservativism appealed to the socially conservative and very patriotic South. The South had been solidly Democratic ever since the harsh Republican Reconstruction after the Civil War. The only way for a politician to have any hope of success was to be a member of the Democratic Party. Thus, even though the South was very conservative, its political leaders were, predictably, Democrats. In addition, the African American vote in the South had been solidly Democratic since the New Deal and the Democratic support of civil rights.

Goldwater in 1964, and succeeding conservative Republican presidential candidates, appealed to these traditional conservatives and began the breakup of the Solid South. Social issues, such as skepticism about civil rights for African Americans (and later affirmative action), support of U.S. policy in Vietnam, law and order, and prayer in public schools, all appealed to conservative southern voters. In 1952, 85 percent of southern whites identified with the Democratic Party; by 1992, 40 percent did. In the 1994 congressional elections, for the first time since Reconstruction, Republicans captured a majority of the southern vote. With this decline in Democrats in the South, the Republicans averaged 66 percent of the southern presidential vote from 1972 to 1988, with Democratic candidates not able to win even one southern state in 1984, 1988, or 2000.[26]

The breakup of the Solid South was only one part of the revolution in electoral politics. Party identification across the country began to change also. The Democrats enjoyed a 47 to 27 percent edge in voter identification in 1952, with 23 percent calling themselves independent. Democratic voter identification rose to a high of 52 percent in the LBJ landslide of 1964, but it then declined to 35 percent in 1992. The 1952 Republican total of 27 percent dipped to a low of 23 percent in 1972 (in spite of the Nixon landslide) and edged back up to 28 percent in 1988.[27]

But the basic realignment of the electorate that would have signaled an enduring Republican majority in partisan identification did not occur. The reason was that, in contrast to previous realigning elections (as in 1932), voters did not switch allegiances from one party to another. Instead, those defecting from Democratic ranks began to consider themselves independents rather than Republicans. The percentage of those who identified themselves as independent of either party rose from 22 percent in 1952 to 39 percent in 2000.[28] The decline in self-identification with either political party was accompanied by widespread disaffection with both parties. In the summer of 1992, one professional opinion poll indicated that 82 percent of Americans felt that "both political parties are pretty much out of touch with the American people."[29]

The decline in party identification, along with the proliferation of presidential primary elections after 1968, combined to make political party support much less important in presidential elections. Richard Nixon raised most of his own money rather than depend on the Republican Party for fund-raising. In the 1968 and 1972 campaigns, he emphasized his own qualifications for office rather than his party allegiance. Neither George McGovern nor Jimmy Carter, though they were Democrats, were closely identified with Democratic Party professionals.

In the 1970s and 1980s, the presidential candidate dominated the political party and named its national chairperson; although, in the 1990s, the party organizations became important as conduits for financial contributions for presidential candidates. This presidential control developed because candidates began to form their own organizations and raise their own money rather than depend on their political parties. Money became more important because expensive television time became essential in reaching voters in primary elections, and political party organizations took second place to TV coverage. Personal organizations in the primary states were put together by individual candidates rather than by party regulars.

Another indicator of party breakdown was the rise in split-ticket voting, with voters voting for a presidential candidate of one party and a congressional candidate of the other party. Ticket-splitting rose from about 12 percent of ballots in 1952 to an average of 25 percent from 1972 to 1988, and to a high of 36 percent in 1992.[30]

Decreasing voter turnout for elections has accompanied the decline of political parties. In the 1950s and 1960s, turnout for presidential elections was about 60 percent of the voting-age population, but in the 1970s it began to decline, and in the 1988 election it was only 50 percent. Part of the reason for the decline was the Twenty-sixth Amendment to the Constitution, which gave the right to vote to all citizens eighteen years old or older. Since young people vote at significantly lower rates than older voters (32 percent for eighteen- to twenty-four-year-olds versus 67 percent for ages sixty-five and above), part of the decline is due to their inclusion in the electorate.[31]

The presidency of George W. Bush intensified the polarization of American politics. Strong feelings on the part of both Democrats and Republicans motivated voters to cast their ballots for the candidate of their own parties in greater percentages than in recent preceding elections. But the increase in partisan voting (and a turnout of 60 percent in 2004) has come at the expense of the ability of the political system to arrive at compromises over important public-policy issues.

THE MEDIA, PUBLIC OPINION, AND THE PERMANENT CAMPAIGN

The presidency began as an office quite insulated from popular opinion, but presidents have always known that public opinion is an important source of their power. President Lincoln declared: "Public sentiment is everything. With public sentiment nothing can fail, without it nothing can succeed."[32] Theodore Roosevelt began the more active use of the "bully pulpit" of the presidency to build public support for his favorite issues. And Woodrow Wilson said of the president's power: "Let him once win the admiration and confidence of the country, and no other single force can withstand him, no combination of forces will easily overpower him. . . ."[33]

PRESIDENTS AND THE MEDIA

Contemporary presidents have the capacity to reach the public in ways that could not have been imagined by these earlier presidents, and they have consciously formed their strategies of governing to exploit that capacity. Throughout most of American history, presidential communication with the American public was indirect. Presidents would give speeches that would be heard by scores or hundreds of people, at most, and word of mouth would carry their ideas further. Reporters would copy their words, opinion leaders around the country would read them, and their reactions would become part of the public opinion about presidents.

At the end of the nineteenth and beginning of the twentieth century, a professional Washington press corps developed to report the actions of a national government that was playing a greater role in the United States and the world. The advent of radio enabled the words of presidents to be heard directly by people throughout the nation, and Franklin Roosevelt effectively used the medium to address the nation in his famous "fireside chats." But FDR's main mechanism for reaching the public remained the Washington press corps. FDR held a total of 998 press conferences and averaged 6.9 per month, more than any other modern president.[34] He averaged no more than two "fireside chat" radio broadcasts per year.[35]

After FDR, the number of press conferences presidents held steadily declined, and John Kennedy began the modern era of presidential communications. The "Kennedy system" was marked by the introduction of live television coverage of press conferences. Television coverage was so appealing to Kennedy because it allowed him to speak directly to the people without his words being selected and interpreted by the Washington press corps. While this was resented by Washington print journalists, presidents now could communicate directly with the public and have greater control over the message that people received. Other elements of the "Kennedy system" included the granting of private interviews to favored reporters and special meetings with representatives of local newspapers to the exclusion of the national press.

The Kennedy strategy of "going public" marked a key turning point in presidents' efforts to control how they are perceived by the public. Political scientist Samuel Kernell argues that the national political system has been undergoing a subtle but basic shift from a system of "institutionalized pluralism" to one of "individualized pluralism." In the older system the political establishment was relatively stable and was dominated by the major power centers of Congress, the political parties, the national press, and the most important broad-interest groups (e.g., big business and big labor unions). A major part of presidential power was the president's personal reputation with this relatively stable constellation of power centers.

But the political landscape changed in the later decades of the twentieth century. With the growth of the welfare state, national public policy affects many more individual citizens than it did in the past. Members of Congress, despite the recent increase of party voting, often behave more as entrepreneurs than as loyal party members. Political parties have declined as the major intermediaries between the public and the government. Presidential candidates are no longer dependent on their party but rather dominate it. All of these developments have been accelerated by breakthroughs in communications technology.

As a result of these developments, especially party breakdown, presidents come to office without a ready-made coalition of a political party and the interest groups associated with it to support their agendas. They must try to cobble together more temporary coalitions of narrower interests for separate policy issues. In trying to put together these more temporary coalitions, they have found that a major tool they can use is "going public"; trying to get groups outside of Washington to use their political power to put pressure on Washington power centers, primarily Congress, to support the president's policy proposals. Thus, presidents have become much more active in developing political support in constituencies outside of Washington as part of their overall governing strategies.

These far-reaching changes in the political environment have had a profound effect on the way presidents have conducted their relations with the American public, as presidents have sought to exploit new communications technology in their efforts to affect public opinion. While the number of formal press conferences has steadily declined since FDR's time, the number of less formal exchanges with reporters has increased, in part because these are much more easily controlled by the White House.[36] The average number of minor public speeches increased by a factor of five between the 1930s and the presidencies of Nixon, Carter, and Reagan.[37] The total number of public appearances by presidents and the amount of their political travel have also steadily increased. Presidents George H.W. Bush, Clinton, and George W. Bush have traveled around the country to advocate their policies and raise money much more than their predecessors.

In their efforts to court the American public, presidents are locked in a love-hate relationship with the various media through which they communicate with the public. The media need presidents as a source for news and entertainment; presidents need the media to communicate with the American people. But each resents the other, because they have conflicting objectives yet are mutually dependent. Reporters often feel they are being manipulated by White House staffers who want to "spin" every story to favor the president. White House staffers feel that reporters are aggressive and cynical and will always undercut what the president is trying to communicate. The White House is focused on presenting the president in the best light and supporting the administration's policies. The press wants to see behind what reporters often consider the manipulation of the White House and report the "real" story behind the White House version of events.

One example of these differing perspectives was President Bush's visit to an aircraft carrier off the coast of California on May 1, 2003, to declare an end to major combat activity in Iraq and to thank the troops for their bravery in accomplishing their mission. The president arrived on the carrier dramatically, flying in the copilot's seat of a Navy jet. One purpose of the event was to thank the troops, but the further White House motivation was to show the president in a heroic setting and to produce photographs that would be used in the president's campaign for reelection. Some in the press emphasized the political nature of the trip and its contrived setting, noting that the aircraft carrier was stopped thirty miles from its port of San Diego—giving the impression of a ship at sea—and that the president could just as easily have arrived by helicopter as by fighter jet. The perspective of some of the press and the White House were clearly at odds about how to interpret the president's actions in this event. Was it a political ploy to present the president as a heroic military leader cheered by the troops, or was it an opportunity to thank the troops for their successful mission of defeating Saddam Hussein in Iraq? It was probably both.[38]

There are many allegations of bias in the press, and all presidents and their staffs get angry at their press coverage. It is doubtful that there is a systematic partisan bias in news coverage of the president (though of course writers of op-ed columns are often explicitly ideological). But the media are systematically biased toward celebrity, personal interest stories, conflict, and scandal; as the saying goes, "if it bleeds, it leads." This interest in what makes news and will engage readers and viewers will predictably be frustrating to presidents and will result in many stories critical of the incumbent president. Presidents must expect to be treated unfairly (from their perspective) by the press, but they are wise not to whine about it publicly (which will be a news story in itself).

In addition to the often adversarial relationship between the media and the president, the increasing velocity of communications is transforming the relationship. At mid-twentieth century, the press was on a schedule with deadlines for morning and afternoon newspapers and fixed times in the early evening for the national network news programs. But in the era of twenty-four hour news stations on television and radio and the increasingly accessible Internet, the news cycle is essentially 24 hours. That is, as soon as a significant event has occurred, it is instantaneously broadcast throughout the world via computer communications, television and radio, and is often covered live.

One important effect of this reality is that there is increasing pressure on presidents to respond immediately to breaking events rather than to take the time to get all of the facts and think through what a measured response ought to be. Secondly, the reporting of news on the Internet has lowered the standards of reporting. Instead of large news organizations, concerned for their reputations for thorough reporting and relying on several sources for a story, individuals can post their own (often biased) version of events immediately. More established news organizations then feel pressure to publish the unsubstantiated stories in order not to be "scooped." This syndrome was broadly visible during the Monica Lewinsky scandal during the Clinton administration.[39]

The media context for the presidency changed fundamentally over the second half of the twentieth century. Relations between the president and media are less formal and more constant. Media outlets have direct feeds from the White House, with reporters present from early morning to late at night. Reporters accompany the president on virtually all trips away from the White House. In addition, everything is on the record when a president speaks in public. As Martha Kumar observes: "Now a President's responses to reporters' questions and his remarks to groups are broadcast live on more than one cable television channel. For a President in the new century, there are no off the record remarks, no statements made on background, or speeches to a limited audience. The presidency today is on the record and broadcast live to audiences around the world."[40]

The new medium of the Internet has transformed American life, and the White House has kept pace in exploiting the new technology. The Clinton administration experimented with online computer access to subscribers to computer services. Computer users could access speech texts and other White House documents and even send e-mail directly to the White House. With the increasing sophistication and availability of computer technology, the George W. Bush administration has improved the White House Web site, vastly increasing the information available and keeping its content up to date.

PUBLIC OPINION

Presidents put a lot of effort into trying to control the image of their administrations in the media, and thereby affect public opinion. How successful are they? What are the limits of presidential control of public opinion?

Modern public polling techniques have become much more sophisticated in the second half of the twentieth century, and by examining these polls historically we can try to understand the waxing and waning popularity of presidents. President Franklin Roosevelt occasionally used polls to gauge public reaction to various public policy directions, and Lyndon Johnson was the first president to have a pollster on the White House staff. In the early 1970s, news organizations relied on private polling organizations, but by the end of the decade every major news organization had its own professional public opinion survey operation. Polling became pervasive in American politics and, in the Carter administration, polling became a permanent part of the White House staff.[41]

Administration sensitivity to public opinion polls is another way in which governing has come to seem like an extension of the presidential campaign. Instead of relying on the "mandate" established in the presidential election, the White House is sensitive to and attempts to affect an ongoing "mandate" as polls are taken throughout a presidential administration and used to defend administration policy. Presidents, however, are not easily able to control their public approval ratings.[42]

While some presidents seem more popular than others, we can detect certain regularities in the pattern of public approval of presidents over the cycle of their terms. In comparing the public approval of presidents, the summary

TABLE 2.1 | EARLY PRESIDENTIAL APPROVAL COMPARED WITH SHARE OF VOTE

President	Popular Vote in First Election	Approval in First Post-Inaugural Poll
Eisenhower	55%	69%
Kennedy	50	72
Johnson	61	71
Nixon	43	60
Carter	50	66
Reagan	51	51
G. H. W. Bush	53	51
Clinton	43	58
G. W. Bush	48	57

Source: George Edwards and Stephen J. Wayne, *Presidential Leadership* (Belmont, CA: Wadsworth, 2003), p. 115.

measure used is the question that has been asked of the public over the past five decades: "Do you approve of the job President _____ is doing as president?" A wide variety of different questions are asked on specific public policy issues, but this is the question that is weighed most heavily by presidents and used by scholars for comparative purposes.

The most certain prediction that we can make about presidential approval ratings is that a president's popularity is likely to decline during the first term. Presidents begin their terms in office with a "honeymoon" period of public support and goodwill. Candidates who have been successful in winning election usually increase their level of public support between the time of election and inauguration. From Eisenhower through George W. Bush (with the exceptions of Reagan and the Bushes), every newly inaugurated president's approval rating was ten percentage points or more greater than his election margin. (See Table 2.1.)

What accounts for this immediate jump in popularity between election and inauguration? Part of it is the halo effect of formally becoming president. Past presidents have taken on mythic stature in the United States. The new president just might be the one to take a place among the pantheon of great presidents: Washington, Jefferson, Lincoln, and Franklin Roosevelt. The irony here is that the strongest public approval of presidential job performance often comes before the president has had any chance to perform on the job. But this makes sense because everyone can hope that the new president will pursue policies they approve of. Campaign promises are often vague and presented as all gain and no pain. That is, everyone can win and there are no losers. There is also the dynamic of high expectations stemming from campaign rhetoric and stirring inaugural addresses. The former merely political candidate takes on the legitimacy of the office of the president, and opinion leaders and the media refrain from criticizing the new president.

But this postinaugural glow is an artificially high level of support, and soon reality and the inevitable decline in public approval begins. The initial approval rating is artificially high because it is usually much higher than the percentage of the electorate who voted for the candidate. But it is also high because the new president has not made any of the hard policy tradeoffs that any presidential agenda necessarily entails. Whenever a policy choice is made, some will be disappointed that their option was not chosen. As more choices are made these disappointments accumulate, and the president's approval ratings slip.

The honeymoon with the public may last several months or half a year, but after the sixth month in office the polls begin to slide and usually decline through the third year of the term before turning up as the election approaches.[43] If the president is reelected, there is no honeymoon with public opinion comparable to the first term. Of course, presidential approval ratings fluctuate during any term depending on the particular president or external events. One of the most important determinants of presidential popularity is the state of the economy, especially inflation and unemployment. Presidents have very little short-term control over these factors. All presidents want a healthy economy, and they do what they can to strengthen economic performance. The problem is that even if most economists agree on the right prescription, presidents can affect economic performance only marginally. Increasingly, the world economy is a major determinant of U.S. economic performance. It is a truism of American politics that presidents are blamed or given credit for the state of the economy regardless of the fact that they are seldom responsible for the country's economic performance.

The other major predictable factors in presidential polls are dramatic international events that involve the United States. These events sometimes produce a "rally effect" in public opinion because the public "rallies around the flag" to support the president as the representative of the United States in a hostile and unpredictable world. The irony of these events is that the rally effect of a jump in approval of the president can occur whether or not the president has acted successfully in an international crisis. For example, Eisenhower's approval rating rose after a U.S. spy plane was downed over the Soviet Union; John Kennedy's approval rose after the Bay of Pigs failure; Jimmy Carter's polls increased after the Iranians took over the U.S. embassy in Tehran and after the Soviet invasion of Afghanistan.[44]

Of course, when presidents act successfully in international crises, as in the Persian Gulf War of 1991, their popularity increases dramatically. If a dramatic international event involving U.S. security is accompanied by an effective speech by the president, the effect of the rally is increased. But even though the effect of these events is fairly predictable, the duration of the public-approval effect is most often short-lived (usually one to four months), and the effect only occurs if the event is dramatic and involves U.S. security.[45] The transience of rally-based popularity was demonstrated dramatically when George H.W. Bush's high approval rating of 91 percent immediately after the Persian Gulf

FIGURE 2.1 | PRESIDENTIAL APPROVAL RATINGS—ANNUAL AVERAGES

Source: Adapted from the Gallup Poll Web site (1999, 2003, 2006); and the *Washington Post* (August 17, 1992), p. A11. Copyright 1992, *The Washington Post,* Reprinted with permission.

War was followed by the largest steady drop of popularity in polling history, followed by his defeat in the 1992 election. (See Figure 2.1.)

The most dramatic and longest lasting rally event occurred immediately after the terrorist bombings of September 11, 2001. President Bush's public approval ratings shot up thirty-five points literally overnight, from 51 percent to 86 percent. Because of the magnitude of the attack on the United States, President Bush's reassuring response to it, the ongoing nature of the threat of terrorism, and the war in Iraq, the president's approval ratings remained at high levels for the next several years. Voter disaffection with the war in Iraq, however, drove his approval rating down to the low 30s in the spring of 2006.

Presidents are not merely reactive to their public approval ratings; along with the increasing sophistication of polling has come its institutionalization in the White House and the importance of the president's aides who interpret their polls. Polling data was initially used by President Roosevelt in the 1930s, and as polling techniques improved, presidents used them more actively. President Nixon assigned one staffer to work on polling. During the Carter administration, pollsters were hired as White House staff, and White House pollsters, such as Richard Wirthlin for Reagan and Dick Morris for Clinton, became important presidential advisers. Despite George W. Bush's disclaimer, "I really don't care what polls and focus groups say," his political adviser Karl Rove paid close attention to the presidential polls. The polling operations were insulated from the president and often located at Republican National Committee headquarters, but the Bush polling operation was as sophisticated and as expensive as that of any of his predecessors.[46] All White House pollsters argue that they use polling not to help decide on policy but merely to help communicate it more effectively. But as polling has improved from merely measuring basic preferences and attitudes of the public to predicting how the public will react to various hypothetical policies, the line inevitably gets blurred.[47]

While the technology and increasing sophistication of public opinion polling allows the president to gauge and thus be responsive to the wishes of the citizenry, there are dangers in relying too heavily on reacting to the latest opinion polls. If presidents become obsessed with the latest poll numbers, they may be tempted to act with a short-term perspective on what will favorably affect their polls rather than on what is in the best interests of the country. They may follow the short-term demands of public opinion rather than take a long-term perspective on what is best for the nation. The real task of leadership is to educate the public about the long-term best interests of the nation, and then to lead the nation in that direction, even if it means short-term sacrifice.

In analyzing these developments, the line between campaigning and governing has become increasingly blurred. Richard Nixon was the first president to realize fully the implications of the changing nature of governing: "The staff doesn't understand that we are in a continuous campaign," he said to his chief of staff, H. R. Haldeman, in 1971.[48] Nixon's successors, especially Reagan and Clinton, also acted on this realization. During his first term Bill Clinton retained some aspects of his campaign organization, experimenting with a central media control center like the "war room" rapid response team of his campaign. The reelection campaign began running TV ads for the president in mid-1995, eighteen months before the election. This campaigning approach continued into his second term as Clinton tried to develop public support for his initiatives.

This "permanent campaign" is a seemingly inevitable consequence of contemporary campaign technology and the sophistication of presidential media specialists. But campaigning and governing have traditionally had different functions. Campaigns are about attacks on the other party, drawing sharp lines between the two sides, and short-term reactions with the goal of winning the election by defeating the opponent. In contrast, once in office, governing ought to be about unifying the country around consensual policies with a long-term perspective on what is good for the country as a whole. The adoption of campaignlike tactics to win approval of particular policies, continual polling, constant money raising, and short-term thinking have a tendency to undercut some of the important functions of governing.[49] Historian Lewis Gould concludes, "The modern presidency has evolved into a perennial campaign, combined with the essential features of a television network and a Hollywood studio. It is demanding labor to elect a president and stage symbolic events, interspersed with policy issues and ritual meetings. Yet these latter activities ought not be confused with real governance."[50]

CONCLUSION

Short-term "pandering" to the public opinion of the moment is the classic problem with democracies, whether during campaigning or once in office. The technology of polling has made the gauging of opinion more immediate and accurate. True leadership, however, will be measured in the long run rather than by short-term popularity. As will be argued in Chapter 8, long-term presidential reputation does not necessarily correspond with popularity while in office. The most striking example of a discrepancy between the two is the presidency of Harry Truman. Truman's poll ratings were among the lowest of modern presidents, yet he is ranked highest by historians among the post–World War II presidents. Part of his historic reputation may even be due to his dismissive attitude toward presidential approval ratings: "I wonder how far Moses would have gone if he'd taken a poll in Egypt? . . . It isn't polls or public opinion of the moment that counts. It is right and wrong leadership."[51]

NOTES

1. See Lester G. Seligman and Cary R. Covington, *The Coalitional Presidency* (Chicago: Dorsey Press, 1989).

2. Nicholas von Hoffman, "Conventional History," *New Republic* (August 26, 1988), p. 26.

3. Stephen J. Wayne, *The Road to the White House, 1996* (New York: St. Martin's Press, 1996), p. 11.

4. Theodore H. White, *The Making of the President, 1960* (New York: Atheneum House, 1961), p. 104.

5. Stephen J. Wayne, *The Road to the White House, 2000* (Belmont, CA: Wadsworth, 2003), p. 12. The Democratic percentage includes the "superdelegates" from the primary states, which amounted to 18 percent of the total delegates.

6. Wayne, *The Road to the White House, 1996*, p. 117.

7. Wayne, *The Road to the White House, 2000*, p. 105. See also James E. Campbell, "Nomination Politics, Party Unity, and Presidential Elections," in James P. Pfiffner and Roger H. Davidson, eds., *Understanding the Presidency*, 3rd ed. (New York: Longman, 2003).

8. See National Association of Secretaries of State, "Election Information," Web site: www.nass.org.

9. Robert L. Dudley and Alan R. Gitelson, *American Elections: The Rules Matter* (New York: Longman, 2002), p. 157.

10. James Reichley, "The Electoral System," in Wayne and Wilcox, *The Quest for National Office*, pp. 5–15.

11. For data on these close elections, see Neal R. Peirce and Lawrence D. Longley, *The People's President* (New Haven, CT: Yale University Press, 1981), pp. 257–258.

12. Jeffrey Toobin, *Too Close to Call* (New York: Random House, 2001), p. 82; Alan M. Dershowitz, *Supreme Injustice* (New York: Oxford University Press, 2001),

pp. 22–25; and Richard A. Posner, *Breaking Deadlock* (Princeton, NJ: Princeton University Press, 2001), pp. 82–85.

13. It is a historical oddity that every time the son or grandson of a president has been nominated for president, he has been elected with fewer popular votes than his opponent. In 1824 John Quincy Adams, the son of John Adams, was elected by the House. In 1888 Benjamin Harrison, grandson of William Henry Harrison, won the electoral vote, despite coming in second to Grover Cleveland in the popular count. George W. Bush is the third direct descendent of a president to be elected, again with fewer popular votes than his opponent.

14. George F. Will, "A Brief Moment," *Washington Post* (December 17, 2000), p. B7. If questions about how a possible change in the Electoral College system might change campaign patterns are of concern, some empirical evidence can be brought to bear. Patterns of campaign activity in recent elections can be measured. For example, in the 2000 election, eight mountain states received no visits by candidates; all of them had few electoral votes and all were solidly Republican. The number of presidential campaign ads in Green Bay (WI) and Grand Rapids (MI) far outnumbered (by more than 5,000) the ads in the New York City or Los Angeles media markets. To win candidates' attention, states must be "in play" and have a significant number of electoral votes. For data on candidate state visits and media market ads, see Alexis Simendinger, James A. Barnes, and Carl M. Cannon, "Pending a Popular Vote," *National Journal* (November 18, 2000), p. 3653.

15. For an analysis of these plans and projections about how they might have affected previous presidential elections, see Dudley and Gitelson, *American Elections*, pp. 147–154.

16. For an analysis of possible unintended consequences of a direct popular election system, see see Dudley and Gitelson, *American Elections*, pp. 149–154. For a thorough analysis of the Electoral College system, see George C. Edwards, *Why the Electoral College is Bad for America* (New Haven, CT: Yale University Press, 2004).

17. Judith A. Best, *The Choice of the People?: Debating the Electoral College* (Lanham, MD: Rowman and Littlefield, 1996), p. 58. The author would like to thank scholars Lara M. Brown, Gerald M. Pomper, and Robert Hardaway for advice and help in understanding the operation of the Electoral College system.

18. Data from Perice and Longley, *The People's President*, p. 243.

19. Interview with the author, Arlington, VA, August 14, 1992.

20. Rhodes Cook, "Perot Positions to Defy a Past Seemingly Carved in Stone," *Congressional Quarterly Weekly Report* (June 13, 1992), pp. 1721–1729.

21. Laurence I. Barrett, "Perot Takes a Walk," *Time* (July 27, 1992), pp. 32–33.

22. Barrett, "Perot Takes a Walk," pp. 32–33.

23. Gerald M. Pomper, "The Presidential Election," in Gerald M. Pomper, ed. *The Election of 2000* (New York: Chatham House, 2001), p. 152.

24. For vote totals, see Wayne, *The Road to the White House, 1996*, p. 320.

25. For critiques of the Bush campaign see Wayne, *The Road to the White House, 2000*, pp. 289–290; and Pomper, "The Presidential Election," in *The Election of 2000*, pp. 140–144.

26. Earl Black and Merle Black, *The Vital South* (Cambridge, MA: Harvard University Press, 1992), p. 295 and passim.

27. Joseph A. Pika, Zelman Mosley, and Richard A. Watson, *The Presidential Contest* (Washington, DC: CQ Press, 1992), p. 125.

28. Wayne, *The Road to the White House, 2000,* p. 75.

29. Richard Morin and E. J. Dionne, Jr., "Majority of Voters Say Parties Have Lost Touch," *Washington Post* (July 8, 1992), pp. 1, A10.

30. Peter F. Galderisi et al., *Divided Government* (Lanham, MD: Roman and Littlefield, 1996), p. 38.

31. Wayne, *The Road to the White House, 2000,* p. 67.

32. George Edwards and Stephen Wayne, *Presidential Leadership,* 5th ed. (New York: St. Martin's, 1997) p. 90.

33. Paul Brace and Barbara Hinckley, *Follow the Leader* (New York: Basic Books, 1992), p. 18.

34. Samuel Kernell, *Going Public* (Washington, DC: CQ Press, 1986), p. 69.

35. Kernell, *Going Public,* p. 106.

36. Martha Joynt Kumar, "Does This Constitute a Press Conference?" *Presidential Studies Quarterly,* vol. 33, no. 1 (March 2003), pp. 221–237.

37. Kernell, *Going Public,* p. 92.

38. The image of Bush in a pilot's gear cut both ways, calling attention to Bush's experience as a pilot in the Air National Guard but also reminding people that his service in the National Guard kept him out of combat in Vietnam. See Jeremy Mayer, "The Presidency and Image Management: Discipline in Pursuit of Illusion," *Presidential Studies Quarterly,* vol. 34, no. 3 (September 2004), p. 620.

39. See the analysis in Joseph A. Pika, John Anthony Maltese, and Norman C. Thomas, *The Politics of the Presidency* (Washington, DC: CQ Press, 2002), pp. 110–114.

40. "The White House and the Press: News Organizations as a Presidential Resource and as a Source of Pressure," *Presidential Studies Quarterly,* vol. 33, no. 3 (September 2003).

41. See Jeremy D. Mayer and Lynn Kirby, "The Promise and Peril of Presidential Polling: Between Gallup's Dream and the Morris Nightmare," in Stephen S. Wayne, ed., *Is This Any Way to Run a Democratic Government?* (Washington, DC: Georgetown University Press, 2003).

42. George C. Edwards argues that presidents are usually not very successful in changing public attitudes. See "The Presidential Pulpit: Bully or Baloney?" in James P. Pfiffner and Roger H. Davidson, eds. *Understanding the Presidency,* 3rd ed. (New York: Longman, 2003), pp. 158, 167; and George C. Edwards, *On Deaf Ears: The Limits of the Bully Pulpit* (New Haven, CT: Yale University Press, 2003).

43. See Brace and Hinkley, *Follow the Leader;* see also Richard A. Brody, *Assessing the President* (Stanford, CA: Stanford University Press, 1991).

44. Brace and Hinkley, *Follow the Leader,* p. 27 and chap. 5. See also Brody, *Assessing the President,* chap. 3. George Edwards argues that many rally events do not produce substantial increases in approval ratings in *The Public Presidency* (New York: St. Martin's Press, 1983), pp. 242–247.

45. Brace and Hinkley, *Follow the Leader,* p. 167.

46. Kathryn Dunn Tenpas, "President George W. Bush and Polling," *The Brookings Review,* vol. 21, no. 3 (Summer 2003), pp. 32–25.

47. Mayer and Kirby, "The Perils and Promise of Presidential Polling."

48. Quoted in Lewis L. Gould, *The Modern American Presidency* (Lawrence, KS: University Press of Kansas, 2003), pp. 150–151.

49. Norman Ornstein and Thomas Mann, eds., *The Permanent Campaign and Its Future* (Washington DC: AEI, 2000), especially the chapter by Hugh Heclo, "Campaigning and Governing: A Conspectus").

50. Gould, *The Modern American Presidency,* pp. 236–237.

51. Brace and Hinkley, *Follow the Leader,* p. 19.

3 CHAPTER | THE WHITE HOUSE STAFF AND ORGANIZATION

One of the defining characteristics of the modern presidency is a large and differentiated White House staff system at the service of the president. This is not merely a group of people serving the president but a collection of bureaucracies: the White House Office, the Executive Office of the President, and several military units, as well as the Secret Service, which is technically in the Department of Homeland Security. This chapter traces the increasing size and complexity of the White House staff in the modern presidency and examines the role of staffers as advisers to the president and occasional implementers of policy. In addition, it argues that the White House needs the firm control of a chief of staff, but that too domineering an approach to the job will result in trouble.

In the nineteenth century, presidents had personal aides and servants. In the early part of the century, these were usually clerical helpers and most often relatives and junior aides who were paid from the president's own pocketbook. At the turn of the century, the functions of such staff began to include liaison with Congress and other political power centers. But presidents still relied primarily on their cabinets and nongovernmental advisers for consultation and advice. President Hoover caused a bit of a stir when he doubled the White House staff from two to four assistants.

The dramatic shift came with Franklin Roosevelt and the birth of the modern presidency. Under Roosevelt, the scope of governmental activity was increased greatly in the effort to fight the Great Depression. Scores of new agencies were created by Congress to administer the various New Deal programs enacted to counteract the effects of the Depression. By the mid-1930s, the executive branch had more than 100 agencies.

Roosevelt decided that he needed more managerial tools to fight the fragmentation of the executive branch and to rein in the "alphabet" agencies of the New Deal. In 1936, he assigned the task of planning a strategy for managerial control to a committee of three public-administration scholars headed by Louis Brownlow. In 1937, the Committee on Administrative Management (the Brownlow Committee), with careful guidance from FDR, announced that "The president needs help." With the principle that the president should be the center of control in the executive branch, its ambitious recommendations proposed more legal power for the president, centralized control of staff agencies (personnel and budget), tighter fiscal controls, extension of the merit system, bringing independent commissions into the purview of the major executive-branch departments, and professional staff help for the president.

These far-reaching proposals were seen as a power grab by Congress, which had just rejected Roosevelt's proposal to "pack" the Supreme Court by increasing its size. The set of recommendations was thus rejected and the proposals were defeated in Congress. Finally, in 1939, two of the proposals were approved by Congress: reorganization power for the president, subject to a legislative veto, and the provision of six administrative assistants who would be officially part of the White House but not subject to Senate confirmation. FDR quickly used his new reorganization power to create the Executive Office of the President (EOP), through Executive Order 8248, and recruited his six top aides over the next several years.

While these two expansions of presidential power were not major changes, the Brownlow Committee report was to have major repercussions over the years. The report articulated the justification for an active White House staff to serve the president and thus laid the foundation for the growth in numbers and power of the White House staff in the modern presidency.

In describing the role envisioned for presidential aides, the report declared:

> These aides would have no power to make decisions or issue instructions in their own right. They would not be interposed between the president and the heads of his departments. They would not be assistant presidents in any sense.... They would remain in the background, issue no orders, make no decisions, emit no public statements.... [T]hey would not attempt to exercise power on their own account. They should be possessed of high competence, great physical vigor, and a passion for anonymity.[1]

Despite the fact that these precepts have gone by the wayside and the White House staff now includes hundreds of people, the norms articulated in the Brownlow Committee report still define the ideal for White House aides.

As the White House staff grew from the relatively small staff of Franklin Roosevelt to more than five hundred in the twenty-first century, presidents have had to confront the problem of how to manage the increasing numbers of people. They have taken different approaches, with some choosing a relatively unstructured, collegial organization and others choosing a more structured, hierarchical approach with a chief of staff to oversee the White House. This chapter examines the contrasting approaches taken by the modern presidents to White House organization.

ROOSEVELT AND TRUMAN: LAYING THE FOUNDATIONS

Franklin Roosevelt's administration began the transformation to the modern presidency in terms of the size and scope of government and the institution-alization of the presidency. Under FDR, the White House staff took on new roles and functions that have been continued and expanded to meet more recent challenges. The initial impetus for this transformation and broadening of the functions of the White House staff included the same two factors that caused the expansion of the role of the federal government in the 1930s and 1940s: the Great Depression and World War II. Under FDR, the federal government came to have more than 150 agencies, with almost 50 reporting directly to the president.

Just as FDR laid the groundwork for the institutional presidency with the creation of the EOP, he also initiated the use of an extensive set of White House aides to help him personally with his conduct of the newly enlarged presidency. FDR made a careful distinction between the institutional staff of the presidency in the EOP and his *personal* staffers, who were to concern themselves inti-mately with his own daily work.[2] In the ensuing decades, this distinction was to become blurred.

Though the number of aides was small compared to recent presidents, with three or four top-level assistants and a total White House staff, including clerical, of less than fifty, the aides acted as an extension of FDR's personal will. He used the high-level personal staffers as "... chore-boys, troubleshooters, checker-uppers, intelligence operatives, and as magnets for ideas, gripes, gossip in the administration, on the Hill, and with groups outside government."[3] The expanded staff was necessary not only because of the increased size of the government but also because of the activist policy role that FDR played as president. But in contrast to more recent presidents, FDR kept his staffers on a very short leash.

Franklin Roosevelt conducted his White House so as to maximize his flex-ibility and sources of information. He gave his personal staff broad assignments but doled out jobs on an ad hoc basis. He did not want his staffers to go into business for themselves, so he gave them conflicting assignments to keep them off balance. He even used people from outside the government to check up on or duplicate his staffers' work.[4] FDR was legendary for his manipulation of his staffers. He thrived on conflict in his personal entourage and used it consciously to his advantage. This was frustrating to his subordinates but useful to Roosevelt. It generated creative conflict and ideas. It kept his channels of information open and kept powerful staffers in check. Roosevelt presided over his own morning staff meetings, and no one short of the president coordinated or integrated the White House staff's work.[5]

Though FDR had a press secretary (Stephen Early), an appointments secretary (Marvin McIntyre), and a special counsel (Samuel Rosenman) for legal and other advice, most of his top staffers were generalists with shifting assignments. Unlike future presidents, he had no specific person to deal with Congress, to recruit political appointees, or to act as liaison with the cabinet or the rest of the executive branch. Roosevelt did all of these things himself and gave specific assignments to different staffers at different times.

FDR's need to dominate his staff, and his insistence on personal loyalty was tinged by a "thin streak of sadism," according to Robert Sherwood.[6] But Roosevelt felt that his assertion of control was necessary to keep his staffers in line. When James Rowe once insisted that he knew the best way to engineer a personnel shift in the government, he said: "Mr. President, you should do it my way and not yours." In putting Rowe in his place, FDR made clear the basic relationship between staffers and the president: "I do not have to do it your way and I will tell you the reason why. The reason is that, although they may have made a mistake, the people of the United States have elected me president, not you."[7] But FDR had a need for loyal staffers, as he commented to a skeptical observer on the role of his intimate, Harry Hopkins, who lived in the White House. FDR said that, if you are president, "you'll be looking at that door over there and knowing that practically everybody who walks through it wants something out of you. You'll learn what a lonely job this is, and you'll discover the need for somebody like Harry Hopkins, who asks nothing except to serve you."[8]

When Harry S. Truman succeeded to the presidency upon FDR's death in April 1945, the war was all but over, though Truman was still to make the fateful decision to drop atomic bombs on Japanese cities. Truman's challenge was to reorient the country from war to peace, guide the economy through demobilization, and to consolidate the Democratic agenda of the New Deal. Truman did not immediately fire FDR's cabinet and White House staff but gradually began to adjust the White House to his own presidential style.

Truman, unlike FDR, was uncomfortable with personal conflict and did not give out overlapping assignments or encourage conflict among his staffers. His White House was more orderly and formal. He held daily staff meetings with his top dozen aides at precisely 9:30 AM, received regular national security briefings, and held weekly meetings with the congressional leadership and Democratic Party leaders. There was never any formal organization chart of the White House, and only the president gave any senior White House staffer a direct order, as future chiefs of staff would.[9]

Truman, reflecting, in part, his path to the presidency but also his own insecurity, was not as sure of himself as FDR. Truman saw himself as a man of modest intelligence but with the willingness to make tough decisions without agonizing deliberation (as in the decision to use the atomic bomb).

This led Truman to delegate much more responsibility than had FDR, an option made more workable by a more fixed and formal White House organization. But the final responsibility and authority rested with him, as was signified by the famous sign resting on his desk in the Oval Office, "THE BUCK STOPS HERE."

The Truman White House began the trend toward functional specialization that has come to characterize the modern presidency. In addition to the press secretary and appointments secretary that FDR had, Truman gave more fixed assignments to individual staffers. As the White House staff began to increase in size, primary aides began to recruit their own staffs and the first layering of the White House staff began.[10]

Truman hired two staffers of special importance to his presidency. The first was John R. Steelman, who was given the title of assistant to the president. Steelman had special responsibility for labor relations, which plagued the federal government after the tight economic controls of World War II. But his broader responsibility was for the coordination of domestic policy agencies. He often performed the role of future chiefs of staff by negotiating and settling disputes among cabinet secretaries that were not of sufficient importance to involve the president directly.

The most eminent aide to Truman was Clark Clifford, who took on Rosenman's title of special counsel. When someone asked what the special counsel did, Clifford answered, "Whatever the president wanted."[11] Clifford's role represented the modern practice of having policy advocates, as opposed to merely coordinators or troubleshooters, in the White House. Clifford saw himself as an advocate for the liberal part of the Democratic agenda, "fighting for the mind of the president."[12] Clifford and his allies were arrayed against the conservatives in the White House, including John Steelman. While Clifford was a major factor in Truman's domestic policy, he was crucial to Truman's foreign policy, where he acted as Truman's personal adviser and as a counterweight to Secretary of State Dean Acheson and Secretary of Defense James Forestall.

Truman asserted an important principle about the role of White House staffers in the modern presidency in an Oval Office meeting in May 1948. At that meeting, Secretary of State George Marshall and State Department officials were discussing with Truman whether the United States should recognize the newly declared state of Israel. Secretary Marshall objected to the presence of Clifford, because he felt that Clifford was merely a political adviser and that his presence was inappropriate at a meeting about serious matters of state. When Marshall angrily objected to Clifford's presence, Truman replied, "Well, General, he's here because I asked him to be here."[13] Marshall was implying more than a difference in expertise; he was also noting the difference between his statutory office and Clifford's merely advisory capacity. The point of Truman's reply was a dual one: presidents can choose to invest their trust in their personal staffers, but the power of those staffers is derivative and entirely dependent on the president's continuing confidence.[14]

EISENHOWER INSTITUTIONALIZES THE WHITE HOUSE

Although FDR began the modern staffing system in the White House and Truman organized it more explicitly, it was under Eisenhower that the White House staff became institutionalized. Before he became president, Dwight Eisenhower had the advantage of having been an executive for many years, directing U.S. forces during World War II and coordinating the Allied effort to victory in the war. During his career he had given considerable thought to leadership in organizations and came to the presidency with firm ideas about how the White House should be organized. He was of the strong opinion that White House organization needed improving:

> For years I had been in frequent contact with the executive office of the White House, and I had certain ideas about the system, or lack of system under which it operated. With my training in problems involving organization it was inconceivable to me that the work of the White House could not be better systemized than had been the case in the years I observed it.[15]

Eisenhower stressed the importance of organization: "Organization cannot make a genius out of an incompetent.... On the other hand, disorganization can scarcely fail to result in inefficiency and can easily lead to disaster."[16] Thus, Eisenhower organized his White House much more formally than either Truman or Roosevelt.

For his immediate staffers, he chose people who were familiar to him from his campaign and his military years, but in general they were more professional in their backgrounds—more experienced in government—than were the staffers of Truman or FDR.[17] He also gave them much more specialized assignments than existed previously in the White House. Eisenhower kept the previous existing positions of press secretary, appointments secretary, and special counsel (though it was more exclusively focused on legal matters than before). But Eisenhower added a number of other positions and organizational systems in the White House. Truman had used one person to coordinate congressional liaison, but Eisenhower elevated the position and created a special office for the function.

With Eisenhower's appreciation for the need to coordinate activities in a large organization, he set up two secretariats for coordination: the secretary to the cabinet and the staff secretary. The cabinet secretary, Maxwell Rabb, and his assistants ensured that cabinet meeting agendas were in the participants' hands in time, that all cabinet papers were in order, and that follow-up to cabinet meetings and decisions was carried out. The staff secretary, Paul Carroll (later Andrew Goodpaster), acted as the coordinator and clearinghouse for all papers and issues that came up to the president. If staff work was incomplete, or if someone who should have seen some papers had not seen them, it was the staff secretary's responsibility to get the job done. In explaining the function of the staff secretary, Eisenhower said: "I look to my staff to keep such things straightened out. I should not have to be my own sergeant major...."[18]

Eisenhower also upgraded the importance of the National Security Council staff, which had been headed by an executive secretary. He created the title of special assistant to the president for national security affairs and appointed Robert Cutler to the position. The special assistant would be responsible for the agenda of the council, briefing the president, and coordinating national security issues for the president.

Perhaps the most important and lasting contribution of Eisenhower to the organization of the presidency was the office of chief of staff, whose function was to oversee and coordinate the much enlarged and more complex staff for the president. The combination of the powers of the office and the personality of its first occupant, Sherman Adams, made it the most powerful position (short of the president) in the government. Adams's official title was assistant to the president, but his function was chief of staff. "I think of Adams as my chief of staff, but I don't call him that because the politicians think it sounds too military," admitted Eisenhower.[19] (See Table 3.1.)

Adams saw his job as making sure that staff work was complete and that any issues brought to the president were ripe for presidential involvement. According to Eisenhower: "A man like that is valuable because of the unnecessary detail he keeps away from the president. A president who doesn't know how to decentralize will be weighed down with details and won't have time to deal with the big issues."[20] Adams spent a considerable amount of time forcing reluctant cabinet secretaries to settle their disputes and turf battles short of the president. "Either you make up your minds or else tell me and I will do it. We must not bother the president with this. He is trying to keep the world from war."[21] As Adams explained his role, "Eisenhower simply expected me to manage a staff that would boil down, simplify, and expedite the urgent business ... and keep as much work of secondary importance off his desk as possible."[22]

Much of Adams's power stemmed from his control of access to the president. Given Eisenhower's preference to be spared details, his absence from the White House much of the time, and his conscious decision to stay behind the scenes, Adams's position became that much more powerful. Despite organization charts and official policy that gave direct access to the president to all cabinet officers and a number of White House staffers, the reality was that Adams usually had final say as to who would see the president and what papers would reach him.

But controlling access was only one of the important roles that Adams played for the president as chief of staff. He took the heat for the president for tough political decisions, such as firing people and negotiating political patronage. He acted as a buffer for the president and organized the White House and cabinet with an iron hand. Immediately after Eisenhower's first heart attack in 1955, Adams ran the executive branch virtually by himself.

Carrying out tough decisions and controlling access are both legitimate and often necessary roles for the chief of staff, but the way they are handled can make a large difference. They can be done in a heavy-handed manner, or they

TABLE 3.1 | CHIEFS OF STAFF TO THE PRESIDENT

President	Chiefs of Staff	Term
Eisenhower	Sherman Adams	1953–1958
	Wilton B. Persons	1958–1961
Kennedy	No chief of staff	
Johnson	No chief of staff	
Nixon	H.R. Haldeman	1969–1973
	Alexander Haig	1973–1974
Ford	Donald Rumsfeld	1974–1975
	Richard Cheney	1975–1977
Carter	Hamilton Jordan	1979–1980
	Jack Watson	1980–1981
Reagan	James A. Baker, III	1981–1985
	Donald T. Regan	1985–1987
	Howard H. Baker, Jr.	1987–1988
	Kenneth Duberstein	1988–1989
Bush, G.H.W.	John H. Sununu	1989–1991
	Samuel K. Skinner	1991–1992
	James A. Baker, III	1992–1993
Clinton	Thomas F. McLarty	1993–1994
	Leon Panetta	1994–1996
	Erskine Bowles	1997–1998
	John Podesta	1999–2001
Bush, G.W.	Andrew Card	2001–2006
	Joshua Bolten	2006–

can be accomplished with a firm hand, but without overt hostility. Cabinet members and staff may chafe under the decision in either case, but hostility and ill feeling will result if the bearer of the bad news is also gratuitously rude. Although Adams ran the White House the way Eisenhower wanted, his tight control and personal style contributed to his eventual undoing. One current joke had it that it would be unfortunate if Eisenhower died and Nixon became president, but a disaster if Adams died and Eisenhower was forced to be president.

Adams's downfall began in June 1958, when it became public that a textile manufacturer and old friend of his, Bernard Goldfine, had on several occasions requested that Adams determine the status of charges against him with federal regulatory agencies. Adams made the calls for Goldfine from the White House to find out the status of the cases but did not suggest any change in agency actions. While the calls in themselves may have been free of improper intent, the very fact that an official of Adams's status, power, and proximity to the president was making them could not help but be taken seriously by any agency in the government. Adams did not seem to be sensitive to the implications or appearance of his calls.

Adams became doubly vulnerable when it was disclosed in congressional hearings that he had accepted gifts from Goldfine, who had paid for hotel rooms for Adams and had given his wife a vicuña coat and an oriental rug.[23] Despite Adams's protestations that he had also given gifts to Goldfine in the context of their friendship, the combination of gifts to Adams with the inquiries from the White House appeared too much like official actions in exchange for gifts.

An additional important cause of Adams's downfall was his personal rudeness to colleagues and others he dealt with on an official basis. To Eisenhower, Adams's curtness was merely his way of communicating in the most efficient manner: "[H]e never added a word to his 'yes' or 'no' if such an answer sufficed. It never occurred to him to say 'Hello.' ... For Sherman Adams this was neither bad manners nor pretense; he was busy." While Adams's brusqueness did not bother his boss, it often did bother his subordinates and others he dealt with. Adams's habitual harshness frequently reduced his secretaries to tears, and at one time he had five of them crying at the same time.[24] Adams treated members of the cabinet and Congress the same way, feeling no need for the usual amenities of human communication. This did not endear him to many, and when he was in trouble and needed friends to defend him, few were willing to come forth. Many in Congress and the executive branch felt that he was an arrogant, power-hungry tyrant who was getting his just deserts.

Even a personal plea and vote of confidence from Eisenhower could not save Adams. After Adams's congressional testimony, in which he argued that he had done nothing wrong, Eisenhower said: "I believe that the presentation made by Governor Adams to the Congressional Committee yesterday truthfully represents the pertinent facts. I personally like Governor Adams. I admire his abilities. I respect him because of his personal and official integrity. I need him."[25] But the plea was seen more as a weakness on Eisenhower's part than an effective defense of Adams. Finally, Adams was persuaded to resign.

KENNEDY AND THE COLLEGIAL MODEL

Although both were popular presidents, John Kennedy and Dwight Eisenhower provide stark contrasts in their personalities and dispositions for organizing the presidency. Kennedy was a young Democrat who took an activist view of the presidency and wanted to "get the country moving again." Eisenhower was an elderly statesman who chose to run as a Republican (he had a choice, Truman even offered to step down if Ike ran as a Democrat in 1948) who wanted to slow the changes the Democrats had begun with the New Deal.

Eisenhower was an experienced organizational leader, while Kennedy had presided over small groups of staffers in the House and Senate.

These contrasts in background were reflected in the two presidents' approaches to staffing and organizing the White House. Whereas Eisenhower wanted issues to be fully staffed out with most of the details settled at subordinate levels, Kennedy wanted issues raised to the presidential level early in the policy development process so he could make personal judgments on defining the alternatives. While Eisenhower wanted to save his energy for the most important decisions, Kennedy wanted to be at "the vital center of action in our whole scheme of government.... [T]he president [must] place himself in the very thick of the fight."[26] Eisenhower felt at home in large organizations and knew how to bend them to his will. Kennedy was slightly suspicious of the career bureaucracy and felt that established organizations would not be flexible enough for bold, new initiatives.

Thus, when Kennedy came to office he immediately abolished many of the committees and organizational systems that Eisenhower had instituted in the White House (though they would reappear in future administrations). The staff secretariat and the secretary to the cabinet were eliminated. The several committees and subcommittees of the National Security Council, including the Operations Coordinating Board, were abolished. Kennedy felt uncomfortable with committee systems and preferred to work with small groups in short meetings that were tightly focused on the problem immediately at hand.

In contrast to Eisenhower's genius for organization and ability to design organizations that would mesh together total strangers and harness them to a common purpose, Kennedy thought in terms of individuals and was able to meld them together into a team through his personal charisma.[27] Eisenhower's staff was a competent, machine-like football team marching down the policy field. Kennedy's staff was a small, fluid basketball team trying to create fast breaks. Kennedy held few cabinet meetings and had no regular staff meetings, preferring to call ad hoc meetings to deal with specific situations.

Because Kennedy rejected much of the organizational apparatus of the Eisenhower White House, he saw no need for its major integrating mechanism, the office of chief of staff. He accepted the advice of his two transition advisers, Clark Clifford and Richard Neustadt, who argued in transition memos that a chief of staff would appear to wall the president off from the rest of the government and the people. Neustadt argued that Kennedy should be his own chief of staff and model his White House after Roosevelt's. Kennedy would be the hub of the wheel for his White House, with a small circle of advisers reporting directly to him. He would be the giver of assignments and the integrator and receiver of all staff reports. No one person short of the president would coordinate the White House staff.[28]

The White House staff did, however, have a first among equals, though not in an organizational sense. Theodore Sorensen had been with Kennedy in the Senate and through the campaign and had coauthored Kennedy's best-selling book, *Profiles in Courage*. Sorensen served as Kennedy's major adviser and coordinator of legislative efforts and domestic policy, but he did not give orders to other staffers, filter their work, or control access to Kennedy. With the memory of Sherman Adams fresh in his mind, Kennedy reminded Sorensen:

> Every man that's ever held a job like yours—Sherman Adams, Harry Hopkins, House, all the rest—has ended up in the shithouse. Congress was down on them or the president was hurt by them or somebody was mad at them. The best way to stay out of trouble is to stay out of sight.[29]

Although it is impossible for so important a presidential aide to remain anonymous, Sorensen took Kennedy's advice and turned down many invitations to give speeches. But Kennedy was not jealous of his staff's publicity in the way that Roosevelt and Johnson were. When McGeorge Bundy received positive press accounts describing his foreign policy duties, Kennedy commented in a humorous though not sarcastic tone, "I will continue to have some residual functions."[30]

The powerful role played by Kennedy's White House staff vis-à-vis the rest of the executive branch, and the beginning of the centralization of control of the government by the president, were shaped in important ways by the Bay of Pigs disaster. The plan to invade Cuba had been charted in the Eisenhower administration, and its major architects and proponents were CIA Director Allen Dulles and his assistant Richard Bissell. They assured Kennedy that social conditions on the island were ripe for overthrowing Fidel Castro, and Kennedy interpreted the military evaluation of the plan's feasibility as favorable. When the operation, with several key Kennedy changes, failed miserably and embarrassed the new president domestically and internationally, Kennedy drew profound lessons that altered his presidency and echoed in future presidencies.[31]

The Bay of Pigs fiasco reinforced Kennedy's suspicions of the career bureaucracies, and he resolved to appoint more of his own people to departments and agencies. He concluded that he had to rely more heavily on his own White House advisers and create a stronger White House capacity to evaluate and oversee the bureaucracy. He would no longer allow the designers of plans to also be their advocates. He moved McGeorge Bundy's NSC office from the Old Executive Office Building to the West Wing (where it has stayed ever since) and encouraged him to set up a "Little State Department" in the White House. He had the Situation Room built in the West Wing basement so that it could serve as the command post in crisis situations, but perhaps more importantly, so its officers could skim off the most important secret cables from the Departments of State and Defense and the CIA.[32]

Similar moves were implemented in dealing with economic policy, which had traditionally been dominated by the Treasury Department and the Bureau of the Budget (BOB). The Council of Economic Advisers that had been created in 1946 and had weathered a threat to its existence in the Eisenhower administration was raised to a new level of importance under Kennedy. His respect for its chairman, scholar Walter Heller, prompted Kennedy to weigh his advice heavily and use the analyses of his relatively small staff, relegating to secondary importance the larger, more established professional staffs of Treasury and BOB.

Kennedy's impact on the presidency was to make it less formal in organizational terms. Yet the secular trend, independent of personality, of greater centralization and White House capacity was furthered during his years in the White House. Future presidents would reject his loose organizational approach but would further intensify his centralizing direction.

While Eisenhower had expanded the White House staff and organized it formally, the Kennedy administration increased the centralization of executive branch policy control in the White House by creating the nascent capacity to develop and formulate policy independent of the major departments and agencies of the executive branch. Kennedy also began to use his brother Robert and Theodore Sorensen as general advisers whose advice cut across all dimensions of policy, foreign and domestic. The changes in structure and decision-making style were evident in the administration's successful handling of the Cuban missile crisis in 1963.

LYNDON JOHNSON'S ONE-MAN SHOW

When Lyndon Johnson took over the presidency after the assassination of Kennedy, he stressed continuity with the Kennedy administration. He did not make any cabinet changes for thirteen months, and he kept on most of the Kennedy staff, at least for a while. While the Kennedy staff was waiting a decent interval before leaving, Johnson was beginning to build his own staff, in effect running two parallel staffs for the first year of his presidency.

Johnson's personal style and psychological makeup determined his approach to his White House staff and organization. He was jealous of his staffers' publicity and deflated their egos whenever they received more attention than he approved of. According to a personal friend, "Lyndon has a clock inside him with an alarm that tells him at least once an hour to chew somebody out."[33] Johnson wanted all of the credit for his administration's accomplishments and demanded absolute loyalty from his subordinates. The volatility of Johnson's moods was reflected in the volatility of his staff. Because of his treatment of his staff, turnover was high, with only two of the twelve top staffers that he had in 1964 still with him in 1968.[34]

Johnson was unwilling to let any aide become too important or to act in authority over the rest of his staff. Thus, he never had a chief of staff. Johnson occasionally asked people to prepare organization charts of the White House staff, but no one was ever successful, because assignments were not fixed or constant and any formulation would be out-of-date by the time it was printed. Bill Moyers commented on one such effort:

> [L]et me briefly say such an exercise is a gross misuse of a good man's time; nothing useful can come of it, since the White House reflects the personal needs of the president rather [sic] a structural design. If there is a design, it is radial—like the

spokes of a wheel radiating out from the hub. Each person has a special relationship to the president and does what the president needs done; you can define very briefly what each man does, but it is impossible to catch the full scope of his duties. In his own mind the president knows what each man does; he doesn't need an organization chart to show him. In our minds, we know what the president expects of us; a chart is irrelevant.[35]

Bill Moyers played an important role for Johnson, both as friend and policy adviser. Moyers ran the 1964 campaign and became the coordinator for domestic policy and legislation in 1965. Moyers played the major role in creating and managing the fourteen task forces that formulated the ideas that were to make up the Great Society initiatives. When George Reedy left the administration in 1965, Moyers became press secretary and left the administration in late 1966.

The other person who played a major role on the domestic side of the Johnson presidency was Joseph Califano, who came to coordinate most of domestic policy, particularly as the war in Vietnam began to escalate and Moyers left. Just as McGeorge Bundy, and later Walt Rostow, coordinated and integrated national security policy, Califano used his position in the White House to oversee the domestic side of the Johnson policy agenda. The role was to provide coordination of programs cutting across departmental boundaries (most did), to provide follow-through on presidential decisions, to spot crises, and to keep the president informed of developments in the executive branch.[36] On the domestic policy side, Califano occasionally had the duty of "knocking heads together" to settle cabinet disputes.[37] Califano's wide-ranging duties, however, did not approach the scope or authority that Sherman Adams had in the Eisenhower administration.

NIXON'S TIGHT HIERARCHY

When Richard Nixon returned to the White House after serving as Eisenhower's vice president and observing the Kennedy-Johnson years, he resolved that his administration would be more formally organized than the Democrats' had been and closer in tone to Eisenhower's. Nixon began his term with intentions of delegating authority to his cabinet secretaries to select their own subordinates and to accomplish the goals of his administration. He would spend much of his time on international affairs; in domestic policy he would take only the big plays. In May 1968, Nixon declared:

For one thing, I would disperse power, spread it among able people. Men operate best only if they are given the chance to operate at full capacity. I would operate differently from President Johnson. Instead of taking all power to myself, I'd select cabinet members who could do their jobs, and each of them would have the stature and the power to function effectively. Publicity would not center at the White House alone. Every key official would have the opportunity to be a big man in his field. On the other hand, when a president takes all the real power to himself,

those around him become puppets. They shrivel up and become less and less creative.... [Y]our most creative people can't develop in a monolithic, centralized
power set-up.[38]

Nixon's initial intentions were echoed by H. R. Haldeman: "Our job is not to
do the work of government, but to get the work out to where it belongs—out to
the departments."[39] Nixon's intentions were reflected in his selection of cabinet
secretaries of stature and independent political standing and a White House
staff that included the disparate viewpoints of liberal Patrick Moynihan and
conservative Arthur Burns.

But disillusionment soon set in. Nixon found that the Democratically
controlled Congress was not about to give him what he wanted, and he shifted
to an administrative strategy to accomplish his goals. He would use all of the
tools of the executive branch at his disposal. Nixon became convinced that a
wide array of forces were intent on frustrating his aims. The Congress would
not pass his proposals, the media were critically hostile, and the career
bureaucracy would drag their collective feet and sabotage his policies. He even
came to the conclusion that his own appointees in the executive departments
had "gone native" and become more concerned with their own power and
standing in their policy areas than in carrying out his priorities.

He decided to rein in the departments and agencies and created several
mechanisms to facilitate White House control. Thus, instead of getting the
work of the administration out to the departments and agencies, Nixon decided
to bring the work of the departments and agencies into the White House, where
he could carefully control policy development and oversee implementation.

Nixon's concept of the presidency was that the executive branch ought to
be at his disposal. As John Ehrlichman put it: "There shouldn't be a lot of
leeway in following the president's policies. It should be like a corporation,
where the executive vice presidents (the cabinet officers) are tied closely to the
chief executive, or to put it in extreme terms, when he says jump, they only ask
how high."[40]

As Nixon became disillusioned with the executive branch, he gave correspondingly greater power to his White House staff. The role of the staff came to
be to buffer the president and to protect his time so that he could read, write,
and ponder the big picture. In Nixon's words, "My disposition is to see that the
president's time is not frittered away. I've found a way to do it. I'm a reader, not
a buller."[41] Nixon's preference for time alone reinforced the tendency of the
White House staff to guard access to him. The line between protecting the
president's time and isolating the president became a fine one. According to
Henry Kissinger,

> Nixon could be very decisive.... But whenever possible Nixon made these decisions
> in solitude on the basis of memoranda or with a few very intimate aides. He
> abhorred confronting colleagues with whom he disagreed and he could not
> bring himself to face a disapproving friend.... He would decide from inside his
> self-imposed cocoon, but he was unwilling to communicate with those who

disagreed.... All this became a vicious circle in which the president withdrew ever more into his isolation and pulled the central decisions increasingly into the White House, in turn heightening the resentments and defiant mood of his appointees.[42]

From the beginning Nixon had wanted a chief of staff to run his White House, and the role came naturally to H. R. Haldeman, a brilliant and hard-nosed organizer who had been with Nixon since his 1960 campaign for the presidency. To the rest of the executive branch and the outside world, Nixon seemed isolated behind his "Berlin Wall" of Haldeman, Ehrlichman, and Kissinger. According to one Nixon staffer, "The White House became an echo chamber that magnified the voice of the president but sacrificed true pitch."[43]

Haldeman was the linchpin in the White House staff system. He became the most powerful White House aide since Sherman Adams and ran the system with an iron hand. He clearly took precedence over the other staffers. "We all knew where we fit. There were five of us that were equal, but as [Bryce] Harlow said: there was a first among equals, and it was clearly me. Nobody questioned it. I never asserted it; I never argued it. I never had to."[44] According to Haldeman, "If I told someone to do something, he knew it wasn't me—he knew exactly what it was; it was an order from the president. They knew an appeal wouldn't get anywhere."[45]

Haldeman's role, as he saw it, was to institute a "zero-defects system" in the staffing operation. He would ensure that all issues and options for the president were fully "staffed out" and that all bases had been touched. Access to the president by anyone except Kissinger was carefully controlled by Haldeman, and cabinet members frequently resented his gatekeeping. When cabinet secretaries actually did get in to see the president, Haldeman would be present to take notes, and the agenda for the meeting would often be presented to the president in such a way as to determine the outcome to the staff's satisfaction but not the visitor's.[46]

He controlled the paper flow and White House staffing. There was a follow-up process (the "tickler" system) that would impose deadlines for staff projects. As the deadline approached, the staffer or his secretary would be reminded, and if the work was not ready or of unacceptable quality, increasingly heavy-handed reminders would hound the person until the work was completed to Haldeman's satisfaction.

The ostensible purpose of the tightly run system was to save the president from nonpresidential details so that he could concentrate on the big picture. The irony was that despite the time that Nixon reserved for thinking great thoughts, he was obsessed with the details of the White House operation, both of substance and style. He was concerned with White House furniture, who had what photographs of former presidents in the Executive Office Building, and he wanted extensive memos to him on what wines would be served at White House functions. He had White House staffers log the comments visitors made on the paintings displayed in the west lobby, and he kept careful inventory of small gifts (cuff links, ash trays, and copies of Six Crises) that were given out to visitors to the White House. There were many memoranda about the White House tennis courts.[47]

Although the Watergate scandals were not caused by the staffing system, both Watergate and the staff organization were reflections of Nixon's psychology and character. Despite the fact that Haldeman was trusted enough by the president to occasionally delay implementation of questionable off-the-cuff orders and demands by an irritated Nixon, there was never any question or doubt in the White House about covering up the initial Watergate break-in. The tone was set by Nixon, and the staff unquestioningly carried out his wishes. The problem was that Haldeman and the staff system he set up faithfully reflected and reinforced Nixon's dark side and need for isolation. Thus, the zero-defects system enabled the Watergate "horrors" to occur and led to the resignations and convictions of top White House staffers and the unprecedented resignation of a U.S. president.

FORD'S AND CARTER'S LESSONS

When Richard Nixon's resignation elevated Gerald Ford to the presidency, as Henry Kissinger said, "the presidency was in a shambles."[48] Ford's challenge was to make a sharp break with the Watergate aspects of the Nixon presidency but to maintain some continuity of leadership and policy. Ford chose to distance himself rhetorically and symbolically from Nixon, proclaiming that "our long national nightmare is over," and being very visible and accessible.

Part of the Watergate baggage that Ford wanted to throw out was the tightly hierarchical White House organization symbolized by H. R. Haldeman. "A Watergate was made possible by a strong chief of staff and ambitious White House aides who were more powerful than members of the cabinet but who had little or no practical political experience or judgement. I wanted to reverse the trend and restore authority to my cabinet."[49] Ford resolved that there would be no powerful chief of staff, and his transition team of advisers concurred with his judgment, though it recommended a "staff coordinator." Ford got along for a while with nine of his top aides reporting directly to him, but after a month of staff squabbling and difficulties in coordination he brought in the ambassador to NATO, Donald Rumsfeld, to fill the role.

Rumsfeld knew he had to bring order to the White House advising system and begin to assert control over access to the president, who was being overwhelmed by his too-open system. Rumsfeld also had to impose order on policy development. Ford had given his vice president, Nelson Rockefeller, jurisdiction over domestic policy and control over the domestic policy staff. One of Rumsfeld's roles was to say no to the vice president, a very delicate task, given his constitutional status and the turf ceded to him by the president. But someone had to make sure that the policies proposed by the administration were consistent with Gerald Ford's conservative philosophy, and Ford did not want to say no to Rockefeller personally. Someone had to say no, and Rumsfeld was the one to do it.[50]

The order brought about by Rumsfeld convinced Ford that the role of a firm coordinator was necessary, and when Ford replaced James Schlesinger at

Defense with Rumsfeld, he gave the task to Richard Cheney, Rumsfeld's deputy. In admitting that the spokes-of-the-wheel approach would not work, Ford said:

> I believe a president has to have a chief of staff who is an expert manager and one who does not seek on his own a high identity—in fact, one who purposely avoids that. That individual has to coordinate everything that transpires in the west wing of the White House and the Oval Office.... If you don't have that kind of person, I don't think the president's job can be well done.[51]

Cheney's approach to the position, which was finally acknowledged to be chief of staff and not the euphemism of staff coordinator, was to maintain very low visibility. He took seriously the prescription of the Brownlow Committee that White House aides should have a "passion for anonymity."

He made no public speeches and talked with reporters only with the understanding that his name would not be used in the articles. Said Cheney: "I had made a very determined decision to keep my head down, and I stuck to it. I thought I could get a hell of a lot more done if I was not a public figure."[52] His low visibility was a source of strength in his role. He did not have a policy agenda of his own, and he was a neutral broker in transferring disparate advice going to the president. In his role, he was not heavy-handed, as Sherman Adams and H. R. Haldeman had been in performing the same role. But his courteous demeanor did not prevent him from asserting firm control over White House policy development and staff.

Cheney imposed order on policy development by guarding against "oh, by the way" decisions. The presidency is always subject to the wiles of cabinet officers and others who try to gain an advantage by getting the president alone in an unguarded minute to push their own policy preferences. If not caught and nipped in the bud, such occurrences can prematurely commit the president to a decision before it has been fully staffed out, and can lead to embarrassing reversals by the president. If an aide or cabinet member wanted to raise an issue with the president, Cheney would insist that it be vetted with all others who had a legitimate say in that policy area.

Cheney recognized the tenuousness of the delicate balance needed to make his approach to the chief-of-staff position successful:

> It's really a matter of trade-offs.... There is no question that to the extent that you involve a number of people in the consultative process before you make a decision, you raise the level of noise in the system. You enhance the possibility of premature disclosures and leaks. You also take more time, cut down in efficiency. On the other side, by encouraging different viewpoints you make sure that the president's got a wide variety of options so he won't be blindsided.[53]

The difference between Cheney's approach to the position of chief of staff and that of Adams and Haldeman was that Cheney was courteous and solicitous, while they were brusque, harsh, and imperious. Cheney maintained a very low profile by design, while they received much press coverage because of their "assistant president" images. Cheney controlled access to the president, while they constricted the flow to a trickle that they personally controlled. Cheney did the "dirty deeds" that a chief of staff must do, but he did not relish the task, while they seemed to revel in asserting their power. Cheney kept his channels to the Hill open, while they never made serious attempts to court Congress. Finally, Cheney worked for Gerald Ford, who consciously tried to be open, while they worked for presidents who, though very different people, each wanted to be buffered and protected from many of the pressures that focus on the presidency.

Jimmy Carter won a narrow victory over Gerald Ford in 1976, but he came to office with the same predilections about Watergate and White House organization. He ran as an outsider, owing little to the Democratic Party. He promised to clean up the "horrible bureaucratic mess" in Washington and never to lie to the American people. He promised cabinet government with access to the president and a White House staff that would not assert itself over cabinet secretaries.

Carter's approach to White House organization reflected his personality. In addition to thinking that Nixon's hierarchical White House, with a strong chief of staff, was a cause of Watergate, he felt that he was smart enough to be his own chief of staff. There was no doubt about his intelligence. He had been a nuclear engineer in the Navy and could comprehend a greater amount of written material than any of his staffers. But according to Jack Watson, Carter was more of a problem solver than a politician, and in his in-depth grasp of policy problems did not understand that "the best is the enemy of the good."[54] He also did not want to choose one from among his Georgia staffers to be in charge of the others.

But the problem of White House organization is more than a question of the intelligence of the president; it is also a matter of filtering information and regulating access. With eight top White House aides reporting directly to Carter and no staff secretary or chief of staff to coordinate policy development, no one short of the president was in charge. As a result, Carter took up his time dealing with policy details that might have been settled at lower levels and settling White House staff and cabinet secretary disputes that no one else had the authority to settle, even if the issues were not of presidential importance.

Another problem was that Carter was unwilling to choose priorities from among his many policy initiatives. Thus, the first year of his administration was rocky, with some victories and some defeats, but with no overall theme that he could use to unify his administration or project to the country.

With that seeming lack of vision haunting his presidency, and an oil shortage that created block-long lines of cars for gas in the summer of 1979, Carter went up to Camp David to reassess his presidency. After talking with many people from all walks of life and seeking advice on his administration, he gave a prime-time speech to the nation and argued that tough decisions had to be made on energy and other policy areas. The same week he also accepted the resignations of five of his cabinet secretaries and designated Hamilton Jordan as his chief of staff. The final recognition that a chief of staff was necessary to coordinate policy development and relations between the White House and the cabinet was a salutary one, but it was undercut by choosing Jordan. Jordan had been with Carter longest and was the closest to him of all of the Georgians; but Jordan was a brilliant campaign strategist, not an organizational genius. However, coordination did improve when Jordan left the White House to run the campaign and Jack Watson was named chief of staff and Alonzo McDonald was named staff director.

Scholars have speculated as to why Carter's White House staff, which was made up of highly intelligent individuals, did not gel into an effective White House team. One of the probable causes was that Carter was unwilling to leaven his Georgian staffers with more Washington insiders. Among his top White House staff, only Zbigniew Brzezinski was not from Georgia and, among the Georgians, only Stuart Eizenstat had previous Washington experience. Former Senator Walter Mondale was a close adviser to Carter personally, but as vice president he could not be expected to hold the White House staff in line.[55]

What the Ford and Carter presidencies proved was that, with the growth of staff in the White House and the expanded functions it is expected to perform for presidents, the modern White House cannot function effectively without a chief of staff. This person does not have to fill the same role as the strong chiefs of the Eisenhower and Nixon presidencies did but must at least coordinate and take charge of the policy process and advice to the president. The two contrasting ways to fill the role of chief of staff were exemplified by the Adams-Haldeman model of the strong chief contrasted with the facilitating model of Cheney-Watkins. The Reagan presidency was to exemplify the best and worst of the two approaches in its first and second terms.

REAGAN'S TWO CONTRASTING TERMS

As it is with all presidents, the shape and role of the Reagan White House staff reflected Ronald Reagan's personality. By all accounts, both friendly and critical, Reagan was extremely passive in his approach to the White House staff. He was not passive with respect to the major direction of his presidency or public policy; his was an active administration. But once the direction was set by Reagan, his aides formulated the policies and carried them out; Reagan was interested only in outcomes and did not want to be bothered with details.

Part of his passiveness was due to his uncritical trust in whatever people told him or what he read that fit in with his world view.[56] This passiveness made him dependent on his staff, who had to make sure he was not unduly influenced by the most recent person he saw.[57] Donald Regan recalled, "I cannot remember a single case in which he changed a time or cancelled an appointment or ever complained about an item on his schedule."[58]

Reagan's hands-off approach to his staff was based on a management philosophy that relied on delegation of authority. In his words: "Surround yourself with the best people you can find, delegate authority, and don't interfere as long as the policy you've decided upon is being carried out."[59] This approach occasionally frustrated administration officials because of Reagan's unwillingness to give them policy guidance. Donald Regan complained: "In the four years that I served as secretary of the treasury I never saw President Reagan alone and never discussed economic philosophy.... I had to figure these things out like any other American, by studying his speeches and reading the newspapers.... After I accepted the job, he simply hung up and vanished." Reagan "laid down no rules and articulated no missions" and thus conferred great "latitude on his subordinates."[60] To David Stockman, Reagan "seemed so serene and passive.... He gave no orders, no commands; asked for no information; expressed no urgency.... Since I *did* know what to do, I took his quiet message of confidence to be a mandate."[61] Stockman observed that, whenever there was an argument, Reagan would smile and say: "Okay, you fellas work it out."[62]

Reagan's passivity and penchant for delegation made his staff crucial to his presidency in a way that was not true of Franklin Roosevelt, John Kennedy, or George H.W. Bush. The unique division of labor in his first term worked in a particularly felicitous way for Reagan. The definition of staff roles began before the inauguration, immediately after the election, when the decisions were made about the structure and organization of the top staff. The outcome was driven by the widespread expectation that Edwin Meese, who had run the campaign, headed the transition, and had run Reagan's gubernatorial office in California, would naturally be named Reagan's White House chief of staff. But others around Reagan judged that Meese, though unquestionably loyal and ideologically dedicated, did not have the organizational talent or discipline to perform well as chief of staff.

Reagan must be given credit for accepting their advice that he needed a Washington insider for his chief of staff and saying no to the loyal Meese. James Baker had supported George H. W. Bush for the presidential nomination in 1976 and 1980, but he turned out to be the architect of the historic Reagan victories of the first year. In order to get Meese to go along with the plan, he had to be convinced that he would still play a major role in the administration. This task was accomplished by a memo initialed by both Baker and Meese that divided up the responsibilities of the two advisers. On the surface, the division was heavily slanted toward Meese, giving him jurisdiction over administration policy, both foreign and domestic. Meese was to have the title of "counselor to the president for policy," along with cabinet rank, and was to participate in all meetings of the full cabinet. He was in charge of "coordination and supervision" of the domestic policy staff and the National Security Council.[63] Thus, Meese was given a very wide range of responsibilities indeed. What was left for Baker?

Baker was to get the formal title of chief of staff and the traditional process and staffing powers of that position. He was given control over "coordination and supervision of White House staff functions, hiring and firing authority over all elements of White House staff, coordination and control of all in and out paper flow to the president and of presidential schedule and appointments," and he was to "preside over meetings of White House staff." Baker also claimed the traditional chief-of-staff office in the West Wing. An addition, written in longhand, ensured that both Meese and Baker had the right to "attend any meeting which Pres. attends—w/his consent."[64]

On the surface Meese had a huge advantage, with cabinet participation and control of foreign and domestic policy; the memo was designed so that Baker received no substance and all process. But in the White House, process often determines policy outcomes, especially with as detached a president as Ronald Reagan, and thus Baker had the advantage over Meese in the administration's policy deliberations.

As chief of staff, Baker hired skilled Washington insiders to help him, and he orchestrated the administration's policy agenda for the first term. He did not seek complete control over access to the president, sharing it with Meese and Michael Deaver, and he exercised his power in a subtle rather than heavy-handed way. With his reputation for pragmatism that invoked the suspicion of the ideological Reaganites, he was careful to keep open his lines of communication to the right wing of the Republican Party, and he assiduously maintained his ties to members of Congress. He was accessible to and trusted by the press and often received favorable news coverage, which he used to the administration's advantage. He thus was attentive to the major constituencies that Reagan would need to accomplish his agenda. Richard Darman was staff secretary and controlled paper flow to the Oval Office.

Michael Deaver, the third member of the troika, had been with Reagan for many years in California and was so close to the Reagans that they considered him almost a son. Deaver became deputy chief of staff, but he was not concerned as much with the substance of policy as with the staging of the president and his presentation to the public.[65] He concerned himself with everything that affected Ronald Reagan as a person: his comfort, his schedule, and the backdrops for his political actions. Perhaps most importantly, Deaver was the primary link to the East Wing, that is, to Nancy Reagan. He would pass on her wishes, either explicitly or as his own ideas, to the West Wing staffers. Baker talked with Deaver daily and thus kept in touch with Mrs. Reagan; he sensitively allied himself with her and accommodated her wishes.

Nancy Reagan was not interested or active in policy across-the-board, but she selectively inserted her views very effectively when she felt that the president's person or reputation was at stake. Several times this affected foreign policy and, quite often, staffing decisions. She played a role in the resignations of cabinet secretaries James Watt, Raymond Donavan, Edwin Meese, and a number of White House staffers, including Donald Regan.[66]

The White House was to change drastically in Reagan's second term, with large-scale changes of personnel at the top. Despite the 1986 tax reform, Reagan's second term brought no sweeping victories comparable to the economic agenda of 1981, and the administration slid into the disaster of the Iran–Contra scandal.

The second term troubles were due, in no small part, to the change in chiefs of staff. Treasury Secretary Donald Regan and Chief of Staff James Baker decided to exchange jobs, and characteristically, Regan, Baker, Deaver, and Nancy Reagan had agreed on the switch before it was presented to Reagan. Characteristically, Reagan agreed to the staff decision and asked no questions.

When Regan came in to run the White House, he had several personal priorities. He wanted to do away with the collegial staffing arrangement of the first term that he felt led to staff conflict and leaks, which it had. He also wanted to make some personnel changes, but most importantly he wanted to "let Reagan be Reagan."

Regan's personal style and career suggested that he would take a different approach to running the White House than had James Baker. Regan had been an officer in the Marines and was used to being CEO of Merrill Lynch. "When I was chief executive and I said, 'Jump,' people asked, 'How high?' As secretary of the treasury, when I said, 'Jump,' people said, 'What do you mean by jump? What do you mean by high?'"[67] According to one of Regan's aides, "He considers the executive branch to be like a corporation. Cabinet members are vice presidents, the president is the chairman of the board, the chief of staff is the chief operating officer."[68] Regan was used to being a principal and did not easily slide into a staff role.

Whereas Baker had brought strong subordinates to work with him, Regan would brook no rivals for influence. The staffers he brought from his days at the Treasury Department were known around the White House as "the mice" because of their meek approach to their boss. According to White House staffers, Regan's personal staff aides were "almost obsequious and scared stiff of him."[69] A former colleague of Regan said: "His weakness is that his ego was so strong he did not pick good subordinates. Or if they were, he broke them. He couldn't stand the competition."[70]

At the same time that Regan was establishing himself as chief of staff, other strong advisers to the president were leaving the White House. Baker and Meese were taking cabinet positions; Deaver was leaving the White House to make money; Darman left with Baker; David Stockman was on his way to Wall Street. Max Friedersdorf and Ed Rollins stayed for a while in the second term, but soon left.

Regan's wanting to "let Reagan be Reagan" led him to think that his own lack of strong policy preferences was a guarantee that he was serving the president's goals and no one else's. But to best serve the president, the White House staff must compensate for his weaknesses. In this case, the president's weakness was his passivity and not being willing to search out alternatives on his own. This placed the responsibility on the staff to ensure that contrasting views were brought to the president's attention. In the first term this was ensured, despite the staff's intentions to protect the president from conflict, because the rivalries among the staff and the struggle between conservatives and moderates could not be entirely suppressed.

Reinforcing the president's conviction that most policy problems were really very simple was another consequence of "letting Reagan be Reagan," but this was not a favor to the president. In criticizing Regan, David Stockman called this "the echo principle" and argued that it shielded Reagan from hard economic realities.[71] According to Richard Darman, one of the advantages of the first-term conflictual triumvirate was that the president was forced to face up to some complex realities. "Seeing the interplay between us, a lot of things happened. First of all, Ronald Reagan learned much more about reality."[72]

But Don Regan was doing his best to stifle this built-in safety valve. He asserted tight control over the White House, controlling access to the president, scheduling, paper flow, public appearances, appointments, and phone calls. Also, unlike other strong chiefs of staff, he attempted to assert control over national security policy. But Regan's heavy-handed attempt to control everything went too far. Long-time Reagan intimate Stuart Spencer observed that Regan "became a prime minister, he became a guy that was in every photo op, he wasn't watching the shop. And he surrounded himself with yes people. Those were all signs of weakness to me."[73]

Contrary to the Brownlowian admonition to have a passion for anonymity, Regan sought the limelight, and was constantly trying to get into photographs with the president that would appear in the newspapers. The most egregious example of this was the official photograph of Presidents Reagan and Gorbachev at the Geneva Summit. The White House photo showed the two leaders sitting on a couch with Don Regan behind them, leaning forward as if he were the orchestrator of their agreement. Regan, who as chief of staff made the final decision, insisted that this be the only photo of the summit agreement released by the White House.[74]

In "letting Reagan be Reagan," Regan acted as if the president were his only constituent. He did not seem to realize that in order to serve the president effectively, a chief of staff needs to cultivate other constituencies, especially Congress and the press. Regan soon alienated members of both houses with his disdain for Congress as an institution and his distaste for politics. He antagonized the press because of his heavy-handed attempts to control leaks and his hostility over unfavorable coverage of the administration. Unlike Baker, he did not realize that the press "serves as a bulletin board" upon which Washington insiders post notices, and use it to his (and his president's) advantage.[75]

Regan had other drawbacks as chief of staff, one of which was not getting along with the First Lady. According to Nancy Reagan, Regan liked the sound of "chief" but not the sound of "staff."[76] Nor did Regan care much for Nancy. "Mrs. Reagan regarded herself as the president's alter ego ... as if the office that had been bestowed upon her husband by the people somehow fell into the category of worldly goods covered by the marriage vows."[77] He also resented the influence of Nancy's astrologer on the management of the presidency. "Virtually every major move and decision the Reagans made during my time as White House chief of staff was cleared in advance with a woman in San Francisco who drew up horoscopes to make certain that the planets were in a favorable alignment for the enterprise."[78] "At times the president's schedule would have to be changed at the last minute, or set for precise timing, at the behest of Joan Quigley, the Reagans' astrologer."[79]

While chiefs of staff traditionally take the blame for the president, Regan wasn't always willing to take the heat for administration failures. After the disclosure of the administration's dealings with Iran and the failed Reykjavik summit, Regan tried to distance himself from the embarrassment. "Some of us are like a shovel brigade that follow [sic] a parade down Main Street cleaning up. We took Reykjavik and turned what was really a sour situation into something that turned out pretty well."[80] What is unsettling about this statement is that Regan is shifting blame for administration embarrassments away from himself and toward the person who was in charge of U.S. performance at the Reykjavik summit: President Reagan. The strong implication here is that Regan saw himself as cleaning up after the president made a mess of things. This public shifting of blame to the president is unacceptable for a White House staffer.

The final straw in Regan's term as chief of staff was the report of the Tower Commission. Despite the fact that Regan denied that he had any control over foreign policy, the Tower Commission held him responsible for the Iran-Contra disaster. According to Brent Scowcroft, Regan claimed to have jurisdiction over foreign-policy advice to the president. "He kept saying he did. One of the reasons McFarlane quit was because Regan wanted McFarlane to report through him."[81]

The Tower Commission that investigated the Iran-Contra scandal did not accept Regan's denials. Although it did not conclude that Regan participated in the scandal or the cover-up, it did hold him responsible for allowing it to happen on his watch. In citing the "failure of responsibility," the board pointed out that ultimate responsibility for the White House staff system belongs to the president, but that Regan was partially responsible for the disaster.

> More than almost any chief of staff of recent memory, he asserted personal control over the White House staff and sought to extend this control to the national security adviser. He was personally active in national security affairs and attended almost all of the relevant meetings regarding the Iran initiative.... He must bear primary responsibility for the chaos that descended upon the White House when such disclosure did occur.[82]

After resisting as long as he could and after much prodding from his wife and other intimates, the president asked for Regan's resignation, but he agreed to wait until several days after the release of the Tower Report as a face-saving gesture. But the coup de grâce was administered by Nancy Reagan immediately after release of the report, when it was leaked to the press from her office that Howard Baker would be Reagan's new chief of staff. As soon as he heard of the press announcement, Regan immediately resigned.[83]

After the resignation on February 27, 1987, Regan's problems were summed up by a former Reagan White House staffer:

> Don never realized that while Wall Street runs one way, Pennsylvania Avenue is a two-way street. He never realized there is a difference between being an elected and an appointed official. He never realized the distinction between being a staff person

and the chief executive officer. He never realized that the White House demands talent throughout, rather than talent derived. He never realized his job was to compensate for the perceived strengths and weaknesses of others, rather than to dominate those weaknesses.[84]

BUSH'S PIT BULL

George H.W. Bush recruited a competent White House staff marked by professionalism and a low-visibility approach to White House service. The best in White House staff service was exemplified by Brent Scowcroft, assistant to the president for national security affairs, who had filled the same role in the Ford administration. Scowcroft was tireless in his service to Bush, and he often provided a personal sounding board to Bush's thoughts about foreign affairs. Another model staffer was Roger Porter, who had served in the Ford and Reagan administrations and was made assistant to the president for domestic and economic policy in the Bush White House. He provided experience, expertise, and sound policy analysis without engaging in public disputes over policy or status or trying to strong-arm members of the cabinet.

Bush's White House staff did not tend to interpose themselves between the president and cabinet secretaries or have major fights with the cabinet departments, because Bush knew his cabinet well, and unlike Reagan, made it a habit to keep in touch with them. So Bush's White House did not have major ego problems or conflicts with the cabinet, with one major exception: his chief of staff, John Sununu.

President Bush, who had a chief of staff (Craig Fuller) when he was vice president, clearly wanted a chief to organize the White House and coordinate policy development. And Sununu performed well many of the traditional chief-of-staff roles. He made the trains run on time. He was the enforcer with respect to White House staffers, the cabinet, and Congress. He fired people, and he took the heat for unpopular decisions.

One common mistake of chiefs of staff that Sununu did not make was to reinforce a presidential weakness, as had Haldeman and Regan before him. He provided a sharp contrast in personal style to the president. He was the president's "pit bull" who would act mean and allow the president to take the "kinder and gentler" stance. Sununu, unlike the three previous strong chiefs of staff, had firm ideological convictions and advocated his own policy preferences. But what would ordinarily be a major drawback in a chief of staff worked to the president's advantage in this case. Sununu was more conservative politically than the president and was willing to play a highly visible role as keeper of the conservative flame and representative of the conservative wing of the Republican Party in the White House. When Sununu would stake out a very conservative position, for instance on environmental policy, it would allow the president to take a more moderate stance, thus reassuring conservatives that their interests were being represented in the White House, while letting the president still claim to be "the environmental president."

The danger of a chief of staff who is also a policy advocate is that advice to the president might be skewed to favor the chief of staff's desired outcome. The other common danger of a strong chief of staff is that access to the president will be constricted. President Bush's style of governing minimized these dangers. He knew enough about the policy issues himself to be able to discount the bias of his staff. And his personal style of frequent communication with members of his cabinet mitigated the danger that he would become isolated, even though Sununu did control access to the Oval Office. The president was often on the phone, touching base with anyone who was involved with current policy issues.

But the president's penchant for keeping in touch, while avoiding the danger of isolation, did not entirely eliminate Sununu's attempts to control communication to the president. Sununu's personal policy agenda made it difficult at times for those in the cabinet or staff who wanted to speak with the president about a different approach to get through Sununu's gauntlet. Senior Bush aides were so upset at being cut off by Sununu that the president was forced to open a post office box at his summer home in Kennebunkport, Maine, as a back channel so that his top advisers could contact him directly without Sununu's censorship.[85] The very fact that President Bush felt compelled to set up a private post office box, physically and organizationally outside the White House, was an admission of organizational failure.

Another indicator of that failure was the Council of Economic Advisers Chair Michael Boskin's attempt to see the president in the fall of 1991. After several unsuccessful attempts to get in to see Bush, on November 20, 1991, Boskin threatened to resign if Sununu did not allow him to talk to the president about economic policy.[86] In these instances John Sununu was not acting as a "neutral broker" of ideas for the president. White House staffers and cabinet secretaries did not have the confidence that their ideas would reach the president intact if they submitted them to the White House staff. Instead, Sununu was seen as a biased filter, screening out ideas he personally did not like.

Despite his rapport with the president and his ability to perform very valuable chief-of-staff functions, Sununu made several strategic errors as chief of staff. One of his soft spots was his stratospheric IQ, which reportedly was 180. But it struck many with whom he worked that he seemed to have to put others down in order to demonstrate how smart he was. White House staffers and assistant secretaries did not appreciate being denigrated in front of their peers when their staff work did not seem to measure up to Sununu's standards. He told one reporter who asked about his interpersonal skills that it "depends how badly the other guy's screwing up."[87]

Sununu really seemed to believe his oft-stated maxim that he had a constituency of only one, the president. Far from being responsible to a constituency of only one, strong chiefs of staff have demonstrated the lesson that serving the president means being able to cultivate other constituencies for his use. Sununu did not recognize this and thus felt free to alienate Congress, the cabinet, the press, and interest groups, as well as his White House subordinates.

It is as if his attitude were, "I am so powerful that I do not have to be nice, or even minimally civil, to other people." In this he was ignoring the old Lebanese proverb that holds, "One kisses the hand that one cannot yet bite."[88] When Sununu got into trouble, those who previously had to kiss his hand turned to bite it.

In defense of his behavior, Sununu echoed other chiefs of staff in claiming he was merely doing the president's bidding. "I'm no freelancer. I meet with the president dozens of times during the day. . . . The president knows I'm following his agenda. . . . I know enough about the president to do exactly what he wants done. Exactly what he wants done."[89] In this statement, Sununu was both claiming presidential authority for all of his own actions and subtly shifting the blame for any of them to the president.

Sununu's explanation for his lack of civility is that each breach of good taste and manners was carefully calculated: "I guarantee you that contrary to the legend, any strong statements on my part are both controlled, deliberate, and designed to achieve an effect. There is no random outburst. It all is designed for purpose. And I think the efficiency of the result is underscored by what we've been able to achieve."[90] This rationalization is consistent with one important role of the chief of staff, playing the heavy for the president, being the enforcer of tough decisions and bringer of bad tidings to others. "I don't care if people hate me, as long as they hate me for the right reasons," said Sununu.[91] But that was the problem. Washington professionals understand that the policy preferences of the president are the responsibility of the chief of staff, and they expect him to be tough for the president. Professionals are willing to accept being beaten in the policy arena, but Sununu's gratuitous ad hominem insults and rude behavior generated resentments much greater than mere policy defeats would have. Sununu acted as if he did not understand the import of his own words.

In spring of 1991, the *Washington Post* reported that the chief of staff had taken more than seventy trips around the country aboard military aircraft. Almost all of the trips were designated (by the chief of staff) as official business, even though the purpose of some of them seemed to be to provide skiing trips for Sununu and his family. None of the twenty-seven trips to his home state of New Hampshire were designated as personal.

When the disclosures caused a public scandal in May 1991, the president (whose early priority was to have an administration above ethical reproach) ordered Sununu to clear all future flights with the White House counsel's office. But in June, Sununu had a White House limousine take him to New York for a stamp auction he wanted to attend and solicited corporations to provide air travel back to Washington and other trips. The president again was forced to restrict Sununu's travel practices.[92]

There is no argument here that Sununu's trips on government planes constituted outrageous or illegal behavior, or that White House staffers should always fly coach. Few would begrudge a few trips on official planes with occasional combinations of business with pleasure. High-level officials in

Congress and the executive branch have done this for decades, and it is standard practice in corporate America. The point is that Sununu abused his privileges and pushed them to excess. His bending of the rules was routine, pervasive, and systematic. He was unable to restrain himself from taking advantage of his position and was unwilling to rein himself in, even after the president was forced publicly to admonish him. By pushing his privileges too far, Sununu became an embarrassment to the president, who was forced to defend him in public. A chief of staff should never put the president in this position.

Sununu's final strategic error was the Don Regan syndrome: Take credit when things go well, and when they turn sour shift blame to the president. At a November 1991 campaign fund-raising speech in New York, President Bush remarked that people in the financial community felt that interest rates charged on credit cards were higher than necessary and that it might spur the economy if they came down a bit. The next day Senator Alphonse D'Amato (R-NY) introduced legislation to impose a legal limit on the interest rates credit-card companies could charge their customers. The economic wisdom of the proposal was challenged in the financial community, and the Dow Jones Industrial Average fell 120 points. The administration had to back away quickly from the proposed legislation and publicly argue against it.

When asked by reporters about this embarrassing episode, Sununu said that the remark about interest rates was not in the president's prepared text but that the president had "ad-libbed" the remarks on credit card interest rates. This attempt to blame the embarrassing remarks on the president was rebutted by Marlin Fitzwater, the president's spokesman. He told reporters that the lines were in the printed text of the speech and were not ad-libbed. Some administration officials even said that Sununu himself was the author of the offending lines.[93]

The issue in this case is not whether the lines were in the speech text or not. The issue is who publicly takes the blame for an embarrassing incident. In this case, Sununu publicly tried to shift blame to the president. If Sununu were lying about the speech text, his behavior was outrageous. But even if he were telling the truth, it is not the role of the chief of staff to publicly blame the president for an administration blunder. The appropriate behavior for the chief of staff is to take the heat in order to protect the president.

Sununu's general attitude toward the press was reflected in his public reaction to a *Washington Post* reporter who covered the story of the credit card flap. After a bill-signing ceremony on the White House lawn, he told Ann Devroy, loudly and in front of others: "You're a liar. Your stories are all lies. Everything you write is a lie."[94]

The final downfall and firing of Sununu took place soon after the credit card incident, which was merely the final straw. The striking thing about Sununu's term as chief of staff is how long he was allowed to stay. It speaks strongly of President Bush's gratitude for Sununu's support in the New Hampshire primary and of the president's personal loyalty to his subordinate, but it also demonstrates that he was performing highly valued functions for the president.

The firing came at a low point in the Bush administration; the economy was doing poorly, the president was sliding in public opinion polls from his huge popularity after the Persian Gulf War, and the administration seemed to be in disarray. Sununu personally could only be blamed for the last of the three, but the scapegoat factor is a real one in Washington. Nevertheless, without Sununu's strategic miscalculations, he could probably have weathered the storm of problems for which he was not solely responsible.

Shortly after Sununu resigned, he was replaced by Secretary of Transportation Samuel Skinner. But in the summer of 1992, when President Bush was faring poorly in the polls and falling behind Bill Clinton, he persuaded James Baker to leave the State Department and return to the White House as chief of staff.

CLINTON'S CIRCUS

In the early months of the Clinton administration, the White House was like a circus in the sense that it had three rings of power, most importantly the president himself, but also First Lady Hillary Rodham Clinton and Vice President Al Gore. The First Lady played a more active role in the administration across the board—politics, personnel, policy—than had any other first lady in history. Certainly other first ladies had been powerful and had played crucial roles in the administrations of their husbands, but not in the comprehensive way that Mrs. Clinton did from the beginning of the administration.

Al Gore had been chosen vice president not for the usual reasons of balancing the ticket in terms of ideology, age, or geography, but because there was a definite simpatico between the two men; their relationship was personal as well as professional. The level of trust between the only two nationally elected officials was unusually high. Thus, Clinton delegated to Gore significant areas of policy for special influence (e.g., foreign policy, science, environmental policy, administrative reform). He also gave Gore a say in personnel, and he consulted him regularly.

The presence of these three circles of power made managing the Clinton White House a special challenge. But in the beginning it was also a circus, in the sense that there was a lack of coordination among White House staffers and the policy agenda. At times there seemed to be no ringmaster other than the president, and the president wanted to think about policy and politics rather than to manage the circus.

Bill Clinton was the first Democratic president to come to office admitting that he needed a chief of staff. Thus, in December 1992 he designated his childhood friend Thomas (Mack) McLarty to be his chief of staff. McLarty had the advantages of unquestioned trust from the president, political experience in Arkansas, and experience as a business executive. In contrast with the domineering chiefs of staff, he was unfailingly courteous and gracious, and he tried mightily to manage the White House for a year and a half. He was not successful for several reasons. He spent only about two-thirds of his time dealing with internal White House management in a position that requires 110 percent of a person's time; the rest of the time he was acting as presidential ambassador to the business community or conservatives on the Hill. He also had to deal with the three rings of power in the White House, a gargantuan coordination challenge. But most importantly, President Clinton did not want to be managed or to delegate the necessary authority to anyone else to manage the White House.

Clinton was an inveterate "policy wonk" who was fascinated by the details of public policy and tended to work over problems endlessly with anyone available; he resisted coming to closure or making final decisions. It seemed that meetings were countless and endless, with nothing ever getting finally decided. As a result, staffers continued to fight for their own preferred policy outcomes and did not hesitate to lobby the president for them. The policy-development process was chaotic, and the White House suffered from a number of minor snafus that might have been avoided with a more disciplined organization.

One of the problems that McLarty had was the active White House involvement of Clinton's 1992 campaign team. Several campaign leaders, including James Carville, Paul Begalla, Mandy Grunwald, and Stanley Greenberg, decided not to take positions in the government but continued to advise Clinton about policy in White House meetings at which they demanded that no White House staffers be present. They argued that in his approach to reduction of the budget deficit Clinton was selling out the constituency that elected him. They wanted more liberal policies and thought that the White House staff, particularly Clinton's economic team, was hijacking the policy agenda.

This caused problems for McLarty and the White House staff. The problem was not that Clinton was getting advice from outside the White House. Presidents often seek the input of those not in the government; and in any case, presidents ought to be able to listen to whomever they choose. The problem was that the campaigners' advice was not being monitored or coordinated with anyone else. The only place where their ideas and professional policy analyses came together was in Clinton's head. The outside ideas were not vetted by White House staffers, departmental policy analysts, or Office of Management and Budget (OMB) staffers. Nor was outside advice balanced with the input of White House staffers on the political, policy, congressional, or budget implications of such advice. McLarty's lack of control over the campaigners' access was a problem for the administration and White House organization. The content of the advice was not a problem; the lack of coordination was.

By the summer of 1994, President Clinton realized that McLarty could not do the job that needed doing in the White House and replaced him with his director of the Office of Management and Budget, Leon Panetta. McLarty was retained in the White House as a senior counselor, the only chief of staff to be retained in the White House after having been, in effect, fired. The fact that Panetta put some more rigor into the White House organization was due not only to his personality, which was more authoritative than McLarty's, but also to Clinton's realization that he had to delegate more authority to his chief of staff to run the White House.

When he took over in July 1994, Panetta asserted more actively some of the traditional prerogatives of the chief of staff. He tightened access to the president so that only one or two staffers, rather than ten, had "walk-in" privileges to the Oval Office. He insisted that the campaigners have access to the president only through him and only as part of the coordinated advice to the president. He insisted that all staff work and decision memoranda go to the president through him and ensured that all staff work was fully prepared before being presented to the president. He took control of White House hiring and payroll decisions. He set tighter, more focused agendas for meetings with fewer people invited and insisted on "closure," that is, coming to a decision about the issue at hand.

With these changes, the Clinton White House became more organized and the policy-making process more coherent. There were fewer minor embarrassments that leaked to the press. In 1995 and 1996, Panetta also was one of the major negotiators with the Republican-controlled Congress. But Panetta's control of the White House was compromised by the role that Dick Morris played in 1995 and 1996. After the devastating defeat in the 1994 congressional elections in which the Republicans gained control of Congress for the first time in forty years, the president sought advice from Dick Morris, who had advised him when he was governor of Arkansas and who helped engineer his reelection in 1982 after he had been defeated for reelection in 1980. Morris, who had been working as a political consultant for Republican members of Congress, began to advise Clinton to moderate the administration's policies, and he drafted speeches for him. Morris's advice was clearly valuable to Clinton, but the problem was that in the early months of 1995 Morris was advising Clinton secretly (under the code name of "Charlie"), unbeknownst to Leon Panetta or the rest of the White House staff.

As with the campaigners in 1993, the problem was not that Clinton was receiving outside advice, but that the advice was not being vetted or balanced with those who would be in charge of implementing the policies. For the president's sake as well as the rest of the executive branch, new policy proposals should be analyzed for their budget and implementation implications as well as for their political appeal. The president needs competing policy advice in order to make the most informed decisions, and he needs administrative advice in order to weigh the policy implications and implementation dimensions of proposals. The regular and frequent access of Morris to the president without the knowledge of White House staffers reduced the effectiveness of the White House staff for the president. Finally, in March and April 1995, Panetta became aware of Morris's role, and Morris along with several people he designated were brought into White House political and policy deliberations. This increased the level of conflict in the White House between more liberal and more moderate advisers, but at least the conflict was in the open and Panetta was fully informed in coordinating advice for the president.

In 1996, Panetta announced that he would retire at the end of the first term to return to California, and shortly after winning reelection, President Clinton designated Erskine Bowles to be chief of staff, in his second term. Bowles was an investment banker from South Carolina who had been head of the Small Business Administration in 1993 and 1994 and was then brought into the White House as a deputy to Leon Panetta. As deputy chief of staff, Bowles conducted a management study of the White House and concluded that the president's time was too fragmented into fifteen-minute time chunks and that he should have several hours of unstructured time in the afternoon to work on his own priorities rather than being dominated by an overcrowded schedule.[95]

Bowles recruited two deputies, each of whom had experience in the first-term Clinton White House. He also designated his own chief of staff and had an executive assistant, a national security assistant, and a press secretary. Even though in some sense all White House staffers report to the president through the chief of staff, this was a more elaborate superstructure for the chief of staff office than had existed in any earlier White House. The general consensus was that Bowles imposed more order on the White House. As one White House staffer put it, "We now have *controlled* chaos."[96]

The bottom line in the White House is always what the president wants. The new order came to the White House management not because Bowles wanted to impose it, but because Clinton, after his experience in the first term, wanted him to. Bowles was replaced by John Podesta in 1998, who managed the White House through the impeachment process and to the end of the Clinton presidency.

GEORGE W. BUSH'S WHITE HOUSE

George W. Bush's transition into office was foreshortened by five weeks because of the delay in an authoritative outcome to the election. Nevertheless, though enjoying about half the time as other newly elected presidents, the Bush team designated the White House staff, named a cabinet, began recruiting personnel, and laid the groundwork for the initial policy agenda with dispatch.

The new administration was acutely aware of the problems the Clinton White House suffered because of the delay in designating the White House staff until immediately before inauguration. Though Andrew Card was the only White House staffer announced before the Supreme Court decision of December 12, the rest of the top of the White House staff was assembled by early December, with directors of major White House offices publicly announced by early January.[97] President George W. Bush's transition into office was one of the shortest but most efficiently run in recent times. Because of the growth of the size and scope of the national government, transitions since the 1970s have been elaborately planned and bureaucratized.

One key to the efficiency of the transition into office was the delegation of transition control to the vice-presidential running mate, Dick Cheney. This avoided the major problems that the Carter team suffered in 1976 when the transition planners clashed with those running the Carter campaign immediately after the election victory. In addition to effective control of the transition, the major asset that Cheney brought to the transition and administration was a

G. W. Bush and the other living presidents at Clinton Library dedication. (© Brooks Craft/CORBIS)

depth of experience in government. After serving in the Nixon administration, Cheney had been deputy and then chief of staff for President Ford, member of Congress from Wyoming, and Secretary of Defense during the administration of George H. W. Bush.

The choice of Cheney as vice-presidential running mate was crucial in several other ways. In contrast to many vice-presidential candidates in U.S. history, Cheney was not chosen primarily for electoral purposes; Wyoming brought few electoral votes, and Cheney was not a dynamic campaigner. Cheney's presence on the ticket was reassuring to voters because of his impressive experience, but his most important contribution would come in governance. As with Clinton's choice of Gore in 1992, Cheney was chosen for his experience, competence, and his relationship with the head of the ticket. While Gore had played an important policy role as vice president, Cheney was to break the mold of vice-presidential importance to an administration. Cheney ran the transition and dominated most of the organizational and policy deliberations early in the administration—so much so that administration officials took pains to emphasize that all final decisions were in fact made by President Bush and that Cheney's role was primarily advisory.

First among White House staffers is the chief of staff, and one of the requirements for an effective chief of staff is Washington experience. The initial chiefs of staffs of each of the previous two presidents, Sununu for George H. W.

Bush and McLarty for Clinton, came with little Washington experience, and each encountered problems as a result. Bush avoided these problems by choosing his longtime friend and veteran of his father's administration, Andrew Card, to be his chief of staff.

Card was an experienced Washington insider and Bush loyalist since 1980. He had worked in the White House for Ronald Reagan and had been a deputy to John Sununu in the George H. W. Bush administration before being appointed Secretary of Transportation; he also ran the 2000 Republican National Convention for George W. Bush. In his experience working for John Sununu and with six other chiefs of staff over two previous administrations, Card experienced firsthand the effects of different approaches to the role. In contrast to his former boss's abusive style, Card's approach to his position was the opposite; he was low key and unfailingly courteous, yet firm and effective in the position. Card was not a policy advocate, and he did not assume a dominating chief-of-staff role. Rather, assisted by his two deputies, he acted as the traffic cop by managing the work flow of the White House, including the president's time and White House personnel.

While Card was the key to managing the White House, the dominant person, short of the president, was clearly Vice President Cheney, whose national experience far outmatched that of President Bush. Cheney put together an impressive staff of his own, including his own national security aides and a domestic policy staff. Cheney's role in the new administration was broad, particularly in foreign policy and in heading up a task force to reduce American dependence on foreign oil and design a new energy policy for the United States. Cheney was also important to the direction of the new administration because President Bush was traveling around the country to sell his tax cut and other policy proposals in public appearances; Bush spent about a third of his first several months in office on the road and set a record among recent presidents of the number of states visited in his first six months in office (33).[98]

Because of Cheney's prominence in the administration, White House officials were careful to emphasize his subordinate position to the president. According to Cheney's counselor, Mary Matalin, "The vice president has no personal or political agenda other than advising President Bush."[99] President Bush frankly addressed the issue when he said: "Dick's doing a good job because he's told me he doesn't want to be president."[100]

After Cheney and Card, the two key aides to Bush were his political strategist, Senior Adviser to the President Karl Rove, and his counselor, Karen Hughes, each of whom had direct access to the president. Hughes had been Bush's closest aide while he was governor of Texas and throughout his campaign for the presidency. When he reached the White House, Bush said, "I want you in every meeting where major decisions are made."[101] She played an important role in creating a sense of order in the White House and crafting Bush's public image. She was in charge of forty-two staffers and the White House offices concerned with the public face of the Bush presidency—the Office of Communications, the Press Office, the Office of Media Affairs, and speechwriting. But most importantly, she had the complete confidence of the president, and this was understood by other White House staffers.

Karl Rove had been Bush's top campaign strategist, and in the White House he played the role of senior political adviser, directing the offices of political affairs and public liaison. While not as close to Bush as Hughes, Rove played the important roles of concentrating on political strategy and tending to Bush's links to the conservative wing of the Republican Party. Rove carefully planned the first weeks of the presidency and the president's initial meetings with members of Congress. Rove also oversaw the political strategy development of the administration and in this capacity coordinated groups of White House staffers who planned the administration's political and policy agenda. At the senior level was the Rove-led "Strategery Group" (named for a humorous television skit on Bush's diction) of the top domestic and national security aides.[102] His purview included the Office of Strategic Initiatives, the Office of Public Liaison, and the Office of Political Affairs. When Hughes left the White House staff in the summer of 2002, Rove's influence increased, and as the 2004 election approached, his presence became more pervasive.

Bush's national security adviser, Condoleezza Rice, was a veteran aide to Brent Scowcroft in the administration of Bush's father and top national security adviser to candidate Bush during the 2000 presidential campaign, where she earned his respect and trust. She was, at forty-six, the youngest person to be national security adviser as well as the first woman in the post. Rice's initial move was to restructure the NSC and cut its staff by a third. She would focus on advising the president, but just as her mentor Scowcroft, she did not plan to dominate the national security policy-making process. In the Bush administration, it would be difficult for *anyone* to dominate the policy process, with such formidable principals on the NSC as Vice President Dick Cheney, Secretary of Defense Donald Rumsfeld, and Secretary of State Colin Powell, each with their own sizable staffs.

Structurally, Bush retained all of the major White House offices of the Clinton administration, including Clinton's National Economic Council, though he dropped some of President Clinton's minor offices and added several of his own.[103] In addition to the Office of Strategic Initiatives and the Office of Faith-Based and Community Initiatives created in 2001, Bush added the USA Freedom Corps in 2002 and the Office of Global Communications in 2003. In late 2001, the Office of Homeland Security was added, though most of its functions were taken over by the Department of Homeland Security when it was created in 2002.[104]

The terrorist attacks of September 11, 2001 changed the Bush White House in important ways in addition to the new Office of Homeland Security. Domestic policy took a back seat to the war on terrorism, and Karl Rove's role became less visible. Karen Hughes shifted her focus to communicating America's purposes to the rest of the world, particularly the Middle East. Vice President Cheney became even more important, though less visible, often weighing in on White House deliberations via secure teleconferencing from an "undisclosed location."

Attorney General John Ashcroft and the Department of Justice became increasingly important in the domestic elements of the war on terrorism and the government's response to domestic vulnerability to terrorism.

After President Bush's victory in the election of 2004, he appointed Condoleezza Rice Secretary of State and Alberto Gonzales Attorney General, but he did not make wholesale changes in his White House staff. Andrew Card remained chief of staff until he was replaced by OMB Director Josh Bolton in 2006. Card was the longest-serving chief of staff since Sherman Adams. George W. Bush's approach to his White House staff was that of a chief executive officer of a corporation. He saw himself as tough minded and able to make decisions quickly and leave the details up to his team. His White House staff was legendary for its tight message discipline and absence of unauthorized leaks.

President Bush preferred short memos, oral briefings, and crisp meetings. His circle of advisers was relatively small. According to the president of the American Enterprise Institute, Christopher DeMuth, "It's a too tightly managed decision-making process. When they make decisions, a very small number of people are in the room, and it has a certain effect of constricting the range of alternatives being offered." Neither did President Bush seek a broad range of outside advice: "I have no outside advice. Anybody who says they're an outside adviser of this Administration on this particular matter [the war on terror] is not telling the truth."[105]

CONCLUSION

The experience with White House organization in the modern presidency has highlighted several important lessons. White House staff and organization will faithfully reflect the president's character but should strive to counter presidential weaknesses. If the president is reclusive (as Nixon was), the staff should try to bring ideas and people to him (as Wilton Persons did for Eisenhower). If the president is too open, the staff should impose some order on access to the president (as Cheney did for Ford). If the president is too focused on details (as was Carter), the staff should encourage him to look at the big picture. If the president is too detached, the staff should bring issues, even unpleasant ones, to the president's attention (as the Baker system did for Reagan, but Regan did not).[106]

Beyond this, we have learned that regardless of personal style or preference, the contemporary White House needs a chief of staff to impose order on policy development, guard access to the president, and settle administration disputes that are not of presidential importance. As the Ford and Carter presidencies demonstrated, someone short of the president must be in charge, or the president will be overwhelmed. No president has successfully run the White House without a chief of staff since 1969, and since 1979 no president has tried.

But if that necessary chief of staff takes a strong and controlling approach to the job, it is a likely prescription for disaster. *Each* of the strong chiefs of staff (Adams for Ike, Haldeman for Nixon, Regan for Reagan, and Sununu for Bush)

- alienated members of Congress
- alienated members of their own administration
- had reputations for the lack of common civility
- had hostile relations with the press

And *each* of them resigned in disgrace, having done harm to their own presidents and the presidency.[107]

A number of lessons about the role of chief of staff can be gleaned from the experience over the past four decades of the presidency. These lessons, which were too often ignored by the domineering chiefs of staff, include:

1. Carrying out the president's wishes will often make some people angry, but gratuitous harshness will not help the president or the chief of staff.
2. It is appropriate to guard access as tightly as the president wishes, but a heavy-handed assertion of personal power will unnecessarily anger members of the cabinet.
3. The chief of staff has a constituency of more than one. This constituency includes both Congress and the press. The president (or chief of staff) will sooner or later need support in Congress, so fences should be mended carefully after congressional feelings have been hurt. Similarly, the president needs favorable press coverage. Having a cordial, professional working relationship with the press may not ensure favorable coverage, but it can help to mitigate bad coverage.
4. The president should not be put in the position of having to defend publicly a White House staffer.
5. A chief of staff cannot do the job in complete anonymity, but people will notice if the chief of staff squeezes into every photo opportunity.
6. As Jack Watson says, the chief of staff is the president's "javelin catcher." The chief of staff should take the heat for the president and under no circumstances publicly shift blame to the president.

This list may seem a bit preachy and obvious. But the lessons bear repeating because they have so often been ignored, particularly by the four domineering chiefs of staff in the modern presidency.

The appropriate approach to the job is exemplified by James Baker, Jack Watson, Richard Cheney, Donald Rumsfeld, Leon Panetta, Erskine Bowles, John Podesta, and Andrew Card (as well as Howard Baker, and Kenneth Duberstein for shorter periods). Each served his president well by performing as an honest broker and coordinator of administration policy. These people were in no way soft or ineffectual. They controlled access to their presidents with firm hands and enforced a discipline on the policy-development process. They performed the other functions of the chief of staff, such as giving credit for success to the president and taking blame for failures, without letting their own egos get in the way. Each demonstrated that the chief-of-staff job could be done without absolute control by one person.

But in the end, there is no salvation from staff. As presidential scholar Bert Rockman puts it: "No system or organization ultimately can save a president from himself when he is inclined to self-destruct. And no system that a president is uncomfortable with will last."[108] A president cannot manage the White House alone, but he must make sure that someone is managing it to his specifications. Presidents must be ruthless in their judgments of aides who are not serving the presidency. If they do not follow these precepts, their presidencies will be vulnerable to being run for others' purposes rather than their own.

NOTES

1. President's Committee on Administrative Management, *Reorganization of the Executive Departments*, 75th Congress, 1st session (1937), S. Doc. 8, p. 5.

2. Richard Neustadt, "Roosevelt's Approach to Staffing the White House," Attachment A, "Memo on Staffing the President Elect" (October 30, 1960), pp. 1–2.

3. Neustadt, "Roosevelt's Approach to Staffing the White House," p. 4.

4. Neustadt, "Roosevelt's Approach to Staffing the White House," p. 5.

5. Neustadt, "Roosevelt's Approach to Staffing the White House," p. 4.

6. Robert E. Sherwood, *Roosevelt and Hopkins* (New York: Harper 1948), p. 537. Quoted in Richard Tanner Johnson, *Managing the White House* (New York: Harper & Row 1974), p. 20.

7. Patrick Anderson, *The President's Men* (New York: Doubleday 1969), p. 79.

8. Michael Medved, *The Shadow Presidents* (New York: Times Books, 1979), p. 198.

9. Clark Clifford, *Counsel to the President* (New York: Random House, 1991), p. 77.

10. See the discussion in Stephen Hess with James P. Pfiffner, *Organizing the Presidency*, 3rd ed. (Washington, DC: Brookings, 2002), pp. 36–48.

11. Clifford, *Counsel to the President*, p. 75.

12. Hess, *Organizing the Presidency*, p. 39.

13. Clifford, *Counsel to the President*, p. 12.

14. Samuel Kernell, "The Creed and Reality of Modern White House Management," in Samuel Kernell and Samuel Popkin, eds., *Chief of Staff* (Berkeley, CA: University of California Press, 1986), pp. 193–232.

15. Dwight D. Eisenhower, *Mandate for Change* (Garden City, New York: Doubleday 1963), p. 87.

16. Eisenhower, *Mandate for Change*, p. 114.

17. Hess, *Organizing the Presidency*, pp. 49–64.

18. Fred I. Greenstein, *The Hidden-Hand Presidency* (New York: Basic Books, 1982), p. 142.

19. Medved, *The Shadow Presidents,* p. 243.

20. Anderson, *The President's Men,* p. 161.

21. Medved, *The Shadow Presidents,* p. 245.

22. Johnson, *Managing the White House,* p. 93.

23. Medved, *The Shadow Presidents,* p. 253.

24. Medved, *The Shadow Presidents,* p. 248.

25. Medved, *The Shadow Presidents,* p. 254.

26. Arthur M. Schlesinger, Jr., *A Thousand Days* (Boston: Houghton Mifflin, 1965), p. 120.

27. Carl Brauer, "John F. Kennedy: The Endurance of Inspirational Leadership," In Fred I. Greenstein, ed., *Leadership in the Modern Presidency* (Cambridge, MA: Harvard University Press, 1988).

28. For an analysis of the Clifford and Neustadt memos, see James P. Pfiffner, *The Strategic Presidency: Hitting the Ground Running* (Lawrence, KS: University Press of Kansas, 1996), pp. 19–21. The Neustadt memo is reprinted in James P. Pfiffner, *The Managerial Presidency,* 2nd ed. (College Station, TX: Texas A&M University Press, 1999).

29. Medved, *The Shadow Presidents,* p. 273.

30. Johnson, *Managing the White House,* p. 132.

31. See the discussion in Hess, *Organizing the Presidency,* pp. 65–77.

32. Bradley H. Patterson, *The White House Staff* (Washington: Brookings, 2000), pp. 49–75.

33. Johnson, *Managing the White House,* p. 180.

34. Johnson, *Managing the White House,* p. 179.

35. Emmette S. Redford and Richard T. McCulley, *White House Operations: The Johnson Presidency* (Austin: University of Texas Press, 1986), p. 52.

36. Anderson, *The Presidents' Men,* p. 447.

37. See the discussion in Anderson, *The Presidents' Men,* pp. 434–449.

38. Hess, *Organizing the Presidency,* pp. 92–93.

39. William Safire, *Before the Fall* (New York: Doubleday, 1985), p. 116.

40. Frederick C. Mosher et al., *Watergate: Implications for Responsible Government* (New York: Basic Books, 1974), p. 44.

41. Hess, *Organizing the Presidency,* p. 103.

42. Henry Kissinger, *White House Years* (Boston: Little Brown, 1979), pp. 45, 482–483.

43. Hess, Organizing the Presidency, p. 104.

44. H.R. Haldeman, interview with author, Los Angeles, CA (May 25, 1983).

45. Haldeman, interview with author.

46. Johnson, *Managing the White House,* pp. 218–221.

47. See the testimony of Alexander Butterfield before the House Impeachment Committee reprinted in Larry Berman, *The New American Presidency* (Boston: Little, Brown, 1987), pp. 264–272.

48. Roger Porter, "Gerald R. Ford: A Healing Presidency," in Greenstein, *Leadership and the Modern Presidency*, p. 200.

49. Porter, "A Healing Presidency," p. 212.

50. See the remarks by Rumsfeld in Kernell and Popkin, *Chief of Staff*.

51. Porter, "A Healing Presidency," p. 212.

52. Medved, *The Shadow Presidents*, p. 340.

53. Medved, *The Shadow Presidents*, p. 339.

54. Jack Watson's remarks at a conference on the "Origins, Development, and Future of the American Presidency," at Gannon University, Erie, PA, April 25, 1987.

55. Q. Whitfield Ayres, "The Carter White House Staff," in M. Glen Abernathy et al., eds., *The Carter Years* (New York: St. Martin's Press, 1984), pp. 144–164.

56. Lou Cannon, *President Reagan: The Role of a Lifetime* (New York: Simon & Schuster, 1991), chap. 10 and p. 181.

57. Hedrick Smith, *The Power Game* (New York: Random House, 1988), p. 305.

58. Donald Regan, *For the Record* (New York: Harcourt Brace Jovanovich, 1988), p. 272.

59. Ann Reilly Dowd, "What Managers Can Learn from Manager Reagan," *Fortune* (September 15, 1986), p. 33.

60. Regan, *For the Record*, pp. 142–143, 144.

61. David Stockman, *The Triumph of Politics* (New York: Harper & Row, 1986), p. 76.

62. Stockman, *The Triumph of Politics*, p. 109.

63. See Smith, *The Power Game*, pp. 314–315. The memo is reproduced in Bob Schieffer and Gary Paul Gates, *The Acting President* (New York: E. P. Dutton, 1989), p. 83.

64. Memo dated November 13, 1980, reproduced in Schieffer and Gates, *The Acting President*, p. 83.

65. See the insightful discussion of Nancy Reagan's role in the Reagan administration by Richard Neustadt, *Presidential Power and the Modern Presidents* (New York: Free Press, 1990), pp. 312–316.

66. Memo dated November 13, 1980, reproduced in Schieffer and Gates, *The Acting President*, p. 83.

67. William R. Doener, "For Rhyme and Reason," *Time* (January 21, 1985), p. 20.

68. Ed Magnuson, "Shake-Up at the White House," *Time* (January 21, 1985), p. 10.

69. Bernard Weinraub, "How Don Regan Runs the White House," *New York Times* (January 5, 1986), p. 33.

70. Cannon, *Role of a Lifetime*, p. 563.

71. Stockman, *The Triumph of Politics*, pp. 18–19, photograph no. 42.

72. Bob Schieffer and Gary Gates, *The Acting President* (New York: E. P. Dutton, 1989), p. 200.

73. Cannon, *The Role of a Lifetime*, p. 721.

74. Maureen Dowd, "Saving Face Means Having It in the Picture," *New York Times* (June 16, 1991), pp. A1, 18.

75. Smith, *The Power Game,* p. 81.

76. Cannon, *Role of a Lifetime,* p. 566.

77. Regan, *For the Record,* p. 288.

78. Regan, *For the Record,* p. 3.

79. Cannon, *The Role of a Lifetime,* pp. 583–588.

80. David Hoffman, "Regan: Chief of Risk" *Washington Post* (February 28, 1987), pp. A1, 16. The rest of Regan's comments were: "Who was it that took this disinformation thing and managed to turn it? Who was it [sic] took on this loss in the Senate and pointed out a few facts and managed to pull that? I don't say we'll be able to do it four times in a row. But here we go again, and we're trying."

81. Cannon, *The Role of a Lifetime,* p. 720.

82. *Report of the President's Special Review Board* (Washington, DC, February 26, 1987), pp. IV-10–IV-11.

83. See the account by Cannon, *The Role of a Lifetime,* pp. 722–732.

84. Hoffman, "Regan: Chief of Risk," pp. 1, 16. Reagan biographer Lou Cannon argued that Regan had four deficiencies as chief of staff: (1) His ego was too large; (2) he held politics in disdain; (3) he did not appreciate Nancy's role in the administration; and (4) he brought the "mice" with him to the White House instead of recruiting a strong staff, as Baker had. See Cannon, *The Role of a Lifetime,* p. 567.

85. *Time* (September 30, 1991), p. 19; and *Newsweek* (December 30, 1991), p. 4. *This Week with David Brinkley,* ABC News, transcript of program of February 2, 1992, p. 13.

86. Bob Woodward, "The President's Key Men," *Washington Post* (October 7, 1992), p. A18.

87. "John Sununu: What Color Is Your Parachute?" *Spy* (March 1992), p. 31.

88. Proverb quoted in *Time* (May 21, 1990), p. 25.

89. Juan Williams, "George Bush's Flying Circus," *Washington Post* (November 24, 1991), pp. C1, C4.

90. Ann Devroy, "Citing Year of Triumph, Sununu Defends Actions," *Washington Post* (December 12, 1990), p. A25.

91. Maureen Dowd, "Sununu: A Case Study in Flouting the Rules," *New York Times* (May 5, 1991), p. 34.

92. *New York Times* (December 4, 1991), p. B12.

93. *New York Times* (November 23, 1991), pp. 1, 10.

94. *New York Times* (November 23, 1991), pp. 1, 10.

95. Karen Breslau, "Clinton Goes Corporate," *Newsweek* (February 17, 1997), p. 38.

96. Breslau, "Clinton Goes Corporate," p. 38, emphasis added.

97. See Stephen Hess with James P. Pfiffner, *Organizing the Presidency,* 3rd ed. (Washington, DC: Brookings, 2002), pp. 164–174; and Martha Kumar, "Recruiting and Organizing the White House Staff," in Martha Joynt Kumar and Terry Sullivan, eds., *The White House World* (College Station, TX: Texas A&M University Press), pp. 360–373.

98. Richard L. Berke, "Bush Shapes His Presidency With Sharp Eye on Father's," *New York Times* (March 28, 2001), p. 1, A13.

99. Eric Schmidt, "Cheney Assembles Formidable Team," *New York Times* (February 3, 2001), p. 1, A8.

100. Eric Schmitt, "Cheney Assembles Formidable Team," p. 1, A8.

101. Mike Allen, "Hughes Keeps White House in Line," *Washington Post* (March 19, 2001), p. 1, A6.

102. Dana Milbank, "Serious 'Strategery'," *Washington Post* (April 27, 2001), p. 1, A5.

103. See the analysis by Bradley H. Patterson in "Preface to the Paperback Edition," in *The White House Staff: Inside the West Wing and Beyond* (Washington, DC: Brookings, 2000), p. vi. Patterson argues that the total personnel count of the White House community is about 5,000 personnel. His count includes estimates for the Secret Service and Military offices and volunteers as well as the rest of the White House offices (pp. vii and 4–5).

104. For an insightful analysis of the structure and functioning of the Bush White House, see Karen Hult, "The Bush White House in Comparative Perspective," paper prepared for the conference on "The Bush Presidency: An Early Assessment," Woodrow Wilson School, Princeton University, April 25–26, 2003.

105. Ron Suskind, "Faith, Certainty and the Presidency of George W. Bush," *New York Times Magazine* (October 17, 2004), NYTimes Web site.

106. Nicholas Lemann, "Remember the Alamo," *New Yorker* (October 18, 2004), 158.

107. James P. Pfiffner, "The President's Chief of Staff: Lessons Learned," *Presidential Studies Quarterly* (Winter 1993), pp. 77–102.

108. Bert Rockman, "The Style and Organization of the Reagan Presidency," in Charles O. Jones, ed., *The Reagan Legacy* (Chatham, NJ: Chatham House, 1988), p. 27.

4 CHAPTER | THE INSTITUTIONAL PRESIDENCY

The decision of how to organize the White House, the functions of the immediate staff, the relations of the staff to the president and to each other are matters of individual presidential choice and personal dynamics. The choice may be conscious, as when Eisenhower chose to create the chief-of-staff position and Kennedy chose not to have a chief of staff, or the decisions may be made by default and depend on day-to-day presidential actions in the White House. Personality dynamics of staff members also have an impact on the relationships; take for example the contrasting styles that James Baker and Donald Regan exhibited as chiefs of staff for the same president.

But as the presidency has grown in size and the reach of the White House has extended deeper into the executive branch, functions have developed that are not at the complete discretion of each new president. For instance, the size and complexity of the White House staff had increased to such an extent that by the 1970s the function of chief of staff was necessary. Presidents Ford and Carter each tried to govern without one, and each admitted defeat.

There are many other functions of the White House that are part of what scholar Hugh Heclo calls its "deep structure," that is, the dimension of the office in which it "is largely a given that a president can change slowly if at all. This structure is a web of other people's expectations and needs."[1] The accumulated functions performed by the presidential staff cannot easily be sloughed off by a new president. For instance, the president needs to coordinate national security policy from his own perspective. This cannot be done at the departmental level. Thus, function of the National Security Council must be performed, under whatever name.

The president can no longer choose not to have a legislative agenda of some sort, and the president's lobbying cannot be delegated to departments and agencies. The president's appointees must be screened for him by his own staffers: No longer do the political parties have the capacity to perform this function. The president's legal needs are too specialized to have them met by the attorney general's office, as they were in the past. During the 2001 transition, Chief of Staff–designate Andrew Card suggested that the new Bush administration would not have an Office of Intergovernmental Affairs. But the constituents of that office—local government officials from throughout the country—mobilized to protect what they considered to be their portal to the White House. Not wanting to alienate an important constituency, Card allowed the office to remain in the White House.[2]

This chapter begins by considering the size and structure of the White House Office and the Executive Office of the President (EOP). While the size of the White House Office has increased over the years, it is difficult to measure the growth precisely. The EOP has housed a number of presidential units since its creation in 1939, and each president has usually added or deleted a unit or two by executive order.

The theme of this chapter is that the size of the White House staff has been growing and its functions have been increasingly institutionalized in the last half of the twentieth century. The subunits in the White House and EOP have been institutionalized by the establishment of continuing functions that survive from president to president. Yet most of the personnel in the majority of the units turn over with each new president. To illustrate the process of institutionalization, this chapter briefly traces the development of several units in the presidency: the Office of Legislative Liaison, the Office of Presidential Personnel, and the Office of Communications in the White House Office; and in the EOP, the Bureau of the Budget, the National Security Council staff, and domestic policy staff.

WHITE HOUSE STAFF AND THE EXECUTIVE OFFICE OF THE PRESIDENT

Two major aspects of White House development are size and complexity. The size of the White House staff has never been easy to determine precisely for two reasons. First, for different purposes it may be relevant to count only staffers close to the president, or only professional-level staffers, or only those in the White House Office. Or it may be relevant to include military support, the Secret Service (which is technically in the Office of Homeland Security), or White House groundskeepers. Second, presidents do not want to seem too imperial and would just as soon be thought of as having small, efficient staffs. This is why all modern White Houses have used workers who have been

TABLE 4.1 | TOP-LEVEL ASSISTANTS TO THE PRESIDENT, 1960–2001

1960	2001
1 Assistant to the President (chief of staff)	1 Chief of Staff
1 Principal Deputy Assistant	2 Deputy Chief of Staff
6 Deputy Assistants	16 Assistants to the President
20 Special Assistants	26 Deputy Assistants
1 Deputy Special Assistant	33 Special Assistants

Source: Data from 1960 are from Paul Light, *Thickening Government* (Washington, DC: Brookings, 1995), p. 154. Data from 2001 are from the U.S. Government Manual Online (http://www.gpoaccess.gov, accessed July 8, 2003).

"detailed" to work at the White House from their own agencies where they are on the payroll. Detailees are usually not counted on the official White House rolls. Persons at the very top levels of the White House staff have some form of the title, assistant to the president. Their increasing numbers over the years can be seen in Table 4.1

Thus, there are many different accounts of the number of White House staff, but one of the most used categories is the number of staffers in the White House Office. By examining these numbers, we can see a trend of increasing size that we might expect to accompany the increased duties and centralization of control of the executive branch in the White House. Looking at the changing size of the White House Office, we can see an increase in the number of staffers from about 60 under FDR, to 300–400 under Eisenhower, to 400–500 under Kennedy-Johnson, up to 500–600 under Nixon-Ford, slightly down to 400–500 under Carter, Reagan, Bush, and Clinton (though if the Office of Administration and Executive Residence are included, as they were in Nixon's time, the numbers are higher than the Nixon administration).[3] In 2001, the total White House support structure, excluding solely EOP units, amounted to about 5,000 government employees with a budget of $750 million. These include personnel in the Military Office (about 2,200 on Department of Defense payrolls) and the Secret Service (about 1,000 now in the Department of Homeland Security), as well as White House workers from the National Park Service (care of the grounds), the National Archives, the General Services Administration, and the Postal Service.[4] None of these latter categories of personnel are counted on most tallies of the White House staff. The White House Office contains the staffers and units closest to the president and is included as a separate unit in the EOP. (See Figure 4.1.)

The Executive Office of the President, created in 1939, is an umbrella organization of offices that serve the institution of the presidency. The EOP is not really a single office, but rather a collection; and it is not really executive, since it contains units that are primarily advisory rather than executing.[5] In addition, the original intention of Roosevelt, to separate his personal staff (the

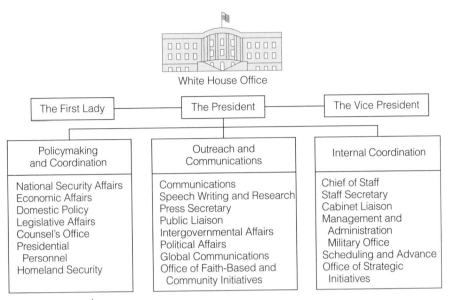

White House Office

| The First Lady | The President | The Vice President |

Policymaking and Coordination	Outreach and Communications	Internal Coordination

National Security Affairs
Economic Affairs
Domestic Policy
Legislative Affairs
Counsel's Office
Presidential
  Personnel
Homeland Security
	Communications
	Speech Writing and Research
	Press Secretary
	Public Liaison
	Intergovernmental Affairs
	Political Affairs
	Global Communications
	Office of Faith-Based and
	  Community Initiatives
		Chief of Staff
		Staff Secretary
		Cabinet Liaison
		Management and
		  Administration
		Military Office
		Scheduling and Advance
		Office of Strategic
		  Initiatives

FIGURE 4.1 | THE WHITE HOUSE OFFICE

Source: Executive Clerk to the President, 1996. The units in the White House Office were specified in personal communication with the author. The functional categories are the author's. Updated by the author.

six staffers the Brownlow Committee called for) from the institutional staff in the Bureau of the Budget and other units, has broken down. The EOP was to contain units that advised the president and coordinated executive branch policy making.

Over the course of the modern presidency, the various units of the EOP have become progressively more responsive to individual presidents, rather than to the continuous office of the presidency, and are now the primary policy makers of the executive branch.

The membership of the units in the EOP changes with each new president; the only unit to have a sizable career civil-service staff with an institutional memory is the Office of Management and Budget (OMB). Since its creation in 1939, the EOP has included more than sixty different units. Most of these had brief stays in the EOP to symbolize presidential concern (e.g., drug abuse, inflation, consumer protection, volunteer service, space exploration, etc.) or to incubate them before transfer to larger, more established departments in the executive branch (e.g., the Office of Economic Opportunity).

The core and continuing units of the EOP perform different functions for the president. Four of them perform coordination and enforcement as well as advisory functions: OMB, the National Security Council staff, the Office of Policy Development, and the Office of U.S. Trade Representative. Each coordinates administration policy for the president and ensures that the narrower

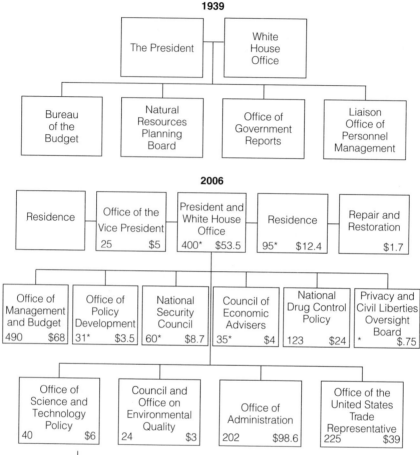

FIGURE 4.2 | EXECUTIVE OFFICE OF THE PRESIDENT AT ITS INCEPTION
AND TODAY

Source: Budget of the United States, Fiscal Year 2006, pp. 979–987. Reprinted from
George C. Edward, Stephen J. Wayne, *Presidential Leadership*, (Belmont, CA:
Wadsworth, 2003) 7th ed. p. 222.

departmental perspectives and turf do not prevail over the president's priorities. Other units of the EOP primarily provide advice to the president and
do not have the independent power or staff to prevail over departments
and agencies. These include the Office of Science and Technology Policy,
the Council of Economic Advisers, and the Council on Environmental
Quality. Finally, some offices perform administrative functions, such as
the Office of Administration and the Executive Residence at the White House.
(See Figure 4.2.)

More than numbers of staffers and separate units are involved in the
institutionalizing of the presidency. The dynamics of centralization and control
have increased the capacity of the White House staff to substitute for

departments and agencies in policy development and expert advice to the president. This can only be accomplished by specialized division of labor to reflect the complexity of the executive branch (which, in turn, mirrors the complexity in the domestic and international environments). The specialization is accompanied by other bureaucratic characteristics, including established decision-making and operating processes, differentiated units, and hierarchical structures.[6] The main difference with more conventional bureaucracies is that there is much less continuity of personnel in the presidency. Virtually all of the White House Office and EOP (with the exception of the OMB, military support, and housekeeping units) turn over with each new president; even secretarial and clerical workers are often cleared out. Institutional memory is sacrificed, but the same functions must be replicated by the next president.

To illustrate the process of institutionalization over the years, this chapter traces the development of several presidential units. In the past, these functions were performed by presidents themselves and their generalist staff aides or outside the presidency entirely, for example, by departments and agencies or political parties. As the presidency expanded and more central control was sought, more functions were drawn into the White House. The process usually began when a president would put one staffer in charge of a function and create a title for him or her. Soon that individual acquired a personal staff, and then a separate office would be created. For the most important functions, this has been a one-way street; once the unit is created, it continues to exist across administrations, regardless of president or political party. The process of institutionalization is illustrated with three units from the White House Office: the Office of Congressional Relations, the Office of Presidential Personnel, and the Office of Communications. We then examine three units from the Executive Office of the President: the OMB, the National Security Council, and the Office of Policy Development.

OFFICE OF LEGISLATIVE LIAISON/OFFICE OF CONGRESSIONAL RELATIONS

Franklin Roosevelt conducted his historic legislative campaign in the first one hundred days of the New Deal by himself with the help of a few White House aides. Despite his legislative activism, no one short of the president coordinated relations with Congress. The first presidential aide to be given informal charge of congressional relations was President Truman's appointments secretary, Matt Connelly, who had two assistants to help him. Truman sent his legislative agenda to Congress each year, and though he was not always successful, the president's legislative priorities were always clear.

When President Eisenhower was elected, he did not intend to be as active in legislation as were his Democratic predecessors. But when he decided not to send a legislative program to the Hill after taking office in 1953, he was criticized by both sides of the aisle. One administration member was told by a member of the House: "Don't expect us to start from scratch on what you people want. That's not the way we do things here. You draft the bills and we work them over."[7] This began the practice of annual legislative programs developed by the White House and sent to the Congress. But this practice also implied an active and professional staff to press the administration's agenda on the Hill.

Thus, Eisenhower was the first to establish a formal legislative liaison unit in the White House. He assigned the task to General Wilton B. Persons, who had experience in congressional liaison in the Defense Department, and several professionals. Persons hosted weekly meetings of legislative leaders with the president and kept in touch with agency legislative liaison operations. Members of Congress being directly contacted by members of the White House staff was very unusual before Eisenhower, but with the development of the Office of Congressional Relations (OCR), it was to become much more commonplace.

Bryce Harlow, who was head of the operation at the end of the Eisenhower administration, was visited by Larry O'Brien after Kennedy was elected. O'Brien was going to handle legislative liaison for the new administration, and he paid a visit to ask Harlow's advice. O'Brien thought he might handle relations with the Hill as a one-person operation, but Harlow quickly disabused him of that fantasy:

> You're about to ruin your president. . . . Let me explain to you why. . . . I average a hundred and twenty-five incoming telephone calls a day. Average. Bob Hampton handles the congressional appointments and presidential appointments. That office handles four hundred incoming calls a day, even now. Now then, when you first come to work in this building, and it's January 20 and it is 12:01, you won't be able to hang up this phone. For your first two years you won't be able to hang it up without it ringing, no matter how many lines you put on it. Now, if you think you can handle all that stuff by yourself and this little girl Phyllis, I'm just telling you, you're going to destroy yourself and destroy your president . . . that's absolutely mad, stark raving mad.[8]

O'Brien took Harlow's advice and expanded the legislative liaison operation into one of the most effective operations in the modern presidency.

His operatives spent much of their time on the Hill cultivating members of Congress and keeping in touch with their concerns. He reined in the rest of the executive branch legislative liaison offices directly to the service of the administration's goals. He held weekly meetings of agency liaison officials and expected regular written reports on their contacts with Congress. One of O'Brien's advantages was that he reported directly to the president rather than through another staffer. According to O'Brien, "For the first time, someone from the White House could sit in the Speaker's office with the congressional leadership and be recognized as a spokesman for the president. You weren't an errand boy or a head-counter, you had the authority to speak for the president."[9]

Richard Nixon had a large congressional liaison operation, but with his conservative legislative goals and his confrontational approach to Congress, it was not able to get him what he wanted from the Democratic Congress. With the congressional reforms in the 1970s, in response to the Nixon administration, Congress became more decentralized. White House relations with Congress became more complex, and presidents had to sell their priorities retail rather than wholesale on Capitol Hill.

The importance of professionalism in congressional liaison was underscored when Jimmy Carter brought in his director of legislative relations, Frank Moore, to conduct relations with Congress. Moore had done a good job with the Georgia legislature, but his lack of Washington experience hurt Carter's dealings with Congress his first year. According to Jack Watson, Moore's first year in the White House was the "most awful case of on-the-job training I have ever seen in my life."[10] President Reagan hired an experienced Washington hand, Max Friedersdorf, to run his congressional liaison, and gave the legislative agenda top priority in his first year. In addition to high-profile lobbying, the Office of Congressional Liaison conducts many routine chores. In the Reagan administration, more than six hundred letters a month would come in from Congress.[11] But when an important congressional vote is at stake, the legislative liaison staff can mobilize most of the White House to call members. Their most effective weapon is a personal call from the president to a wavering member.

While Congress has always been important to presidents, congressional relations has been at the center of much of the modern presidency. From the momentous to the routine, presidents cannot do without the multifaceted services of a professional legislative liaison operation. The number of professionals increased from six in the Kennedy years to thirteen under President Reagan. The contemporary Office of Legislative Affairs includes a total contingent of thirty to forty people.[12]

OFFICE OF PRESIDENTIAL PERSONNEL

For most of the nineteenth and first part of the twentieth century, the recruitment of political appointments for the president was mediated by the political parties. Patronage was a sustaining force for the party system, and presidents were tightly tied to the parties. But with the coming of the modern presidency, the political recruitment function slowly began to be taken over by the White House.

Several factors led to this centralization. The political parties began to decline with the proliferation of primary elections and the increasing independence of presidential candidates from the parties. With an activist federal government, there was a greater need by presidents for control of policy rather than merely partisan control of the government.[13] The need for policy control necessarily implied a greater degree of professionalism in presidential appointments. These factors led to the formalization of a political-recruiting capacity in the White House.

Harry Truman was the first president to assign the recruitment function to one person, and Eisenhower created the position of special assistant for personnel management. White House recruitment began to be more systematic when Kennedy divided his "talent hunt" operation from the political patronage function. John Macy wore two hats in serving Lyndon Johnson as political personnel recruiter as well as chairman of the Civil Service Commission. The Nixon administration saw the development of professionalism in recruiting when White House Personnel Operation (WHPO) Director Frederic Malek brought in professional "headhunters" from the private sector to do recruiting for the president. Malek also increased the size of the White House operation from about twelve to thirty, ending up with a full complement of sixty in his office.

President Ford changed the name from WHPO to the Presidential Personnel Office, and Jimmy Carter was the first presidential candidate to begin organizing a personnel search operation (the Talent Inventory Program) before he was elected. But the largest and most sophisticated personnel recruitment effort of the modern presidency was organized by Pendleton James for the Reagan administration. James had been a recruiter in the Nixon administration and was a professional private-sector recruiter when Reagan convinced him to take the job. James was given the title of assistant to the president, a signal of the importance that Reagan attached to the personnel recruitment task. In the first years of the Reagan administration, James had one hundred people working for him, though the number dropped by about half after the administration was fully staffed.

The large number of people on his staff stemmed from the broad approach to personnel recruiting and the importance attached to it by the Reagan administration. The administration screened candidates for jobs very closely, determined to hire only those who were firmly committed to the policy goals of the administration. The number of political appointees had increased over the 1960s and 1970s, demanding greater resources. But the OPP also took on the job of screening candidates for lower-level political appointments (not requiring presidential nominations) in order to control more tightly the implementation of presidential priorities. This centralization of power was unprecedented and required a more elaborate operation than had existed in the White House before. The new Clinton administration sought to emulate the Reagan personnel operation and had 130 people working in the OPP in the early months of 1993. The first years of President George W. Bush's political recruitment operation were run by his longtime friend, Clay Johnson. The Bush administration was a pioneer in using new, Web-based technology to have applicants for jobs enter their own data that would then be fed into a central database.[14]

The modern presidency has seen the personnel recruitment function develop from a one-person job to a very sophisticated and systematic operation supported by the latest computer capabilities and scores of professionals. Although the size of the operation will depend on presidential preferences and the initial recruitment task of the president, a professional personnel office is now a permanent fixture in the White House.[15]

OFFICE OF COMMUNICATIONS

All presidents have realized that the press has an important impact on the success of presidential campaigns, and later on public support of the president in office, and the most effective presidents have cultivated relations with the press. By the end of the nineteenth century, a professional press corps was developing in Washington with a focus on covering the presidency and the federal government. While all presidents and their top aides have had regular relationships with the press, it was not until Franklin Roosevelt that a president formally designated one staffer (Stephen Early) to be his press secretary.[16] When Truman came to office he continued to have press conferences, but he also began to permit radio broadcasts of excerpts of his news conferences. Eisenhower held fewer news conferences than Truman but did allow the recording of press conferences to be broadcast on television.

John Kennedy was an innovator in the development of a public relations capacity in the White House. He introduced the first live televising of presidential press conferences, beginning in his first month in office.[17] Kennedy was to make several other innovations that would be of lasting significance. He held private interviews with members of the media and special informal gatherings with invited members of the press. The White House also began to cultivate the local press throughout the country, not merely the Washington press corps. These innovations marked the recognition that in order to portray the president most favorably, the White House would have to be active in managing the image of the administration and not just passively let the press decide what to cover.

The duties of the press secretary were broadened under Kennedy and Johnson, but it was the Nixon administration that began the systematic organization of these innovations. Realizing that the duties of the press secretary were much broader than merely handling the Washington press corps, Nixon created the White House Office of Communications, headed by Herbert Klein. The Washington press corps was to be handled by the press secretary, while the Communications Office would develop the potential of television, further exploit radio opportunities, arrange more briefing sessions for the press, and develop outreach to local media around the country. Kennedy's new techniques were to be lasting, and Nixon's newly created White House organizations to exploit those techniques were to become a permanent fixture of the presidency.

Just as Gerald Ford tried to run his White House without a chief of staff, he decided to downgrade the Communications Office and placed it under the press secretary. But just as he later decided a chief of staff would be necessary, he also decided to restore the Office of Communications, with speech writing, television, and a research office included. Carter also put the communications function under the press secretary, calling it media relations. In 1978, its purview was broadened under Gerald Rafshoon.[18]

Ronald Reagan was known as "the Great Communicator," and the public presentation of the president was a major tool in the advocacy of the administration's policies. The White House communications capacity was organized under Assistant to the President for Communications David Gergen and included a television office, a speaker's bureau, and research and writing sections. The White House also developed the capacity for the electronic distribution to local radio stations of presidential speeches and White House news releases. The Reagan White House is acknowledged to have been masterful in its use of the media to project to the nation the story that it wanted to convey.

The presence in the White House of a large communications office reflects the combination of two factors. One is the importance of communications to the modern president's policy agenda. Public statements reflect the commitment of the president to certain policies, and the way they are communicated to the public affects how they are received. But these policy-making decisions are communicated using complex technology that requires a high level of professionalism to conduct effectively. The other factor is the development of different media outlets (national TV networks, local TV stations, local and national radio, daily newspapers, weekly news magazines, the Internet, etc.), which has led to the differentiation of the organization that must service these various outlets. These multiple audiences are why the White House Office of Communications has grown in size and complexity. The office run by Herbert Klein in 1969 with four aides had developed by 1988 into a large staff that supervised five separate subunits.[19] The cause of growth is not merely bureaucratic empire builders seeking more power and money, but rather a presidential response to a more complex environment driven by new technologies.

The continued existence of the White House Office of Communications is ensured. The president is no longer free to decide not to have an Office of Communications, whether it is combined with the press secretary functions or separate. As Jody Powell, President Carter's press secretary, put it:

> That's got to be done. Whether the press secretary should be the person to do it is a good question. . . . You had literally hundreds of people involved . . . not only with "Meet the Press" and those shows but "Good Morning Idaho" and "Hello Atlanta" . . . that takes a lot of coordination. You've got to free the people up. You've got to tell them where to go. You've got to make sure that they say what they're supposed to say when they get there. . . . There's no doubt in my mind . . . that those [Panama Canal] treaties would never have been approved . . . but for that sort of operations. . . .[20]

The need to deal with the media will continue to be important to presidents, and it will be done by professionals on the president's immediate staff.

The organizational structure of the Office of Communications was changed with different presidencies, but its primary functions have remained to project the president's message to the American people and to coordinate the administration's efforts to do so. As Ann Lewis, President Clinton's director of communications, put it:

> [T]he role is really to take what the president is doing today [and throughout the administration] and get it to the largest number of people. . . . [M]aybe that's through intergovernmental, through state and local elected officials; maybe it's

back to a cabinet agency like HHS [Health and Human Services]. But it's every other way of communicating the message other than the press. The press has its own operation.[21]

The stress of performing the communications job for the president is reflected in the turnover in the position. Since its creation in 1969, twenty-two people have directed the Office of Communications, an average term of less than eighteen months. In contrast, there have been approximately the same number of press secretaries since 1929.[22] Karen Hughes's communications role in the Bush White House was enhanced with the onset of the war on terrorism, when the White House Coalition Information Center was created for her to help shape the nation's image abroad. The Center was subsequently converted to the Office of Global Communications in the White House Office.

BUREAU OF THE BUDGET/OFFICE OF MANAGEMENT AND BUDGET

The Bureau of the Budget (BOB) was created by the Budget and Accounting Act of 1921. It gave the president the capacity to formulate an executive budget that would be considered as a whole in Congress, rather than as separate appropriations requests from the many agencies of the executive branch.[23]

BOB was placed in the Treasury Department, and its small staff of twenty or thirty was used to achieve economies and efficiencies over the next two decades. The bureau was transformed, however, when it was transferred to the newly created Executive Office of the President in 1939. Its role was to help give the president some managerial control over the agencies of the executive branch, many newly created during the New Deal. During World War II, it also played an important role in coordinating the war effort. BOB emerged from World War II, with a staff of 600 and a managerial as well as a budgetary role, as the right arm of the president in dealing with the executive establishment.

BOB's major role has been to formulate the president's budget by refining agency budget requests before they go to Congress for consideration. This function is accomplished by its budget examiners, who become experts in the agencies they oversee and know where cuts can be achieved with the least harm to essential programs. BOB also conducts "central legislative clearance" by examining all legislative requests from agencies to ensure they are in accord with the president's program before they go to the Hill. By the 1950s, BOB had developed a professionalism and institutional memory that was a great help to the presidency.

But in the 1960s, Presidents Kennedy and Johnson believed that the bureau was not as useful as it might be for innovation and the new ideas and programs of the New Frontier and the Great Society. They began to pull domestic policy making into the White House and create the capacity for new initiatives under White House staffers Theodore Sorensen, Bill Moyers, and Joseph Califano.

President Nixon came to office with the purpose of reducing the domestic functions of the government and cutting programs. He felt that BOB, with its history of coordinating agencies and building new programs, would not be responsive to his new priorities. He thus decided to reorganize BOB and change its name to the Office of Management and Budget (OMB) to signify its new functions. To ensure political control, a new layer of political appointees, the program assistant directors, was inserted between the career budget staff and the director's level. These four new positions covered the functional areas of the budget and were intended to make the bureau more directly responsive to presidential political priorities. Nixon also gave his first director of OMB, George Shultz, an office in the West Wing of the White House to signify his status both as personal presidential adviser and director of the institution of OMB.

In 1973, Shultz's successor, Roy Ash, was given the title of assistant to the president as well as director of OMB.[24] The role of OMB was changed during the Nixon administration to support his controversial impoundment policies, to exert greater control over the executive branch, and to take a higher-visibility role in publicly asserting the president's budgetary proposals. During the Carter administration, another layer of political appointees, executive associate directors, was added to the leadership of OMB.

In the Reagan administration, OMB Director David Stockman played the major role in the administration's fiscal agenda of cutting taxes and programs on the domestic side of the government. The huge deficits generated by the administration's fiscal policy necessitated a top-down control of the budget and the ability to respond immediately to changes in budget assumptions. Thus, Stockman changed the role of OMB staffers by creating the capacity to analyze immediately, by computer, changes he was negotiating with Congress, and he put new emphasis on liaison with Congress to defend the administration's budget policies.

In the George H.W. Bush administration, OMB Director Richard Darman played a major role in formulating administration domestic policy as well as presiding over OMB. He continued the trend toward using budget documents to justify the administration's policies and counterproposals from Congress rather than as objective statements of the finances of the federal government. Under Clinton, Leon Panetta as OMB director was a major force in the administration's domestic and economic policy before he took over as the chief of staff. His deputy, Alice Rivlin, was appointed director when he left, and when she was appointed to the Federal Reserve Board, Franklin Raines took over for Clinton's second term. In the George W. Bush administration, OMB director Mitch Daniels took the lead in defending the administration's tax cut proposals; in 2003 he was succeeded by Joshua Bolten. When Bolten became the president's chief of staff in the spring of 2006, the president appointed Rob Portman to be director of OMB.

Since its inclusion in the Executive Office of the Presidency, the budget bureau has played an active and crucial role as the right arm of the president in policy and management. In contrast to most of the other agencies discussed in this chapter, it has not become more institutionalized since it was established as a large bureaucracy by the end of World War II. It has, however, become more responsive to presidents over the years by becoming more involved with the personal political priorities of individual presidents at the cost of its role as custodian of the institutional presidency. But this responsiveness has developed because presidents have wanted it to play that role. To survive, OMB had to make a choice between responsiveness and decay. It chose to survive and has thus remained at the heart of White House centralization of control over the executive branch, a trend that has been going on since 1960. One key difference remains, however: Even though it has more political appointees than ever before, the bulk of its staff are still career civil-service workers. A high level of professionalism is necessary because of the expertise and institutional memory that is necessary for OMB to perform its function effectively.

NATIONAL SECURITY COUNCIL STAFF

The National Security Council (NSC) was created in 1947 and was intended to ensure that the president would take into account professional military advice in planning national security policy. Harry Truman was suspicious of the congressional creation and did not use it much until the Korean War in 1950. The council itself has four statutory members: the president, vice president, secretary of state, and secretary of defense. The council merely advises the president and thus has little independent power; the influence of the NSC usually relates to the clout of the NSC staff and its director. In Truman's time there was an executive secretary who ran the staff. When Eisenhower came to office, he decided to raise the importance of the NSC staff and gave its director the title of special assistant to the president. The influence of the staff was ensured when Eisenhower built an advisory system of interagency sub-committees organized around the NSC staff. With his military background, Eisenhower was not dependent on his staff director for expertise, and the NSC staff was no threat to the domination of foreign policy by Secretary of State John Foster Dulles.

John Kennedy dismantled much of the NSC machinery, but after the Bay of Pigs invasion failed he leaned more heavily on his national security assistant, McGeorge Bundy. He brought Bundy's office into the West Wing of the White House and encouraged him to form a "Little State Department" to give independent advice to the president. Bundy's small staff of fifteen to twenty professionals acted as a neutral conduit of information and advice for the president, but it clearly marked the centralization of policy advice in the White House, a development that continued under Lyndon Johnson.

During the Nixon administration, the White House capacity for advice to the president independent of the Departments of State and Defense was firmly established. The NSC staff under Assistant to the President for National Security Affairs Henry Kissinger was to become much more than a neutral conduit of information and advice; it was to become the central formulator of the Nixon administration's foreign policy. Kissinger reorganized the NSC policy development process at the very beginning of the administration to ensure his domination of the committees and subcommittees set up to deal with

policy planning and implementation. But in addition, Kissinger and his staff
became the chief formulators of the major initiatives of the Nixon administration. Kissinger himself played the major negotiating role in the opening to
China, the Strategic Arms Limitation Talks (SALT) with the Soviet Union, and
the Vietnam peace talks. To support these unprecedented roles for the national
security adviser, the NSC staff grew to more than fifty professionals, but if
detailees (temporary workers from the other agencies) are included, the real
staff strength approached two hundred.[25]

Under Jimmy Carter, NSC staff strength was cut a bit, but the assertiveness
and strongly held views of Zbigniew Brzezinski ensured that the NSC adviser
would play a powerful role in the administration. Despite Carter's assurances
to Secretary of State Cyrus Vance, Brzezinski and his staff prevailed in many
important aspects of foreign policy and process. The friction between the two
men and their staffs finally led to Vance's resignation.

Ronald Reagan came to office determined to cut the influence of the
national security adviser and the NSC staff, and the White House was organized to have Richard Allen report to the president through Edwin Meese. The
original intent was to restore the secretary of state to preeminence as the foreign
policy spokesman for the president, but the White House staff did not trust
Alexander Haig. When Reagan intimate William Clark came from the State
Department to the White House to be assistant to the president for national
security affairs, the locus of national security policy making returned to the
White House, where it would stay throughout Reagan's term. The Iran-Contra
affair demonstrated the dangers of too much secrecy and centralized control in
a White House staff that was not sufficiently supervised by the top levels of the
White House. Although the Reagan administration NSC staff had a budgeted
full-time staff of about sixty professionals, its full strength was at the levels of
the Kissinger staff, about 180.[26]

President George H.W. Bush had one of the most tightly knit national
security teams in the recent past. James Baker as secretary of state, Richard
Cheney as secretary of defense, and Brent Scowcroft as national security
adviser had all worked together before the Bush administration and trusted
each other. This experience was invaluable during the successful conduct of the
Gulf War in 1990–1991. Bill Clinton chose the low-key Anthony Lake as
national security adviser, who did not try to dominate the foreign policy process but worked without much visible conflict with Secretary of State Warren
Christopher and Secretaries of Defense Les Aspin and William Perry. The size
of the NSC staff was reduced in the Clinton administration to lower levels than
it was in the Reagan administration, and the relationship between the national
security departments and the White House staff returned to a more even balance than it had been during the Nixon, Carter, or Reagan administrations.
President George W. Bush's national security adviser, Condoleezza Rice, had
worked on the NSC staff for Brent Scowcroft in the administration of George
H. W. Bush. It was decided during the transition to reduce the size of the NSC
staff, in part because of Vice President Cheney's experience and staff resources.
Rice served well through the Afghanistan war, but she was criticized during the

run-up to the Iraq war for not guiding the national security policy process firmly enough. But Rice was at a disadvantage, given the dominating roles played by Vice President Cheney and Secretary of Defense Rumsfeld in national security policy making.

Military and foreign policy advice have always been central to the presidency, but since World War II the coordination of the huge national security bureaucracies has become a major challenge. That challenge was met with the creation of the National Security Council and the growth in ensuing decades of its staff. The failure of the attempt by President Reagan, in 1981, to downgrade the NSC staff demonstrates that a strong, central, integrating capacity for national security policy in the White House is unavoidable.

OFFICE OF POLICY DEVELOPMENT (DOMESTIC POLICY STAFF)

Until the 1960s, domestic policy was not considered a separate category of the presidency. The New Deal proposals of Roosevelt were virtually all domestic policy, and FDR and his top advisers developed the legislative initiatives in the White House and sent them to Congress. Truman had a legislative staffer, but he put no one in charge of domestic policy per se. Eisenhower's aides worked on different aspects of domestic policy, but with no separate designation. Ted Sorensen took care of much of the domestic agenda for John Kennedy, though he was involved with foreign policy, speech writing, and other functions as well. The immediate forerunner to a formal domestic policy staff was Joseph Califano, whose primary job was coordinating Great Society legislation and implementation for Lyndon Johnson.

After experimenting with domestic advice from conservative Arthur Burns and liberal Patrick Moynihan, Richard Nixon decided that he wanted a formal White House capacity to formulate and coordinate domestic policy, similar to the role that the NSC played in national security policy. When the budget bureau was reorganized into OMB, President Nixon created the Domestic Council, which was to be chaired by the president and included cabinet secretaries and EOP officials. John Ehrlichman was to be its director, and he recruited a staff of sixty to seventy by 1972, including a deputy and six assistant directors.[27] The council itself seldom met, but the staff met often and acted, in effect, as the president's agent with respect to domestic policy. That is, Ehrlichman acted for the president and convinced cabinet members to go along.[28]

Watergate led to the decline of the power of the Domestic Council, and it did not recover much in the Ford administration when the president delegated his domestic agenda to Vice President Nelson Rockefeller. Because President Ford was a fiscal conservative, there was not much on the domestic agenda, and much of the policy-making action on the domestic side was dominated by the newly created Economic Policy Board. But when Jimmy Carter came to office, there were a number of domestic policy initiatives he wanted to pursue, and he reconstituted the function under the name of the Domestic Policy Staff. The staff was headed by Assistant to the President Stuart Eizenstat, who acted as an honest broker with the cabinet and advised the president. Eizenstat and his staff of forty to fifty were influential advisers to Carter but did not have the independence or authority that Ehrlichman had in the Nixon administration.

In the Reagan administration, the name of the domestic staff was changed to the Office of Policy Development (OPD), with a staff of about forty under Martin Anderson, who reported to Edwin Meese. The main priorities of the new administration were economic and budgetary and were developed through the Legislative Strategy Group and David Stockman's OMB. The OPD developed second-level domestic policy initiatives but also played an important role in staffing the cabinet council system of the first term and in staffing the Domestic Policy Council during the second term. Under President George H.W. Bush, the Domestic Policy Council continued, with the domestic policy staff headed by Roger Porter, whose title included both domestic and economic policy. Domestic policy, however, was also heavily influenced by OMB Director Richard Darman and Chief of Staff John Sununu.

President Clinton created a large Domestic Policy Council, but he did not meet with it often, if ever. A domestic policy staff existed in the White House, but did not function as a major force in policy making. Clinton's National Economic Council staff, however, did play an important role in domestic policy making.

Similarly, in the George W. Bush administration, the domestic policy staff, headed by Margaret Spellings, dealt with some of the domestic initiatives of President Bush, though it did not dominate the Bush domestic policy agenda. According to scholar Karen Hult, "As in past presidencies, under Bush, 'domestic policy' is less a coherent policy area than a collection of odds and ends whose importance will vary with circumstances and with the priorities of each administration."[29]

Thus, the existence and legitimacy of a domestic policy capacity with a specialized staff is firmly established in the White House. Some presidents may use it more (Nixon), and others may use it less (Reagan), but the option to do away completely with a domestic policy capacity in the White House is not likely to be taken by any president. The function of domestic policy coordination and the capacity to develop new initiatives are too important to a president.

CONCLUSION

Since the beginning of the modern presidency, the White House staff has grown as the federal government has taken on more functions in our society. In the 1930s, the national government did not have a space program, run a large-scale military establishment, project its force around the world, provide Social Security or Medicare benefits for most Americans, have an interstate highway system, regulate air traffic, or play an active role in education. As the tasks of government increased, the size of government grew in both personnel and budget.

In order to be effective and serve presidential needs, the White House has had to respond to the greater complexity of its environment. The executive branch is much more fragmented now that it has to deal with the many functions of modern government, and the White House has reflected that fragmentation in its internal specialized units. Congress, though it is made up of roughly the same number of legislators, has expanded its functions as the federal government has grown, and it has also increased its own staff resources to deal with the executive branch. The White House has had to respond to these changes, as well as to the increased fragmentation in Congress, since the reforms of the 1970s.

Thus, the proliferation of offices in the presidency, while striking when viewed in isolation, becomes much more understandable when seen as a series of responses to a changing political and governmental environment. The offices examined in this chapter follow a similar trajectory of growth. Responding to pressures in the political system, the president informally assigns tasks to White House aides, the function is then formalized in a White House office, the office becomes institutionalized, and finally it becomes indispensable to the effectiveness of the presidency.

NOTES

1. Hugh Heclo, "The Changing Presidential Office," in James P. Pfiffner, ed., *The Managerial Presidency*, 2nd ed. (College Station, TX: Texas A&M University Press, 1999), p. 24.

2. Martha Joynt Kumar, "Recruiting and Organizing the White House Staff," in Martha Kumar and Terry Sullivan, *The White House World* (College Station, TX: Texas A&M University Press, 2003), p. 369.

3. These general estimates are drawn from John Hart, *The Presidential Branch* (New York: Pergamon Press, 1987), p. 101; Gary King and Lyn Ragsdale, *The Elusive Executive* (Washington, DC: CQ Press, 1988), pp. 205–206, Table 4.2; and Samuel Kernell and Samuel Popkin, eds., *Chief of Staff* (Berkeley: University of California Press, 1986), p. 201.

4. Bradley H. Patterson, *The White House Staff* (Washington, DC: Brookings, 2000), pp. vii, 345.

5. Hugh Heclo, "The Executive Office of the President," in Marc Landly, ed., *Modern Presidents and the Presidency* (Lexington, MA: Lexington Books, 1985).

6. See the analysis by Margaret J. Wyszomirski in "The Discontinuous Institutional Presidency," in Colin Campbell and Margaret J. Wyszomirski, eds., *Executive Leadership in Anglo-American Systems* (Pittsburgh: University of Pittsburgh Press, 1991), pp. 85–108.

7. Richard Neustadt, "The Presidency and Legislation: Planning the President's Legislative Program," *American Political Science Review* (December 1955), p. 1015.

8. LBJ Library, oral history interview of Bryce Harlow by Michael L. Gillette, pp. 51–52 of the transcript.

9. Patrick Anderson, *The Presidents' Men* (New York: Doubleday, 1969), p. 307.

10. Jack Watson's remarks at a conference on the "Origins, Development, and Future of the American Presidency," at Gannon University, Erie, PA, April 25, 1987.

11. Bradley Patterson, *The Ring of Power* (New York: Basic Books, 1988), p. 154.

12. Patterson, *The White House Staff* (Washington, DC: Brookings, 2000), p. 115.

13. G. Calvin Mackenzie, "Partisan Presidential Leadership: The President's Appointees," in L. Sandy Maisel, ed., *The Parties Respond* (Boulder, CO: Westview Press, 1990).

14. Terry Sullivan, "Already Buried and Sinking Fast," in Kumar and Sullivan, *The White House World,* pp. 335–341.

15. For analyses of presidential recruitment of political appointees, see James P. Pfiffner, "Presidential Appointments: Recruiting Executive Branch Leaders," in G. Calvin Mackenzie, *Innocent Until Nominated* (Washington, DC: Brookings, 2001), pp. 50–80; and James P. Pfiffner and Bradley H. Patterson, "The Office of Presidential Personnel," in Kumar and Sullivan, *The White House World,* pp. 165–192.

16. See the analysis of Samuel Kernell, *Going Public* (Washington, DC: CQ Press, 1986), pp. 63–76.

17. Kernell, *Going Public,* p. 70.

18. Samuel Kernell, "The Evolution of the White House Staff," in John E. Chubb and Paul E. Peterson, *Can the Government Govern?* (Washington, DC: Brookings, 1989), pp. 211–217.

19. Kernell, "The Evolution of the White House Staff," p. 217.

20. Patterson, *The Ring of Power,* p. 189.

21. Martha Kumar, "The Office of Communications," in Kumar and Sullivan, *The White House World,* p. 264.

22. Kumar, "The Office of Communications," in Kumar and Sullivan, *The White House World,* p. 253. For an analysis of the development of the structure and function of the press secretary and the Office of Communications, see this chapter and "The Office of the Press Secretary" in the same book.

23. For a full analysis of the development of BOB/OMB since 1939, see James P. Pfiffner, "OMB: Professionalism, Politicization, and the Presidency," in Campbell and Wyszomirski, eds., *Executive Leadership in Anglo-American Systems,* pp. 195–218. For a longer-term perspective on the development of BOB/OMB, see James P. Pfiffner, *The President, the Budget, and Congress: Impoundment and the 1974 Budget Act* (Boulder, CO: Westview, 1979).

24. Margaret J. Wyszomirski, "The De-Institutionalization of Presidential Staff Agencies," *Public Administration Review* (September/October 1982), pp. 448–458.

25. Joel M. Woldman, "U.S. Presidential National Security Advisers: Changing Roles and Relationship," *Congressional Research Service Report No. 87–334F,* (Washington, DC: Library of Congress April 15, 1987), p. 34. See also Patterson, *The Ring of Power,* p. 99; and John Prados, *Keepers of the Keys* (New York: Morrow, 1991), p. 493.

26. Woldman, "U.S. Presidential National Security Advisers," p. 37; Patterson, *The Ring of Power,* p. 339.

27. Margaret Wyszomirski, "The De-Institutionalization of Presidential Staff Agencies," pp. 448–458.

28. Margaret J. Wyszomirski, "The Roles of a Presidential Office for Domestic Policy: Three Models and Four Cases," in George C. Edwards, Steven A. Shull, and Norman C. Thomas, eds., *The Presidency and Public Policy Making* (Pittsburgh: University of Pittsburgh Press, 1985), pp. 130–150.

29. Karen Hult, "The Bush White House in Comparative Perspective," paper prepared for the conference on "The Bush Presidency: An Early Assessment" (Woodrow Wilson School, Princeton University), April 25–26, 2003, p. 23.

5 CHAPTER | THE CABINET AND THE EXECUTIVE BRANCH

The Constitution declares that the executive power shall reside in the president and mentions "executive departments," but it does not go into detail about the structure or organization of the president's branch of government. This chapter analyzes the major components of the executive branch—the cabinet, political appointments, departments, and agencies—with the emphasis on how the president uses these tools of governance. Presidents have often tried to use their cabinets as collegial sounding boards, but the experience of recent presidents has not often lived up to that ideal. Relations between cabinet secretaries and the White House staff have often been strained, and this chapter analyzes the causes and consequences of the dominance of the White House staff in the contemporary presidency.

Political appointees provide managerial and policy leadership in the executive branch. Some of the appointments are presidential, but some are controlled by cabinet secretaries and agency heads. Recent presidents have centralized the control of these appointments in unprecedented ways. Most presidents come to office harboring suspicions of the career government bureaucracies. This chapter examines the role of the 1.8 million civil servants (and 1.4 million in the active-duty military) who serve the country at the direction of the president.

The theme of this chapter is that presidents have asserted much more centralized control over the cabinet and the executive branch in recent decades and that, contrary to some assertions, executive branch bureaucracies are quite responsive to presidents. Nevertheless, presidents will still be frustrated because they must share power with Congress, and they are subject to the constraints of public law and the broader forces in the political system. The modern presidency exerted more centralized control over the executive branch at the end of the twentieth century, but presidential control continues to be necessarily incomplete because of the role of Congress in the separation of powers system.

ORIGINS OF THE CABINET

The "president's cabinet" as an institution is based on practice and precedent, for it has no basis in the Constitution or law (though some laws refer to cabinet officers). The Framers decided not to saddle the president with any council of advisers, and the Constitution merely allows the president to "require the Opinion, in writing, of the principal Officer in each of the executive Departments, upon any Subject relating to the duties of their respective Offices" (Article II, Section 2). The cabinet departments were begun when Congress, at President Washington's request, created three departments of government in the summer of 1789: the Departments of State, War, and Treasury.[1] While Washington continued to seek advice from his former associates, the use of his cabinet secretaries as a more formal advisory system was precipitated by the refusal of the Senate to perform the advisory role that Washington had expected. Washington went to the Senate in 1790 to seek its advice on a treaty with the Indians, but the Senate rejected his overture. Consequently, Washington turned to his department heads for advice, and since then no president has relied on the Senate for advice with respect to treaties or appointments.

Washington consulted with his departmental secretaries about matters of state, and in 1791 began meeting with them as a group. He even suggested that when he was traveling, Alexander Hamilton, Thomas Jefferson, and Henry Knox meet in his absence if any issues arose that might require his attention.[2]

Although the term "cabinet" in the U.S. government was not used until 1794, Washington began in 1793 to seek regular advice from his department heads: the secretaries of state, treasury, and war, and Attorney General John Jay (though the Justice Department was not created until 1870).

After the Federalist period, presidents began to choose cabinet members with whom they were not close associates, and they began to seek advice from others as well. Andrew Jackson, for instance, did not even meet with his official cabinet for his first two years in office, preferring to seek advice from old friends who became known as his "Kitchen Cabinet." James Polk, on the other hand, met with his department heads 350 times during his one term in office. Throughout the nineteenth century, presidents more or less used their cabinets as a primary advisory mechanism.

The cabinet in the United States must be distinguished from the cabinet in a parliamentary system, where cabinet members are also members of parliament. Political parties choose ministers from among the leadership of the controlling party in parliament. They retain their full voting membership in the legislature at the same time that they are the cabinet ministers in charge of the executive departments (ministries). They are thus dependent on their party in the legis- lature, where party loyalty is expected, and the prime minister is the first among equals. In the United States, however, cabinet secretaries are wholly dependent on the president for their positions, and the Constitution forbids membership in both branches at the same time. Cabinet secretaries serve at the pleasure of the president, who can dismiss them at any time. The U.S. cabinet as such has no formal power. Its relationship to the president was reflected by Abraham Lincoln, who is said to have announced a vote in his cabinet: "Seven nays and one aye, the ayes have it."

THE CABINET AS A DELIBERATIVE BODY

Modern presidential candidates often referred to "cabinet government" as an ideal to which their administrations would adhere. In the U.S. context, the term refers to the delegation of a certain amount of authority to cabinet secretaries and to presidential consultation with the cabinet as a deliberative body. The idea has much appeal. The U.S. government is so complex that no one person can understand it all, and the regular advice of the experts who head the major departments and agencies cannot help but be salutary to a president. In addi- tion, the synergy of a team of highly competent people deliberating on the complex issues of governance and proffering their best collective advice to the president can be compelling.

Harry Truman expressed this ideal when he decided to replace Roosevelt's cabinet appointments with his own: "The cabinet is not merely a collection of executives administering different governmental functions. It is a body whose combined judgment the president uses to formulate the fundamental policies of the administration."[3]

Of all modern presidents, Dwight Eisenhower came closest to achieving the U.S. ideal of cabinet government. He consciously chose his cabinet appointees to be part of a team, selecting a group of men of similar back- grounds. His cabinet was a homogeneous collection of, as one magazine put it, "eight millionaires and one plumber."[4] Eisenhower believed in the efficacy of the deliberation of the full cabinet on matters of importance. He told his cabinet: "My hope will be to make this a policy body, to bring before you and for you to bring up subjects that are worthy of this body as a whole."[5] Eisenhower expected that members of his cabinet would not confine their advice to their own policy areas but would speak out on the broad issues facing his administration.[6]

Eisenhower also believed in delegating matters not clearly of presidential importance to his line officers (officials who have the authority to make policy decisions) in the cabinet rather than having his White House staff make the decisions. Eisenhower's White House aide, General Goodpaster, recalled: "In the Eisenhower White House, the president would deal only with the great issues. . . . I remember that when important issues came up in staff meetings, Eisenhower would interrupt and say 'Excuse me, but that is not a staff matter. I will take that up with the secretary of defense, or interior. . . .'"[7]

The seriousness with which Eisenhower took cabinet deliberations was demonstrated by his establishment of a cabinet secretariat to prepare agendas for cabinet meetings and make sure that all background papers were in the hands of secretaries well before cabinet meetings. Members of the secretariat also made a record of each meeting and followed up on presidential decisions to ensure cabinet compliance.[8]

But even Eisenhower's cabinet did not always live up to his ideals of cabinet government. According to one participant, Elliot L. Richardson, seldom were matters of importance put before the collective body for deliberation and decision by the president. Vice President Richard Nixon, whom Eisenhower included in cabinet deliberations, recalled that most cabinet meetings were "unnecessary and boring."[9] If the pressures of the U.S. political system prevented even Eisenhower's cabinet from fully living up to his cabinet government ideal, most post–World War II presidents did not even come close. The incentives in the system all run against collaboration. Cabinet secretaries would prefer to do their special pleading one-on-one with the president, rather than putting their own priorities on the table for general discussion by the full cabinet.

Possibly because of his background as a member of Congress with a small staff, and in contrast to Eisenhower's experience with military staff systems, John Kennedy preferred working with small groups. From the beginning of his presidency, Kennedy believed that the cabinet should meet for little more than symbolic reasons. "Cabinet meetings are simply useless," he declared. "Why should the Postmaster General sit there and listen to a discussion of the problems of Laos?"[10] Even his close adviser and brother, Attorney General Robert F. Kennedy, felt that full cabinet meetings were of such little use that he attended only about half of them.[11]

Kennedy preferred to bring together smaller groups of people who were directly involved with an issue, whether members of his cabinet or White House staff. But more importantly, he wanted people whose judgment he could trust at these meetings. After the Bay of Pigs invasion, he felt he could not rely on people based on their experience or the positions they held; he wanted people at the table whom he personally knew.[12]

Lyndon Johnson kept Kennedy's cabinet for the first thirteen months of his administration before he began to replace them with his own appointees. In the earlier years of his administration, Johnson met with his cabinet regularly, though at times they were not as productive as he hoped. George Reedy recalled LBJ's cabinet meetings: "Cabinet meetings were held with considerable regularity, with fully predetermined agendas and fully prewritten statements. In general, they consisted of briefings by cabinet members followed by a later release of the statements to the press. It was regarded by all participants except the president as a painful experience."[13]

In the latter years of his administration, marked by controversy about the continuing war in Vietnam, President Johnson came to distrust even his own cabinet members. As he told President-elect Richard Nixon in December 1968, "Let me tell you, Dick, I would have been a damn fool to have discussed major decisions with the full cabinet present, because I knew that if I said something in the morning, you could sure as hell bet it would appear in the afternoon papers."[14]

Richard Nixon began his presidency with the intention of rejecting the Democrats' more casual approach to the cabinet and return to a model closer to Eisenhower's. His initial intention was to delegate personnel selection and most of domestic policy to his cabinet and concentrate most of his own energy on foreign affairs. "I've always thought this country could run itself domestically without a president. All you need is a competent cabinet to run the country at home. You need a president for foreign policy."[15] Nixon wanted a strong cabinet to run the government for him. He intended that his cabinet secretaries would be experienced leaders who would use their independent judgment in advising him and running their departments.

But Nixon soon became disillusioned with his cabinet appointees and felt that they were too attached to their own policy and organizational interests and not committed enough to his reelection. After his landslide reelection in 1972, Nixon demanded the resignation of his entire cabinet and their political subordinates, a devastating blow to the loyal political appointees who had faithfully served in the administration and had worked for his reelection. In his second term, Nixon replaced his first-term cabinet with people who had less independent political stature of their own and were more personally loyal to him.[16] Nixon's first-term experience changed his mind about the possibilities of cabinet deliberation and delegation: "Cabinet government is a myth and won't work, . . . a president should never rely on his cabinet . . . no [president] in his right mind submits anything to his cabinet. . . ."[17]

Nixon's disdain for his cabinet appointees was reflected in their frustration with him. Many of them felt that, as cabinet secretaries, they had a certain claim on the president's time to discuss issues that fell within their jurisdictions. Secretary of the Interior Walter J. Hickel, in a letter to Nixon shortly before he was fired, said, "Permit me to suggest that you consider meeting, on an individual and conversational basis, with members of your cabinet. Perhaps through such conversations we can gain greater insight into the problems confronting us all, into solutions of these problems."[18] Nixon's attitude toward his cabinet led to his sweeping proposal for the restructuring of White House–cabinet relations, which would have placed several layers of counselors between the president and most cabinet secretaries.

Gerald Ford, in reacting to the Nixon administration, wanted to restore the status of the cabinet; he made himself much more accessible to his cabinet and refurbished its stature. But just as his "spokes of the wheel" White House organization gave way to a chief-of-staff system, after a year his cabinet declined in importance. The Ford administration did, however, make use of a cabinet subcommittee, the Economic Policy Board (EPB), to deliberate about economic policy. The EPB was a frequently used forum in the Ford presidency and included both White House staffers and members of the cabinet.[19]

In reaction to Nixon's centralized control and neglect of his cabinet secretaries, Jimmy Carter intended to "restore the cabinet to its proper role as the president's first circle of advisers."[20] Carter promised that his White House staffers would clearly be subordinate to members of his cabinet and not dominate them as the Nixon staff had. Carter's White House aide and later chief of staff, Jack Watson, articulated four principles of cabinet government: (1) Cabinet officers should be free to select their own subordinates; (2) they should be able to set their own priorities; (3) they should be able to administer their own agencies free of White House interference; and (4) the president should delegate significant policy-making authority to cabinet secretaries.[21]

Carter's early intentions did not escape the reality of executive branch politics. According to his domestic policy adviser, Stuart Eizenstat, the cabinet was important for expertise, information, and implementation, but it was not effective as a collective decision-making body. In the beginning of his administration, Carter held cabinet meetings weekly, but the cabinet's effectiveness as an advisory body soon declined, and meetings decreased in frequency. By the middle of the Carter administration, the White House staff began to feel that some members of the cabinet were not fully on board with the president's program but were pursuing their own policy priorities on the Hill. This feeling led Carter to demand the resignations of all of his cabinet appointees and accept the resignations of five in the summer of 1979.

During President Reagan's transition into office, Caspar Weinberger wrote an op-ed piece for the *Washington Post* describing how Reagan's cabinet system was intended to work. The president would

> meet with his cabinet appointees on a regular basis with a planned agenda . . . to discuss with them all of the major problems facing the government that week, as well as some of the longer range problems, and to take counsel with his appointees not just on subjects relating to each member's department, but on an overall basis aided by a collegial discussion, arguments and differing points of view, presented by all members of this small group.[22]

Weinberger's description fit squarely into the traditional post–World War II cabinet ideal. But this idealized version of cabinet government did not work for Reagan any better than it had for his immediate predecessors. The Reagan administration was one of the most staff-directed and centralized presidencies in the modern era. Administration policy, budget priorities, and political personnel selection were tightly controlled by the White House staff. The people who planned the Reagan presidency self-consciously learned lessons from the experiences of Nixon and Carter with their cabinets. They were determined that Reagan would not make the same mistakes (as they saw it) of delegating personnel discretion to cabinet secretaries or of allowing budget priorities to be driven by departmental needs.

To ensure central control of policy development but also to include cabinet secretaries, they organized a cabinet council system. Seven cabinet councils were formed around specific policy areas (economic affairs, commerce and trade, resources and environment, human resources, management and administration, food and agriculture, and legal policy), and the cabinet secretaries responsible for these areas would meet with White House staffers to develop policy. The important part of this system was to get the White House staff and cabinet members sitting down together to discuss policy. Though some of the councils were much more active than others and not all major policy initiatives went through the system, it was a useful contribution to White House–cabinet relations and helped to avoid some of the usual fighting between the two groups. By the beginning of the second term, however, it was evident that the seven-council system was too cumbersome and time-consuming. So the seven councils were reduced to two: economic policy and domestic policy. Along with the National Security Council, these were intended to be the primary policy development mechanisms for the administration, though as in the first term, the issues of highest priority were handled directly by top White House aides.

President George H.W. Bush, unlike his immediate four predecessors, did not claim that he would install cabinet government when he became president. Yet he had a closer working relationship with his cabinet both because he knew them personally and liked to keep in touch and because he was familiar with the policies he expected them to implement. As president-elect, Bush had said he wanted cabinet members to "think big" and "challenge the system." "I want them to be frank; I want them to fight hard for their position. And then when I make the call, I'd like to have the feeling that they'd be able to support the president."[23]

Early in his administration, members of the cabinet enjoyed a certain amount of leeway, and some took initiatives without first clearing them with the White House.[24] But the influence of individual cabinet secretaries did not extend to the cabinet as a collective body. Cabinet meetings were "used more for a briefing session" than for policy deliberations, according to David Bates, secretary to the cabinet.[25] Bush's national security team was particularly effective, with little of the institutional and personal rivalries that marked the administrations of Nixon, Carter, and Reagan.[26]

During his transition, President-elect Clinton spent a considerable amount of time choosing his cabinet. He brought candidates to Little Rock and met with them individually for hours to ensure that he felt comfortable with them personally and in policy terms. He believed that his cabinet appointments were important because they would send a symbolic message of inclusion to the country about his priorities. He said he wanted to appoint "a cabinet that looks like America." He had to scramble to meet his self-imposed deadline of December 24 for completing his cabinet designations, but he did appoint a more diverse cabinet than any of his predecessors, with four African Americans, two Latinos, and three women, including the nation's first woman attorney general, Janet Reno. His careful selection paid off in that only four positions turned over during his first term (including the accidental death of Commerce Secretary Ron Brown in an air crash).

For his second term, Clinton replaced seven of his cabinet secretaries, an about-average turnover for a second term. In his second-term appointments, Clinton continued to value diversity, with two Latinos, three African Americans, and four women, including Madeleine Albright, who was the first woman appointed secretary of state. He also appointed a Republican to be secretary of defense, former Senator William Cohen of Maine. In addition to the secretaries of the fourteen cabinet departments, President Clinton accorded "cabinet-level rank" to eleven other officials. Other presidents had granted cabinet rank to officials other than the secretaries of departments, but not to the extent that Clinton did. President George W. Bush, in contrast, gave cabinet rank to only five officials who were not cabinet secretaries.[27]

President Clinton's use of his cabinet as a symbol of the representative nature of his administration and his unprecedented granting of cabinet status to many other administration officials was consistent with his disinclination to use the cabinet as a working group or deliberative body. Twenty-five people is too many for a working meeting. The same point held for Clinton's National Economic Council, with eighteen members, and his Domestic Policy Council, with twenty-three members. Clinton also added nine officials as participants in National Security Council meetings (see Chapter 7). The large size of these policy groups emphasizes the symbolic nature of their memberships. Actual policy deliberations were most often conducted in informal subsets of the groups' members along with the staffs of the groups who actually did most of the policy development work.[28]

Clearly, the main policy initiatives of the Clinton administration were run out of the White House, not in the departments or in the cabinet policy groups set up by the president. For instance, the economic program of his first term was formulated by Robert Rubin, director of the National Economic Council. After he was appointed treasury secretary, Rubin continued to play the dominant role in economic policy. The national health-care planning task force symbolized Clinton's approach, with 500 people set up in the White House led by First Lady Hillary Rodham Clinton and directed by White House adviser, Ira Magaziner. President Clinton's approach to his cabinet was indicated by the fact that, in the four years of his first term, he had formal cabinet meetings only eighteen times, an average of fewer than five per year.[29] He of course met with members of the cabinet many times, but not often as a deliberative body.

The George W. Bush cabinet-selection committee consisted of only four people: the president-elect, Vice President–elect Dick Cheney, Transition Director Clay Johnson, and Andrew Card. The whole cabinet was named by the first week in January, and seven were confirmed on the first full day of the administration, January 21. Without echoing President Clinton's promise to appoint a cabinet that "looks like America," Bush recruited a cabinet equally diverse by contemporary standards. Bush appointed three women (Ann Veneman at Agriculture, Gale Norton at Interior, and Christine Whitman at

EPA—designated as part of the cabinet), two African Americans (Colin Powell at State and Roderick Paige at Education), one Arab American (Spencer Abraham at Energy), one Hispanic (Mel Martinez at Housing and Urban Development), and one Asian American (Norman Mineta at Transportation, also a Democrat who had been secretary of commerce in the Clinton administration). Only six of the fifteen were white males. The diversity of the cabinet reflected both the increasingly qualified pool of minorities in the United States and the signal that Bush wanted to send that would draw minority voters from the Democratic Party to the Republican Party.

Despite Bush's care in recruiting an experienced and well-credentialed cabinet, he was not about to reverse the trend of the past four decades of power gravitating to the White House. Early in his administration, all of the policy priorities were dominated by White House staffers rather than led from the cabinet. The administration began with monthly cabinet meetings and frequent contact between cabinet members and the White House staff, but that did not translate into policy clout.

For instance, the administration's education initiative was handled by the domestic policy adviser, Margaret LaMontagne Spellings rather than Education Secretary Roderick Paige, who had been the superintendent of schools in Houston. On medical issues, such as government financing of prescription drugs, the patients' bill of rights, and stem-cell research, the action was in the White House rather than with Health and Human Services Secretary Tommy Thompson. The administration's tax cut proposals were not led by Treasury Secretary Paul O'Neill but by White House staffers, particularly the National Economic Council director, Lawrence Lindsey. Vice President Cheney dominated the administration's energy policy proposals rather than Secretary of Energy Abraham.[30]

President Bush had one of the most stable (post-WWII) cabinets during his first term, with only two positions changing hands. Yet in the transition to his second term, President Bush changed more of his cabinet than had his predecessors, replacing nine cabinet secretaries. In the second-term shifts, Bush placed several of his close White House advisers in the cabinet to assure adherence to his priorities. Condoleezza Rice became secretary of state, Margaret Spellings became secretary of education, and Alberto Gonzales became attorney general.

In his second term, Bush kept Donald Rumsfeld at Defense, signaling continuity with the first-term national security policy and war in Iraq. At State he replaced Colin Powell, who had always been suspected of disloyalty by the White House staff, with his confidant and national security adviser, Condoleezza Rice. He also replaced John Ashcroft as attorney general with his long-time counselor and White House counsel, Alberto Gonzalez. These three cabinet posts were filled with executives very close to Bush, but with regard to the rest of the cabinet, he continued the first-term practice of centralized control. As one high-level White House official said during the transition from the first to the second term: "The Bush brand is few priorities, run out of the White House, with no *interference* from the Cabinet. . . . The function of the

Bush Cabinet is to provide a chorus of support for White House policies and technical expertise for implementing them." (emphasis added).[31]

The principal role of cabinet secretaries continued to be implementation rather than initiation or primary advice. This does not mean that cabinet secretaries are now ciphers, just that policy initiation and advice, which had been the primary role of cabinet secretaries up through the Eisenhower administration, are now the primary province of White House staffers.

Since the Eisenhower administration, presidents have been disappointed in their attempts to use their cabinets as a deliberative body. The synergy that should result when presidents convene these highly intelligent men and women, all with the highest ideals of serving the president and the nation, is somehow missing. Why is the ideal of the cabinet as the president's primary advisory body so difficult to achieve? Part of the problem is size. The cabinet now has fifteen members in addition to the president and vice president and others whom presidents often invite to cabinet meetings.[31]

But the more important impediment to true collegial deliberation is that each cabinet secretary feels a strong need to defend departmental political and policy interests, and is thus unwilling to expose his or her special interests to the crossfire of fellow cabinet officers who may be battling for the same turf and resources.[32] As FDR's secretary of commerce, Jesse H. Jones, declared: "My principal reason for not having a great deal to say at cabinet meetings was that there was no one at the table who could be of help to me except the president, and when I needed to consult him, I did not choose a cabinet meeting to do so."[33]

CREATING THE DEPARTMENT OF HOMELAND SECURITY

The creation of the Department of Homeland Security was the largest reorganization of the executive branch of the government since the National Security Act of 1947 created the Department of Defense, the Central Intelligence Agency, and the National Security Council. The terrorist attacks of September 11, 2001, convinced President Bush that central coordination and focus were necessary to coordinate the nation's response to the new terrorist threats within the United States. In order to implement his plans, Bush created the Office of Homeland Security in the Executive Office of the President and appointed Governor Tom Ridge of Pennsylvania to be its director.

Ridge would have the responsibility of coordinating the many functions and agencies in the executive branch that would play important roles in preventing terrorism and dealing with its aftereffects. As White House "czar" of homeland security, Ridge had the advantage of direct access to the president and would not be bound by close monitoring from Congress. On the other hand, he would not have direct control of the agencies he would be coordinating and could authoritatively affect neither their budgets nor their personnel. Congressional critics of the administration's approach to homeland security pointed out these weaknesses in the Bush plan and also argued that such an important function as homeland security should involve Congress more directly. A number of proposals for the creation of a cabinet department were bandied about, but they ran into turf battles among the affected agencies.

After resisting the proposals for a new department, President Bush realized that some form of a departmental reorganization was likely to be adopted by Congress, and he decided he would be better able to control the outcome if the administration came up with its own proposal. So in the spring of 2002, an administration team worked in secret, and in June President Bush publicly proposed the creation of a new Department of Homeland Security. The House quickly passed the president's proposed reorganization, but the Senate was split over the bill's provisions that gave the president power to override personnel protections and union rights for employees who would be transferred to the new department. Both Republicans and Democrats filibustered rival plans for the new department during the impasse in the Senate in the fall of 2002, preventing passage of the bill until after the 2002 elections gave clear control of the Senate to the Republicans and the Republican plan was passed.[34]

The new department was officially created, and Tom Ridge was confirmed as its first secretary in January 2003. It would be the third-largest department after Defense and Veterans Affairs, with a budget of nearly $30 billion and 170,000 employees brought together from nine cabinet departments and twenty-two different agencies across the executive branch. The mission of the department was to help prevent domestic attacks by terrorists, to reduce vulnerability to terrorism, and to minimize the damage and assist in the recovery from any attacks that might occur. The structure of the department included five major divisions.

In addition to the five major divisions, two important agencies were transferred to the department. The Coast Guard, a uniformed service, had been in the Department of Transportation and has national defense responsibilities; its commandant would report directly to the secretary of DHS. The Secret Service had been in the Department of Treasury; its most important function is the protection of the president, but it also has important responsibilities in the areas of currency and credit card fraud. Though the Secret Service in effect works directly for the president, its director organizationally reports to the secretary of DHS. (The organization of the DHS is shown in Figure 5.1.)

The creation of DHS was important politically in order for the administration to control the outcome of congressional action, and it was important symbolically to demonstrate the government's commitment to protect American citizens. But the effectiveness of the new department would depend on the skill of its leadership, the commitment of its employees, and the ironing out of the thousands of administrative details that are involved in any large reorganization. With employees scattered throughout the Washington region and the rest of the United States, it would be a challenge to transform any such large conglomeration of separate agencies, each with its own history and culture, into a smoothly functioning organization.

FIGURE 5.1 | MAJOR DIVISIONS OF THE DEPARTMENT OF HOMELAND SECURITY

Department of Homeland Security: Major Divisions

- Border and Transportation Security
- Emergency Preparedness and Response
- Science and Technology
- Information Analysis and Infrastructure Protection
- Management

Other Major Units

- Coast Guard
- Secret Service

The growing pains of the newly established department became evident when Hurricane Katrina struck the Gulf Coast in 2005. The Federal Emergency Management Agency (FEMA), which had been folded into the new DHS, had suffered from a loss of resources and professional personnel because the primary mission of DHS was protection from terrorism rather than recovery from natural disasters. In the aftermath of the storm, FEMA was not able to mobilize or coordinate sufficient resources to prevent the flooding of New Orleans from becoming a human as well as a natural disaster.

DEPARTMENTAL SECRETARIES VERSUS THE WHITE HOUSE STAFF

The inability of presidents to take advantage of their cabinets as collective, deliberative bodies is rooted in cabinet members' individual roles as departmental secretaries and the consequent rise of the White House staff as the president's primary advisers. Departmental secretaries are the highest-ranking appointed positions in the executive branch and are the line officers of the government. As line officers they possess statutory authority to carry out their duties, and they make major decisions about the allocation of resources and the deployment of personnel. In contrast, the power of White House staffers is derived from their personal relationship to the president; they do not have independent legal authority. Given this official status of cabinet secretaries and the resources at their command, why have they been overshadowed by the White House staff in the modern presidency? The answer lies in the roles they play in the political system and the need of presidents to control the government. (See Table 5.1.)

The role of departmental secretaries is Janus-like in that it requires them to "face" both the president, as the person who appointed them and at whose

TABLE 5.1 | CABINET DEPARTMENTS: DATE OF CREATION, PERSONNEL, AND BUDGET IN FY2003

Department	Year	President	Personnel	Budget
State	1789	Washington	28,244	$11 billion
War/Defense	1789	Washington	636,000 (civilian)	358 billion
Treasury	1789	Washington	116,675	358 billion
Interior	1849	Polk	70,037	10 billion
Agriculture	1862	Lincoln	114,040	73 billion
Justice	1870	Grant	105,953	22 billion
Commerce (formerly part of Commerce and Labor, 1903)	1913	Wilson	39,000	6 billion
Labor (formerly part of Commerce and Labor, 1903)	1913	Wilson	17,274	71 billion
Housing and Urban Development	1965	Johnson	10,500	37 billion
Transportation	1966	Johnson	59,189	52 billion
Energy	1977	Carter	16,000	20 billion
Health and Human Services (formerly part of Health, Education and Welfare, 1953)	1980	Carter	65,000	502 billion
Education (formerly part of HEW, 1953)	1980	Carter	4,620	60 billion
Veterans Affairs	1988	Reagan	211,764	60 billion
Homeland Security	2003	Bush	179,241	28 billion

Source: Budget of the United States, FY2004 (OMB Web site: http://www.whitehouse.gov/omb/budget).

pleasure they serve, and their departments. This places them in a bind: They must prove themselves loyal to the president, yet at the same time they must be effective leaders of their own departments. To be effective in implementing programs and advocating presidential priorities, departmental secretaries must provide effective leadership for their departments. But this requires loyalty to departmental staff and career civil servants as well as to the president. The irony is that at times cabinet secretaries can be of most use to the president by paying close attention to the needs of their own departments and their constituencies.

White House staffers often complain that cabinet secretaries tend to be special pleaders, and they are mostly correct in that evaluation. According to Miles' Law: Where you stand (concerning policy) depends on where you sit (organizationally).[35] Thus, cabinet secretaries are virtually always advocates for their own departments. Just as this is predictable, it is also mostly legitimate. If departmental secretaries do not defend their programs, who will do it with credibility? Department heads cannot be expected to judge impartially the merit or priority of their own programs. The secretary of health and human services is obliged to make the best case for the value of medical research and public-health programs. The secretary of transportation is equally obliged to assert the priorities of air-travel safety.

But departmental advocacy stems from resource as well as policy grounds. In order to do an effective job, department heads need resources, money, and people, and they will fight for those resources. This is why Charles G. Dawes, the first director of the budget bureau and Calvin Coolidge's vice president, said: "Cabinet secretaries are vice presidents in charge of spending, and as such are the natural enemies of the president."[36]

The differences in perspective of cabinet secretaries and White House staffers become more understandable if you consider the reasons why each group is selected. Although White House staffers are recruited based on personal loyalty to the president, there are a number of criteria that are considered in putting together a cabinet. The appointments of cabinet secretaries are often the first signals of how a president will act in office. Thus, these early decisions are fraught with symbolic importance. A newly elected president may want to unite the political party by naming a member of the opposite ideological wing to the cabinet. A president may even appoint a member of the other party, as did President Kennedy in naming Douglas Dillon to be treasury secretary, or Eisenhower his first secretary of labor, Martin Durkin. Carter's first secretary of energy, James Schlesinger, had been secretary of defense in the Nixon and Ford administrations. President Clinton's secretary of defense was former Republican Senator William Cohen; George W. Bush asked Bill Clinton's secretary of commerce, Norman Mineta, to stay on to be his secretary of transportation.

Traditionally, presidents have paid attention to geographic and religious distribution in selecting their cabinets. Some departments are typically filled with representatives of certain constituencies: The Department of Agriculture is usually headed by a former farmer, Interior by someone from the West, Treasury by someone from the financial community, and so on. Presidents have also demonstrated their commitment to racial diversity by naming African Americans or Latinos to cabinet posts. Recent presidents have usually named at least one woman to their cabinets, and President Clinton appointed five. With these different criteria affecting the choice of cabinet secretaries, it is predictable that the collective members of the cabinet will not be as personally close to the president as will the senior White House staff.

The roles that departmental secretaries play for the president are diverse. Each must be an effective political representative for the president with the public and an effective lobbyer with Congress, which controls departmental budgets and programs. Each must effectively manage the department's bureaus and agencies, and be an effective leader of the career and political officials of the agency, as well as a visible symbol of the president's commitment to that particular policy area. The internal management function is challenging because most departments are more like holding companies of different bureaus and agencies than single-purpose agencies. This calls for adept use of budgetary, organizational, and personnel skills by the secretary. At times these levers of control are sufficient, but in other cases bureaus have ties to sympathetic members of Congress who may try to influence departmental policy independent of the secretary.

Because of these multiple obligations, departmental secretaries often seem to be "captured" by the interests of their departments and swayed by their career personnel, who have a stake in the well-being of their programs. According to Nixon aide John Ehrlichman, departmental secretaries go off and "marry the natives." Of course, the perspective of the departmental secretary is that he or she is faithfully serving the president's best interests and that White House staffers have their own agendas that they claim presidential authority to pursue. The frustrations of presidential appointees in the agencies is expressed by Donald Devine, former Reagan administration director of the Office of Personnel Management: "The president's staff at times pursues its own interests, not necessarily the president's. . . . If the agency head is loyal to the president, he should never be dictated to by the White House staff. Otherwise, every clerk in the White House will feel at liberty to call him and tell him the president wants this or that."[37]

In explaining departmental advocacy, the background of departmental secretaries is also a factor. They have often spent most of their careers becoming experts in the policy area they are now administering. But lack of absolute loyalty to the president by department secretaries is inherent in the American political system, both because of the reasons for their recruitment and because they are legally bound to carry out the law and may be called before Congress to account for their actions and justify their budgets.

From the White House perspective, however, these forces are not sufficient reason when cabinet secretaries do not seem to be toeing the administration line. As one Kennedy White House staffer put it, "Everybody believes in democracy until he gets to the White House and then you begin to believe in dictatorship, because it's so hard to get things done. Every time you turn around, people resist you and even resist their own job."[38] From the White House perspective, only advisers close to the president have the breadth of perspective to make the cross-cutting policy decisions that are necessary at the top of the federal government. In the words of Stuart Eizenstat, Jimmy Carter's domestic policy adviser: "No matter how good a cabinet secretary is there is a certain predictability to the outlook and response of his agency. The White House staff, as opposed to the cabinet, is perhaps the only arm of the president that offers some integrative capacity."[39]

The perspective of cabinet secretaries, however, is different. They often feel that they are forced into the role of advocacy because they so seldom get to see the president. According to one executive branch official:

> [D]omestic cabinet members are so rarely with the president that when they do have a chance to see him, they have to advocate and plug their departmental program. . . . But precisely at such times, the senior White House aide present can adopt or strike a pose as the more objective, rational statesman taking a non-advocate and more

"presidential" position. . . . The White House aide knows, on the other hand, that he can see the president later that day or the next, and so can afford to play a more reasonable and restrained role in such meetings.[40]

The natural friction between cabinet secretaries and White House staffers is exacerbated by differences in age and stature, with young White House aides often having the clout to be able to tell senior administration officials what to do. Jeb Stuart Magruder, a young Nixon staffer, put it this way:

> From our perspective in the White House, the cabinet officials were useful spokesmen when we wanted to push a particular line—on Cambodia, on Carswell, or whatever. From their perspective, however, it was often a rude awakening to have Jeb Magruder or Chuck Colson calling up and announcing, "Mr. Secretary, we're sending over this speech that we'd like you to deliver." But that was how it was. Virtually all the cabinet members had to accept that they lacked access to the president and that their dealings would be with Haldeman and his various minions.[41]

These differing perspectives represent the inherent tensions in the modern presidency. Cabinet secretaries are the line officers of the executive branch, and they are pulled by strong centrifugal forces. White House staffers enforce the presidential need to have greater control of the large and complex executive branch.

Since the 1970s, the centralization of control of the executive branch in the White House has been a continuing reality in domestic as well as foreign policy. In 1971, Senator Ernest F. Hollings stated the perceived reality:

> It used to be that if I had a problem with food stamps, I went to see the secretary of agriculture, whose department had jurisdiction over that program. Not any more. No, if I want to learn the policy, I must go to the White House and consult John Price. If I want the latest on textiles, I won't get it from the secretary of commerce, who has the authority and responsibility. No, I am forced to go to the White House and see Mr. Peter Flanigan. I shouldn't feel too badly. Secretary [of Commerce] Stans has to do the same thing.[42]

The fragmenting forces in American politics have intensified with the growth of the scope and size of government. The modern presidency has dealt with this fragmentation by increasing the size and power of the White House staff. Regardless of campaign promises, the reality of the modern presidency is that the White House staff will continue to compete with and often overshadow departmental secretaries.

PRESIDENTIAL APPOINTMENTS

Cabinet secretaries are the president's most important line officers, but they comprise only a very small percentage of the total number of political appointments that presidents make. Most government officials in most nations in the world are not temporary political appointees but rather are appointed for indefinite periods, often for their careers. So are most government employees in

TABLE 5.2 | POLITICAL APPOINTMENTS AVAILABLE TO PRESIDENTS

Presidential Appointments

PAS (requiring Senate confirmation)*	1,125
PA (not requiring Senate confirmation)	20
White House Staff (no confirmation)	636
Agency Head Appointments	
Noncareer Senior Executive Service+	720
Schedule C (GS-15 and below)#	1,428
Part-Time Presidential Appointments	
PAS (requiring Senate confirmation)	490
PA (not requiring Senate confirmation)	1,859
Total Presidential Appointments	6,278

*Includes 185 Ambassadors, 94 U.S. district attorneys, 94 U.S. marshals.
+Up to 10 percent of career Senior Executive Service (SES) positions can be filled with political appointees. Legally made by agency head, but the president can instruct his appointees whom to appoint.
#Lower-level political positions requiring policy-making or confidential duties. Legally made by agency head, but the president can instruct his appointees whom to appoint.
Source: Bradley H. Patterson and James P. Pfiffner, "The Office of Presidential Personnel," in Martha J. Kumar and Terry Sullivan, *The White House World* (College Station, TX: Texas A&M University Press, 2003), p. 166.

the United States. What sets the United States apart from other modern industrialized democracies is the number of political appointees available for each newly elected president. The European parliamentary democracies of Britain, France, and Germany change only a maximum of several hundred officials with a change in party control of the government. A U.S. president, however, can make almost 4,000 full-time appointments to the executive branch, and more than 2,000 part-time, more than any other modern democracy. (See Table 5.2.)

The purpose of these presidential appointees is to help lead the 1.8 million civilian employees and 1.4 million active-duty military personnel who comprise the executive branch. The premise is that the American people elect the president but that the president cannot manage the government alone, and thus he or she can appoint executives and managers to help lead, direct, and control the executive branch of government. When the people elect a president, they also, by implication, help select the people the president will appoint to lead the government.

The Framers of the Constitution were greatly concerned with the quality of those chosen to run the government, believing that their character would determine the overall quality of the U.S. government. Those Framers favoring a strong executive wanted to give the president exclusive authority to make appointments. But those distrustful of executive power preferred to give the appointment power to the Senate. At the end of the Constitutional Convention, the issue was finally settled by the compromise calling for presidential nomination and Senate confirmation of the major appointments to the executive branch.[43]

Senate confirmation hearings on particular nominees can be grueling for the nominee and tense for the administration. Occasionally there will be an acrimonious fight and the Senate will reject a nominee, such as George H.W. Bush's nomination of John Tower to be secretary of defense in 1989. But such rejections are very unusual. From 1789 to 1990, only fifteen cabinet nominations (and twenty-seven Supreme Court nominees) have been formally rejected by the Senate, and only four of these occurred in the twentieth century.[44] No president since Herbert Hoover has been forced to withdraw more than 1 percent of his nominations, and no president since FDR has had more than six nominations rejected by the Senate.[45]

There is a tension in the modern nation-state between political responsiveness and technical competence. The American government of the twentieth century is a huge, fragmented, and highly complex collection of organizations. Government organizations put satellites into space, search for cures for cancer and AIDS, make judgments about patents for biotechnology, control nuclear missiles and regulate nuclear energy, and make sure that computers generate accurately the millions of Social Security checks that go out each month. Running these programs is no job for amateurs.

So each new president is faced with the duty to appoint competent professionals to leadership positions in the government. But presidents also face pressures to reward political supporters with government jobs. Before the modern presidency, the job of recruiting presidential appointees was dominated by the political parties. From the early nineteenth century presidents had used patronage—that is, government jobs—to build support for their political parties. When the party's candidate won, the party faithful expected that they would be rewarded with jobs.

The modern appointments system, though greatly changed, still has some resemblance to the traditional patronage system. The major changes stem from two factors: the decline of political parties and the need for expertise in the government. The types of people now needed to run the government must be highly qualified, and their qualifications must be more than mere party loyalty. The people needed to fill technical positions in defense systems, nuclear energy, biotechnology, patents for intellectual property, space exploration, or strategic defense are "unlikely to be found hanging out at party headquarters on election night."[46]

The other major developments that have affected presidential appointments are the decline of political parties and the simultaneous rise of the White House staff. As the White House staff grew in size, importance, and influence in the modern presidency, political parties enjoyed less control of traditional patronage. As the number of primary elections increased, political parties lost control of the nominating process, and thus when presidents were elected, they owed less in the way of patronage to the parties. In making appointments, presidents were unwilling to accept whomever happened to be a loyal party worker but wanted to recruit people who would be loyal to them and who were competent enough to the do the jobs for which they were recruited.

Presidents began to designate White House staffers to specialize in political recruitment. Harry Truman put one person in charge of presidential appointments. John Kennedy had his three-person "talent hunt." Richard Nixon had Frederic Malek put together a thirty- to forty-person White House personnel office. Jimmy Carter's transition operation had its "Talent Inventory Program." Ronald Reagan's Office of Presidential Personnel had 100 people at work during the first months in office. President Clinton had 130 people recruiting presidential appointees in the early months of 1993. As the White House personnel operation grew in size, it also increased in professionalism, with people directing it who had had professional executive recruiting experience in the private sector. Clay Johnson, President George W. Bush's political recruiter, used unprecedented technological innovations in putting much of the applications process online.

In the contemporary presidency, the professionalism and competence of the Office of Presidential Personnel is crucial, especially at the very beginning of a presidency. In order for a new president to take control and give direction to the government, appointees must be in place to provide leadership to the many bureaucracies. At the beginning, efforts must focus on the top 300 or so positions in the executive branch: the cabinet and immediate subcabinet (undersecretaries, deputy secretaries, and assistant secretaries). But the need for speed in making these appointments is countered by the volume of work that must be done.

Each new administration is besieged by people who want government jobs. Those who have worked in the campaign expect special consideration, and members of Congress are not at all reticent in recommending constituents or staffers for appointments in the new administration. In recent administrations, thousands of applications and recommendations flowed into transition headquarters. President George H.W. Bush's director of the Office of Presidential Personnel, Chase Untermeyer, reported that the Bush administration received more that 45,000 applications and recommendations in its first five months in office.[47] The Clinton transition team received up to 2,000 applications per day during the transition period, and expected to receive a total of 100,000.[48] It ended up with 95,000 resumes in its personnel database.

The Office of Presidential Personnel must separate out the wheat from the chaff in the applications. But even the chaff cannot be ignored with impunity. If the recommendation comes from the Hill, the president's personnel office must write cordial letters explaining why Senator X's favorite nephew is not qualified to be assistant secretary for research in the energy department. A contemporary president cannot afford to begin an administration without a large and professional personnel operation.

With the volume of applications for presidential appointments, what criteria are used to narrow down the list of final nominations? The sine qua non of presidential appointments is loyalty. But the definition of loyalty has shifted over the years. Loyalty used to be defined by party service. If one was a good Republican or Democrat, that was deemed sufficient to attest to one's loyalty. But party affiliation began to decline in importance as the need for professional competence rose. President Eisenhower, a professional public servant for all of his career, felt very uneasy with the claims of partisanship. John Kennedy and Richard Nixon both said early in their terms that competence was more important than partisanship; they wanted the person best qualified for the job.

But recent presidents have felt an increasing need for loyalty in presidential appointees in order to control the government. In their initial commitment to cabinet government, both Presidents Nixon and Carter delegated to their cabinet appointees the authority to select their immediate subordinates (the subcabinet), even though these were presidential appointments. But several years into their administrations, both came to feel that they had delegated away too much presidential leverage. When conflicts between cabinet departments and the White House staff arose, the White House felt that the presidential appointees out in the agencies were loyal to the cabinet secretary who appointed them rather than to the president. Each administration tried to pull the appointment authority back into the White House, but once appointment authority has been delegated, trying to bring it back to the White House is like trying to put toothpaste back into the tube after it has been squeezed out.

In 1980, top Reagan advisers decided before they took office that they would control political appointments in the White House. Pendleton James, Reagan's first personnel recruiter, was given an office in the West Wing and the title of assistant to the president; both actions were unprecedented and intended to symbolize the importance that the administration gave to personnel. They argued that policy control was not possible without personnel control.

In order to ensure White House primacy, the Reagan administration insisted that all presidential appointments be tightly controlled by the White House. Cabinet secretaries could suggest candidates for their management teams, but final decisions would be made in the White House. In another unprecedented action, they insisted that all political, not just presidential, appointees be cleared through the White House. These included noncareer Senior Executive Service (SES) and Schedule C appointments, which are technically at the discretion of the agency head.

The other component of the Reagan administration plan to control the government was their definition of loyalty. A loyal Republican heritage was insufficient. People who had worked for the Nixon and Ford administrations were called "retreads." The right wing of the Republican Party wanted people in the administration who were committed "Reaganites" and who were committed to the conservative policy agenda. Those who were not "movement conservatives" felt that the criteria were an unfair "litmus test" that excluded loyal Republicans who were competent and qualified for positions because of their service in previous Republican administrations. The tension between professionalism and ideological commitment characterized the appointment process for the first year of the administration.[49]

In the George H.W. Bush administration, the definition of loyalty shifted from ideological to personal loyalty to, and past service with, George Bush. An administration "scrub team" went over potential nominations to ensure that those with past service to Bush were not passed over. The Bush administration paid more attention to professional competence and delegated more discretion to its cabinet secretaries in choosing their immediate subordinates than Reagan had but still insisted that agency heads find jobs for campaign workers at the Schedule C level.

The main criterion for personnel selection in the Clinton administration (aside from competence) was diversity, often known as the "EGG" standard, standing for ethnicity, gender, and geography. The Clinton White House played a very active role in selecting political appointees throughout the government. Although the White House accepted suggestions from departmental secretaries, the lists submitted were often rejected for lack of diversity. One of the results of this commitment to diversity was a greater percentage of women and African Americans than served in any previous administration. Another result was a slower appointment process than any other administration.

As the White House has taken a larger and more controlling role in the political appointment process, the time it takes to get the top levels of the executive branch staffed has increased. It took President Kennedy an average of 2.1 months from inauguration day to fill a position, but since then the period steadily increased to 8.5 months for President Clinton in 1993. In 2001, President George W. Bush's appointments pace was the slowest on record.[50] The reasons for the increasing time necessary to staff an administration include the new ethics laws, closer scrutiny by presidential recruiters, more thorough FBI checks, and more drawn out Senate confirmation procedures.

Several trends have marked the development of the political appointments process in the modern presidency. As the government has grown in size and complexity, the number of political appointees has grown, at the PAS level (presidential appointments requiring Senate confirmation) as well as at lower levels. From the 1930s to the 1970s, the White House gradually took control of appointments from the political parties by developing a professional recruitment capacity in the White House. Since the 1970s, appointments have been more tightly controlled by the Office of Presidential Personnel, with much less leeway for department and agency heads to choose their immediate subordinates. All of these factors point to the importance of a professional White House recruitment office that is ready to go immediately after a presidential election.

THE EXECUTIVE BRANCH BUREAUCRACY

The modern career bureaucracy that makes up most of the executive branch is the successor to the spoils system of the nineteenth century, where the party faithful were rewarded with jobs. President Andrew Jackson provided the

TABLE 5.3 | MORE OFFICIALS AT THE TOP LAYERS OF THE EXECUTIVE BRANCH

Position	1960	2004
Secretary	10	15
Deputy Secretary	6	24
Under Secretary	15	53
Assistant Secretary	87	256
Deputy Assistant Secretary	78	535

Source: Adapted from Paul Light, *Thickening Government* (Washington, DC: Brookings, 1995), pp. 191–193. Updated by Paul Light on Brookings Web site, 2006.

justification for the spoils system by arguing that all government jobs were essentially simple and that incumbents of government positions tend to abuse their power. In the middle decades of the nineteenth century, presidents newly coming to office brought with them party loyalists to fill the government jobs. The spoils system helped to build political parties in the United States, but reformers argued that spoils led to incompetence, inefficiency, corruption, and the need to train a new cadre of campaigners to do government jobs every four years. Presidents complained that they spent too much time making patronage decisions and acting as petty job brokers. (See Table 5.3.)

The arguments of the reformers came to fruition when Charles Giteau, a disappointed office seeker, assassinated President Garfield in 1881. This act galvanized the Congress to pass the Pendleton Act of 1883, which created the merit system under which civil servants would be chosen on the basis of ability rather than party affiliation. The act also forbade executive branch officials from making personnel decisions—hiring, firing, promotions, demotions—on the basis of party. It also created the Civil Service Commission to run personnel recruitment for the government and act as a watchdog for the protection of merit principles throughout the government.

Initially, the Pendleton Act covered only 10 percent of the civil service, with presidents having the option of including, by executive order, other categories of workers ("blanketing in"), thus protecting their own political appointees from being dismissed by the next president. By the 1930s, over 70 percent of government workers were in the civil service, and by the 1980s, well over 80 percent were covered.

The tradeoff for the protections of the merit system for civil servants was the commitment to "neutral competence." That is, professional civil servants would be selected on the basis of competence, but they would be neutral with respect to political party. They would be responsive to any president, regardless of party. But as the system of protections against political abuse grew—for instance, limits on demoting or firing personnel—the system was seen to be

FIGURE 5.2 | THE GOVERNMENT OF THE UNITED STATES

Source: United States Government Manual, 2002/2003 (Washington, DC: Government Printing Office), www.gpoaccess.gov; updated by author.

more insulated from political control. And complaints about the insulation and lack of responsiveness of "the bureaucracy" were increasingly heard. (See Figure 5.2.)

Modern presidents have tended to be skeptical of the career bureaucracy. When Eisenhower was elected, Republicans felt that the career people promoted during the past twenty years of Democratic control would be biased against the new administration. His administration thus created a new category of political appointments, Schedule C positions, which would be at lower levels (GS-15 and below) in the agencies. Those committed and loyal in a partisan way to the president would no longer be limited only to the highest positions in the executive branch.

John Kennedy was doubtful whether the leadership of the career services, who had developed their careers during the Eisenhower years, would be flexible or bold enough to develop proposals for the "New Frontier" and to "get the country moving again." After the Bay of Pigs disaster, Kennedy became even more suspicious of the judgment of career executives and began to centralize control in the White House. Lyndon Johnson prodded the budget bureau to think boldly in designing his Great Society legislation, but he was never fully satisfied by their efforts.

Richard Nixon had a legendary distrust for the career bureaucracy. He regarded them as "built-in establishmentarians fighting for the status quo," and told his White House aides: "We have no discipline in this bureaucracy. We never fire anybody. We never reprimand anybody. We never demote anybody. We always promote the sons-of-bitches that kick us in the ass." According to Nixon aide John Ehrlichman, the Nixon White House waged "guerrilla warfare" with the bureaucracy.[51]

Jimmy Carter ran for president as an outsider complaining about the "horrible bureaucratic mess in Washington." Part of his motivation and support for the 1978 Civil Service Reform Act came from the desire to make it easier to fire civil servants. Ronald Reagan also ran a "bureaucracy bashing" campaign, promising to "get the government off our backs." He recruited a number of political appointees who were openly hostile to the agencies to which they were appointed and did his best to cut spending and personnel for the domestic agencies of the government. President George H.W. Bush provided a sharp contrast to his immediate predecessors with his respect for career professionals and his ideals of public service.

Notwithstanding the attitudes of some newly elected presidents, their distrust of career civil servants is mostly misplaced. The vast majority of career professionals believe in the Constitution and respect the outcome of elections. Political executives have the necessary managerial tools to motivate career civil servants. Presidential appointees control promotions and can heavily influence the career prospects of people in their agencies. They can, although with some difficulty, fire people who are incompetent or who resist legitimate directives. Each agency head can also move most top career executives to different assignments because of the personnel authority granted in the 1978 Civil Service Reform Act. There will always be scattered instances of resistance to any policy, regardless of the incumbent party, but these are unusual. Presidents Clinton and George W. Bush did not bash the bureaucracy (though they both attacked Washington) in their campaigns for office. The Bush administration during the run-up to the war in Iraq in 2002, however, felt that the intelligence agencies (especially the CIA) were not sufficiently responsive to the administration's policy goals. A new unit in the Office of the Secretary of Defense, the Office of Special Plans, was created to analyze intelligence data from a different perspective than the CIA brought to bear.[52]

Most presidential appointees gradually come to have a high respect for their career subordinates. This reality is reflected in the responses of presidential appointees to questions about the competence and responsiveness of career executives they worked with. From 77 to 92 percent of them rated career executives as "responsive" or "very responsive" (four or five on a five-point scale). Most administrations are marked by a "cycle of accommodation" in which new political appointees gradually gain respect for the career subordinates with whom they work.[53]

But this responsiveness does not guarantee that presidents will always get everything they want from the executive branch. Congress, especially when it is of the opposite political party, can be depended on to compete with the president for control of administration. Congress holds the key levers of power over much of the bureaucracy and is often willing to use that power. The very existence of programs depends on the enabling legislation that creates programs and agencies, and most programs face periodic reauthorization. Each agency's budget must be defended every year, and the purse strings can be very specific.

Presidential appointees can be compelled to testify before congressional hearings that can be used to put pressure on agencies. Political power is also wielded by organized interest groups who can weigh in on issues affecting them directly. Even presidential appointees will be pulled by these centrifugal forces.

Thus, presidents will often be frustrated by outside political forces when they are seeking to achieve their policy goals. But the source of these frustrations is most often not "those damn bureaucrats" but the power of Congress and opposing political factions in the broader society. Bureaucrats may respond to these diverse political forces, but they seldom initiate them and by themselves can seldom effectively resist presidential wishes. If bureaucrats, in and of themselves, could effectively counter presidential wishes, the Reagan administration would not have been able to achieve the budget and personnel cuts in domestic agencies that it accomplished in 1981 and 1982.

The career bureaucracy is the implementer of almost all programs and policies of presidents and the national government. But the separation-of-powers system ensures that presidents will not have exclusive control of the executive branch. It is thus not the independent power of bureaucrats that frustrates presidents; it is the division of powers guaranteed by the Constitution.

CONCLUSION

The reality of the modern presidency is the domination of policy and administration in the executive branch by the White House. Presidents Nixon, Ford, Carter, and Reagan all came to office with expectations that their cabinets would play a greater role in their administrations than they ultimately did. This chapter has explained some of the reasons that these presidents' expectations were not met.

The causes of the centralization of policy control in the White House relate to broad historical forces in American politics. Ever since the Progressives saw the presidency as the engine of national progress, public expectations of the president have continued to grow. The New Deal and World War II expanded the size of the national government and the role of the government in the economy. The resulting fragmentation of power led presidents to want to pull together the threads of control in the White House. The proliferation of primaries and the rise of the personal, rather than party-dependent, candidate for president led to the need for personal loyalty and responsiveness in modern presidents.

The causes of White House staff domination of the executive branch stem from the administrative incentives of presidents and the advantages of personal staff over institutional bureaucracies. White House staffers are physically closer and immediately responsive to presidential wishes; they can drop everything and concentrate on the needs of the moment. In contrast to cabinet officials, they have no managerial duties to distract them, no budgets to balance, people to hire, or programs to run. No congressional mandates constrain them, nor will they be called to testify on the Hill. No wonder presidents tend to rely on their White House staffs rather than cabinet officers.

But these advantages bring with them drawbacks for the ongoing government on which presidents and their successors must depend. Cabinet departments possess the institutional memory, expertise, planning capabilities, and orderly policy processes to run the ongoing programs that are necessary to all modern governments. Insofar as presidents ignore these essentials, their decisions will be less well informed and government programs will be less well administered.

When too much policy making is pulled into the White House, presidential capacity can be stretched too thin. Matters best handled at lower levels can create problems that bog down presidents and create expectations that the president should solve every problem that arises. When political appointees penetrate the career bureaucracies too deeply, the capacity of the career services to do their jobs is undercut. Loyalist political appointees may not have the expertise to run technical programs.

The short-term perspectives of appointees may distort longer-term planning and rob the government of the ability to serve the next president equally well. The more leadership positions at lower levels that are taken by political appointments, the fewer talented career civil servants will stay in the government throughout their careers. Insofar as presidential appointees manage agencies with a close coterie of intimates to the exclusion of career executives, the capacity of agencies to serve the next president will be undercut. David Stockman, as director of OMB, and James Baker, as secretary of state, were justly praised for their competence. But their failure to include career executives in much of their policy deliberations left their agencies weaker than if they had fully used their career subordinates and tried to strengthen the institutional capacities of their agencies.

The centralization of power and control in the White House is understandable and, to a certain extent, inevitable. The calls of some reformers to cut drastically the size of the White House staff or to delegate most policy making to departmental secretaries are based on assumptions that no longer hold. We cannot go back to the time when the president personally knew all of the White House staffers or when cabinet secretaries could expect to discuss their agencies' matters regularly with the president. But it would not hurt to tilt back slightly in that direction. The analysis of this chapter leads to three paradoxes of the modern presidency:

1. With respect to the cabinet: The best way for a president to "control" the executive branch is to delegate most issues that are not clearly presidential to department and agency heads. Presidential involvement should be selective.

2. With respect to political personnel: The president should play a positive role in setting the tone for recruiting political appointees but should delegate the selection of most subcabinet appointments to department and agency heads. Personal or ideological loyalty to the president does not guarantee the effective implementation of presidential priorities.

3. With respect to the permanent bureaucracy: The career bureaucracy is often seen by new presidents as an obstacle to the achievement of presidential priorities. But cooperation with the career services is essential to accomplishing presidential goals, and enlisting the bureaucracy's enthusiastic support can enhance the probability of presidential success.[54]

NOTES

1. For a history of the U.S. Cabinet, see R. Gordon Hoxie, "The Cabinet in the American Presidency, 1789–1984," *Presidential Studies Quarterly* (Spring 1984), pp. 209–230; for a developmental perspective on the cabinet, see Ronald C. Moe, "The President's Cabinet," in James P. Pfiffner and Roger H. Davidson, *Understanding the Presidency*, 3rd ed. (New York: Longman, 2003), pp. 197–215.

2. Hoxie, "The Cabinet in the American Presidency," p. 212.

3. Michael Nelson, ed., *Congressional Quarterly Guide to the Presidency* (Washington, DC: CQ Press, 1989), p. 978.

4. *New Republic* (December 15, 1952), p. 3, Stephen Hess with James P. Pfiffner, *Organizing the Presidency*, 3rd ed. (Washington, DC: Brookings, 2002), p. 51. The one "plumber" was Martin P. Durkin, who had been president of the AFL United Association of Plumbers and Steamfitters.

5. Fred I. Greenstein, *The Hidden-Hand Presidency* (New York: Basic Books, 1982), p. 106.

6. Dwight D. Eisenhower, *Mandate for Change* (New York: Doubleday, 1963), p. 99.

7. Andrew Goodpaster, "Jimmy Carter on the Presidency" (Washington, DC: The Wilson Center, 1984), transcript of remarks, p. 16.

8. For an analysis of the operation of the cabinet secretariat by one of its participants, see Bradley Patterson, *The President's Cabinet* (Washington, DC: American Society for Public Administration, May 1976), pp. 107–114.

9. See Elliot L. Richardson and James P. Pfiffner, "Creating a Real Cabinet," *USA Today Magazine* (September 1990), pp. 10–12.

10. Arthur Schlesinger, Jr., *A Thousand Days* (Boston: Houghton Mifflin, 1965), p. 688.

11. Edwin O. Guthman and Jeffrey Shulman, eds., *Robert Kennedy in His Own Words* (New York: Bantam Books, 1988), p. 53.

12. Guthman and Shulman, *Robert Kennedy in His Own Words*, p. 54.

13. Nelson, *Congressional Quarterly Guide to the Presidency*, pp. 978–979.

14. Richard Nixon, *RN: The Memoirs of Richard Nixon* (New York: Grosset & Dunlap, 1978), p. 357.

15. Rowland Evans, Jr., and Robert D.Novak, *Nixon in the White House* (New York: Random House, 1971), p. 11.

16. Nelson Polsby, "Presidential Cabinet Making: Lessons for the Political System," *Political Science Quarterly* (Spring 1978), pp. 15–16.

17. Joan Hoff-Wilson, "Richard M. Nixon: The Corporate Presidency," in Fred I. Greenstein, ed., *Leadership in the Modern Presidency* (Cambridge, MA: Harvard University Press, 1988), p. 170.

18. Nelson, *Congressional Quarterly Guide to the Presidency*, p. 979.

19. Roger Porter, *Presidential Decision Making* (New York: Cambridge University Press, 1980).

20. Joseph Califano, *Governing America* (New York: Simon & Schuster, 1981), pp. 26–27.

21. Joel Havemann, "The Cabinet Band—Trying to Follow Carter's Baton," *National Journal* (July 16, 1977), p. 1105.

22. Caspar W. Weinberger, "Yes, Washington, We *Can* Have Cabinet Government," *Washington Post* (November 25, 1980).

23. David Hoffman, "Watkins, Bennet Named to Cabinet; Bush Orders New Team to Think Big, Avoid Kiss-and-Tell Books," *Washington Post*, January 13, 1989.

24. For examples of initiatives taken without White House clearance, see John P. Burke, *Presidential Transitions: From Politics to Practice* (Boulder, CO: Lynn Rienner Publishers, 2000), pp. 238–239.

25. Burt Solomon, "When the Bush Cabinet Convenes . . . It's a Gathering of Presidential Pals," *National Journal* (July 1, 1989), p. 1704.

26. For an analysis of the cabinet and White House staffs of Presidents George H. W. Bush and Bill Clinton, see Stephen Hess with James P. Pfiffner, *Organizing the Presidency*, 3rd ed. (Washington, DC: Brookings, 2002), chap. 10, pp. 146–174.

27. White House Web site: http://www.whitehouse.gov/government/cabinet.html (accessed July 22, 2003). For the Clinton cabinet designates, see *United States Government Manual 1996/1997* (Washington, DC: Government Printing Office, 1997), p. 89.

28. See James P. Pfiffner, *The Strategic Presidency: Hitting the Ground Running*, 2nd ed. (Lawrence, KS: University Press of Kansas, 1996), pp. 155–159.

29. Number of meetings provided by the Office of Cabinet Affairs, March 4, 1997.

30. Ellen Nakashima and Dana Milbank, "Bush Cabinet Takes Back Seat in Driving Policy," *Washington Post* (September 5, 2001), p. 1, A12.

31. Jim VandeHei and Glenn Kessler, "President to consider changes for new term," *Washington Post* (November 5, 2004), p. 1. One set of Washington Post headlines seemed to reflect the insignificance of the Cabinet to the second-term Bush White House: "Secretary Who? The President's Invisible Cabinet . . . Condi, Rummy and the Nobodies." Michael Grunwald, "Secretary Who? The President's Invisible Cabinet." *Washington Post* (May 21, 2006).

32. For an analysis of why cabinet government does not work, see Shirley Warshaw, *Power Sharing: White House-Cabinet Relations in the Modern Presidency* (Albany, NY: State University of New York Press, 1996).

33. Nelson, *Congressional Quarterly Guide to the Presidency,* p. 980.

34. For an analysis of the politics of the creation of the department, see Richard S. Conley, "Presidential and Congressional Struggle over the Formation of the Department of Homeland Security," in Richard S. Conley, ed. *Transforming the American Polity: The Presidency of George W. Bush and the War on Terrorism* (Englewood Cliffs, NJ: Prentice Hall, 2004).

35. Rufus Miles was assistant secretary for administration of the Department of Health, Education, and Welfare for many years, as well as a public administration scholar.

36. Richardson and Pfiffner, "Creating a Real Cabinet," p. 12.

37. Donald Devine, "So You Want to Run an Agency," *Policy Review* (Winter 1989), p. 9.

38. Thomas Cronin, *The State of the Presidency* (Boston: Little, Brown, 1980), p. 223.

39. Goodpaster, "Jimmy Carter on the Presidency," p. 17.

40. Cronin, *The State of the Presidency,* p. 284.

41. Jeb Stuart Magruder, *An American Life: One Man's Road to Watergate* (New York: Atheneum, 1974), p. 102.

42. Harold Relyea, "Growth and Development of the President's Office," in David C. Kozak and Kenneth N. Ciboski, eds., *The American Presidency* (Chicago: Nelson-Hall, 1985), p. 135.

43. An excellent analysis of the Framers and the appointment power can be found in Charles Ross, "The Accidental Elite: Senate Confirmed Federal Executives" (PhD diss., George Mason University, 1993), chap. 2.

44. See Rogelio Garcia, "Cabinet and Other High-Level Nominations That Failed to Be Confirmed, 1789–1989," *Congressional Research Service Report No. 89–253 GOV* (Washington, DC: Library of Congress, April 14, 1989).

45. Morris Fiorina, *Divided Government* (New York: Macmillan, 1992), p. 97.

46. G. Calvin Mackenzie, "Partisan Presidential Leadership: The President's Appointees," in L. Sandy Maisel, ed., *The Parties Respond* (Boulder, CO: Westview Press, 1990), p. 283.

47. Interview with Chase Untermeyer, The White House, June 6, 1990.

48. *U.S. News & World Report* (February 1, 1993), p. 9.

49. For analysis of the presidential appointments process, see James P. Pfiffner, "Nine Enemies and One Ingrate: Presidential Appointments During Transition," in G. Calvin Mackenzie, ed., *The In and Outers: Presidential Appointees and the Problems of Transient Government in Washington* (Baltimore: Johns Hopkins

University Press, 1987); James P. Pfiffner, "Presidential Appointments: Recruiting Executive Branch Leaders," in G. Calvin Mackenzie, ed., *Innocent Until Nominated: The Breakdown of the Presidential Appointments Process* (Washington, DC: Brookings, 2001), pp. 50–80; and Bradley H. Patterson and James P. Pfiffner, "The Office of Presidential Personnel," in Martha Kumar and Terry Sullivan, *The White House World* (College Station, TX: Texas A&M University Press, 2003), pp. 165–192; James P. Pfiffner, *The Strategic Presidency: Hitting the Ground Running* (Lawrence, KS: University Press of Kansas, 1996), chap. 3, "Personnel Control: Staffing the Administration."

50. For a detailed analysis see Pfiffner, *The Strategic Presidency*, chap. 8 and conclusion. For the 2001 data, see G. Calvin Mackenzie, "The Real Invisible Hand: Presidential Appointees in the Administration of George W. Bush," in Kumar and Sullivan, *White House World*, pp. 326–334.

51. The first quote is from *Public Papers of the Presidents 1971*, p. 448. The Ehrlichman quote is from the presidential transcripts made from the Watergate recordings, quoted in Thomas Cronin, *The State of the Presidency* (Boston: Little, Brown, 1980), p. 223.

52. Evan Thomas, Richard Wolffe, Michael Isikof, "(Over)Selling the World on War," *Newsweek* (June 9, 2003), p. 29.

53. See James P. Pfiffner, "Political Appointees and Career Executives: The Democracy-Bureaucracy Nexus in the Third Century," *Public Administration Review* (January/February 1987), pp. 57–65; these data have been replicated by the Presidential Appointee Initiative of the Brookings Institution. Responses of political appointees through the 1990s are comparable to the responses through 1984.

54. James P. Pfiffner, "Can the President Manage the Government?" in James P. Pfiffner, ed., *The Managerial Presidency*, 2nd ed. (College Station: Texas A&M University Press, 1999), p. 3.

6 CHAPTER | THE PRESIDENT AND CONGRESS

In dividing constitutional powers among the branches, the Framers intended legislative power to reside in Congress and gave the president only minimal tools to affect the legislative process. In the modern presidency, however, one of the president's main roles is that of "chief legislator." This transformation is the result of broad-scale economic and societal changes in the United States. The turning point was Franklin Roosevelt's famous "100 Days." Since then, presidents have developed the institutional capacity to influence and sometimes dominate the legislative process. But more importantly, both the public and Congress now expect that presidents will have a legislative agenda and will actively fight for it on Capitol Hill.

Modern presidents are much more active in the legislative process; however, this does not mean that they dominate Congress. The success rate of presidents with legislation on which they take a position usually ranges between 50 and 80 percent and typically declines over the course of a term. This chapter examines the constitutional and political fundamentals of presidential relations with Congress and then presents contrasting examples of how modern presidents have tried to influence Congress and the legislative agenda. The varying success rates of the modern presidents demonstrate that, despite increased presidential power, the balance the Framers designed in the Constitution still exists (at least in domestic policy), often to the frustration of presidents.

CONSTITUTIONAL FUNDAMENTALS

For the president to achieve public-policy goals and deliver on campaign promises, Congress must at least go along with, and more often actively support, the president. Even in national security policy, where the president has most leeway, money must be appropriated, and Congress can thwart presidential initiatives if it is provoked to do so. In most policy areas, legislation must be passed to initiate and implement policies.

The Framers of the Constitution, however, did not make this an easy task. In their fear of allowing power to be concentrated in any one branch of government, they separated powers and provided each of the three branches with checks on the other two. This would be accomplished, according to James Madison in Federalist No. 51, by "giving to those who administer each department the necessary constitutional means and personal motives to resist encroachments of the others."

In dividing governmental powers, the Framers gave the legislative power to the Congress. Article I, Section 1 provides that "all legislative Powers herein granted shall be vested in a Congress of the United States, which shall consist of a Senate and House of Representatives." Section 8 of Article I enumerates the substantive powers of Congress and gives Congress the power "to make all Laws which shall be necessary and proper for carrying into Execution the fore-going powers." The president's legislative powers are minimal. Article II provides for the president to inform Congress on the state of the union, to recommend "necessary and expedient" measures to Congress, to convene both Houses on extraordinary occasions, and to adjourn them in cases of disagreement between them. The Constitution also gives the president the power to veto legislation, the most effective formal power of the president in the legislative process.

In addition to the formal provisions for dividing the legislative power, the structure of government virtually guarantees conflict between the two branches. They have different constituencies. The president and vice president are elected by a national constituency, while each member of the House represents one congressional district of about 500,000 people and each senator represents one state. Local and regional interests often pull Congress, or important parts of it, in different directions than where the president wants to go.

Differing terms of office were designed to ensure that a popular wave of public opinion could not easily change the entire leadership of the country. Only one-third of Senate seats are up for election in any presidential election year. And even though all House seats are at risk each presidential election year, turnover in the House seldom exceeds 20 percent, and it is most often much less than that. In addition, House seats are not often heavily influenced by the presidential election, and this has especially been the case in recent decades. In fact, the political dynamics of House elections in the twentieth and early twenty-first centuries almost guarantee frustration for presidents, who most often lose support in the House during midterm elections.

In presidential election years, voter turnout is greater, and the party of the winner of the presidency often benefits by a gain in seats in the House. In the

TABLE 6.1 | MIDTERM LOSSES AND GAINS BY THE PRESIDENT'S PARTY

Year	President's Party	House	Senate
1934	D	+9	+10
1938	D	−71	−6
1942	D	−55	−9
1946	D	−55	−12
1950	D	−29	−6
1954	R	−18	−1
1958	R	−48	−13
1962	D	−4	+3
1966	D	−47	−4
1970	R	−12	+2
1974	R	−48	−5
1978	D	−15	−3
1982	R	−26	+1
1986	R	−5	−8
1990	R	−8	−1
1994	D	−52	−8
1998	D	+5	0
2002	R	+6	+2
2006	R	−29*	−6

*Seven house races were still undecided on November 17, 2006.
Source: Congressional Quarterly Weekly Reports (December 19, 1992), p. 3896; updated by author.

off-year elections, turnout is usually significantly lower, and the advantage of the additional voters for the president is missing. In addition, voters may be disillusioned by presidential performance, or the opposition party may be particularly active. Unusual circumstances in 1998 with the impeachment of President Clinton led to the Democrats gaining five seats in the House. This gain by the president's party was so unexpected that it precipitated the resignation of Speaker of the House Newt Gingrich. The unexpected also occurred in 2002 when Republicans gained seats in the House and Senate.[1] (See Table 6.1.)

The midterm congressional elections of 2006 returned to the normal pattern, and the Democrats took control of the House for the first time since 1994. But 2006 was also unusual in that national issues, particularly the war in Iraq, seemed to have a significant impact on the congressional elections. Usually congressional elections focus on local issues and candidates. But in 1994 the Republicans had "nationalized" the midterm elections by making their opposition to President Clinton a major factor in the race, and they won the House and the Senate convincingly. In 2006 the Democrats nationalized the elections by making President Bush and the war in Iraq the major issue in their campaigns. The Democrats, who benefited from unusually high voter turnout, were successful in capturing the House by a significant margin and in achieving a majority of 51 over the Republicans in the Senate.

Congress and the president are also likely to be in conflict because of the different characteristics of the two branches. Congress is necessarily collegial because of the principle of one vote per member. The executive branch, however, is hierarchical because the president holds most of the authority. The president can thus present a much more coherent and unified facade than can Congress, where disagreements are public and often dramatic. It is often said that public policy making is like producing sausages. The difference between the two branches is that in the executive branch the public only sees the end product, whereas in Congress the public gets to witness the ingredients (political fights, compromises, etc.) that go into the machine, as well as the product. This gives the president a rhetorical advantage in fights with Congress.

VETO POWER

The most powerful formal legislative power granted to the president is the right to veto a law that has been passed by both houses of Congress. To do so, the president returns the bill to the house of its origin with a message explaining the objections. The president's veto can be overridden, but only by the vote of a two-thirds majority of each house.

If, however, Congress sends a bill to the president and then adjourns within ten days (Sundays not included), the president can veto the bill by doing nothing. This "pocket veto" procedure is useful for presidents because it cannot be overridden. For it to be reconsidered, the bill must be reintroduced when Congress comes back into session and passed anew. Although some presidents have tried to exercise a pocket veto during short congressional recesses or at the end of a session, it is generally used at the end of a Congress.[2]

Early presidents did not use the veto power very actively, and some felt that it should be used only to protect the constitutional prerogatives of the president. George Washington vetoed only two bills, and John Adams and Thomas Jefferson did not use the veto at all. Andrew Jackson used the veto twelve times, more than the total number of vetoes cast until that time, and established that the veto could be used to disapprove any bill the president did not think was wise. After the Civil War, the veto came into much more common use, with Cleveland using it 414 times in his first term.

The veto is a powerful tool because it is so difficult to override. The president needs merely to get the votes of one-third plus one vote in either House for a veto to be sustained. Since a president can usually find this many votes among his party cohorts in Congress, only 107 of 2,569 vetoes were overridden between 1789 and 2001.[3] From 1988 to 1992, the Democratic Congress was able to override only one of President Bush's thirty-seven vetoes,

TABLE 6.2 | PRESIDENTIAL VETOES (1789–2006)

President	Regular Vetoes	Pocket Vetoes	Total Vetoes	Vetoes Overridden
George Washington	2	—	2	—
John Adams	—	—	0	—
Thomas Jefferson	—	—	0	—
James Madison	5	2	7	—
James Monroe	1	—	1	—
John Q. Adams	—	—	0	—
Andrew Jackson	5	7	12	—
Martin Van Buren	—	1	1	—
William H. Harrison	—	—	0	—
John Tyler	6	4	10	1
James K. Polk	2	1	3	—
Zachary Taylor	—	—	0	—
Millard Fillmore	—	—	0	—
Franklin Pierce	9	—	9	5
James Buchanan	4	3	7	—
Abraham Lincoln	2	5	7	—
Andrew Johnson	21	8	29	15
Ulysses S. Grant	45	48	93	4
Rutherford B. Hayes	12	1	13	1
James A. Garfield	—	—	0	—
Chester A. Arthur	4	8	12	1
Grover Cleveland	304	110	414	2
Benjamin Harrison	19	25	44	1
Grover Cleveland	42	128	170	5
William McKinley	6	36	42	—
Theodore Roosevelt	42	40	82	1
William H. Taft	30	9	39	1
Woodrow Wilson	33	11	44	6
Warren G. Harding	5	1	6	—
Calvin Coolidge	20	30	50	4
Herbert Hoover	21	16	37	3
Franklin Roosevelt	372	263	635	9
Harry S. Truman	180	70	250	12

President	Regular Vetoes	Pocket Vetoes	Total Vetoes	Vetoes Overridden
Dwight D. Eisenhower	73	108	181	2
John F. Kennedy	12	9	21	—
Lyndon B. Johnson	16	14	30	—
Richard M. Nixon	26	17	43	7
Gerald R. Ford	48	18	66	12
Jimmy Carter	13	18	31	2
Ronald Reagan	39	39	78	9
George H. W. Bush	29	15	44	1
William Clinton	36	1	37	2
George W. Bush*	1	—	1	1
Total	1,485	1,066	2,551	106

*Bush vetoes were through 2006.
Source: Office of the Clerk of the House of Representatives, "Presidential Veto" http://clerk.house.gov/histHigh/Congressional_History/vetoes.html

and the Republicans were only able to override two of President Clinton's thirty-eight vetoes from 1995 to 2001. While 2,500 vetoes between 1789 and 2001 may seem like a lot, the total number of bills vetoed by presidents amount to only about 2.6 percent of the more than 92,000 bills that have been passed and sent to the president.[4] As we would expect, vetoes are more likely when the president and Congress are not controlled by the same party. For instance, in his first two years in office President Clinton cast no vetoes; but after the Republicans captured Congress in 1994, he vetoed seventeen measures during the rest of his first term, with one veto being overridden by Congress.

Yet this very effective and seemingly powerful tool, when depended on too heavily, is a sign of weakness. That is, a president who is able to convince the Congress to pass his agenda, or who is able to modify bills to his liking before passage, is in a much more powerful position than one who must wait until an unacceptable bill is presented to him and then exercise his formal veto power. President Ford used a veto strategy, vetoing sixty-eight bills and having twelve overturned. But by resorting to the veto strategy, he reflected the weakness of his situation, being an unelected president following the Watergate scandals and facing the liberal Democratic Congress brought into office in the 1974 elections. (See Table 6.2.) The opposite situation was illustrated during unified government under President George W. Bush. He did not veto a single bill until halfway through his sixth year in office, a record matched by no president since Thomas Jefferson.

One legislative technique that came into frequent use in the modern period is called the "legislative veto." It has no constitutional foundation, but it has been written into legislation since 1932. The legislative veto is used when Congress is delegating power to the executive branch to make decisions in a broad program area. The legislation provides that whenever the power is used in a specific instance, such as passing a regulation or shifting funds among appropriation accounts, that Congress (or one house or a committee) be notified of the specific action and have the chance to disapprove that one application of the general delegated power. It was a technique intended to give Congress some control when a broad grant of discretion was delegated to the president, and it was used some 250 times between 1932 and 1980.[5]

Presidents, however, objected to its increasing use and argued that it was an unconstitutional restraint on the executive power. In 1983, the Supreme Court agreed with this argument in *Immigration and Naturalization Services v. Chadha*.[6] The Court ruled the legislative veto unconstitutional, arguing that it violated the separation of powers principle. It said that if Congress wanted to change legislation once passed, it must present it to the president as specified in the Constitution and give him a chance to veto it. While the formal decision stood, the legislative veto provided the kind of flexibility useful to both branches, and after 1983 the technique continued to be used both formally and informally.[7]

Although the Framers considered giving the president an absolute veto, one that could not be overridden, they never considered an "item veto," allowing the president to veto part of a bill while approving the rest of it. This type of partial veto, however, was included in the Confederate Constitution and has been adopted in the constitutions of forty-three of the fifty states. The item veto gives governors quite a bit of flexibility, particularly in appropriations legislation, in that they can strike out one or several projects from a broad bill that includes hundreds of itemized expenditures. Contemporary presidents have sought such power, and Presidents Ronald Reagan and George H. W. Bush proposed constitutional amendments to give it to the president, arguing that it would allow them to save the taxpayers' money by vetoing unwise "pork barrel" projects. But it was to Bill Clinton that Congress gave this legislative power. In the spring of 1996, Congress passed a law granting to the president, in effect, an item veto for spending measures. The procedure, technically called "enhanced rescission," allowed the president to reduce appropriation bills (or cancel part of narrowly targeted tax cuts) by rescinding, within five days, the portion to which he objected. These portions would then be sent back to Congress, which could then pass them separately within thirty days; but these bills would be subject to a regular veto, which would have to be overridden by the usual two-thirds majority in order for them to become law. Proponents of the item veto argued that such power would help reduce the deficit, but most federal spending is in uncontrollable expenditures such as entitlements, rather than in appropriations measures. Their expectation was also that presidents will be more fiscally responsible than Congress, an unproven assumption. But one of the effects of this innovation was to give the president significant potential new power in bargaining with individual members of Congress. The president might very well pressure members for support on large spending measures by threatening relatively smaller projects in their districts with an item veto.

During 1997 and 1998, President Clinton used the item veto sparingly and in a relatively nonpartisan way. But several cases challenging the constitutionality of the act were making their ways through the courts, and the Supreme Court decided in June 1998 that the act violated the Constitution. Justice John Paul Stevens, writing for a 6–3 majority, stated that the "cancellations pursuant to the Line Item Veto Act are the functional equivalent of partial repeals of Acts of Congress that fail to satisfy Article I, S.7." Although proponents of the item veto in Congress said that they would devise a grant of item veto power that passed constitutional muster, the Supreme Court decision made it much more difficult. The irony remains that Congress was willing to grant such a significant power that could only be used against congressional decisions.[8]

SIGNING STATEMENTS

Article I, Section 1 of the Constitution begins: "All legislative Powers herein granted shall be vested in a Congress of the United States, which shall consist of a Senate and House of Representatives." Article II of the Constitution provides that "the executive Power shall be vested in a President of the United States of America," and that "the President shall be Commander in Chief of the Army and Navy of the United States." Despite the Article II provision that the president "shall take Care that the Laws be faithfully executed," signing statements have been used to argue that Article II provisions trump Article I of the Constitution.

The idea of presidential signing statements begins with the reasonable presumption that each coordinate branch of government should have a role in interpreting the Constitution and its own constitutional powers. As James Madison said in Federalist No. 49, "The several departments being perfectly co-ordinate by the terms of their common commission, none of them, it is evident, can pretend to an exclusive or superior right of settling the boundaries between their respective powers." Thus, within the checks and balances of the Constitution, no single branch has the final say as to what the Constitution says or what public policy shall be. Each branch has a role in interpreting the Constitution, but each is subject to checks and balances from the other two branches.

Presidents since James Monroe have occasionally issued statements upon the signing of bills into law, though it was unusual for the first 150 years of the Republic. Most of these signing statements were rhetorical and meant to show presidential support for the legislation or occasionally to record publicly presidential reservations about the law. Rhetorical signing statements began to increase with the Truman administration. But the more important use of signing statements has been to register questions about the constitutionality of the law in question. The use of signing statements for this purpose began to be taken seriously during the Carter and Ford presidencies, but they took a significant jump during the Reagan presidency, during which they were used in a strategic manner to signify presidential disapproval of parts of a law.[9] (See Table 6.3.)

TABLE 6.3 | PRESIDENTIAL SIGNING STATEMENTS

President	Constitutional	Interpretive	Rhetorical	Total
Hoover	1	0	11	12
Roosevelt	0	3	48	51
Truman	3	7	108	18
Eisenhower	9	7	129	145
Kennedy	1	0	79	80
Johnson	11	2	289	302
Nixon	6	2	181	169
Ford	10	0	120	130
Carter	24	8	215	247
Reagan	71	23	94	276
Bush, G. H. W.	146	30	38	214
Clinton	105	21	265	391
Bush, G. W.				755*

*as of May 2006.

Source: Christopher S. Kelley, "'Faithfully Executing' and 'Taking Care'—The Unitary Executive and the Presidential Signing Statement," paper presented at the American Political Science Association annual convention, 2002. The 755 total for G.W. Bush is from: Charlie Savage, "Bush Challenges Hundreds of Laws," *Boston Globe* (April 30, 2006), Web site.

An important change was instituted in 1986 when the Reagan administration arranged with West Publishing Company to publish signing statements in the "Legislative History" section of *The United States Congressional Code and Administrative News* (USCCAN), which provides information about the background for the development of a law that might be relevant to its future interpretation by courts. Attorney General Edwin Meese explained that the purpose of the administration's action was so that the president's thinking when signing a bill into law "will accompany the legislative history from Congress so that all can be available to the court for future construction of what that statute really means."[10]

Such a purpose seems reasonable, because it merely calls to the attention of the courts the president's perspective on the law. This benign interpretation of signing statements, however, was undercut by Meese's later statement of the intent of signing statements in 2001, in which he said that in addition to expressing the president's view of a law, it would also indicate "those provisions of the law that might not be enforced."[11] There is a big difference between expressing an opinion on the meaning of a law and refusing to enforce the provision of a law of which a president disapproves. Presidents Carter, G. H. W. Bush, and Clinton occasionally used signing statements to indicate that they had reservations about the laws they were signing and might not enforce.

President George W. Bush, however, used signing statements to an unprecedented extent (as shown in Table 6.3). The total signing statements of all previous presidents included fewer than 600 challenges to the bills they signed (one signing statement can contain more than one challenge). President Bush issued more than 800 challenges in signing statements in his first six years in office.[12] He also used signing statements in unprecedented ways to assert the unilateral and unreviewable right of the executive to choose which laws to enforce and which to ignore. For instance, he has used them to indicate that he does not feel bound by all of the provisions of laws regarding reporting to Congress pursuant to the PATRIOT Act; the torture of prisoners, whistle-blower protections for the Department of Energy, the number of U.S. troops in Columbia, the use of illegally gathered intelligence, and the publication of educational data gathered by the Department of Education.[13]

Another way in which President Bush has used signing statements was to assert that he could withhold information from Congress and refuse to comply with laws requiring the executive branch to report information to Congress. In a signing statement accompanying the Intelligence Authorization Act for FY2002, for example, President Bush stated that he would construe the law "in a manner consistent with the President's constitutional authority to withhold information the disclosure of which could impair foreign relations, the national security, the deliberative processes of the Executive, or the performance of the Executive's constitutional duties."[14] That is, the administration would treat requirements in the law as "precatory" (that is advisory) rather than mandatory.

The point is not the reasonableness of the president's goals—for example, protecting national security—the problem is the assertion that the president alone has the right to make the determination of what is or is not constitutional. And if the president refuses to report his secret activities to Congress, there can be no independent check on the executive, as was the case with warrantless surveillance by the National Security Agency before it was revealed by the *New York Times* in 2005.

When President Bush signed into law the reauthorization of the Patriot Act (discussed in more detail later in the chapter), he also issued a signing statement claiming that "the executive branch shall construe the provisions . . . that call for furnishing information to entities outside the executive branch [i.e., Congress] . . . in a manner consistent with the president's constitutional authority to supervise the unitary executive branch and to withhold information. . . ."[15] Thus President Bush did not consider himself bound by any part of the law that he deemed might impinge on his own constitutional powers. The term "unitary executive branch" was repeated often in signing statements by President Bush and seemed to be intended to convey the assertion that the president has exclusive control of executive branch agencies and that Congress may not legislate regarding administrative matters. Over the course of U.S. history, however, Congress has often passed laws directly affecting the administration of the executive branch.

One problem with signing statements of this sort is that presidents can use them to achieve what the Framers decided not to give the president: an absolute veto. The constitutional process calls for bills to be passed by Congress and presented to the president for his signature or veto. But a signing statement, in effect, allows the president to sign the bill and later to decide if he does not want to comply with part of the law. It also allows the president to achieve, in effect, an item veto, which the Supreme Court has declared unconstitutional. In the passage of legislation, members of Congress often vote for a bill because of the assurances that certain provisions have meaning. But if the executive can unilaterally decide not to enforce whatever portion of laws it believes infringe on its constitutional power, the votes of members of Congress are effectively nullified.

The belief that he could selectively enforce the law pursuant to his signing statements may be part of the reason that President Bush did not issue any veto for the first five and a half years of his administration, a record unmatched since Thomas Jefferson. An example of the potentially unchecked nature of signing statements occurred when President Bush strongly opposed and threatened to veto the Detainee Treatment Act forbidding torture sponsored by Senator John McCain (R-Ariz). It was passed by both Houses of Congress by veto-proof majorities. President Bush signed the law in a ceremony at the White House with John McCain, symbolizing the administration's abjuring of using torture to obtain information from prisoners.

In his signing statement, however, President Bush indicated that he did not feel bound by the law: "The executive branch shall construe Title X in Division A of the Act, relating to detainees, in a manner consistent with the constitutional authority of the President to supervise the unitary executive branch and as Commander in Chief and consistent with the constitutional limitations on the judicial power...."[16] Thus the president reserved for himself the right to ignore the law when he deemed it to conflict with his commander-in-chief role, but he avoided the constitutional process of having to subject his veto to a possible override by Congress. Since the administration had previously asserted that Congress could not limit the way in which the executive treated prisoners, the implication was that it would not consider itself bound by the provisions of the law. It also seemed to claim in the signing statement that it could avoid judicial review.

The implications of these sweeping claims to presidential authority are profound and undermine the very meaning of the rule of law. Despite the Constitution's granting law-making power to the Congress, if the president maintains that presidential executive authority and the commander-in-chief clause can overcome virtually any law that constrains the executive, the executive was claiming unilateral control of the laws. If the executive claims that it is not subject to the law as it is written but can pick and choose which provisions to enforce, it is essentially claiming the unitary power to say what the law is. The "take care" clause of Article II can thus be effectively nullified. As Humpty Dumpty told Alice in this exchange from *Through the Looking Glass.*

> "When *I* use a word, it means just what I choose it to mean—neither more nor less."
> "The question is," said Alice, "whether you *can* make words mean so many different things." "The question is," said Humpty Dumpty, "which is to be master—that's all."[17]

The master in the U.S. constitutional system was intended to be the three branches of government, not just one.

The claim to such power might also be considered by a president to be retroactive, such as when President Bush decided that the provisions of the Foreign Intelligence Surveillance Act that required warrants for surveillance of communications in the U.S. did not bind him when he ordered NSA to conduct warrantless wiretaps (see Ch. 8). According to this precedent, any president could retroactively decide that some provision of a law was an unconstitutional infringement of his constitutional power and decide not to "faithfully execute the law in secret."

Defenders of President Bush's use of signing statements said that there was nothing to worry about, because President Bush would only use his claimed authority when necessary. But this misses the constitutional point. Precedents do not expire when one president leaves office. Even if one posits that the current president is a fine person of upstanding character who would not abuse executive power, future occupants of the Oval Office may not be of such character. As James Madison said in Federalist 10, "enlightened statesmen will not always be at the helm."

The Constitution does not give the president the right to decide not to execute the law. If there is a dispute about the interpretation of a law, the interaction of the three branches in the constitutional process, including the politics of passage, the choice to veto, and the right to challenge laws in court are all legitimate ways to deal with differences in interpretation; and each has a long record of use throughout U.S. history. But the assertion by the executive that it alone has the authority to interpret the law and that it will enforce the law at its own discretion is a dangerous claim.

In the summer of 2006, a prestigious task force of constitutional experts of the American Bar Association recommended a resolution on singing statements that stated:

> Resolved, That the American Bar Association opposes, as contrary to the rule of law and our constitutional system of separation of powers, the issuance of presidential signing statements that claim the authority or state the intention to disregard or decline to enforce all or part of a law the President has signed, or to interpret such a law in a manner inconsistent with the clear intent of Congress.[18]

THE PRESIDENT AS LEGISLATIVE LEADER

Early presidents were not very active in the legislative process. George Washington proposed only three specific laws to Congress, and after he was frustrated in seeking advice from the Senate about an Indian treaty, he carefully avoided the appearance of participation in legislative activities. Members of his cabinet, however, did attempt to influence legislation, and cabinet secretaries of Thomas Jefferson even helped formulate legislation.[19] For most of the rest of the nineteenth century, presidents, particularly the Whigs in the 1840s, who believed in legislative supremacy, were not active in the legislative process.

Lincoln was aggressive about legislation and presidential constitutional prerogatives, but after his administration Congress returned to domination for the rest of the century. Just as the federal government was not active in the national economy, so were presidents not active in the policy arena.

In the nineteenth century, in fact, Congress dominated the government to such an extent that the young scholar, Woodrow Wilson, entitled his doctoral dissertation *Congressional Government,* arguing that congressional domination of the national government after Lincoln led to ineffectual governance.[20] The twentieth century, and a more active federal government, brought changes in the presidency. President Theodore Roosevelt, with his activist view of the powers of the presidency, argued that "a good executive under the present conditions of American political life must take a very active interest in getting the right kind of legislation."[21] But even Roosevelt was hesitant to intrude too visibly in the legislative process. "Are you aware," he wrote to a critic, "... of the extreme unwisdom of my irritating Congress by fixing the details of a bill, concerning which they are very sensitive...."[22]

Foreshadowing the modern presidents, William Howard Taft's first attempt to present legislation formally to Congress was greeted with resentment for his meddling in the legislative process.[23] Woodrow Wilson, with the model of the British prime minister in mind, played an aggressive role in the legislative process, working with members in drafting some legislation in the White House. He symbolized his activism by personally addressing Congress in 1913, the first time a president had formally addressed Congress since Thomas Jefferson.[24]

But the real breakthrough for presidential participation in the legislative process was the unprecedented, and since unequalled, legendary "100 Days" of Franklin Roosevelt. Roosevelt was elected with the hope that he could do something about the Great Depression that was wracking the country. The stock market crash of 1929 had left the nation's economy in a shambles, with almost a quarter of the work force unemployed. Roosevelt was able to provide the leadership the country needed to regain its confidence.

Immediately after he was sworn into office on March 4, 1933, Roosevelt declared a bank holiday and, on March 9, called the Seventy-third Congress into special session to pass the Emergency Banking Act. Over the next 100 days, Congress passed a flurry of laws meant to deal with the economic crisis. All of the bills save one were drafted in the White House, with occasional participation by members of Congress, and while some amendments were considered, none of the proposals emanating from the White House was fundamentally changed. The president, for the first time, was acting as a prime minister in controlling the legislative agenda and directing the legislative process.[25]

The legislation passed during this historic period in 1933 between March 9 and June 16 included, among other laws:

Emergency Banking Act (to reform the banking system)

Civilian Conservation Corps (jobs for unemployed youth)

Abandonment of the gold standard (increasing the money supply)

Federal Emergency Relief Act (national welfare program)

Agricultural Adjustment Act (national agricultural policy)

Emergency Farm Mortgage Act (refinanced farm mortgages)

Tennessee Valley Authority Act (provided a government corporation to develop the Tennessee Valley)

Truth in Securities Act (required full disclosure of the financial situation of a firm selling new securities)

Home Owners Loan Act (refinanced home mortgages)

National Industrial Recovery Act (public works program and a system of industrial regulation)

Farm Credit Act (reorganized federal farm credit programs)

Emergency Railroad Transportation Act (coordinated the national railroad system)[26]

The significance of the 100 days was not just the number of laws passed but their effect in changing the role of the federal government in the economy and reversing the fundamental nature of the role of the federal government in the economic life of the nation.

Roosevelt's impressive legislative juggernaut was unequaled in American history, and it has not been matched since. The only periods of comparable importance were Lyndon Johnson in 1965 and Ronald Reagan in 1981. Johnson took advantage of the nation's grief over the death of Kennedy and the huge Democratic legislative majority that was elected in 1964 to push through Congress his Great Society legislation and to launch the War on Poverty, creating scores of programs and expanding the role of the federal government in social welfare areas in unprecedented ways.

In 1965 Johnson and his legislative cohorts pushed through a prodigious amount of legislation, and Congress refused only three of the eighty-three major bills of the administration. The laws created included, among others:

Medicare and Medicaid

Civil Rights Act of 1964

Elementary and Secondary Education Act

Higher Education Act

War on Poverty

Head Start

Air Pollution Control Act

Educational Opportunity Act

Safe Streets Act

Model Cities

Department of Housing and Urban Development

Department of Transportation

National Endowment for the Arts

National Endowment for the Humanities

Federal Water Pollution Control Act[27]

It is significant that four future conservative Republican presidents (Nixon, Ford, Reagan, and G. H. W. Bush), though denouncing active government, did not move to repeal any of the major components of the New Deal or the Great Society. After the elections of 1994, however, Republican-controlled congresses and the George W. Bush administration did attempt to cut back some of these programs.

President Reagan's triumph in 1981 was not due to the volume of legislation passed by Congress but to the far-reaching nature of the changes enacted. They included the largest tax cut in history, the largest peacetime increases in defense spending, and major cuts in the funding of domestic programs. Reagan's legislative victories symbolized a major change toward a more conservative direction of public policy and a change in attitude about the role of the federal government in the economy.

These historic legislative landmarks, however, were initial victories that came early in each president's term and were not followed by equivalent success. Each suffered legislative setbacks and frustrations at the hands of Congress. Thus, periods of cooperation between the president and Congress in passing major legislative programs are unusual in American history. The typical relationship is one of conflict and occasional victories by presidents, along with occasional thwarting of their wishes by Congress—much as the Framers seemed to intend.

The Political Fundamentals

Although Roosevelt's participation in the legislative process was active and intense, it was not institutionalized. He approached relations with Congress in an ad hoc manner, delegating to members of his cabinet and White House staff specific assignments to lobby Congress on particular pieces of legislation. It was left to his successors to institutionalize presidential participation in the legislative process.

When Harry Truman took over from FDR, he continued an activist approach to legislation and began the practice of formulating detailed legislative packages to send to Congress on an annual basis. Even though the Republicans in the Eightieth Congress elected in 1946 were not very cooperative in passing his legislative proposals, Truman continued to submit legislation in the spirit of FDR's New Deal.

President Eisenhower initially declined to send a legislative agenda to Congress, but under pressure from public and congressional expectations, he began to formulate an annual legislative program. To assist him and to serve as a buffer to demands from his own partisans on the Hill, Eisenhower established the Office of Congressional Relations (OCR) as a unit in the White House

Office. In 1960, when Larry O'Brien, who was going to handle legislative liaison for John Kennedy, came to ask the advice of Eisenhower's OCR director, Bryce Harlow, he was convinced of the necessity to retain the formal structure, organizing his operation much as Harlow had. O'Brien effectively led Kennedy's and Johnson's legislative liaison operation teams in pushing the liberal legislation championed by these activist presidents. Since then, the OCR has become an institutionalized unit in the White House Office and has played an important role in lobbying Congress for each succeeding administration.

The OCR cajoles members of Congress and occasionally twists arms, but presidential success in the legislative arena is most often determined by the fundamental political realities of the American political system. The basic reality is that the president is in a constitutionally weak position with respect to passing legislation, and the major factor that can bridge the constitutional gap is the party system. To get the votes to pass laws, presidents must start with the members of their party in each house. That is why the partisan balance is so important to a president's policy priorities. If presidents could determine only one factor to help their programs with Congress, it would be the number of members of their party in each house.

While presidents can count on their party members for a core of support in legislation they propose, they cannot count on consistent or unanimous support. This contrasts with parliamentary systems of government, in which party discipline is expected. In important legislative votes, the failure to vote with the party can result in exclusion from the party and being dropped from the ballot at the next election. Thus, on important issues, a prime minister can almost always count on the vote of members of his or her party in the parliament. In the United States, however, members of Congress run for office on their own and declare their membership in one political party. The political party cannot even prevent a person from running for office under the party banner. In 1990, David Duke ran a racist campaign for governor of Louisiana as a Republican, despite attempts by the national Republican Party to prevent him from using their party as a vehicle for his campaign.

If party members refuse to adhere to the party platform, or to vote with the party in Congress, there are few sanctions that can be imposed to punish them. But more importantly, the norms of Congress dictate that members' first allegiance is to their own political interests, even if constituent interests conflict with their party's position. While party cohesion in Congress has been increasing for the past decade or so, it does not solve the problem of lack of party discipline for presidents. While higher levels of party polarization can help presidents with their own party, it can also hurt them with members of the other party.

What this means to presidents is that they cannot count on the full vote of their party's contingent in Congress. In fact, even in key votes, presidents cannot count on support from members of their own party more than two-thirds of the time. But they can count on substantial opposition from the other party most of the time.[28] Thus, U.S. presidents are in the position of having to seek votes actively on most significant bills they support or oppose. The greater

TABLE 6.4 | PARTISAN SUPPORT FOR PRESIDENTS IN CONGRESS, 1953–2003*

	House		Senate	
	President		President	
	Democrat	Republican	Democrat	Republican
Democrats	71%	33%	70%	31%
Republicans	26%	66%	32%	72%

*On roll-call votes on which the winning side was supported by fewer than 80 percent of those voting.

Source: George C. Edwards and Stephen J. Wayne, *Presidential Leadership*, 7th ed. (Belmont, CA: Thomson Wadsworth, 2006), p. 339.

the margin of party members that presidents have in each house, the better their chances are when they begin to seek a majority of votes on any particular measure. (See Table 6.4.) While large majorities of partisans in each house help, there is no guarantee of legislative success. Nor is the lack of large partisan majorities necessarily fatal.

Recent trends in partisan voting have moved Congress closer to parliamentary patterns of support for the executive. With the polarization of congressional parties (explained later in this chapter), each party has increased its party discipline. For instance, "party voting," that is, when a majority of Democrats opposes a majority of Republicans, increased in the House from about 20 percent in the 1970s to 65 percent in the 1990s; in the Senate the increase was from 40 to 60 percent.[29] This has resulted in part from the increased power the parties have delegated to their leaders in Congress (especially the House). Party leaders have more tools to enforce discipline, and with narrow margins in Congress, the parties have greater incentives to prevent defections. Under House Speaker Dennis Hastert, enforced support for Bush administration initiatives was intensified by his insistence that before he would allow a bill to come to the floor for a vote, a "majority of the majority" must support it. That means that a cross-party coalition in support of a bill will not guarantee its coming to a vote unless a majority of the Republicans support it. The consequence is that fewer moderate measures make it through Congress.

Popularity with the public is one factor that may help a president in dealing with Congress, and presidents follow their public opinion polls carefully. The link between presidential popularity and success with Congress, however, is tenuous. It may be a necessary, but not sufficient, condition for congressional victories for the president. Public popularity certainly helped make possible FDR's 100 Days, Lyndon Johnson's huge victories in 1965, and Ronald Reagan's 1981 budget victories. Falling public popularity hurt President Truman from 1949 to 1952, and President Nixon in 1973 and 1974. But relatively high sustained public approval did not guarantee legislative success to presidents Eisenhower or Reagan in their second terms or George H.W. Bush in his first two-and-one-half years in office.

PRESIDENTIAL SKILLS

Given the inevitable difficulties presidents will have with Congress, what can they do to increase their chances of success with their legislative agendas? Despite fundamental constitutional and political problems, presidents can affect the fate of their proposals in Congress, and there is a rich lore on how presidents ought to handle Congress. One thing that a president can do is take a strategic approach to the administration's legislative agenda. This involves choosing which measures to put forth: Should they be ambitious or narrowly cautious? It involves volume: Should a president push many measures or concentrate on only a few? It involves timing: In what order and at what pace should measures be sent to Congress? A narrowly focused agenda with only a few major policy items can be called a "rifle" strategy, in contrast to a "shotgun" strategy in which many agenda items are pushed in Congress.

There is no one formula that will guarantee success, because presidents come to office with different political assets and at different times in the country's political history. President Johnson was successful with many legislative proposals, while President Carter was criticized for sending too many things to Congress at one time. President Reagan achieved impressive victories in his first year by concentrating on only a few priorities of sweeping character.

One generalization that seems to hold for modern presidents is that measures sent to Congress early in their first terms have a better chance of being passed than if they wait until later to send their most important initiatives. Scholar Paul Light has calculated that, from 1961 to 1978, 72 percent of those measures sent to Congress in the first three months of an administration eventually became law. During the second three months the rate of success dropped to 39 percent, and in the third three months to 25 percent.[30]

Several factors account for this predictable decline in legislative effectiveness. A new president usually enjoys a "honeymoon" with the public at the beginning of an administration, when the country wants to see the new president succeed. This feeling of goodwill is often reflected in Congress, which is willing to be more open-minded about presidential proposals than later in the term. Presidential popularity almost inevitably falls after the beginning of an administration, and as the midterm elections approach, members of Congress will begin to get nervous about their reelections and will be less likely to be sympathetic to presidents. According to Lyndon Johnson: "I keep hitting hard because I know this honeymoon won't last. Every day I lose a little more political capital. That's why we have to keep at it, never letting up. One day soon, I don't know when, the critics and the snipers will move in and we will be at stalemate. We have to get all we can, now, before the roof comes down."[31] The beginning of a term is also the best time to take advantage of the "mandate" of the voters from the election. Any mandate applies more to the person of the president than to any specific policy preferences, but managed skillfully, a claim for a mandate can be used to the president's advantage.

An example of the Johnson "treatment." President Lyndon B. Johnson was legendary for his ability to persuade members of Congress to support his bills. This series of photographs shows him in action with Democratic Senator Theodore E. Green of Rhode Island. (George Tames/New York Times Pictures)

Presidents are also well-advised to "court" Congress, that is, build up a reservoir of goodwill that can be called upon when it is needed in a close vote. Most presidents, being successful politicians, are sensitive to the need to pay their respects to members of Congress as individuals and Congress as an institution. At the beginning of administrations, they often invite members of their own party (and sometimes the opposition) to the White House for various political and social functions. Presidents Truman through Ford used to invite members of Congress to social gatherings on the presidential yacht, the *Sequoia,* for dinner, drinks, socializing, and even (in Truman's case) poker games. These were not occasions for arm-twisting or lobbying for specific votes, but rather for low-key socializing and building up the rapport that might help in later situations.

It is the job of OCR to keep in touch with members of Congress and be sensitive to their political needs. OCR also helps the president dole out favors to the administration's best advantage. Presidents consciously use a variety of carrots and sticks to reward friends and to punish political enemies. Social invitations to the White House are used to help cement support on the Hill. Those who do not vote with the president are removed from invitation lists.[32] Members of Congress can be invited to a photo session with the president and sent autographed copies of photos of them with the president.

They can be invited for flights on Air Force One or be given tickets to the presidential box at the Kennedy Center. Favors can also be arranged for key constituents, such as tours of the White House or birthday greetings from the president. Campaign help from popular presidents is in high demand during election years, and presidential campaign trips are used to good effect. President Kennedy once excluded a California congressman from a speech platform in his own district because of the member's failure to consistently

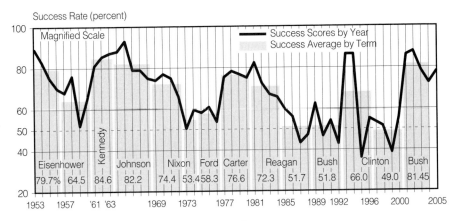

Success Rate (percent)

Success Rate History

Eisenhower		Johnson		Ford		Bush	
1953	89.0%	1964	88.0%	1974	58.2%	1989	62.6%
1954	82.8	1965	93.0	1975	61.0	1990	46.8
1955	75.0	1966	79.0	1976	53.8	1991	54.2
1956	70.0	1967	79.0			1992	43.0
1957	68.0	1968	75.0	Carter			
1958	76.0			1977	75.4%	Clinton	
1959	52.0	Nixon		1978	78.3	1993	86.4%
1960	65.0	1969	74.0%	1979	76.8	1994	86.4
		1970	77.0	1980	75.1	1995	36.2
Kennedy		1971	75.0			1996	55.1
1961	81.0%	1972	66.0	Reagan		1997	53.6
1962	85.4	1973	50.6	1981	82.4%	1998	50.6
1963	87.1	1974	59.6	1982	72.4	1999	37.8
				1983	67.1	2000	55.0
				1984	65.8		
				1985	59.9	Bush	
				1986	56.1	2001	86.7%
				1987	43.5	2002	87.8
				1988	47.4	2003	78.7
						2004	72.6
						2005	78.0

FIGURE 6.1 | PRESIDENTIAL SUCCESS WITH CONGRESS

Source: Congressional Quarterly Weekly Reports, December 19, 1992, p. 3896; December 21, 1996, p. 3428; January 3, 1998, p. 13; January 9, 1999, p. 86; December 14, 2002, p. 3275; December 11, 2004; January 9, 2006.

support the president's foreign policy legislation.[33] Small mementos are also used consciously and effectively. Members of Congress prize cufflinks with the presidential seal, and Richard Nixon kept careful track of who received them.[34]

Presidents often present to key supporters and members of Congress the pens they use to sign bills into law, which are mounted and framed along with a reproduction of the first page of the law that was enacted. Lyndon Johnson, wanting to make the most of these opportunities, often used multiple pens to sign the different letters of his name and the date of the signing. He set what must be a presidential record by using seventy-two pens to sign the Economic Opportunity Act of 1964; each pen was presented to one of those who worked with him on passage of the bill. One indicator of President Carter's rational rather than political approach to being president was his refusal to use more than two pens to sign legislation.[35]

Personal appeals for votes from the president can be very effective, because no member of the president's party wants to say no directly to the president, and no one wants to be subject to presidential wrath. President Reagan was able to win a key vote for his budget package in the spring of 1981 by placing a personal call to a member of Congress from Pennsylvania during a call-in radio talk show. A call from the president can even be effective with members of the opposition party. In March 1993, President Clinton was searching for votes on a bill and called Republican Senator James Jeffords, who was in Damascus, Syria. Senator Jeffords admitted that the call had an impact on him. "It was unbelievable," said Jeffords, "No matter how long we've been around the Hill, there's nothing more exciting than a call from the president."[36]

Presidents can even occasionally be persuasive when the vote they want seems to conflict with the political self-preservation of members of Congress. In August 1993, President Clinton was desperate for one vote in the House to break a 216–216 tie in order to pass his deficit-reduction budget package, the centerpiece of his first-year agenda. Every Republican had voted against it, and Clinton made a personal appeal to Democratic Representative Marjorie Margolies-Mezvinsky of Pennsylvania to save his agenda. Despite grave reservations about the feelings of her constituents about tax increases, she cast the tie-breaking vote for the president. Unfortunately, her loyalty to the president cost her the election in 1994, when she was defeated by her Republican opponent, who exploited her loyalty to Clinton and her vote for the tax-increase portion of his deficit reduction package.[37]

But personal appeals must be an unusual occurrence or their effectiveness will be diluted. According to a Carter aide: "You see, you have to be careful when you use the president. A visit with the president or a call from the president has to be an event in the life of a senator or representative, or it loses its magic. Or they say, 'Why should I give you a commitment? I want to talk to the president. John has talked to the president. And George has talked to the president. Are you taking us for granted?' You've got to be sure that you don't squander him."[38] The same point holds for patronage appointments or support on pork barrel projects. In an important battle for a key vote on an important bill, the president might trade a nomination for an appointment or make an administrative decision on the location of a federal project. But if these favors are used too freely, everyone will expect the same treatment, and there are not enough appointments or projects to please everybody.

Using appointments or projects as sticks to punish uncooperative members of Congress should be done sparingly. The principle is: Once in a while to make a point is acceptable, but not too often. Presidents do not want to be seen as too heavy-handed or too quick to seek revenge. But it is useful to be seen "cracking heads" occasionally to get what you want. When the Reagan administration wanted to get the vote of a Republican representative from Pennsylvania on a vote for selling planes to Saudi Arabia, the director of public affairs for the president said: "We just beat his brains out. That's all. We just took Jepson and beat his brains out."[39]

In another example, President Clinton decided to get tough after Democratic Senator Shelby of Alabama publicly opposed and consistently voted against his budget package in the spring of 1993. The administration transferred a NASA space program involving more than $300 million and ninety jobs from Alabama to Texas. To add insult to injury, Senator Shelby received only one ticket to a White House reception for Alabama's championship football team while his fellow senator from Alabama received more than twenty-five. Shelby subsequently switched his affiliation to the Republican Party.

CASES OF PRESIDENTIAL LEADERSHIP

This section considers several cases of presidential leadership of Congress to illustrate the different relationships recent presidents have had with Congress. The Kennedy and Johnson cases show the different approaches to the Democratic Congress that each president employed. Nixon and Reagan took different approaches to achieving their agendas in the face of divided government. Jimmy Carter, despite a Democratic Congress, had mixed success with his legislative agenda. The next case shows Bill Clinton first facing a Democratic Congress, which gave him mixed support, and then a Republican Congress with which he had a much lower success rate and several confrontational showdowns. The final case shows how George W. Bush, with a minimal electoral mandate, was able to achieve legislative success with Congress.

KENNEDY AND THE HOUSE RULES COMMITTEE: BEHIND-THE-SCENES LEADERSHIP

The 1960 election was a squeaker. Kennedy won by a very narrow margin and could claim no mandate with which to convince the Congress that his program was the overwhelming preference of the American electorate. The congressional elections were no help for Kennedy's liberal agenda; the Democrats lost twenty-one seats in the House. Despite having served in both houses of Congress, Kennedy was not able to use his experience to create early legislative victories.

The overall partisan margins in Congress were substantial and should have been reassuring to the Democrats, with a 262–174 advantage in the House and a 65–35 majority in the Senate. But the political reality was that a conservative coalition of Republicans and southern Democrats had made a common cause since the 1930s of defeating liberal, and especially civil rights, legislation. (The same coalition would combine three decades later, in 1981, to pass Ronald Reagan's conservative agenda.) The reason that the southern Democrats were so conservative was that the South had been a conservative region but was solidly Democratic, and no budding ambitious politician could have won running as a Republican. So southern conservatives ran as Democrats and were returned year after year to Congress, since the South, for all practical purposes, was a one-party region. The combination of this certain longevity with the seniority system in Congress magnified the power of the southern block beyond its mere numbers. The member with the most seniority on a committee was automatically its chair, and many key committees were chaired by southern conservative Democrats. In 1964, the twenty-one House committee chairmen averaged 76.6 years of age.[40]

The House Rules Committee is the "traffic cop" for all House legislation and has to act on each bill before it goes to the floor for consideration. Since the House has so many members, allowing legislation to be introduced in a free-for-all fashion would lead to chaos. Thus, House procedures provide that each piece of legislation has to have a "rule" from the rules committee that specifies when it will be taken up and under what conditions of amendment and debate. In the early 1960s, when the committee chair held most of the reins of power, the chairman of the rules committee was the conservative Howard Smith of Virginia. In addition to Smith, the other key member was a fellow conservative, William Colmer of Mississippi. Neither Smith nor Colmer, though Democrats, had supported Kennedy in the campaign, and together with the six Republicans on the rules committee, they would be able and willing to block any legislation they deemed too liberal—what amounted to most of Kennedy's legislative agenda.

Not even Speaker of the House Sam Rayburn had the power to overcome this procedural barrier to getting legislative proposals out of committee and onto the floor of the House for a vote, where Kennedy's proposals would at least have a chance. So Rayburn and Kennedy decided soon after the convening of the Congress, and even before Kennedy was inaugurated, to attempt to enlarge the rules committee by three members, two Democrats (who would be liberals) and one Republican, which would give the liberal supporters of Kennedy a thin 8–7 majority that would vote to get Kennedy's legislative proposals to the floor for a vote by the whole House.

Kennedy was well aware of the sensitivities of members of the House who might resent a president interfering with its internal procedures, so Kennedy decided not to take a visible role in the conflict. In a public statement, he said merely: "It is no secret that I would strongly believe that the members of the House should have an opportunity to vote ... on the programs which we will present—not merely the members of the rules committee.... But the responsibility rests with the members.... I merely give my view as an interested citizen."[41] But when it became clear that the fight would be close and victory was not ensured, Kennedy entered the fight behind-the-scenes and put the full lobbying power of his new administration behind the vote on enlarging the rules committee. As head legislative liaison, Larry O'Brien took head counts and was very active in using all of the tricks of his trade to win votes, including patronage and promises of executive branch action.

Members of the cabinet were also pressed into service to change the minds of those who would have opposed the new rules. At the end, Kennedy made several personal phone calls to try to persuade wavering members. The final vote was victorious for the Kennedy forces, with 217–212 in favor of expanding the rules committee. Sixty-four Democrats voted against the rules change and twenty-two Republicans voted for it.

The striking thing was that even with all of the stops pulled and an all-out effort by a newly elected president and House leadership, the margin of victory was only five votes. This foreshadowed the future difficulties the administration would have with much of its liberal agenda. Members of the conservative coalition, who were briefly defeated in the fight over the rules committee, would combine again to frustrate liberal Kennedy initiatives in Medicare, federal aid to education, creation of an urban affairs department, and most visibly, civil rights legislation. Experience with Congress during his first two years in office led Kennedy to be pessimistic about the use of presidential power to get his way with legislation: "Party loyalty or responsibility means damn little. They've got to take care of themselves first." The Congress, Kennedy said, "looks more powerful sitting here [in the White House] than it did when I was ... one of a hundred in the Senate."[42]

This early experience with Congress explains in part Kennedy's reluctance to introduce bold and sweeping legislative proposals. The president's brother, Robert F. Kennedy (his attorney general), argued that the House rules committee fight was indicative of Kennedy's lack of influence with Congress, particularly southern conservatives. "[H]ere we had Sam Rayburn and, therefore, the Texas delegation.... [W]e had the maximum strength.... [Y]et we only won it by a couple of votes.... How much more difficult it was when the odds were much higher against us!"[43]

LBJ's ACTIVIST APPROACH: THE 1964 CIVIL RIGHTS ACT

For the eighty years between the withdrawal of Union troops from the South in 1876 until 1956, no civil rights legislation had been passed by Congress. Southern conservatives, all Democrats, had been able to prevent any consideration of legislation through the skillful use of parliamentary tactics. As national attitudes began to change in the mid-twentieth century and the civil rights movement began to become more active, liberals began to make some progress in Congress, though not with major breakthroughs. The Civil Rights Act of 1957 was historic, not for its substance, for its provisions were substantially watered down by the time conservatives allowed its passage, but for the very fact that it was passed at all. The 1960 Civil Rights Act was passed in a similarly weak state.[44]

As president, John Kennedy favored civil rights legislation, but his election in 1960 was very close, and he needed the support of southern Democrats in Congress and southern states' votes for his reelection in 1964. Though he supported civil rights as president, he was unwilling early in his term to introduce serious legislation to change the reality of segregation in the country.

But his attitude changed in May 1963, when the city police chief of Birmingham, Alabama, Bull Connor, used police dogs, fire hoses, and cattle prods to break up nonviolent demonstrations. The televised film of these brutal tactics moved the nation, and John Kennedy decided to send to Congress a serious civil rights bill.

The bill, written in June 1963, would enforce equal access to all public accommodations and would cut off federal funds to states that allowed segregation in their schools. The bill was being considered in the House judiciary committee when Kennedy was assassinated in Dallas in November 1963.

When Johnson became president after the assassination, he was in a relatively weak position because of the way he had become president. He had succeeded to the office rather than being elected in his own right, and thus he could not argue that he had a mandate for his policy agenda. He also faced the same partisan, regional situation in Congress that Kennedy had faced. Johnson did, however, have several advantages with respect to civil rights. First, he was a southerner, and his decision to support civil rights for blacks would not hurt him as much in the South as it would have the northeastern Kennedy. Secondly, Johnson had been Senate majority leader and was a masterful legislative tactician. He would have to use all of his skills in seeking passage of Kennedy's civil rights bill, which he decided to back without any of the compromises that had been expected to water down the bill.

The first step Johnson had to take was to get the bill through the House. Since the judiciary committee, which had jurisdiction, was chaired by liberal northern Democrat Emanuel Celler, the bill was dealt with favorably. The real problem was the House rules committee. Despite the expanded membership, its chairman, Howard Smith of Virginia, was going to use every trick at his disposal to prevent the bill from being considered before the full House, where it would have passed. In the past, when he wanted to block civil rights legislation, Chairman Smith would disappear from the Capitol and go out to his farm in rural Virginia, thus preventing the committee from meeting. When he used this tactic in opposing the 1957 Civil Rights Act, his staff said that he had to return to his farm to inspect a barn that had burned down. When Speaker Sam Rayburn heard this he said, "I knew Howard Smith would do most anything to block a civil rights bill, but I never knew he would resort to arson."[45]

Smith was using his wiles again in 1963 to fight the Kennedy-Johnson proposal. Since the bill could not be considered by the floor unless it was reported out by the rules committee, the only way to pry the bill from Smith's clutches was to have a majority of House members sign a discharge petition, which would force the bill to floor consideration. By Christmas 1963, the petition was still fifty votes short of the needed majority, but Johnson and the leadership in the House put enough pressure on unwilling members and Smith that Smith finally bowed to the inevitable and allowed the bill to go to the floor before the discharge petition forced him to do it. On the floor of the House, the bill's proponents were able to defeat every amendment in the ten days of debate, and it passed the House on February 10, 1964, by a 290–130 margin.

But the Senate brought an even tougher battle. Senator James O. Eastland of Mississippi was chair of the judiciary committee and had been able to use his powers as chair to kill more than 100 proposed civil rights bills in the 1950s and 1960s. But his powers as chair were effectively evaded when the Senate leadership, which held much of the same scheduling power as the rules committee held in the House, was able to place the bill directly on the Senate calendar, thereby bypassing the judiciary committee completely.

The roadblock to Senate floor consideration and a vote on the civil rights bill, which was likely to pass if it came up for a vote, was the filibuster. Unlike the House, which due to its greater numbers must be run more tightly, the Senate, through Rule XXII, allows unlimited debate by members before a measure is brought to a vote. The only route around a filibuster is a vote for cloture, which took a two-thirds majority to pass (changed to three-fifths in 1975). A vote for cloture places a limit on debate and allows a bill to be brought to the floor for a vote. The filibuster is a parliamentary tactic that can be used by a few senators to prevent legislation from coming to a vote, and a failure to win cloture keeps the filibuster alive and prevents a vote on a bill.

There is no requirement that debate has to be relevant to the legislation under consideration, and senators in marathon talkfests would read from the Bible or cookbooks, merely to keep the floor until, on the verge of exhaustion, they would yield the floor to a colleague who would keep up the fight. Leadership tactics to fight a filibuster included round-the-clock sessions to wear out the talkers, but the filibusterers were often up to the challenge, with the record being held by Democratic Senator Strom Thurmond of South Carolina in the filibuster against the Civil Rights Act of 1957, who talked for more than twenty-four hours.[46] Cloture is very difficult to achieve because many senators feel that it is one of the few tactics they can use as a last resort to protect their own vital interests.

By use of the filibuster, or its mere threat, southern conservatives had been able to stop civil rights legislation from being considered by the Senate for years, and senators had never been able to get the votes to invoke cloture to end the debate on a civil rights bill. In the 1964 battle, Johnson knew that the southerners would use the filibuster, and he arranged for the decks to be cleared by getting the Senate to pass all the legislation he wanted considered in the first half of 1964 so that a filibuster would not create pressure to give up the civil rights fight merely to get other legislation considered.

So Johnson let the filibuster drone on through April and the beginning of May before he made his move to get the necessary votes for cloture. In his move, Johnson called in favors from years as Senate majority leader and used all of his leverage as president. To get the necessary votes, Johnson knew he had to enable moderate Republicans to vote for the bill. To convince them and to provide them political cover, Johnson courted his old colleague, minority leader Everett McKinley Dirksen of Illinois, and maneuvered so that Dirksen would get credit for his contribution to the civil rights victory. "I deliberately tried to tone down my personal involvement . . . so that a hero's niche could be carved out for Senator Dirksen, not me."[47]

Senate Democratic whip Hubert Humphrey represented Johnson in negotiations with Dirksen to work out a compromise that would satisfy both the civil rights advocates and Republican moderates. During May and early June an acceptable compromise was worked out, and on June 10 the Senate, for the first time in its history, used a cloture vote to force consideration of a civil rights bill. The historic breakthrough civil rights bill went through Congress and was signed by Johnson on July 2, 1964.

When Johnson was elected in his own right—by a landslide—in the November 1964 elections, he went on to push through his Great Society legislative agenda, which was historic in its scope and volume. But his sweeping success—eighty of eighty-three of his major proposals were enacted in 1965—was due in large part to the Democratic majorities in Congress that came in with him after the 1964 elections. In the Eighty-ninth Congress, the Democrats had a 295–140 majority in the House and a 68–32 advantage in the Senate. While the legislation of the Eighty-ninth Congress was of historic proportions, the battle for the 1964 Civil Rights Act demonstrated that presidents usually have to fight for what they get from Congress. It also showed how skillful a fighter Lyndon Johnson was before the 1964 elections.

RICHARD NIXON: THE POLITICS OF CONFRONTATION

In 1968, Richard Nixon was elected in a very close race, winning only 43.4 percent of the vote to Hubert Humphrey's 42.7 percent (with third-party candidate George Wallace winning most of the remainder). Despite his lack of a majority at the polls, Nixon believed that he had a mandate from the people because the electorate of the presidency is national, while the electorate of Congress is confined to individual states and congressional districts. Nixon initially intended to be an activist president, but when he tried to get the Congress to go along with his conservative proposals, he became disillusioned. He found that the Democrats who controlled Congress, many of whom had voted for the Great Society legislation of Lyndon Johnson, were not about to be accomplices in its dismantling. Nixon's response to his inability to dominate the domestic agenda of the country was to "*take over* the bureaucracy and *take on* the Congress."[48] That is, Nixon used his powers as chief executive officer of the government, to their fullest extent, to achieve his policy goals. He also used, to the fullest extent, his constitutional powers as president against the Congress. In the end, he pushed some of his claimed authority beyond legal and constitutional bounds.

One of the main levers of power in government is the control of the money to run programs. That is why the Framers split the power of the purse between the two branches, giving Congress the power to appropriate money, subject to presidential veto, and to the president the authority to spend the funds in carrying out the laws. Nixon decided that if he could not get Congress to make the cuts and programmatic changes in the budget that he proposed, then he would do it himself by refusing to spend money that had been provided by Congress in law.

Other presidents, in order to save money and to cancel particular projects within broader programs had also refused to spend appropriated funds.

Presidents Truman, Eisenhower, and Kennedy cancelled some military spending, and President Johnson impounded some domestic funds, though he released them when Congress made a fuss. With these precedents in mind, President Nixon decided to make impoundment the cornerstone of his domestic budget policy by refusing to spend funds on programs he disapproved of, regardless of the law or Congress.[49]

But Nixon's impoundments departed from the actions of all previous presidents in several important ways:

1. He impounded larger amounts than any previous president, from 1969 to 1972 impounding 17 to 20 percent of controllable expenditures.[50]
2. He refused to spend funds despite explicit expressions of intent by Congress in law, and preambles to laws, that they be spent.
3. He tried to use impoundment to eliminate entire programs, rather than merely individual projects within larger programs.
4. He withheld funds from programs that were not included in his budget proposal to Congress, though Congress had not yet acted on his proposed budget.
5. He claimed to have the constitutional power to impound funds.

According to Nixon, "The Constitutional right of the President of the United States to impound funds, and that is not to spend money, when the spending of money would mean either increasing prices or increasing taxes for all the people—that right is absolutely clear."[51] No other president had ever made that claim.

What is important about Nixon's constitutional claim is that if it were true, Nixon would be free to ignore the will of Congress and the law of the land. Thus, President Nixon proceeded to impound funds from programs that he thought should not be funded, and his actions were challenged in federal courts throughout the country. One of the cases that finally got to the Supreme Court provides a useful illustration of Nixon's interpretation of the Constitution.

In the fall of 1972, Congress and the president were engaged in a battle over spending priorities, with the president seeking to cut expenditures. When Congress refused to grant him the unilateral authority that he had requested to cut spending for fiscal year 1973, he decided to veto the Federal Water Pollution Control Act amendments that provided $11 billion in 1973 and 1974 for building water-pollution abatement plants. His grounds for the veto were that it was too much money to spend. So far things were perfectly constitutional, but when both houses of Congress voted to override his veto, he decided to impound the funds anyway. He instructed the Environmental Protection Agency to expend less than half the funds provided in the legislation.

As might be expected, this action was appealed in federal court along with scores of other impoundment cases. The Nixon administration did not fare well when its impoundment actions were examined by judges. The administration was not able to convince even one judge to declare that the president had the power to impound funds unilaterally. Some cases were dismissed on the basis of

standing or justiciability, but none were won on their merits by the administration. The court of appeals found that

> when the executive exercises its responsibility under appropriation legislation in
> such a manner as to frustrate the Congressional purpose, either by absolute refusal
> to spend or by a withholding of so substantial an amount of the appropriations as to
> make impossible the attainment of the legislative goals, the executive trespasses
> beyond the range of its legal discretion....[52]

The Supreme Court also decided against President Nixon in a 9–0 decision. It
decided the case on the legislative provisions of the Water Pollution Control
Act, but made a broad statement about the arguments of the Nixon
administration:

> As conceived and passed in both Houses, the legislation was intended to provide a
> firm commitment to substantial sums within a relatively limited period of time in an
> effort to achieve an early solution of what was deemed an urgent problem. We
> cannot believe that Congress at the last minute scuttled the entire effort by pro-
> viding the Executive with the seemingly limitless power to withhold funds from
> allotment and obligation.[53]

The alarming aspect of the use of impoundment by President Nixon is that
it amounted to a unilateral and absolute veto power for the president. If the
president could refuse to spend money appropriated in law, even after an
override of a veto, the president would possess a power that was explicitly
rejected by the Framers.

In reaction to the Nixon claims to impoundment power, Congress passed
the Congressional Budget and Impoundment Control Act of 1974. The act
reformed the congressional budget process and severely limited the president's
ability to impound funds. In the future, presidents would have to submit their
proposed impoundments to Congress before they could legally take effect.

The impoundment controversy was not the only way that President Nixon
decided to confront Congress. He also attempted to assert a pocket veto during
a five-day Christmas recess, when Congress had made provisions to receive any
regular veto message. He appointed an acting director to the Office of Economic Opportunity in order to avoid the Senate's confirmation authority.
When the acting director began to dismantle the agency and impound funds
while the laws for its existence and funding were still on the books, he was
taken to court. President Nixon lost both of these court battles over his constitutional power.

Nixon also confronted the Congress over presidential war powers,
resulting in the passage, over his veto, of the War Powers Resolution of 1973.
He asserted a blanket authority for executive privilege with respect to the
Watergate tapes, but he was rebuffed by a 9–0 decision of the Supreme Court.
These assertions of presidential power by the Nixon administration were the
culmination of what some called the "Imperial Presidency."[54] Congressional
reaction to them, in laws that limited actions by the executive and reformed
internal procedures in Congress, transformed relations between the branches,
though all of the reforms did not have the results intended by their proponents.

JIMMY CARTER: THE MORAL EQUIVALENT OF WAR

When Jimmy Carter was elected, Democrats in Congress held high expectations for a productive legislative relationship. The Nixon period of divided government was ended, with the presidency and both houses of Congress controlled by the Democrats: 292–143 in the House and 61–38 in the Senate. Carter intended to be an activist president and had a number of legislative proposals to tackle major policy problems, such as welfare reform, health care, the tax system, and energy.

The major legislative effort in his first year was energy legislation. Since the 1973 oil embargo by OPEC (Organization of Petroleum Exporting Countries), U.S. dependence on foreign nations for oil had become obvious and worrisome, but the United States had not been able to do anything to change it. Between 1973 and 1976 the price of gasoline almost doubled, but still the United States increased its dependence on imported oil from 35 percent to almost 50 percent.[55]

Carter had talked about the energy problem in his presidential campaign, but he had not laid out specific proposals or made it a centerpiece of his drive for the presidency. After the election, he designated James Schlesinger, an economist who had been appointed secretary of defense by President Nixon, to take charge of the administration's energy policy and to be his secretary of energy when the department was created in 1977. Carter gave Schlesinger ninety days from the inauguration to come up with a comprehensive proposal to deal with the nation's energy problems. This was a tight time frame, given the complex nature of the policy problem as a technical issue and the formidable political obstacles that would have to be overcome if basic changes were to be proposed.

Schlesinger and his team carried out the task virtually in complete secrecy. This was useful from a technical perspective, since the issues were so complex, and politically it kept the various provisions from being leaked piecemeal and shot down before they could be formally presented. But from another political perspective, the secrecy was a major hindrance. Members of Congress, who would have to vote on all of the provisions, were not brought into the process or even informed of the provisions. They felt left out, and they did not have advance warning to formulate their own reactions or explain them to their constituents. But even Carter administration officials whose jurisdictions would be affected by the policies were not informed until very late. Two weeks before the plan was unveiled, Vice President Mondale, CEA Chairman Charles Schultze, and OMB Director Bert Lance had not been informed of the plans.[56]

Schlesinger's plan was ready in the required ninety days, and on April 18 Carter appeared in a nationally televised speech to announce his energy package. Carter preached to the American people that they had been wasteful in the past and that his plan would call for sacrifice. "Ours is the most wasteful nation on earth. We waste more energy than we import." His energy plan would "test the character of the American people" and would amount to "the moral equivalent of war."[57] By his secrecy and rhetoric, Carter was staking the administration's prestige on passage of the energy package. Two days later he presented the specifics of his proposal to a joint session of Congress.

The major elements of the proposal included a gasoline tax increase (if gas consumption exceeded the previous year's), a tax on gas-guzzling cars, a tax on crude oil, conservation tax credits, continued control of natural-gas prices (with some price increases), utility rate reforms, mandatory industrial conversion from oil to coal, and the development of alternative energy sources such as nuclear and solar power.[58] One of the problems was that all of the elements did not fit neatly into one piece of legislation. The plan had 113 interlocking provisions that fit together in a complex way and affected different parts of the economy in different ways.[59]

Another problem was that there was no natural constituency for the legislation. Even though most observers would admit that dependence on foreign oil had hurt the U.S. economy and was a potential threat to U.S. security, there was no consensus about what to do about it. The Carter plan promised diffuse benefits (i.e., everyone would benefit a little through a sounder economy) but concentrated costs. Costs would be borne by consumers in the form of higher prices for car fuel and heating oil, and the plan would hurt producers by cutting into their profits. In his appeal to the public, Carter was not able to convince people that the crisis was as bad as he judged it to be or that his package was the solution to the problem. Industries that opposed the legislation were very effective in lobbying Congress, and oil-producing states had powerful representatives on the Hill. Carter complained that "The influence of the special interest lobbies" was "almost unbelievable, particularly from the automobile and oil industries."[60]

The administration wanted the legislation considered in Congress as a single package rather than in separate pieces, a difficult task because the various provisions fell into the jurisdictions of seventeen House committees and subcommittees. But Speaker of the House Thomas P. "Tip" O'Neill was able to manage this tactical problem by creating a special Ad Hoc Select Committee on Energy. The administration bill passed the House relatively intact (except for the gas-tax increase) by early August 1977. The Senate, however, was another story. The package was split into five separate bills to be considered by the Energy and Natural Resource and the Finance Committees. Carter did not have the help in the Senate that he got from Speaker O'Neill in the House, and the debate dragged on over two months, with an attempted filibuster by liberals, who did not want to see natural-gas prices deregulated. The Senate finally passed an energy bill in late October, but several key provisions of the Carter package were significantly changed. The Senate voted to deregulate natural gas, and it rejected the crude-oil tax, the gas-tax increase, and the declining rate structures for utilities.[61]

Carter renewed his efforts in 1978 and was much more effective in his approach to Congress. A conference committee was created to consider the different House and Senate bills, and compromises were worked out over the next eight months. The several provisions were put together in a five-part package that passed in the Senate but survived in the House by only one vote. The bill got through Congress on October 15, 1978, a year and a half after Carter had presented his proposals to Congress. The National Energy Act provided for the gradual deregulation of natural gas, a major change from Carter's original intention. It increased energy taxes a bit and required that electric power plants convert to coal. It required states only to *consider* restructuring of rates for utilities, and it included a number of other conservation measures.[62]

Thus, President Carter got an energy package passed, but it did not contain a good portion of what he had proposed in 1977. What problems prevented Carter from getting most of what he wanted in the most important legislative priority of his first year in office? The first problem was the nature of the policy itself. Energy policy is complex, and the Carter proposals did not guarantee a solution to the problem of dependence on foreign oil. Second, the plan distributed a lot of pain without enumerating concrete benefits that were certain to follow.

But changed relations between the presidency and Congress also affected the outcome. The reaction of Congress to the Nixon administration made the institution less willing to be cooperative with any president, even a Democrat. The internal reforms of the 1970s had fragmented power within the Congress. The leadership held less power to coerce their party troops to go along, and there were more individual members who wanted a piece of the action. Thus, presidents had to retail, rather than wholesale, their appeals for support on legislation. That is, they had to deal with many individual members rather than with only a few leaders. Carter expressed his frustration in his memoirs: "I learned the hard way that there was no party loyalty or discipline when a complicated or controversial issue was at stake—none. Each legislator had to be wooed and won individually. It was every member for himself, and the devil take the hindmost!"[63]

But Carter was also at fault. Part of the lack of party loyalty to Carter may have resulted from Carter's decision to run for president as an outsider rather than as a traditional Democratic party regular. Despite his effectiveness in electoral politics, Carter held a disdain for bargaining with Congress and communicated this in his dealings with its members. He felt that his policy proposals were best for the country and that members of Congress ought to support them on their merits without special efforts by him to court their votes or bargain for support. His first legislative liaison team was inexperienced, and the administration committed some early mistakes that alienated some members of Congress.

By the end of 1977, the Carter administration had learned many of the hard lessons about Congress and was much more effective in its relations with the Hill. Carter's overall legislative record compares favorably with the other modern presidents, but his early mistakes with Congress kept him from being as successful as he might have been.[64]

RONALD REAGAN: THE FY1982 BUDGET JUGGERNAUT

In 1980, Ronald Reagan won a resounding electoral victory over Jimmy Carter and promised to cure the economy of high inflation and balance the budget by 1984. He promised to cut taxes, to drastically reduce domestic spending, and to restore America's military forces. No one doubted his intentions, but many doubted his ability to make good on these campaign promises. Skeptics said the momentum of federal spending, combined with the power of both the Democrats in Congress and of the beneficiaries of federal programs, would be too powerful even for a popular president to reverse.

But contrary to most expectations, Reagan was able to accomplish much of his agenda, though not with his charisma alone. The historic budget victories of Reagan's first year were the result of careful planning, singleness of purpose, and speed of execution. At the same time, broader forces favored the administration: There were no major foreign policy crises, the electorate was in the mood for a change, the economy was in a mess, and the Democrats were in disarray.[65]

David Stockman, who had spent two terms as a member of Congress from Michigan, began planning for the budget changes before the election. Stockman's intimate knowledge of the budgetary process, his command of the budget details, and his skills in congressional procedure were crucial to the Reagan budget victories. As soon as Stockman took over as director of OMB, he put the staff to work reversing their efforts to construct the last Carter budget and planning the drastic changes that Reagan sought.

The capture of the Senate by Republicans for the first time since 1954 made the task of the administration much easier. Senate backing of early Reagan proposals could be taken virtually for granted. The House was another matter because it was controlled by the Democrats by a 243–192 majority. The new administration contemplated drastic changes, and getting the Democratic House to go along was a major challenge. The soft spot in Democratic control of the House was the block of forty-seven conservative southern Democrats in the Conservative Democratic Forum, better known as the "Boll Weevils." In its campaign to win House support for its budget priorities, the White House decided that these members were particularly vulnerable to administration pressure.

The administration used its most important asset, the president, very effectively. The public campaign was conducted by a series of formal presidential addresses, as well as hundreds of informal comments to the press. In a televised address February 5, 1980, the president warned of an "economic calamity of tremendous proportions" if Congress refused to pass his program. On February 18, he addressed a joint session of Congress to present his "Program for Economic Recovery" along with an inch-thick document explaining his approach to fiscal and monetary policy. This was followed by another address to Congress on March 10 and the release of "Fiscal Year 1982 Budget Revisions," the detailed OMB proposals. During the same period, members of the cabinet and the Council of Economic Advisers were also pushing the administration's proposals throughout the country.

The first crucial votes on the administration program came in the House on May 7, when the first concurrent resolution came up for a vote. The purpose of the resolution was to lay out the total revenues, spending, and deficit targets for the next fiscal year. In a tactical maneuver, the Republicans had succeeded in forcing consideration of the package of budget cuts and spending priorities as a whole rather than in pieces that might have been defeated one at a time by the

Democrats. After several weeks of intense lobbying by the administration sixty-three Democrats defected, and the House passed the budget package for the first concurrent resolution 253–176. These first crucial votes demonstrated the Reagan team could control the Democratic House in the budget battle.

The details of the cuts still had to be worked out in the reconciliation package in June. The Democrats put together a package that provided 85 percent of what the administration wanted, but with a smaller deficit. But the Republicans refused the compromise and proposed a substitute called "Gramm-Latta II" for the administration's vehicle. The administration again pulled out its heavy guns to lobby the House Democrats. The president himself called or telegraphed each of the sixty-three Democrats who had voted with him on the first budget resolution, and compromises were made to capture enough votes to win. Again the Republicans were able to keep the proposals in one package rather than allowing separate voting on different pieces, and the reconciliation measure passed 232–193 on June 26. After being passed by the Senate, the omnibus reconciliation package cut from the budget a total of $35.1 billion in 1982 and $130.6 billion by fiscal year 1984.

The other major part of the Reagan economic plan was a large tax cut predicated on the "supply-side" theory that a cut in taxes would stimulate the economy enough to wipe out the deficit in the near future. The Democrats also were preparing a tax-cut package, but the administration was determined to win. What resulted was a bidding war to include the most "sweeteners" and "ornaments" on the "Christmas tree bill" to attract the most votes in the House. According to David Stockman: "The basic strategy was to match or exceed the Democrats, and we did. . . . Do you realize the greed that came to the forefront? . . . [T]he hogs were really feeding. The greed level, the level of opportunism, just got out of control."[66]

After another massive lobbying effort by the administration, including a televised presidential address that helped create public pressure on Congress, forty-eight House Democrats defected to vote for the administration's tax-cut bill. In the Senate, thirty-seven of forty-seven Democrats voted for the bill. The total five-year loss to the treasury would amount to $750 billion.

President Reagan's first budget defied the predictions of scholars and old Washington hands alike. Very few predicted that he would be able to make such drastic shifts in priorities so suddenly. The changes included what House Budget Committee Chairman James Jones called "clearly the most monumental and historic turnaround in fiscal policy that has ever occurred."[67] The measures included the largest spending cuts in U.S. history, affecting hundreds of programs. It included the largest peacetime buildup of military spending. It also included the largest tax cuts in history.

The problem, of course, was that the domestic cuts neither made up for the military increases nor for the loss of revenues to the treasury. The immediate results of this fiscal policy, plus the recession of the early 1980s, were unprecedented deficits of over $200 billion that approached 6 percent of GNP (Gross National Product). At the end of Reagan's term in office, the national debt had nearly tripled and approached $3 trillion.

No one can dispute the historic nature of the changes made, or the skillful way the Reagan administration "hit the ground running" and accomplished its major priorities in its first nine months in office. But as with Franklin Roosevelt and Lyndon Johnson, Ronald Reagan could not maintain his string of victories throughout his term. Reagan's conservative policy victories galvanized opposing political forces, limiting his ability to continue winning further conservative initiatives. Even Republicans in Congress were not willing to back many of his budget proposals after the first few years. Reagan's legislative success steadily declined after 1981 until it fell below 50 percent in his last year in office.

Clinton and Two Congresses: A Study in Contrast

Clinton and the 103rd Congress: Winning Battles and Losing Wars   There are several perspectives from which to evaluate the way a president deals with Congress; at the personal level, presidents can be relatively skilled or clumsy; at the agenda level, they can put together a policy agenda designed to make the most of a particular congressional situation; and at the environmental level, they can decide whether the time is ripe for constructive legislative cooperation or confrontation. President Clinton had a mixed record in his first two years in office both in terms of his overall legislative record and in the way he approached his policy agenda.

Earlier, this chapter discussed how presidents were urged to "court" Congress. At the personal level, Clinton was an impressive lobbyer of Congress. He took pains to court members of both parties with invitations to the White House and personal phone calls. He combined the personal affability of Ronald Reagan with the detailed policy expertise of Jimmy Carter. In addition, he was empathetic and could communicate that he understood and sympathized with the perspective of his listener. He was willing to compromise on substance as well as pass out favors in seeking the votes he needed. His personal politicking was crucial in several very close votes on his initial budget agenda, twisting arms and making deals to win last-minute votes that he won by only one vote in both the House and the Senate. His active and public campaign for the North American Free Trade Agreement (NAFTA) was effective in winning congressional approval despite the opposition of the Democratic leadership on the Hill.

Earlier in this chapter, it was also argued that presidents should focus their initial agendas tightly by using the "rifle strategy" to narrow their agendas and not to include so many issues that priorities are not clear. In this respect, the new Clinton administration did not do as well. The campaign had raised a number of issues that Clinton promised would be priorities if he were elected. Despite his promise to "focus like a laser beam" on economic policy, the new administration was not ready to go with its economic plan until February 1993. This delay allowed the press to focus on minor embarrassments like the withdrawal of his first nominee for attorney general and his proposal to allow gay citizens to serve in the military. Clinton did sign the Family Medical Leave

Act and the "motor voter" voting registration bills, as well as issue several executive orders early in his term.

His economic package included a five-year deficit-reduction package of spending cuts and tax increases amounting to about $500 billion. It was skillfully introduced to Congress and the public and was well on the way to passage when the momentum was interrupted by Clinton's introduction of a "stimulus" package of less than $20 billion. The Republicans were able to label the package as "pork" and to stop it with a filibuster. This small defeat of the administration slowed momentum on the whole budget and made success more problematic. The budget fight was finally won by the administration without a single Republican vote in the House or Senate, and it came down to a 217–216 victory in the House on the reconciliation bill and a 50–50 tie in the Senate that was broken by the vice president's vote. Thus, the administration's initial agenda did not have the level of timing, coherence, and momentum that would have helped them. Even Leon Panetta, Clinton's OMB director and later chief of staff, admitted: "There were so many initiatives and so many efforts that were made that we lost the message...."[68]

At the systemic level (the political environment and tenor of the times), the mood of the country was not ripe for large new public programs, which doomed the Clinton health plan. Health-care reform was a centerpiece of the 1992 campaign, and the administration was determined to introduce basic reform that included at least covering those who were uninsured. To signal how important health care was, the president appointed Hillary Rodham Clinton to be in charge of the huge effort that involved a White House task force of five hundred people.

This major priority was finally defeated in the fall of 1994, for a number of reasons. Not only was the plan not ready for unveiling until September 1993 when Clinton gave a well-received speech to Congress, but the draft bill was not finished until a month later. In the spring of 1994, interest groups and Republicans campaigned against the plan. But perhaps most important, the health-care reform plan was exceedingly complex, calling for the creation of organizations that did not yet exist. The consequences of the reform plan were not clear, and the public felt uncertain enough about it to turn against it. The complexity arose from the administration's attempt to rely on private-sector employer mandates, create universal coverage, and have no-cost increase—all in the same package. The resulting proposal was so complex that it was vulnerable to Republicans' charges that it was too much "big government."

Thus, Clinton's legislative record in his first two years was decidedly mixed. He won major victories in his budget package and the NAFTA votes; he won other victories in the Brady Bill (waiting period for handgun purchases), motor voter, Medical Leave Act, and Hatch Act changes; but he was defeated in the centerpiece of health-care reform. This seems to conflict with his legislative support scores of 86.4 percent in each of his first two years, according to *Congressional Quarterly*[69]—the highest since LBJ's 1965 record. But the score is misleading, as the above analysis implies, probably because the Democrats were able to structure votes so that if they were not going to win, they would not schedule a vote. Also, health care was abandoned without even a vote in the full House or Senate.[70]

But given the political environment in 1993–1994, we should not be surprised that Clinton had a mixed record in his legislative priorities. He was elected with a 43 percent plurality, he ran behind most members of Congress, he had fewer Democrats in Congress than other recent Democrats, and his party lost seats in the election. Combine these negatives with a very ambitious policy agenda and you have a prescription for high conflict and low success. Clinton won a significant number of legislative victories, but the broader war for public approval was lost when voters rejected the administration in the 1994 congressional elections and turned Congress over to the Republicans.

CLINTON AND THE 104TH CONGRESS: LOSING BATTLES AND WINNING THE WAR   Clinton's mixed success with the 103rd Congress was a cakewalk when compared with his relations with the Republican-controlled 104th Congress. The irony, however, was that despite his frustration and much lower success rate with the 104th Congress, his record led to his reelection in 1996. How did this amazing turnabout occur?

The 1994 elections were widely seen as a rejection of the Clinton administration and the Democrats in Congress. Despite the relatively small margin of votes that switched, virtually all of the switches went in the Republicans' favor. They took control of the House of Representatives and of the Congress for the first time in forty years. They gained fifty-two seats in the House and eight seats in the Senate, giving them margins of 230–204 and 53–47, respectively. (Later defections of Democrats gave the Republicans a 55–45 advantage in the Senate and a 232–202 advantage in the House.) Not one Republican incumbent lost an election. The Republican sweep of Congress was also reflected in Republican victories in state legislatures and governorships.

The Republicans in Congress, led by newly elected Speaker of the House Newt Gingrich, believed that they had a clear mandate from the voters. They had campaigned on an agenda of issues, known as the "Contract with America," and they were determined to push their conservative priorities through Congress. The seventy-three freshmen in the House were particularly determined and loyal to Speaker Gingrich, to whom most felt that they owed their elections. The conservative agenda in the contract included a balanced-budget amendment to the Constitution, transforming welfare entitlements into block grants to states, a tax cut, a missile defense system, cuts in capital gains taxes, and term limits for members of Congress.

During the first several months in 1995, the House worked overtime to pass the contract items, creating an impressive record. In April, President Clinton was reduced to the point of insisting to the press that he was still "relevant" to the policy processes. As the contract items went to the Senate, however, they were slowed down by the relative ideological moderation of the Senators and the procedural constraints of the Senate, which is subject to filibusters that can effectively bring the Senate to a halt.

By the summer of 1995, the Republicans had been insisting on balancing the federal budget within seven years, and Clinton felt that this was important enough to the public that he had to agree in principle. In doing this, he was able to shift the debate from *whether* to balance the budget to *how* to balance the budget, as well as to highlight the differences between himself and the Republicans in Congress.

In the fall of 1995, the Republicans passed a budget for fiscal year 1996 that would have put the budget on a path toward balance; but it also contained serious cuts in the projected expenditures for programs in education, environment, Medicare, and Medicaid. Clinton said that he was also for a balanced budget, but that he would not accept the Republicans' formula. He said that he was protecting important programs from extreme cuts and vetoed the Republicans' budget. The Republicans stood firm, arguing that they were elected to implement conservative priorities and that they would not make the changes in priorities that Clinton demanded. Their problem was that they did not have the votes to override the president's veto.

With no budget passed to fund much of the government, the government would have to shut down all programs that did not yet have appropriations except those necessary to protect life or property. Ordinarily in such a situation, a continuing resolution is passed, allowing the government to operate at present levels of funding until appropriations are finally passed. But the Republicans thought that Clinton would cave in and agree to their priorities rather than shut the government down. They were wrong. Clinton refused to change his mind, and the government shut down for six days in October and again for about two weeks at the end of the year. In January 1996, Senate Majority Leader Robert Dole convinced the Republicans to agree to continuing resolutions until regular appropriations could be passed.

The first session of the 104th Congress ended with Clinton having the lowest success rating of any president in the *Congressional Quarterly* survey of presidential success: 36.2 percent.[71] The partisanship of the session was also reflected in the highest party unity scores since 1954 when *Congressional Quarterly* began recording them. The majority of the Republicans voted against a majority of the Democrats in 62.4 percent of the total votes in the Senate and 56.4 percent of the time in the House.[72]

But this dismal legislative record set the stage for Bill Clinton's amazing comeback in 1996. The public saw the government shutdown as irresponsible and extreme on the part of the Republicans. Clinton's approval ratings began to rise above the 50 percent level, and in the 1996 spring primaries he did not have to run against any Democratic challenger. During the spring of 1996, little legislation was passed, although appropriations measures were enacted to fund the government's programs.

By summer, members of Congress were intensely engaged in reelection bids, and members of both parties wanted positive legislative records to run on. Republicans could also see that their confrontational tactics had not worked, and they began to soften their stances and cooperate with Democrats to pass legislation before the fall elections. Thus in the spring and summer of 1996, a number of significant pieces of legislation passed, including an increase in the minimum wage, the phasing out of some farm benefits, deregulation in the telecommunications industry, and changes in portability of health insurance.

Even though there was no lovefest between the two parties, they saw the necessity of cooperation for their mutual benefit. Thus, the legislative record of the second session of the 104th Congress was significantly better than the first session, and the president's success score took the largest single-year leap in the history of the survey to 55.1 percent, though this was significantly lower than most post-WWII presidents.

The 1996 congressional campaigns reflected the change in public attitude from the 1994 elections. In 1994, Democratic candidates were trying to distance themselves from their president for fear that association with him would hurt their chances for reelection. Republican congressional candidates were attacking Clinton as a "big government" liberal and promising to cut government severely if they were elected. In 1996, Democrats were clamoring to have President Clinton campaign for them, and even Republicans were taking credit for compromises with him, such as the minimum wage increase.

Clinton himself ran a strong campaign in 1996, staying consistently well ahead of Robert Dole, who suffered from the age factor and a lackluster campaign. Even though Clinton won the election 49 percent to Dole's 42 percent, the Republicans maintained control of both the House and the Senate.

Thus, Bill Clinton's first-term legislative record was a paradox. In the 103rd Congress, working with the Democratic majority, he had near-record legislative support scores but a mixed policy record, and he lost the war for congressional elections. Against the 104th Congress, his legislative success was much lower, but he was able to prevail in the broader war over the policy agenda of the Republican Congress and win reelection easily, a feat that no one could have predicted at the beginning of the 104th Congress.

PRESIDENT GEORGE W. BUSH AND CONGRESS: LEGISLATING WITHOUT A MANDATE

Claims to policy mandates from the voters are suspect in American politics, though presidents often claim them. The claim is most credible if the president wins election in a landslide and brings to Congress large majorities of his own party on his coattails, as happened with Franklin Roosevelt and Lyndon Johnson. Even Ronald Reagan's impressive victory over Jimmy Carter, which was accompanied by the Republicans capturing the Senate for the first time in several decades, was claimed as a mandate for the ambitious policy agenda of Reagan's first year in office. By these general criteria, George W. Bush did not have much of a mandate; he won half-a-million fewer votes than his opponent; and the Republicans lost seats in both houses of Congress. The Senate was evenly split 50–50, and the Republicans retained a narrow margin in the House (222–211, with two independents).

During the presidential campaign of 2000, candidate Bush set a moderate tone by asserting that he was a "compassionate conservative" and advocating educational proposals that often appealed to Democratic voters. He promised to "change the tone" in Washington by taking a bipartisan approach to governing, as he had in Texas. While arguing for more defense spending and a national missile defense, privatizing part of Social Security, and a large tax cut, the emphasis was not on the more conservative aspects of his policy agenda. In his initial policy proposals, however, he pursued a conservative agenda that pleased his Republican base in the House of Representatives and the electorate.[73] According to the conventional wisdom, a president in such a weak legislative position would adopt a legislative strategy that sought to build a coalition of moderates in the middle of both parties and build out toward the wings to assure passage of key legislation. But instead of that strategy, President Bush's approach to his initial policy agenda was to appeal to his partisan base and then try to win over enough Democratic votes to prevail.

The new administration had learned the lessons of previous presidential transitions that an initial policy agenda is most likely to be successful if the agenda is relatively tightly focused rather than scattershot or too lengthy. But the new Bush administration also learned from his father's transition into power. His close political adviser Karl Rove said that he had heard President Bush say, "I saw what happened to my dad, who got elected and said, 'What do we do?'"[74] Consequently, President Bush had a clear policy agenda and kept his focus on relatively few priorities: his tax cut, a faith-based initiative, education, a defense buildup, and an energy policy. But he also decided that he did not need to moderate the substance of his policy proposals because of the thinness of his political mandate.

President Bush's first and largest legislative initiative was to propose a large tax cut, as he had promised in the campaign. The administration's proposal was for a $1.6 trillion cut over ten years that included reducing the top brackets, eliminating the estate tax, reducing the marriage penalty, and increasing child credits. Democrats argued that most of the benefits would go to the relatively well-off and that the overall size of the reduction in revenues would threaten the projected surpluses; they favored a smaller cut that was targeted at lower income levels. The House passed Bush's plan, but the Senate held out for a smaller cut. After negotiations, the Senate went along with the House to vote for a $1.35 trillion cut, an important policy victory for the president.

In another of Bush's top priorities, he established, by executive action, a White House Office of Faith-Based Initiatives to facilitate the use of federal funds for social purposes to be administered by faith-based organizations. He also proposed changes in law to allow federal funds to be administered through the faith-based organizations. His purpose was to overcome the usual presumption against allocating government money for religious purposes. Democratic Senator Joe Lieberman favored the initiative, but many other Democrats feared that the funds would be used for religious purposes and thus violate the separation of church and state. Though the proposal was generally supported by conservatives, some religious conservatives thought that federal dollars might change the priorities of religious organizations. There was not enough consensus in Congress to pass the necessary changes in law to fully fund the initiative.

In other administration priorities, Bush proposed privatizing part of the Social Security system by setting aside a portion of contributions to the system for private investment in personal retirement accounts. As part of a plan to improve U.S. energy production, he favored opening the Arctic National Wildlife Refuge for oil drilling, a proposal that was opposed by Democrats and environmentalists.

To moderate the conservative cast to his policy agenda, Bush also pursued the education reform proposals he emphasized in his campaign. He called for more aid to the states for education but also for accountability through testing of students. If student test scores did not perform up to standards in public schools, the government would provide parents with vouchers to send their children to other schools, including private or religious schools. Democrats objected to the voucher provisions but supported other parts of the Bush proposal. After becoming bogged down in the Senate, the education bill (without vouchers) was finally passed, with the support of Senator Edward Kennedy, in December 2001.

In the late spring of 2001, the president had won an important victory in his large tax cut and was turning to his other priorities when his political power was dealt a blow. Senator James Jeffords, a third-term Republican from Vermont, had been a moderate, but loyal Republican. But he had felt increasingly out of place in the conservative Republican Party of the 1990s. After voting for the Bush tax cut, he switched his affiliation to Independent and caucused with the Democrats in the Senate.[75] Consequently, in the middle of the first session of the 107th Congress, party control of the Senate shifted from the Republicans to the Democrats. With the 50–50 split after the election, the Republicans could count on a tie-breaking vote from the vice president. But with the Democrats controlling 51 votes to the Republicans' 49, control of the Senate agenda, along with chairmanships of all the committees, went to the Democrats, who would not be as sympathetic to President Bush's priorities.

At 180 days in office, President Bush enjoyed public approval of 57 percent, not bad, but lower than other post–WWII presidents except for Bill Clinton at 45 percent.[76] In late summer, President Bush won two victories in the House—on his comprehensive energy plan and on a patients' bill of rights. But victories in the Senate were going to be much more difficult with the new Democratic majority.

Thus in the summer of 2001, the Bush administration began to recalibrate its policy priorities to adjust to Democratic control in the Senate and looked forward to some difficult policy battles in the fall. Then on September 11 came the terrorist attacks that transformed the Bush presidency and the nation's priorities. The lack of mandate from the 2000 election suddenly became irrelevant; Osama bin Laden and his attack on the United States provided President Bush with a stronger mandate than in the election. The nation was at war, and President Bush used his newly created mandate effectively in the national security arena and skillfully as political capital.

The terrorist attacks transformed American politics quickly and changed Congress from an arena of partisan brawls to one of bipartisanship and shared concern.[77] Central to the new atmosphere was the threat of terrorism and the need for presidential leadership. On September 14, Congress passed a joint resolution that gave the president broad discretion to "use all necessary and appropriate force" to pursue the perpetrators of the terrorist attacks in Afghanistan.

Congress also gave the executive broad new powers for the domestic fight against terrorism. The most important and sweeping law, passed by Congress in mid-October and signed by the president later in the month, was entitled the "Uniting and Strengthening America by Providing Appropriate Tools Required to Intercept and Obstruct Terrorism Act of 2001," or more briefly the "U.S.A. PATRIOT Act." (often referred to simply as "the Patriot Act") The bill broadened the definition of who might be considered a terrorist and gave the attorney general expanded powers to deal with suspected terrorists. Congress also passed antiterrorism measures proposed by Attorney General John Ashcroft, with broad, bipartisan support. Congress also passed a $40 billion emergency spending bill, a $15 billion airline-bailout bill, and a bill to hire 30,000 airport security personnel.[78]

The creation of the Department of Homeland Security, though initially opposed by the president, was shaped by the administration's plan and was considered a victory for the White House. Perhaps most importantly for the administration, in the fall of 2002 President Bush was able to win bipartisan approval of a congressional resolution to attack Iraq. The vote came in October, just prior to the 2002 elections, and Democrats were afraid to go into the congressional elections being charged by their Republican opponents as being soft on terrorism or Saddam Hussein. (See Chapter 7 for details.)

After passage of the Iraq resolution, President Bush engaged in an unprecedented level of campaigning for Republicans leading up to the 2002 elections. During the fall of 2002, he made ninety campaign appearances, raised $144 million, and in the last five days of the campaign traveled to fifteen different states.[79] Bush's efforts paid off when the Republicans regained control of the Senate and actually gained seats in the House—only the second time since 1934 that the president's party gained seats in the off-year elections. The election was interpreted as a victory for Bush, whose intense campaigning efforts were seen as key to the Republicans' victories.

Overall, given his lack of an initial mandate, President Bush was remarkably successful with Congress during his first two years in office. Though his policy achievements before 9/11 were mixed (big win on taxes, small win in education, delay with faith-based initiative, defeat on environment and Social Security reform), his congressional support scores, as measured by the *Congressional Quarterly*, were among the highest of post-WWII presidents at 87 and 88 percent for his first two years.[80]

He won strong bipartisan support for his national security initiatives, including two resolutions giving him broad wartime discretion in Afghanistan and Iraq. He was able to count on the disciplined Republican House to pass his proposals with a narrow majority, and he was often able to win enough votes in the Senate to give him victories.

In sum, President Bush's first term success with Congress was due to a combination of the following factors:

1. Democratic restraint in accepting the outcome of the 2000 election
2. A focused initial agenda, skillfully pursued
3. Public reaction to the terrorist attacks on 9/11 and President Bush's reassuring performance in the immediate aftermath
4. Democratic timidity in the face of public support for the war on terrorism
5. President Bush's skillful use of the national security issue to gain public support for his foreign and domestic priorities

After he won the 2004 election, President Bush declared that he had increased his political capital and intended to use it: "I earned capital in the campaign, political capital, and now I intend to spend it. It is my style."[81] His most ambitious policy initiative was his proposal to revamp the Social Security system so that it would include individual, private accounts that could be invested in the stock market and would not be dependent on tax revenues. The difficulty was that conversion to the new system would be very expensive, and the proposal did not deal with the fiscal shortfall that was predicted for the Social Security system after the retirement of the baby boom generation. Other domestic priorities included tax simplification, eliminating 150 government programs, further tax cuts, tort law reform, and extension of the No Child Left Behind education act.

Despite President Bush's extensive travel and campaigning in support of his Social Security proposals, there was insufficient support to even bring a proposal to Congress. But more importantly, the situation in Iraq continued to deteriorate so that domestic priorities got overwhelmed by division in the country over the wisdom of continuing the U.S. occupation. President Bush's poll numbers began to slide, and in spring of 2006 they reached the low 30s in presidential approval. With his political capital thus depleted substantially since his 2004 election, President Bush shifted to a damage-control mode and proposed few new domestic initiatives.

THE PRESIDENCY AND A POLARIZED CONGRESS

In the latter decades of the twentieth century, divided government—when one political party does not control both houses of Congress and the presidency—seemed to lead to "gridlock." With Republican presidents and Democratic Congresses through much the period after 1968, the two parties had difficulty addressing some of the most pressing national problems (e.g., the budget deficits and policy toward the Soviet Union). Scholars sought the roots of divided government and decried its effects.[82] But after Republicans took control of Congress in 1994 and President George W. Bush won the presidency in 2000, Republicans controlled both Congress and the presidency. The result, however, was not entirely what was expected. Polarization between the two parties had increased to such an extent that politics became bitter and fractured.

Republicans were able to get their way, but only with heavy-handed tactics that embittered Democrats. The development of polarization—that is, Republicans becoming more conservative and Democrats more liberal—had profound implications for governance in the American political system.

THE ROOTS OF CONGRESSIONAL POLARIZATION

Important changes swept Congress in the latter half of the century as it was transfromed from a Democratic-dominated institution with significant overlap between the parties, to an ideological and polarized battleground with virtually no middle ground.[83] The roots of polarization began with Republican success in breaking up the "solid" Democratic South. With general urbanization and black migration to the north in the 1960s, the partisan complexion of the South began to change. The Republican Party was becoming a viable political party and beginning to attract more voters.[84] Partisan realignment in the South was further encouraged by the Civil Rights Act of 1964 and the Voting Rights Act of 1965, both of which increased the number of black voters, who voted overwhelmingly Democratic.[85]

Conservative whites began to identify with the Republican Party, sending more Republican representatives to Congress. The creation of majority-minority districts concentrated more liberal blacks in a few congressional districts while more conservative whites ended up in districts that voted Republican. The result of this realignment was that the Democratic Party in Congress lost its "Dixicrat" (conservative southern Democrats) members and became more homogeneously liberal.[86] The conservative coalition of Republicans and conservative southern Democrats, which had been thwarting Democratic presidents since FDR, began to decline in importance; the conservative southerners were now in the Republican Party.

The increasing liberal consensus among the Democrats in Congress led the Democratic caucus in the House to become more cohesive and, through control of committee membership, assert its liberal policy views more effectively (e.g., on civil rights, old-age assistance, health care, housing, and other federal programs).[87] As the Democrats in the House became more ideologically similar (i.e., liberal), their leadership became more assertive in the use of parliamentary tactics and evoked the ire of Republicans by denying them procedural rights in ways that were perceived as unfair.[88] In the 1980s, Newt Gingrich led the outraged Republicans in the House to develop Republican candidates, particularly in the south, which culminated in the 1994 election landslide that put the Republicans in charge of Congress for the first time in 40 years.[89] Thus, Republican domination of southern congressional delegations led to a more homogeneous, liberal Democratic party in Congress, which led to more polarized parties and finally to the Republican takeover of Congress.[90] This polarization was exacerbated and perpetuated by bipartisan gerrymandering that reinforced the polarizing trend.

Redistricting, among other factors, has led to in increasing proportion of safe seats, with fewer congressional districts "in play," that is, that might be won by either party. According to Gary Jacobson's analysis, the number of safe seats increased significantly between 1992 and 2002: Democrats' safe seats increased from 142 to 158, and Republicans' safe seats increased from 139 to 356.[91] Thus the total number of safe seats was 356 of 435, but the number of House races that were actually competitive were many fewer than that.[92] In the 2004 elections, 83 percent of House races were won by margins of 20 percent or more, and 95 percent of districts were won by more than 10 percent.

Redistricting, from the 1970s through 2004 in the South and elsewhere, led to safer districts, which along with the advantages of incumbency, led to the election of more liberal Democrats and more conservative Republicans. If congressional districts are competitive, with elections won and lost by small margins, candidates must move to the middle of the ideological spectrum to try to capture a majority of votes. But safe seats put moderate candidates of both parties at a disadvantage. Turnout for primary elections is low, and most of those who actually vote are committed partisans; that is, true believers who hold more extreme views than most voters in their parties. Thus in order to get nominated and then to remain in office, members must please their respective wings or be outflanked by more extreme candidates.[93]

Once in office, the advantages of incumbency help keep the more extreme members in office for longer periods of time. But even more important than advantages for individual incumbents (e.g., name recognition, media coverage, travel to the district, raising money, etc.) is the advantage gained through safe partisan majorities of congressional districts ensured through skillful drawing of district boundaries, that is, gerrymandering.[94] Thus the advantages of incumbents who sought reelection, always considerable, have become even more effective. From 1984 to 1990, House members seeking reelection were successful 97 percent of the time, and in 2002, 98 percent were successful. Senators were a bit more vulnerable, but still quite successful, winning 86 percent of bids for reelection from 1982 to 2003 and 95 percent in 1996.[95] In 2004, aside from the redistricted Texas, 99 percent of House incumbents won reelection, with only three incumbents being defeated.[96]

The Consequences of Partisan Polarization

In the middle of the twentieth century, the two political parties in Congress were not ideologically monolithic. That is, each party had a significant number of members who were ideologically sympathetic to the other party. The Democratic Party contained a strong conservative wing of members, the southern "Boll Weevils," who often voted with the conservative Republicans. The Republican Party contained a noticeable number of moderates, mostly from the northeast, the "Rockefeller Republicans," who would often vote with the Democrats. These cross-pressured members of Congress made up between one fifth and one third of each house of Congress from 1950 to the mid-1980s.[97]

In the last fifteen years of the twentieth century, the cross-pressured members of each party all but disappeared. Bond and Fleisher have calculated the number of liberal Republicans and conservative Democrats in Congress from the 1950s through the 1990s and have documented their decline. The number of conservative Democrats in the House has decreased from a high of 91 in 1965–66 to a low of 11 in 1995–96. In the Senate, the high of 22 in the early 1960s was reduced to zero in 1995–96. Liberal Republicans similarly fell from a high of 35 in the early 1970s to a low of 1 in 1993–94 in the House, and a high of 14 in 1973–74 to a low of 2 in 1995–96 in the Senate.[98] This disappearance of the middle is a convincing demonstration of ideological polarization in Congress.

What the above data mean in a practical sense is that each of the political parties in Congress is more ideologically homogenous and that there is greater ideological distance between the two parties. Thus there is less need to compromise in a moderate direction when reaching a consensus within each party. And it is correspondingly more difficult to bridge the ideological gap between the contrasting perspectives of the two parties. Finding middle ground where compromise is possible becomes much more difficult. It is more likely that votes will be set up to highlight partisan differences and used for rhetorical and electoral purposes rather than to arrive at compromise policies.[99]

The traditional norms of courtesy, reciprocity, and comity that marked the 1950s and 1960s in Congress began to break down in the 1970s.[100] Reflecting broader divisions in U.S. politics over the Vietnam War and Watergate, life in Congress became more contentious. Legislative language had traditionally been marked by overly elaborate politeness in order to manage partisan and sometimes personal conflict. But instances of harsh language and incivility became more common and more partisan in the 1970s and 1980s. In the House, the Republicans felt increasingly suppressed by the majority Democrats through the rules of debate and legislative scheduling and, under the leadership of Newt Gingrich, began to use obstructionist tactics to clog up the legislative process.[101] The predictable Democratic response was to tighten up the rules even more to deal with disruptive tactics. After Republicans took control of Congress in 1994, relations between the parties continued to deteriorate.

Once Democrats were in the minority, they also complained that Republicans systematically excluded them from important conference committee negotiations between the two houses and that the procedural rules were used against them in ways that exceeded the Democrats' partisan use of procedures in the later years of their domination of Congress. Republican Senator John McCain commented on the partisanship of the procedural battles, "The Republicans had better hope that the Democrats never regain the majority."[102]

Former Tennessee Senator and Republican National Committee chair William Brock attributed the incivility, with "less dialogue, less comity, and more partisanship," to safe districts and the resulting polarized politics.

> Consistently now in general elections, well over 90 percent of congressional races are virtually uncontested. . . . If a candidate need talk only to those who are most fervent in support of the party, he or she doesn't have to listen to, or even speak to, people at the center, much less those of the other party. . . . We're increasingly moving to a political system that looks, and feels, like a political barbell: one where all the weight is at the ends of the spectrum, leaving those in the center with little voice or opportunity for impact.[103]

196CHAPTER 6: THE PRESIDENT AND CONGRESS

Thus the partisan polarization that had its roots at mid-twentieth century had reached destructive levels during President Bush's second term. Congressional scholars Thomas Mann and Norman Ornstein argued that during the Bush presidency, Congress was "the broken branch":

> The majority [Republicans] saw itself more as a group of foot soldiers in the president's army than as members of an independent branch of government.... The attitude of the majority party leaders that the president's program trumped everything, including institutional comity and basic fairness, accompanied a general decline in institutional identity.... A very aggressive assertion of executive power was met with institutional indifference in Congress.[104]

After the 2006 elections, President Bush's influence in Congress was significantly diminished when the Democrats took control of the House by a considerable margin and the Senate was almost evenly balanced between the two parties.

CONCLUSION

Modern presidents have had varying degrees of success with Congress. President Kennedy's liberal policies did not get enacted until the Johnson administration. After Johnson's Great Society legislative victories, he lost favor in Congress over Vietnam and decided not to run for a second term of his own. President Nixon's confrontational actions did not accomplish most of what he attempted, and he ended up resigning in disgrace after Watergate. President Ford's vetoes deflected the Democrats' policies but did not achieve his own agenda. President Carter did not achieve as much as he might have had he handled his congressional relations differently. President Reagan's initial budgetary leadership quickly dissipated, and confrontation with Congress marked most of his term. President Bush's virtually unbroken string of vetoes did not bring him a strong record on which to run in 1992. President Clinton had mixed success with Congress, and his confrontations with the Republican 104th Congress played a role in his reelection. President George W. Bush was very successful with Congress on national security issues, but had a mixed record in domestic affairs.

In evaluating how different presidents have dealt with Congress, it is important to remember that the Framers put Congress in Article I of the Constitution for a reason: they expected that Congress would dominate the national policy agenda. It is easy to lose sight of this historical reality when considering the modern presidency. Presidents now have many more resources to influence Congress, they are regularly active in doing so, and we expect them to try. But despite our expectations, and the famous legislative victories of Presidents Franklin Roosevelt, Lyndon Johnson, and Ronald Reagan, the president remains in a relatively weak position with respect to Congress. Even the most successful presidents could not sustain their initial string of victories, and their legislative performance soon fell off. Public popularity of presidents can help them when it is high and undermine them when it is low, but popularity by itself cannot guarantee legislative success. President George W. Bush's support from a partisan, Republican Congress was notable. But his dominance was primarily in the national security area, and it began to dissipate after the 2006 elections.

NOTES

1. Nelson W. Polsby, "How to Spin the 2002 Election," *The Forum* vol. 1, no. 3 (2003), article 1.

2. Constitutional law on the use of the pocket veto is not settled. It is clear that the pocket veto is not available over a three-day recess, though some presidents have claimed that they can exercise it in a recess of five days. The question of an adjournment between sessions of one Congress is uncertain. See Jay R. Shampansky, "The Pocket Veto: A Legal Analysis," *Congressional Research Service, Report 90-43A* (Washington, DC: Library of Congress, January 11, 1990).

3. See Office of the Secretary of the Senate, *Presidential Vetoes, 1789–1991* (Washington, DC: Government Printing Office, 1991), update to 1992 by Gregory Harness, Head Reference Librarian, 1993.

4. Gary L. Galemore, "Veto Overrides by Congress 1969–1988," *Congressional Research Service Report No. 89–436 GOV* (Washington, DC: Library of Congress, July 20, 1989), pp. 2–3.

5. Larry Berman, *The New American Presidency* (Boston: Little, Brown, 1987), p. 42.

6. *INS v. Chadha* (1983); Louis Fisher, "A Political Context for Legislative Vetoes," *Political Science Quarterly* 93 (Summer 1978), pp. 241–254.

7. Louis Fisher, "Congress as Micromanager of the Executive Branch," in James P. Pfiffner, ed., *The Managerial Presidency* (Pacific Grove, CA: Brooks/Cole, 1991).

8. See Ronald Moe, "Prospects for the Item Veto at the Federal Level: Lessons from the States," (Washington, DC: National Academy of Public Administration, February 1986). For an analysis of the demise of the item veto, see Robert J. Spitzer, "The Item Veto Dispute and the Secular Crisis of the Presidency," *Presidential Studies Quarterly* (Fall 1998).

9. Christopher S. Kelley, " 'Faithfully Executing' and 'Taking Care'—The Unitary Executive and the Presidential Signing Statement," paper presented at the American Political Science Association annual convention, 2002.

10. Marc N. Garber and Kurt A. Wimmer, "Presidential Signing Statements as Interpretations of Legislative Intent: An Executive Aggrandizement of Power," *Harvard Journal on Legislation* vol. 24, p. 367. Quoted in Kelley, "Faithfully Executing," p. 15.

11. Christopher S. Kelley, " 'Faithfully Executing' and 'Taking Care'—The Unitary Executive and the Presidential Signing Statement," paper presented at the American Political Science Association annual convention, 2002, p. 32.

12. American Bar Association, Task Force on Presidential Signing Statements and the Separation of Powers Doctrine (July 2006), p. 14; ABA Web site.

13. "Examples of the President's Signing Statements," *Boston Globe* (April 30, 2006), Web site. See also, Charlie Savage, "Bush Challenges Hundreds of Laws," *Boston Globe* (April 30, 2006), Web site.

14. Weekly Compilation of Presidential Documents, vol. 37, p. 1834 (2001), quoted in Philip Cooper, "George W. Bush, Edgar Allan Poe, and the Use and Abuse of Presidential Signing Statements," *Presidential Studies Quarterly*, vol. 35, no. 3 (September 2005), p. 523.

15. Quoted by Charlie Savage, "Bush Shuns Patriot Act Requirement," *Boston Globe* (March 24, 2006), Web site.

16. The White House, "President's Statement on Signing of H.R. 2863, the 'Department of Defense, Emergency Supplemental Appropriations to Address Hurricanes in the Gulf of Mexico, and Pandemic Influenza Act, 2006.'" December 30, 2005. Found on White House Web site, http://www.whitehouse.gov.

17. Lewis Carroll, *The Annotated Alice* (annotated by Martin Gardner), (NY: Bramhall House, 1960), p. 269.

18. American Bar Association, Task Force on Presidential Signing Statements and the Separation of Powers Doctrine, August 8, 2006; www.abanet.org.

19. Michael Nelson, ed., *Guide to the Presidency* (Washington, DC: CQ Press, 1989), p. 1118.

20. Woodrow Wilson, *Congressional Government: A Study in American Politics* (New York: Meridian Books, 1956).

21. Nelson, *Guide to the Presidency*, p. 461.

22. James Sundquist, *The Decline and Resurgence of Congress* (Washington, DC: Brookings Institution, 1981), pp. 129–130.

23. James Sundquist, *The Decline and Resurgence of Congress*, p. 130.

24. Nelson, *Guide to the Presidency*, p. 461.

25. See the discussion in James Sundquist, *The Decline and Resurgence of Congress*, pp. 129–136.

26. Adapted from Nelson, *Guide to the Presidency*, p. 462.

27. Berman, *The New American Presidency*, p. 252.

28. George C. Edwards, III, *At the Margins* (New Haven, CT: Yale University Press, 1989), p. 40.

29. John E. Owens and Burdett A. Loomis, "Qualified Exceptionalism: The US Congress in Comparative Perspective," *Journal of Legislative Studies*, vol. 43, no. 2 (June 2006).

30. Paul Light, *The President's Agenda* (Baltimore: Johns Hopkins University Press, 1982), p. 45.

31. Light, *The President's Agenda*, p. 52.

32. Cary Covington, "Guess Who's Coming to Dinner: The Distribution of White House Social Invitations and Their Effects on Congressional Support," *American Politics Quarterly* 16:3 (July 1988), pp. 243–265.

33. Theodore Sorensen, *Kennedy* (New York: Bantam Books, 1965), p. 392.

34. See testimony reprinted in Berman, *The New American Presidency*, p. 268.

35. Nigel Bowles, *The White House and Capitol Hill* (Oxford, England: Clarendon Press, 1987), pp. 105, 213.

36. Richard L. Berke, "Courting Congress Nonstop, Clinton Looks for an Alliance," *New York Times* (March 8, 1993), p. B8.

37. See Burdett A. Loomis, *The Contemporary Congress*, 3rd ed. (Belmont, CA: Wadsworth, 2004), chap. 1.

38. Edwards, *At the Margins*, p. 72.

39. Edwards, *At the Margins*, p. 87.

40. Charles and Barbara Whalen, *The Longest Debate* (New York: New American Library, 1985), p. 30.

41. Sorensen, *Kennedy*, p. 381.

42. Sorensen, *Kennedy*, p. 387.

43. Edwin O. Guthman and Jeffrey Shulman, eds., *Robert Kennedy in His Own Words* (New York: Bantam Books, 1988), p. 52.

44. This section is based on the article by Robert D. Loevy, "The Presidency and Domestic Policy: The Civil Rights Act of 1964," in David C. Kozak and Kennedth N. Cioski, eds., *The American Presidency* (Chicago: Nelson-Hall, 1985), pp. 411–419.

45. Whalen and Whalen, *The Longest Debate*, p. 92.

46. William Safire, *Safire's Political Dictionary* (New York: Random House, 1968), pp. 226–227. In 1993, Republican Senators were able to hand President Clinton a significant defeat when they conducted a filibuster to prevent a vote on an economic stimulus package that was pushed by the new administration. Because the Democrats held only fifty-seven seats in the Senate, they could not muster the sixty votes necessary to invoke cloture and cut off debate.

47. Lyndon Johnson, *The Vantage Point* (New York: Holt, Rinehart, and Winston, 1971), p. 159.

48. Richard Nathan, *The Plot That Failed* (New York: John Wiley, 1975), p. 8.

49. For a full treatment of the impoundment issue, see James P. Pfiffner, *The President, the Budget, and Congress: Impoundment and the 1974 Budget Act* (Boulder, CO: Westview Press, 1979).

50. Nile Stanton, "The Presidency and the Purse: Impoundment 1803–1973," *University of Colorado Law Review* (1973) in U.S. Congress, Senate, *Congressional Record* (December 14, 1973), pp. S22925, S22926.

51. *Weekly Compilation of Presidential Documents*, 9 (5), pp. 109–110.

52. 489 F.2nd. p. 492 (December 10, 1973).

53. *Train v. New York City* 420 U.S. 136, in Pfiffner, *The President, the Budget, and Congress*, p. 103.

54. Arthur M. Schlesinger, *The Imperial Presidency* (Boston: Houghton Mifflin, 1973).

55. Jimmy Carter, *Keeping Faith* (New York: Bantam Books, 1982), p. 71.

56. Haynes Johnson, *In the Absence of Power* (New York: Viking Press, 1980), p. 189.

57. Barbara Kellerman, *The Political Presidency: The Practice of Leadership* (New York: Oxford University Press, 1984), p. 190.

58. See Charles O. Jones, *The Trusteeship Presidency* (Baton Rouge: Louisiana State University Press, 1988), pp. 135–143; Michael J. Malbin, "Rhetoric and Leadership: A Look Backward at the Carter National Energy Plan," in Anthony King, ed., *Both Ends of the Avenue* (Washington: American Enterprise Institute Press, 1983), pp. 212–245; and Kellerman, *The Political Presidency*, pp. 185–219.

59. Jones, *The Trusteeship Presidency*, p. 138.

60. Carter, *Keeping Faith*, p. 99.

61. Malbin, "Rhetoric and Leadership," pp. 224–227.

62. Kellerman, *The Political Presidency*, p. 209.

63. Carter, *Keeping Faith*, p. 80.

64. For a more complete analysis of the Carter administration's early relations with Congress, see James P. Pfiffner, *The Strategic Presidency*, 2nd ed. (Lawrence: University Press of Kansas, 1966), chap. 6.

65. For a more complete analysis of the Reagan budget victories in 1981, see James P. Pfiffner, "The Reagan Budget Juggernaut," in James P. Pfiffner, ed., *The President and Economic Policy* (Philadelphia: ISHI Press, 1986), pp. 108–134.

66. William Grieder, "The Education of David Stockman," *Atlantic* (December 1981), p. 51.

67. *Congressional Quarterly Weekly Report* (August 1, 1981), p. 1371.

68. Ruth Marcus, "Administration Now Sees Its Record at Risk," *Washington Post* (January 24, 1995), pp. A1, A6.

69. *Congressional Quarterly Weekly Report* (December 21, 1996), p. 3428.

70. For a detailed analysis of Clinton and the 103rd Congress, see James P. Pfiffner, "President Clinton and the 103rd Congress: Winning Battles and Losing Wars," in James Thurber, ed., *Rivals for Power: Presidential-Congressional Relations* (Washington, DC: CQ Press, 1996).

71. *Congressional Quarterly Weekly Report* (December 21, 1996), p. 3427.

72. *Congressional Quarterly Weekly Report*, p. 3432.

73. Stephen J. Wayne, "Bush and Congress: The First Two Years," paper presented at the conference, "New Challenges for the American Presidency," sponsored by the Institute of United States Studies at the University of London and the Eccles Centre for American Studies at the British Library (May 12–13, 2003), London. See also David Broder, "No Moderate in GOP Clothing," *Washington Post* (April 18, 2001), p. A21; Gloria Borger, "Pleased as Punch," *U.S. News & World Report* (April 9, 2001), p. 35; Adam Clymer, "Not So Fast," *New York Times* (April 1, 2001), p. E1; Bob Herbert, "The Mask Comes Off," *New York Times* (March 26, 2001), p. A23; Dan Balz, "Bush Protects His Right Flank," *Washington Post* (February 12, 2001), p. 1, A13.

74. Both quotes from Richard L. Berke, "In the White House, a Sense of What History Can Teach," *The New York Times* (January 9, 2001), p. 1, A18.

75. The transcript of Jeffords's announcement was printed in *The New York Times* (May 25, 2001), p. A18.

76. *USA Today* (July 13, 2001), p. 8A. DDE-69%; JFK-66%; RN-58%; JC-67%; RR-60%; GHWB-66%.

77. John C. Fortier and Norman J. Ornstein argue that the first four months after 9/11 were marked by "hyper bipartisanship." See "Congress and the Bush Presidency," paper presented at the conference, The Bush Presidency: An Early Assessment, Princeton University, April 25–26, 2003.

78. Barbara Sinclair, "Patriotism, Partisanship and Institutional Protection: The Congressional Response to 9/11," paper presented at the conference on The Presidency, Congress and the War on Terrorism, University of Florida, Gainesville (February 7, 2003).

79. Fortier and Ornstein, "Congress and the Bush Presidency," p. 39.

80. *Congressional Quarterly Weekly Report* (December 14, 2002), p. 3275.

81. Mike Allen, "Confident Bush Vows to Move Aggressively," *Washington Post* (November 5, 2004), p. 1.

82. See James P. Pfiffner, "Partisan Polarization, Politics, and the Presidency: Structural Sources of Conflict," in James A. Thurber, ed. *Rivals for Power*, 3rd ed., (Lanham, MD: Rowman and Littlefield, 2006), pp. 33–58.

83. Nelson Polsby, *How Congress Evolves: Social Bases of Institutional Change* (NY: Oxford University Press, 2004).

84. Polsby, *How Congress Evolves*, pp. 80–94.

85. For analyses of the changing electoral make-up of the South and the partisan implications, see: Earl Black and Merle Black, *The Vital South* (Cambridge, MA: Harvard University Press, 1992).

86. Polsby, *How Congress Evolves*, p. 94.

87. Polsby, *How Congress Evolves*, pp. 80, 150.

88. See Burdett A. Loomis and Wendy J. Schiller, *The Contemporary Congress*, 4th ed. Belmont, CA: 2004), pp. 150–160.

89. For an analysis of the 1994 elections and the 104th Congress, see James P. Pfiffner, "President Clinton, Newt Gingrich, and the 104th Congress." in *On Parties: Essays Honoring Austin Ranney*. Eds. Nelson W. Polsby and Raymond E. Wolfinger (Berkeley, CA: Institute of Governmental Studies Press, 2000), pp. 135–168.

90. Polsby puts it this way: "...air conditioning (plus other things) caused the population of the southern states to change [which] changed the political parties of the South [which] changed the composition and in due course the performance of the U.S. House of Representatives leading first to its liberalization and later to its transformation into an arena of sharp partisanship, visible among both Democrats and Republicans." *How Congress Evolves*, p. 3.

91. Gary C. Jacobson, *The Politics of Congressional Elections*, 6th ed. (NY: Longman, 2004), p. 252.

92. Charlie Cook, "Value of Incumbency Seems to Be Growing," *National Journal* (March 20, 2004), p. 906.

93. Quoted in Jeffrey Toobin, "The Great Election Grab," *The New Yorker* (December 8, 2003), p. 76.

94. Bruce Oppenheimer argues that individual incumbency advantage has been decreasing and that very high reelection rates of House incumbents is primarily due to the partisan loading of districts. See "Deep Red and Blue Congressional Districts: The Causes and Consequences of Declining Party Competitiveness," in *Congress Reconsidered*, 8th ed. edited by Lawrence Dodd and Bruce Oppenheimer (Washington: Congressional Quarterly, 2005), pp. 135–158.

95. Loomis and Schiller, *Contemporary Congress*, p. 66.

96. In Florida, if an incumbent is not opposed, his or her name does not appear on the ballot. Thus the candidate is "automatically reinstated in Washington" without any constituent have to cast a ballot in his or her favor. David S. Broder, "No Vote Necessary," *Washington Post* (November 11, 2004), p. A37.

97. Jon R. Bond and Richard Fleisher, "The Disappearing Middle and the President's Quest for Votes in Congress," *PRG Report* (Fall 1999), p. 6.

98. Bond and Fleisher, "The Disappearing Middle," p. 7. The authors calculate their ideological scores from the rankings of liberal and conservative groups, Americans for Democratic Action (liberal) and American Conservative Union (conservative).

99. On the decrease of the number of moderates in Congress see also Binder, "Going Nowhere," APSR, p. 526.

100. See Eric M. Uslaner, *The Decline of Comity in Congress* (Ann Arbor, MI: University of Michigan Press, 1993).

101. Eric M. Uslaner, "Is the Senate More Civil than the House?" in Burdett A. Loomis, ed., *Esteemed Colleagues: Civility and Deliberation in the U.S. Senate* (Washington: Brookings, 2000), pp. 32–55.

102. Charles Babington, "Hey, They're Taking Slash-and-Burn to Extremes!" *Washington Post* (December 21, 2003), p. B1, B4.

103. William Brock, "A Recipe for Incivility," *Washington Post*, June 27, 2003, p. B7.

104. Thomas E. Mann and Norman J. Ornstein, *The Broken Branch* (NY: Oxford University Press, 2006), p. xi.

The President and National Security

Of all the constitutional powers and political roles of the president, perhaps the most vital is the direction of national security policy. As John Kennedy said: "The big difference [between domestic and foreign policy] is between a bill being defeated and the country being wiped out."[1] In the mid-twentieth century, the pressures of the Cold War with the Soviet Union tended to make U.S. policy makers view all aspects of foreign policy, not only military policy, as aspects of national security policy. Later in the century, increasing global economic interdependence, including balance-of-trade issues and energy dependence, made the performance of the American economy a vital element of national security.

This chapter considers three major aspects of the presidency with respect to national security: the constitutional powers of the president, the growth of the institutional capacity of the White House to dominate foreign policy, and the leadership styles of different presidents in crisis situations. The chapter has a dual theme: centralization of control in the presidency and the constitutional balance with Congress. The modern presidency has seen the development of a large and expert National Security Council staff, whose policy-development functions often overshadow the Departments of State and Defense. This increased control has favored the president in the struggle with Congress over the direction of U.S. foreign policy. In the 1970s, Congress used its own constitutional authority to assert its prerogatives. But President Reagan and particularly George W. Bush reasserted presidential prerogatives. After 9/11 President Bush made extraordinary claims to presidential authority that will be examined later in this chapter.

In formulating the Constitution, the Framers were faced with the dilemma of designing a government not too weak to act, as under the Articles of Confederation, but one that was not so strong that it would abuse its power. With respect to the chief executive, the office had to be powerful enough to defend the nation and lead the government in times of emergency. But the danger was that a too-powerful president might abuse power, as had the various monarchs in European history who were fresh in the minds of the Framers. James Madison felt that executives were particularly vulnerable to the temptation to win glory for themselves through war: "It is in war, finally, that laurels are to be gathered; and it is the executive brow that they are to encircle. The strongest passions and most dangerous weaknesses of the human breast, ambition, avarice, vanity, the honorable or venial love of fame, are all in conspiracy against the desire and duty of peace."[2] This fear of overweening executive ambition for war was echoed by John Jay in Federalist No. 4, where he wrote that ". . . there are *pretended* as well as just causes of war . . . absolute monarchs will often make war when their nations are to get nothing by it, but for purposes and objects merely personal, such as a thirst for military glory, revenge for personal affronts, ambition, or private compacts to aggrandize or support their particular family or partisans" (emphasis in original).[3] Thus the Framers were determined that the power to take the nation to war would not be entrusted to one executive, and so the "power of the sword" was split between the president and Congress.

In this division, the president's power was designated by the conferring of an office, the "Commander in Chief of the Army and Navy." Other foreign policy powers included the right to "receive ambassadors from other nations" and the right to make treaties, subject to advice and consent of the Senate. In contrast, Congress was given a number of specific powers and duties: "To declare War, grant Letters of Marque and Reprisal. . . . To raise and support Armies. . . . To provide and maintain a Navy, To make Rules for the Government and Regulation of the land and naval forces. . . . To provide for calling forth the militia."

This formula for sharing the foreign-policy and war-making powers between the president and Congress led the distinguished presidency scholar Edward S. Corwin to declare that the constitutional provisions constituted an "invitation to struggle" for the control of foreign policy.

The argument of this chapter is that the presidency has come to dominate the foreign policy of the United States and that this trend accelerated in the post–World War II years of the Cold War. Advances in the technology of communication and warfare have made this inevitable. After the "imperial presidencies" of Johnson and Nixon, Congress began to assert itself in many aspects of foreign policy, but the war-making power is still dominated by the president. An important aspect of this domination is the increasingly centralized White House control of the formulation of foreign policy. What in the past had been the main responsibility of the executive branch Departments of State and Defense came to be dominated after 1960 by the president's assistant for national security affairs. In the final part of the chapter, these themes are illustrated with contrasting examples of crisis decision making by several presidents.

THE WAR POWER

The most far-reaching power of modern chief executives is the ability to engage their nations in war, especially in an age when millions of lives may be lost and the destructive potential of nuclear weapons has the frightening capacity to make much of the globe uninhabitable. In deliberating over the war power, the delegates to the Constitutional Convention were concerned that one person not be able to commit the country to war. An early draft of the Constitution provided that Congress be given the power to "make war." But on August 17, 1787, the word "declare" was substituted, "leaving to the Executive the power to repel sudden attacks."[4] The deliberation of the Framers that day indicated a consensus that the executive was not to be entrusted with the power to initiate war:

> Mr. Sherman: "The Executive shd. be able to repel and not to commence war."
> Mr. Gerry "never expected to hear in a Republic a motion to empower the Executive alone to declare war."
> Mr. Elseworth: "It shd. be more easy to get out of war, than into it."
> George Mason: "was agst giving the power of war to the Executive, because not (safely) to be trusted with it. . . . He was for clogging rather than facilitating war."[5]

In the debate over the Constitution, James Madison wrote that the "fundamental doctrine of the Constitution" was

> That the power to declare war is *fully* and *exclusively* vested in the legislature; that the executive has no right, in any case, to decide the question, whether there is or is not cause for declaring war; that the right of convening and informing Congress, whenever such a question seems to call for a decision, is all the right which the Constitution has deemed requisite or proper . . . [for the president].[6]

Alexander Hamilton, one of the foremost exponents of a strong executive in the constitutional debate, defined the commander-in-chief power in Federalist No. 69:

> It would amount to nothing more than the supreme command and direction of the military and naval forces, as the first general and admiral of the Confederacy; while that of the British king extends to the *declaring* of war and to the *raising* and

regulating of fleets and armies—all which, by the Constitution under consideration, would appertain to the legislature.[7]

Hamilton defined the war power as "when the nation is at peace, to change that state into a state of war; whether from calculations of policy or from provocations or injuries received: in other words, it belongs to Congress only, to go to war."[8] There can be little doubt that the Framers intended to give the war power to Congress.

Despite this clear intention on the part of the Framers, the exigencies of international relations, precedents set by strong presidents, and the technologies of the twentieth century have all combined to make the president the dominant decision maker with respect to committing the nation to war. Congress has at times been more hawkish than the president and has often consciously delegated sweeping powers to the president for purposes of national security. When there has been a difference of opinion over the wisdom of military action, it is most often the president who has prevailed.

While the president has committed U.S. troops to combat more than 100 times over the past two centuries, most of these actions have been relatively minor incidents intended to protect American lives or property from pirates or revolutionary factions rather than attacks on sovereign nation-states.[9] Congress has declared war only five times in the nation's history:

The War of 1812 (fought against the British)

The War against Mexico in 1846 (to acquire disputed territory)

The Spanish-American War in 1898 (over Caribbean and Pacific parts of the Spanish Empire)

World War I in 1918 (to prevent Germany from dominating Europe)

World War II in 1941 (to defeat Germany and Japan)

The United States has also engaged in major undeclared wars, including the Civil War, that for various political and legal reasons were never declared by Congress.

With respect to the constitutional balance between the president and Congress, the important issue is whether the decision to go to war is shared, as intended by the Constitution. It is to be expected that, in times of war, power will flow to the chief executive. There is a need for unified leadership of the country in times of threat, and the president commands the bureaucratic apparatus to wage war: the military services, intelligence-gathering agencies, and the diplomatic capacity of the State Department. In addition, Congress has been willing to delegate sweeping powers to the president during wartime as the nation rallies behind the commander in chief.

The major wars of the twentieth century have been different in kind from the military conflicts of the nation's first century. World War I involved the massive mobilizing of the nation's resources, and Congress delegated unprecedented control of the national economy to President Wilson under the Lever Food and Fuel Act and over the executive branch in the Overman Act.

In 1945 President Franklin Roosevelt went to the Yalta conference to negotiate with Winston Churchill and Joseph Stalin about the organization of Europe after World War II. (© Bettmann/CORBIS)

WORLD WAR II

World War II saw even more far-reaching power delegated to and claimed by President Franklin Roosevelt. The 1930s were a time of isolationist fervor in the United States, when the public was fearful of being drawn into the coming European war. But as Hitler began to conquer much of eastern Europe, occupied France, and threatened England, President Roosevelt became convinced that the United States would have to enter the war to save England and, ultimately, the United States. At Prime Minister Winston Churchill's desperate request as a "matter of life or death," Roosevelt traded with Britain fifty U.S. destroyers of World War I vintage for rights to military bases in the Atlantic and Caribbean. He did not ask the Senate to ratify a treaty, because he knew it would likely be defeated, but rather accomplished the trade through executive order after consulting with congressional leaders. In 1941, Congress passed the Lend-Lease Act, giving Roosevelt the authority to continue his economic trades and delegating unprecedented economic and military powers to him, short of authorizing direct military intervention.

Roosevelt's task of convincing the nation that war was the only way to protect U.S. security was solved by the Japanese attack on Pearl Harbor, Hawaii, on December 7, 1941. Congress immediately declared war on Japan and Germany, and the United States committed its full economy and military might to defeat the Axis powers. Roosevelt's powers during the war were even more sweeping than those delegated to Wilson. He directed the economy, created executive branch agencies, and exercised wide-ranging emergency powers. He even threatened to ignore a law (concerning price controls) passed by Congress if it were not revised to meet his objections. The war ended with many emergency powers of the president still in effect, but their exercise was not seen as necessary by President Truman.

KOREA

When North Korean troops invaded South Korea on June 24, 1950, President Truman, after consulting with his advisers but not Congress, decided to commit U.S. troops to defend South Korea. Within a few days, the United Nations Security Council had met and called for an international effort to drive the North Koreans back above the thirty-eighth parallel. Truman claimed the authority to send troops under the commander-in-chief power and the UN resolution. On June 27 he met with a delegation from Congress that expressed support for his actions, though some complaints were made that he should have asked for formal congressional approval. With general political support from Congress, Truman decided not to ask for formal approval so as not to risk a split vote or a debilitating debate.

As U.S. forces under General Douglas MacArthur were successful in pushing back North Korean forces over the thirty-eighth parallel, pressure began to grow for the full defeat of North Korea and the reunification of the country under noncommunist rule. When MacArthur pushed farther north toward the border with Communist China—the Yalu River—China entered the war and drove U.S. forces back to the south, beginning a protracted war of stalemate. MacArthur's public disagreement with the president over the conduct of the war provoked Truman to fire him, asserting in a very visible way the primacy of civilian control of the military under the U.S. Constitution.

Congressional support for Truman's early actions in the war gradually evaporated as the war waged on, and U.S. forces suffered heavy casualties after the entry of the Chinese. Public and congressional disenchantment with the war eventually forced the United States to disengage. After a prolonged period of negotiations, and after Eisenhower had been elected president, an armistice was signed on July 27, 1953. But an important constitutional precedent had been set by Truman's failure to consult Congress and ask for its approval to engage in war in Korea.

VIETNAM

The United States had been supporting the French in Vietnam during the Eisenhower administration, though Eisenhower refused to commit U.S. forces when the French were finally defeated by nationalist forces at Dien Bien Phu in 1954. John Kennedy felt that the United States had to counter communist movements worldwide, and by the time of his death he had sent more than 16,000 military advisers to support the South Vietnamese government. Lyndon Johnson had promised in the presidential campaign of 1964 to limit U.S. military involvement, but by the summer of 1965 he had begun the escalation of military actions against the communist North Vietnam and Vietcong guerillas in the South. In 1965, he changed the U.S. role from support of the South Vietnamese government to direct participation in the war by bombing North Vietnam and ordering 50,000 more U.S. troops to the South. Eventually U.S. troop strength was increased to 500,000 troops.

Johnson derived his authority to commit the United States to war in Vietnam from the Tonkin Gulf Resolution. The resolution was based on reports of an attack on U.S. ships in the Gulf of Tonkin that it was later learned probably did not occur. Johnson, however, reported the incidents to Congress as unprovoked attacks on U.S. military forces and asked for approval of an administration-prepared joint resolution from Congress to sanction U.S. retaliation. Congress quickly passed the resolution, which read in part:

> The Congress approves and supports the determination of the President, as Commander-in-Chief, to take all necessary measures to repel any armed attack against the forces of the United States and to prevent further aggression . . . [T]he United States is, therefore, prepared, as the President determines, to take all necessary steps, including the use of armed force, to assist any member or protocol states of the Southeast Asia Collective Defense Treaty requesting assistance in defense of its freedom.[10]

Although this was not a declaration of war, President Johnson used it as the functional equivalent when he was questioned about the appropriateness of the U.S. presence in Vietnam. In addition, he pointed out the willingness of Congress to continue to appropriate funds for military action.

As with Korea, Congress and public opinion supported the president's actions at the beginning of U.S. involvement. But as the war wore on, and the numbers of U.S. soldiers killed in action mounted, public opinion began to change, and congressional dissent grew in stridency. U.S. public opinion was so split over the war that Johnson decided that he would not run for reelection in 1968.

President Nixon came to office with promises to end the war, but when it became clear that his definition of "peace with honor" necessarily entailed years of further fighting, congressional opposition grew. With the battlefield deaths of thousands more U.S. soldiers and the invasion of Cambodia in May 1970, Congress was provoked to try to force the president to end the war. After a series of legislative skirmishes in which Congress tried to legislate an end to U.S. military action in Vietnam and Cambodia, the Nixon administration signed a cease-fire agreement in Paris on January 27, 1973.

The war in Vietnam was the second major nondeclared war after World War II, though the president had congressional approval in the Tonkin Gulf Resolution. Members of Congress, however, believed that President Johnson used the resolution to justify a much broader involvement than was contemplated when it was passed. The resolution was made in response to a minor naval incident and was used to conduct a major ground and air war. In the eyes of many in Congress, the president had used the resolution as a blank check to pursue his own policies, in spite of congressional opposition.

THE WAR POWERS RESOLUTION OF 1973

In response to what it believed was the abuse of presidential military power by Presidents Johnson and Nixon, Congress passed the War Powers Resolution over President Nixon's veto. Its proponents intended it to correct the constitutional balance and restore the rightful congressional role in committing the nation to war.

The War Powers Resolution provided that the president is permitted to send U.S. forces into combat, "or into situations where imminent involvement in hostilities is clearly indicated by the circumstances," *only* pursuant to (1) a declaration of war, (2) a specific statutory authorization, or (3) a national emergency created by attack upon the United States, its territories or possessions, or its armed forces. It provides that the president shall consult "in every possible instance" before committing U.S. troops to hostilities. It requires that the president report to Congress in writing within forty-eight hours on any commitment or substantial enlargement of U.S. combat forces abroad. If U.S. forces were committed and there was no approval by Congress, the resolution requires that they be withdrawn within sixty days, with the possible extension of thirty more days if the president certifies to Congress that there is an unavoidable military necessity.

The experience with the operation of the War Powers Resolution has generally been unsatisfactory. Beginning with President Nixon's veto, presidents have felt that the law infringes on their constitutional powers as commander in chief. In most instances of the use of military forces since 1973, presidents have reported to Congress only "consistent with" the War Powers Resolution, not "pursuant to" it. This has preserved their position that the law is not constitutional yet prevented them from being accused of violating its provisions to report to Congress.

From the perspective of Congress, the experience has not been satisfactory either. The law has not been successful in forcing presidents to consult with Congress before introducing military forces abroad, though Congress has mostly been informed immediately before or after the fact, as would have been the case even without the law. The law has not been successful in reasserting Congress's power of the sword, though some argue that it has acted as a restraining influence in how long presidents feel able to leave U.S. troops committed overseas. Senator Thomas Eagleton even argued that the War Powers Resolution provides the president with an undated blank check to use U.S. forces for ninety days without any regard to Congress. He believed that the war powers clause of the Constitution was a more reliable check on the chief executive.

President Ford reported military actions to Congress in three minor actions, as well as his unilateral decision to send troops to rescue the crew of the USS *Mayaguez* when it was captured by Cambodians in 1975. Forty-one soldiers lost their lives in the rescue mission. President Carter informed Congress after he had sent a small force to attempt to rescue the U.S. hostages in Iran in 1979. The mission was aborted when a helicopter crashed and eight soldiers lost their lives.

President Reagan resisted consulting with Congress about the military actions he initiated overseas. When he decided to increase the number of U.S. troops on a peace-keeping mission in Lebanon in 1982 and 1983, however, he felt the need to negotiate the terms of their stay with Congress. Congress agreed to an eighteen-month period that troops could stay in Lebanon, but after 241 Marines were killed in a terrorist bombing in October 1983, the president withdrew the troops. In 1983, when President Reagan sent U.S. troops to invade Grenada and oust a newly installed Marxist government without reporting to Congress under the provisions of the War Powers Resolution, Congress voted that the sixty-day clock had started when the invasion began. The troops, however, were brought home soon after they had taken control of the island, and the timing became irrelevant.[11]

But the ticking-clock provision (the sixty-day period that troops are permitted to remain without congressional approval) points to a key weakness of the War Powers Resolution. The problem is that if presidents do not want to officially report their actions according to the provisions, Congress will have to do it for them. But Congress is then faced with the problem of seeming to oppose a presidential action that may be publicly popular. Often it has not had the resolve to do this, as was evident in the case of U.S. reflagging of Kuwaiti tankers in the Persian Gulf in 1987.

Iran had been attacking Kuwaiti oil tankers in the Persian Gulf, and Kuwait had appealed to the United States and the Soviet Union for protection. President Reagan decided to preempt Russian presence in the Gulf by providing naval escorts for the Kuwaiti tankers, which would be allowed to fly the U.S. flag. It was quite evident that U.S. naval forces that were deployed to the Gulf were in danger from possible hostilities by Iran, but the president refused to report the action to Congress and start the sixty-day clock ticking. A number of initiatives to begin the clock by Congress failed to gain adequate support. Members of Congress did not want to take the responsibility for undermining the president, but they did not want to legitimize his actions either. They wanted the option to criticize the president if anything went wrong, without being implicated in his actions. Luckily, in this case, U.S. forces did not become involved in a military fight with Iran.

A key problem with the procedures set up by the War Powers Resolution is that Congress by its inaction can force the president to remove forces from combat. Thus, Congress does not have to take political responsibility for its actions and make tough decisions about war and peace and whether to support the president or not. It can merely wait and decide whether to back the president, if the action is successful, or blame the president, if his actions fail. Presidents naturally resent this unwillingness of Congress to take responsibility. There have been a number of proposals to revise the War Powers Resolution to make it more workable, but none have been acceptable to presidents.

Some scholars have argued that the Supreme Court *Chadha* decision, which invalidated the legislative veto, also invalidated the War Powers Resolution provision that requires the president to withdraw troops if Congress does not approve of a troop deployment within ninety days. This allows Congress to force presidential action without any specific law that would be subject to a presidential veto. Constitutional law scholar Louis Fisher, however, argues that the War Powers Resolution does not delegate any congressional authority to the president and thus cannot contain a legislative veto (which, by definition, delegates congressional power to the president). Congress did pass a separate bill to allow a joint resolution (which requires a presidential signature or a veto override to take effect), but the concurrent resolution remains in the War Powers Resolution.[12]

THE PERSIAN GULF WAR

When the forces of Saddam Hussein invaded and occupied Kuwait in August 1990, President George H. W. Bush decided that it was imperative for the United States to respond militarily in order to protect Saudi Arabia and its oil fields from capture by Iraq. After convincing the Saudis to accept U.S. troops, he deployed about 200,000 troops in defensive positions along the Saudi-Kuwait border. Though he did not consult Congress, after it was back in session each house passed resolutions of support for the president's actions. By then the president had widened U.S. goals in the Gulf to include forcing Iraq to leave Kuwait.[13]

During the fall of 1990, President Bush became convinced that the U.S. policy of economic sanctions against Iraq would not be successful in forcing Iraq out of Kuwait. When the president announced immediately after the 1990 elections that troop levels in the region would be doubled, it was clear that the administration was preparing for an offensive action against Saddam Hussein. Concerns were raised throughout the country and in Congress that the United States might engage in war prematurely, and there were questions about whether the aims of a possible war were worth the likely price in U.S. lives.

The Democratic leadership in Congress was faced with a dilemma. Memories of the 1964 Gulf of Tonkin Resolution were still in its collective memory, and Congress did not want to give the president a blank check to pursue policies over which Congress would have no control. On the other hand, members of Congress wanted to support the president's defensive actions in Saudi Arabia without endorsing an offensive to throw Saddam Hussein out of Kuwait. They did not want to appear to undermine the president or the troops, but they were not willing to endorse a war.

The president's dilemma was that it would be politically useful to get a congressional declaration of support, and it would strengthen his hand against Saddam Hussein. On the other hand, weak support or a split vote would be worse than no vote at all and would encourage Saddam Hussein in his aggression.

Finally, in early January 1991, a resolution of support for the president's actions was debated in Congress. The president won heavily in the House, 250–183, but with a closer vote of 52–47 in the Senate. The resolution that was passed authorized the president to use U.S. armed forces to implement the UN resolution to force Iraqi forces out of Kuwait. The resolution was not a formal declaration of war, but, according to Speaker of the House Tom Foley, the action constituted "the moral and constitutional equivalent of a declaration of war."[14]

The congressional action thus fulfilled the constitutional requirement that Congress participate in the decision to commit the United States to war. But President Bush maintained publicly, even after the war, that he had the constitutional right to make the decision without congressional action. "Though I felt after studying the question that I had the inherent power to commit our forces to battle after the UN resolution, I solicited congressional support before committing our forces to the Gulf war."[15]

This was an extraordinary claim, on the part of President Bush, to presidential war power to the exclusion of Congress. Over the history of the United States, most presidential military actions taken without congressional approval were either minor or taken under pressure in which a quick military response was necessary. This is the type of action Bush took immediately after the invasion of Kuwait by Saddam Hussein. Despite the military implications of this action, there was no constitutional objection by Congress. It was only when the offensive option was considered that the issue of war powers was raised. Even President Truman's actions in Korea were taken in response to a sudden invasion, and the U.S. push into North Korea was decided in the heat of a shooting war.

But President Bush's decision to take the offensive against Saddam Hussein was prepared over a number of months. It was quite obvious to all that the United States was preparing for a major military offensive. If the president would not admit that such a situation fell under the war declaration clause of Article I of the Constitution, it is hard to see what independent role the Congress would have in committing the nation to war.

While some might be willing to trust the goodwill and judgment of a president like George H.W. Bush to make vital decisions of war and peace by himself, the separation of powers system was designed to prevent the exercise of arbitrary power by anyone who might occupy the office of president. That is why the Constitution divides the war power between Congress and the president. As Justice David Davis argued in *Ex Parte Milligan* (1866):

> This nation, as experience has proved, cannot always remain at peace, and has no right to expect that it will always have wise and humane rulers, sincerely attached to the principles of the constitution. Wicked men, ambitious of power, with hatred of liberty and contempt for law, may fill the place occupied by Washington and Lincoln; and if this right is conceded, and the calamities of war again befall us, the dangers [to] liberty are frightful to contemplate.[16]

OTHER CONSTITUTIONAL POWERS

Besides the commander-in-chief power, the most important constitutional power of the president in foreign affairs is the authority to negotiate and sign treaties. Article II gives the president the authority "by and with the Advice and

Consent of the Senate, to make treaties, provided two-thirds of the Senators present concur." The most important international commitments of the country are made by treaties, for example, international alliances of mutual protection, the conclusion of wars, and territorial agreements.

Early in his presidency, George Washington attempted to consult with the Senate on the provisions of a treaty he was negotiating with the Creek Indians. The Senate delayed its reply and did not satisfy Washington with its eventual action. After that time, Washington interpreted the clause "advice and consent" to include merely the submission for Senate consent treaties he had negotiated and not consultation with the Senate during negotiations. The precedent has remained as constitutional practice ever since, even though political caution may convince presidents to consult with some members of the Senate during negotiations. The Senate may, however, make changes in treaties negotiated by the president and leave to him the decision whether to sign them or not. This happened when President Carter negotiated the treaty with Panama that phased out U.S. control over the Panama Canal. The Senate insisted on several changes in the understanding, and Carter was forced to accept them in order to win a close vote (68–32) for ratification of the treaty in 1978.

While virtually all treaties (about 99 percent) are approved by the Senate, ratification is not automatic, and about 15 percent are approved only after changes demanded by the Senate.[17] The most famous instance of a treaty being rejected by the Senate was the Treaty of Versailles that ended World War I. President Wilson had gone to Europe to negotiate the treaty himself and had failed to consult or even inform the Senate of the terms he was negotiating. One of the provisions that was included, at the insistence of Wilson, was the creation of the League of Nations. When it became clear that the Senate would not approve any treaty that included the league, Wilson continued to insist on it, and the treaty went on to defeat in the Senate.

The ability of a president to end a treaty agreement was allowed by the Supreme Court after President Carter decided, in 1978, to establish full diplomatic relations with the People's Republic of China and terminate the Mutual Defense Treaty of 1954 with the Republic of China (Taiwan). Senator Barry Goldwater filed suit in federal court to challenge Carter's action, arguing the Senate had to approve of treaty terminations. In 1979, the Supreme Court refused to review lower court decisions that had ruled against the senator, which had the effect of letting the president's action stand.

The authority to terminate a treaty does not, however, include the authority to change the accepted interpretation of one. In 1985, the Reagan administration decided that it was going to develop parts of its "Strategic Defense Initiative" that included a space-based antimissile system. Opponents of the administration in Congress objected that this would violate the 1972 Antiballistic Missile (ABM) Treaty with the Soviet Union. The Reagan administration disagreed. This new interpretation of the 1972 treaty constituted a break with the interpretation of the three previous administrations, but the administration argued that the executive branch was the sole judge of what a treaty meant. Members of the Senate argued that the president could not unilaterally change the understanding of treaty terms that had been the basis for initial Senate ratification of the treaty.

After about a year of confrontation and argument, the administration abandoned its attempt to reinterpret the treaty and proceeded with development of the aspects of the Strategic Defense Initiative (SDI) that fell within the previously existing interpretation of the 1972 treaty, but without conceding the principle that the president was bound by the original interpretation of treaties. President George W. Bush later persuaded Russian Premier Putin that the development of a space-based defense by the United States would not threaten Russia, and the United States withdrew from the treaty in 2002.

Of course all agreements between nations are not weighty enough to create a formal treaty for each agreement, so for issues of a minor or routine nature the president relies on executive agreements. There is no clear distinction between the two types of agreement except the label and whether it has to be submitted to the Senate for ratification. But the lack of need for Senate approval constitutes a temptation for presidents to accomplish their aims that might not get through the Senate by the use of an executive agreement. The use of executive agreements has proliferated since World War II, with over 10,000 agreements having been made that constitute about 95 percent of all U.S. international agreements.[18] (See Table 7.1.)

When the Senate discovered that the Nixon administration had made a number of secret executive agreements with significant policy implications in its first two years in office, the Congress passed the Case Act of 1972, requiring the executive branch to report all executive agreements to Congress within sixty days. When it became clear that not all agreements were being reported, legislation was passed in 1977 requiring that Congress be informed of any agreement, written or oral, that might constitute a commitment on the part of the United States.[19]

By virtue of the constitutional provision that the president shall "receive Ambassadors and other public Ministers," the president also has the authority to decide which foreign governments the United States will recognize as legitimate. This also implies the ability to conduct the diplomacy of the United States. While the recognition power is most often routine, at times it can be an important policy-determining prerogative. Theodore Roosevelt made the decision to recognize the rebelling government of Panama, making it possible for the United States to build the Panama Canal. Franklin Roosevelt decided, over heavy opposition in the United States, to recognize the government of the Soviet Union in 1933. President Truman decided, over the objection of Secretary of State George Marshall, to recognize the newly declared state of Israel in 1948. Jimmy Carter decided to establish full diplomatic relations with the People's Republic of China in 1977.

The president's constitutional power to appoint ambassadors and other officials of the executive branch also gives the president additional control over foreign and national security policy. The Senate's right to confirm appointments does not often impinge on the president's discretion, but it occasionally provides some leverage. President Carter nominated Theodore Sorensen to be

TABLE 7.1 | TREATIES AND EXECUTIVE AGREEMENTS APPROVED BY THE UNITED STATES, 1789–1996

Year	Number of Treaties	Number of Executive Agreements
1789–1839	60	27
1839–1889	215	238
1889–1929	382	763
1930–1932	49	41
1933–1944 (F. Roosevelt)	131	369
1945–1952 (Truman)	132	1,324
1953–1960 (Eisenhower)	89	1,834
1961–1963 (Kennedy)	36	813
1964–1968 (Johnson)	67	1,083
1969–1974 (Nixon)	93	1,317
1975–1976 (Ford)	26	666
1977–1980 (Carter)	79	1,476
1981–1988 (Reagan)	125	2,840
1989–1992 (G. H.W. Bush)	67	1,371
1993–2000 (Clinton)	209	2,048
2001–2002 (G. W. Bush)	21	262

Note: Varying definitions of what compromises an executive agreement and its entry-into-force date make the above numbers approximate.

Source: Data for 1989–1992 from Harold W. Stanley and Richard G. Niemi, *Vital Statistics on American Politics* (Washington, DC: CQ Press, 2003), p. 337. Reprinted from George Edwards and Stephen Wayne, *Presidential Leadership*, 7th ed. (Thomson Wadsworth, 2006), p. 479.

director of the Central Intelligence Agency in 1977, but when it became clear that influential members of the intelligence community would make confirmation problematic, Carter withdrew the nomination. President Bush's first nomination for secretary of defense, John Tower, was defeated in the Senate over a variety of allegations about his personal life and conflicts of interest. This was the first time that a president's choice for his initial cabinet was defeated in the Senate.

Congressional power of the purse has been used increasingly in post–World War II years to influence national security policy. The authorization for defense programs had been on a standing basis, but between 1961 and 1983 Congress increased the percentage of required annual authorizations from 2 percent to 100 percent.[20] Actual appropriations requests from the executive branch have been increasingly altered after the president's budget gets to Congress. In 1970, 180 programs were changed in the authorization process, and 650 in appropriations. By 1988, the changes were 1,184 in authorization and 1,579 in appropriations.[21] Congress has also been deeply involved in decisions over procurement and acquisition of weapons systems. At times disagreements with the executive branch stem from policy differences about the desirability and effectiveness of different systems, but at other times they reflect traditional pork-barrel politics, with members of Congress taking care of their own districts.

These congressional actions, among others, have been seen by the executive branch as "micromanagement" of the implementation of national security policy. While this close control of some aspects of national security management by the Congress is frustrating to the president, some of it is a legitimate response to abuses of power and some is encouraged by factions within the executive branch.[22]

The irony of congressional involvement in the management and implementation of national security policy is that Congress has greater control over more and more details of policy management. In contrast, Congress has less control over the major issues of war and peace.

THE NATIONAL SECURITY COUNCIL DOMINATES THE EXECUTIVE BRANCH

The president has always been in charge of U.S. foreign policy and of the executive branch departments charged with the formulation and implementation of national security policy. During the first 150 years of the Republic, presidents have most often used their secretaries of state and war as their principle advisers in foreign and national security policy.

But after World War II a new institutional apparatus was created to deal with national security policy. The National Security Act of 1947 (amended in 1949) created the Department of Defense to give unitary leadership to the military services, the Central Intelligence Agency to replace the Office of Strategic Services, and the National Security Council (NSC) to advise the president.

Ironically, the purpose of early proposals for an NSC, and part of the reason for its creation, was to force the president to consult with military experts in order to ensure more coherent strategic policy and to give a greater role to the military. President Truman soon ensured that he would have complete control of the NSC by insisting that its office be in the Old Executive Office Building (OEOB), immediately adjacent to the White House, rather than in the newly built Pentagon across the Potomac River. He also made the NSC a component of the Executive Office of the President in 1949.[23]

The purpose of the NSC was "to advise the president with respect to the integration of domestic, foreign, and military policies relating to the national security."[24] Its membership consists of the president, vice president, secretary of state, and secretary of defense. The director of central intelligence and the chairman of the Joint Chiefs of Staff are statutory advisers to it. President Clinton in 1993 also included as "standing participants" at National Security Council meetings several officials not included by law: the secretary of the treasury, U.S. representative to the UN, chief of staff, assistant to the president for economic policy, and the assistant to the president for national security affairs (who has always been a participant).[25] President George W. Bush included his chief of staff, counsel to the president, and assistant for economic affairs and occasionally the attorney general and director of OMB. (See Table 7.2.) In contemporary usage, the term NSC refers to the staff of the council that is directed by the assistant to the president for national security affairs.

Fully aware that support for creation of the NSC in the Republican Congress stemmed from a desire to limit exclusive control of security policy by the president, Harry Truman insisted that its offices be located in the OEOB and purposely downplayed its importance by attending only about one-fourth of its meetings before mid-1950. But after the beginning of the Korean War in June 1950, NSC meetings were held weekly and the president presided at them most of the time.[26]

President Truman presided over the creation of the NSC and ensured that it would be a tool of the president, but President Eisenhower institutionalized it. From his experience in World War II, he valued thorough staff work and an orderly policy process, so he established a highly regularized process of policy development in the NSC. Within the NSC system, major roles were played by the Planning Board (at the assistant secretary level), which developed policy-planning papers, and by the Operations Coordinating Board (at the under-secretary level), which ensured implementation of policy decisions by the president. Ideas would have to be walked up a "policy hill" in their development, through the committees to the top where they would be considered by the NSC. When the president had made a decision, they would be walked down the other side of the hill to ensure proper implementation.[27]

Eisenhower used his NSC as he used his cabinet: as a deliberating body where policy options would be fully discussed and any difference among advisers or the different departments and agencies would be ironed out. There was never any doubt that final decisions belonged to the president, and as they were made, they were duly recorded and followed up by the OCB. Eisenhower upgraded the role of executive secretary of the NSC by creating the position of special assistant for national security affairs to manage the NSC staff. Eisenhower's first special assistant, Robert Cutler, firmly believed that his role was to coordinate the national security policy process. He believed that he was in charge of the National Security Council staff rather than national security policy, a distinction that would be lost on some future national security assistants.[28]

While the processes of the NSC were orderly and ensured presidential control and follow-through, the system was criticized in Congress as being too cumbersome and bureaucratic. Senator Henry Jackson held hearings, which

TABLE 7.2 | ASSISTANTS TO THE PRESIDENT FOR NATIONAL SECURITY
AFFAIRS

President	Appointee	Term
Truman	Sidney Souers (executive secretary)	1947–1953
Eisenhower	Robert Cutler	1953–1955
	Dillon Anderson	1955–1956
	Robert Cutler	1957–1958
	Gordon Gray	1958–1961
Kennedy	McGeorge Bundy	1961–1963
Johnson	McGeorge Bundy	1963–1966
	Walt Rostow	1966–1968
Nixon	Henry Kissinger	1969–1974
	(simultaneously secretary of state and national security adviser)	1973–1975
Ford	Henry Kissinger	1974–1975
	Brent Scowcroft	1975–1977
Carter	Zbigniew Brzezinski	1977–1981
Reagan	Richard Allen	1981–1982
	William Clark	1982–1983
	Robert C. McFarlane	1983–1986
	John Poindexter	1985–1986
	Frank Carlucci	1986–1987
	Colin Powell	1987–1989
Bush, G. H. W.	Brent Scowcroft	1989–1993
Clinton	Anthony Lake	1993–1997
	Samuel Berger	1997–2001
Bush, G. W.	Condoleezza Rice	2001–2005
	Stephen Hadley	2005–

reported that "the root causes of difficulty are found in overcrowded agenda, overly elaborate and stylized procedures, excessive reliance on subordinate interdepartmental mechanisms," and his committee recommended that the process be "deinstitutionalized."[29]

When John Kennedy came to office he intended to do precisely that. He disbanded the interagency committees of the NSC and replaced the regular meetings with a more ad hoc approach to dealing with discrete issues one at a time. Kennedy preferred smaller and more informal meetings to larger, formal ones. He increased the influence of the special assistant when he moved McGeorge Bundy into a West Wing office after the Bay of Pigs disaster. His choice of Bundy was also significant because Bundy was a substantive expert on foreign policy who played an active role in policy making, not merely a process manager, as were previous special assistants. Bundy stayed on in the beginning of Lyndon Johnson's presidency and was later replaced by Walt Rostow.

The role and relationship to the president that Bundy had initiated with Kennedy was enlarged and brought to its peak by Henry Kissinger. From the beginning, Kissinger intended to dominate national security policy making, and he engineered the return to a more formalized process in order to do it. Pursuant to a plan that President Nixon signed the day of his inauguration, he established interdepartmental groups (IGs), at the assistant secretary level, and the Senior Review Group (SRG). The IGs were chaired by State Department officials, but the SRG was chaired by Kissinger himself, and no policy proposal could get to the president until it had passed through Kissinger's hands.

While Kissinger's control of the process was virtually complete, this was possible only because Richard Nixon wanted it that way and had full confidence in Kissinger. Nixon intended to be his own secretary of state because he distrusted the State Department as too tied to the eastern establishment and felt that his own foreign policy experience was sufficient for the conduct of foreign policy.

Kissinger recruited a first-rate staff from throughout the government and academia. In effect, he created a counter-bureaucracy in the White House to give him an independent policy-formulation capacity. He could use the Departments of State and Defense, but he was not dependent on them. He had his own staff and policy-development capability. Soon after the inauguration, Kissinger began to establish "backchannels" of communication in which key communications from his agents throughout the world could be directed directly to the White House and bypass the State Department.

In addition to his control of the policy-making process, Kissinger changed the traditional role of NSC adviser by becoming the public spokesperson for administration policy and completely overshadowing Secretary of State William Rogers. So complete was Kissinger's domination that he personally conducted the diplomacy for Nixon's highest-priority foreign policy initiatives: the opening to China, peace talks with the Vietnamese, and Strategic Arms Limitation Talks (SALT) with the Russians. Finally, Kissinger was made secretary of state in fact as well as function. His deputy at the NSC, Brent Scowcroft, became assistant to the president for national security affairs and remained in that position during the Ford administration.

Jimmy Carter came to office determined to restore the traditional role of secretary of state as the primary foreign policy spokesperson for the president, and made that promise to Cyrus Vance when he nominated him. But his appointment of Zbigniew Brzezinski to be assistant to the president for national security affairs made the fulfillment of his promise impossible. Brzezinski had an aggressive personality and strong preferences in foreign policy. By the second year of the administration, there were open disputes between the two highest foreign-policy appointees of Carter. Their disputes extended to the substance of policy (with Brzezinski taking a much harder line than Vance), as well as to who would speak for the administration short of the president. Predictably, this led to incoherence in the Carter administration's foreign policy and ended in the resignation of Vance after the failed hostage rescue attempt.

Ronald Reagan, in his 1980 campaign, decried this disarray in the nation's foreign policy, declaring that if he were elected he would restore the primacy of the secretary of state:

> The present administration has been unable to speak with one voice in foreign policy. This must change. My administration will restore leadership to U.S. foreign policy by organizing it in a more coherent way. An early priority will be to make structural changes in the foreign policy-making machinery so that the secretary of state will be the president's principal spokesman and adviser. The National Security Council will once again be the coordinator of the policy process.[30]

Accordingly, he appointed the formidable Alexander Haig to be secretary of state and the self-effacing Richard Allen to be his adviser for national security affairs. While Haig declared his intention to be the president's "vicar" in foreign affairs, Allen was relegated to reporting to the president through Edwin Meese. Allen was soon eased out of his position, and Haig's deputy, Judge William T. Clark, came to head the NSC staff, with Robert C. McFarlane as his deputy. Despite the naming of George Shultz to be secretary of state, this marked the beginning of the takeover of the nation's foreign policy by the NSC staff.

Under NSC advisers McFarlane and John Poindexter, the NSC staff undertook the sale of missiles to Iran in exchange for U.S. hostages and the diversion of funds from the sales to the Contra rebels in Nicaragua. The arms-for-hostages deal was inconsistent with several U.S. laws and directly contradicted official U.S. policies, though much of it was carried out with the explicit approval of the president. The diversion of funds to the Contras violated U.S. law, and President Reagan denied any knowledge of the illegal activities. In these activities, the NSC staff, which candidate Reagan had promised to make subordinate to the State Department, took control of U.S. foreign policy in the vital areas of the Middle East and Central America.

In the Iran case, it did so with presidential approval but against the strong objections of the secretaries of state and defense. In the Contra case, it acted without the knowledge of the secretaries of state and defense and also without the president's explicit authority. After the Report of the President's Special Review Board (the Tower Commission) was given to the president, the NSC policy process was overhauled in order to ensure that the lack of accountability did not lead to similar incidents in the future.

National security policy leadership was well integrated and as smooth as it has ever been during the administration of George H.W. Bush. The principals, Secretary of Defense Cheney, Secretary of State James A. Baker, and National Security Adviser Brent Scowcroft, had worked with each other before in the Ford administration and each was close to President Bush. Scowcroft was the classic "neutral broker" among the other principals; he did not have strong policy preferences in opposition to other actors, and he faithfully presented their views to the president. He gave his personal advice to the president but did not bias the process to favor his own views. The effectiveness of their collaboration was exhibited in the Gulf War of 1991. President Clinton's national security advisers, Anthony Lake and Sandy Burger, led Clinton's national security council staff with policy expertise, but they did not attempt to dominate the policy-making process as had Henry Kissinger or Zbigniew Brzezinski.

As George W. Bush's national security adviser, Condoleezza Rice, began her job in the White House intending to cut the NSC staff by a third and was overshadowed by the other principals on the national security team, Secretary of Defense Donald Rumsfeld, Secretary of State Colin Powell, and particularly by Vice President Cheney, who, as a former chief of staff and secretary of defense, played a major role in national security policy. But over the first two years of the administration, the president's national security advisory team underwent significant changes as a consequence of the war on terrorism and planning for the war in Afghanistan. Condoleezza Rice rose from a low-key adviser and tutor to an influential actor within a very senior and more experienced national security team.

But Rice's important role in deliberations over war in Afghanistan began to wane over the next year, in the run-up to the war in Iraq. She was still a central adviser and confidant to President Bush, but national security policy decision making came to be dominated by Vice President Cheney and Secretary of Defense Rumsfeld. Colin Powell and the State Department were marginalized, and the traditional national security policy process was short-circuited. At the beginning of President Bush's second term, Rice was appointed Secretary of State, and her deputy, Stephen Hadley, became national security adviser. Hadley was also overshadowed by Cheney and Rumsfeld in administration policy making.[31]

The development of the national security policy process since 1947 has led to the centralization of control of policy in the White House. While the control of executive branch foreign policy by presidents is one of their constitutional responsibilities, much of the expertise and organizational machinery for policy development and implementation lies with the Departments of State and Defense. The temptation is to try to run everything out of the White House, but significant assets are lost when the cabinet departments are ignored. They contain the institutional memory and professional expertise that is essential to a sound foreign policy. To ignore these assets can very well lead to disaster, as it did in the Iran-Contra scandal.

PRESIDENTIAL LEADERSHIP AND CRISIS DECISION MAKING

We now examine four sets of presidential national security decisions to show how different presidents react in crisis situations:

Eisenhower and Johnson on Vietnam

Kennedy on Cuba in 1961 and 1962

Carter and Reagan on Iran

Bush Wars in Afghanistan and Iraq

These cases highlight different aspects of presidential leadership, advisory structures, and approaches to decision making.

Two Decisions on Vietnam: Eisenhower and Johnson

These two cases on Vietnam highlight the contrasting decision-making approaches of Presidents Eisenhower and Johnson. Eisenhower's formal process led him to keep the United States out of Vietnam. Johnson's less formal approach led him to conclude that the U.S. military had to become heavily engaged in Vietnam.

Vietnam I: Eisenhower in 1954
The United States had been involved with Vietnam since the end of World War II, and it had been supporting French interests that stemmed from their colonial control of Vietnam in the nineteenth century. Vietnamese nationalists fought the Japanese occupation during World War II and shifted their opposition to the French after the war. By 1954, the Vietnamese resistance had taken on a communist ideology, and the French were faced with a military defeat at Dien Bien Phu. The United States had been giving the French military aid, but U.S. forces were not directly involved in fighting the Vietnamese. In the early months of 1954, President Eisenhower was faced with the decision of whether to commit U.S. forces to support the French against the communist rebellion.

Eisenhower held weekly meetings of the National Security Council during the crisis period where the issues of U.S. intervention were discussed. The United States did not want to abandon its long-time ally France, and it particularly did not want Vietnam to fall under the control of a communist government that might ally with Russia and China and aid the subversion of other countries in Southeast Asia. On the other hand, the communist nationalists had wide support in Vietnam, and it was not clear how much of a military commitment would be necessary to keep the communist insurgency from taking control of the country.

In considering the French request for military aid and U.S. interests in the region, the president and his advisers made a thorough analysis of the implications and consequences of a U.S. commitment. The NSC meetings were marked by spirited debate and vigorous give-and-take. The process was designed to highlight any differences of opinion and force proponents to defend their positions. Participants were willing to disagree with the president. The role of Robert Cutler, Eisenhower's special assistant for national security affairs, was to ensure that no differences among the group were ignored and that all alternatives were thoroughly explored.[32]

Eisenhower's NSC process, which had been criticized for being too formal, had the advantage of ensuring that all points of view were examined. Part of this was due to Eisenhower's personality and leadership style. According to Eisenhower, "I know of only one way in which you can be sure that you've done your best to make a wise decision. That is to get all of the people who have partial and definable responsibility in this particular field . . . in front of you and listen to them debate."[33] Eisenhower's final decision was that he would not commit U.S. forces directly in order to aid the French, because if the United States did, "the Vietnamese could be expected to transfer their hatred of the French to us" and the "war in Indochina would absorb our troops by divisions!"[34]

VIETNAM II: JOHNSON IN 1965 Eleven years later, President Lyndon Johnson was faced with the decision of whether to commit U.S. combat forces to Vietnam. When the French left Vietnam, President Kennedy decided that it was in the U.S. interest to continue to try to keep Vietnam from being controlled by a communist government, and he sent 16,000 U.S. military personnel to act as advisers to the government of South Vietnam, who were fighting Vietcong guerillas and forces from North Vietnam. Lyndon Johnson believed that U.S. interests demanded continued support for the government of South Vietnam, but he was unwilling to make a public commitment until after the 1964 election, which he won in a landslide over Barry Goldwater.

The key decisions to escalate the U.S. military commitment were made by Johnson and his advisers in early 1965. When communist forces attacked an American air base at Pleiku, Johnson ordered retaliatory air strikes against the North. Soon after that, the decision was made to undertake sustained bombing of the North, and not only in response to specific incidents. Without fanfare, ground and support troops were sent to protect U.S. air bases. By July 1965, U.S. troops in Vietnam had increased to 180,000, and President Johnson had committed the United States to large-scale military action in South Vietnam.

One of the striking aspects of the series of decisions that resulted in the open-ended commitment of U.S. troops to Vietnam, with a peak of 500,000 troops and 58,000 U.S. deaths, was the lack of rigorous analysis of the full implications of the 1965 decisions. The meetings called by the president during the early spring took place in a crisis atmosphere, and the discussions were "singularly devoid of analysis."[35] There was little exploration of the differences of opinion among his advisers, and there was no analysis of the long-term implications of the commitment of combat forces.

Johnson dominated the NSC meetings and did not encourage the presentation of differing views, as Eisenhower had.[36] There were significant differences of opinion about the wisdom of escalating the war. General Maxwell Taylor, Senator Mike Mansfield, and George Ball all expressed reservations, but their objections were never thoroughly explored and defended at a full meeting of Johnson's advisers. When Mansfield expressed disagreement with the decision for a U.S. air strike, Johnson reacted so emotionally against him that Mansfield communicated his future disagreements with Johnson by way of private memo rather than by speaking up at meetings. McGeorge Bundy laid out differences among his advisers in a memorandum on July 1, 1965, but the memo was not taken up at the next-day NSC meeting.[37] The meetings often ended with an unwarranted feeling of unanimity about the direction of U.S. policy in Vietnam.

While it is not obvious that Johnson's final decisions about Vietnam would have been any different had his NSC process been more systematic, scholars Fred Greenstein and John Burke describe the process as an "organizational shambles," one "marked by the absence of regular meetings and routinized procedures, shifts in the membership of advisory and other decision-making groups, a reliance on out-of-channel advocacy, and other impediments to rigorous policy analysis."[38] Had Johnson insisted that his advice be more systematically organized, at least the broader implications would have been more fully explored and the decisions would have been better informed. The system also suffered because Bundy took the role of advocate rather than the role of neutral broker or process manager, whose job it was to ensure that all points of view were forcefully expressed and fully explored.[39]

These two cases on Vietnam illustrate important differences between the two presidents. Eisenhower was an experienced military leader, and his White House national security decision-making structure was designed to explore the full implications of important decisions in a deliberative manner. Lyndon Johnson's main strength was domestic politics, and his approach to decision making was much less formal than Eisenhower's. Johnson's personal style led to his domination of meetings and the unwillingness of subordinates to voice their doubts about the wisdom of LBJ's inclinations.

It is also striking that Eisenhower, the military leader of the victorious allies in World War II, was skeptical of the efficacy of U.S. military action in Southeast Asia, while Johnson was much more optimistic. Of course, the historical context of the two decisions was different, with the Cold War hotter in the 1960s than the 1950s. But in retrospect, Eisenhower's reticence was more farsighted than Johnson's optimism about the role of U.S. military forces in the political and military context of Vietnam.

Two Decisions on Cuba: Kennedy's Lessons

The following two cases in which John Kennedy made crucial decisions about Cuba also contrast a less formal with a more structured process. They illustrate how Kennedy learned from his experience, leading to a more successful outcome in the 1963 missile crisis than in the Bay of Pigs disaster in 1961.

CUBA I: BAY OF PIGS, 1961   In 1959, Fidel Castro led a revolution in Cuba that overthrew the discredited Batista regime and drew Cuba into the communist camp. The Eisenhower administration saw this as a threat to U.S. interests, and after urging by Vice President Nixon, the CIA began in the spring of 1960 to plan to overthrow the Castro regime. Anti-Castro exiles were organized into a military force and trained in Guatemala, with the hope of invading the island to wrest control from Castro.

When President Kennedy came to office, he was briefed on the plans and gave his approval for further planning. In March 1961, the fully developed plan was presented to the president. It called for an invasion of the island at the city of Trinidad, on the central Cuban coast, with the invading brigade of Cuban exiles being supported by U.S. air cover. The invasion was expected to precipitate a popular uprising against Castro and lead to his overthrow. The fallback, in case the invading forces were not victorious, was for the surviving exiles to retreat into the adjoining mountains and organize guerilla resistance to the Castro regime.

Kennedy was reluctant to provoke a confrontation with Russia, which was supporting Castro, and decided that no U.S. forces would be allowed to participate and that the "noise" level should be kept down by moving the invasion away from the major city to the Bay of Pigs. But he was also reluctant to stop the plan. During the 1960 presidential campaign, he had criticized the Eisenhower administration for not moving more vigorously against Castro, and he did not want to be accused of being soft on communism. It would have been difficult to keep secret a decision not to move forward because the disappointed exile brigade would have talked to the press, and he would have been accused of passing up a chance to get rid of Castro.

So the modified plan for the invasion was approved, and in April 1961 the invasion took place, but not according to plan. Kennedy relented and allowed one U.S. supporting air mission to take out Castro's air force, but the attack was not fully successful. He did not provide further air cover or allow any other U.S. participation. Castro's air force took control of the skies and defeated the hapless invading force. The switch of the location of the invasion meant there was a swamp between the invaders and the mountains, closing off any means of escape.

The whole incident was a disaster. Kennedy was criticized from the right for not providing sufficient support to ensure a U.S. military victory and the throwing out of Castro. He was attacked from the left for the U.S. backing of an invasion of a sovereign nation. Kennedy took full public responsibility, but his private reaction was, "How could we have been so stupid?"[40]

The answer was that the president had not explored fully enough all of the implications of his decision. Because of secrecy concerns, he did not allow full staffing-out of the decision, even by experts in the CIA. He asked the

Joint Chiefs of Staff for an analysis of the CIA invasion plans but did not allow them to staff it out fully. Their assessment was the chance for success of the operation was "fair," which Kennedy took to mean reasonably good. But the military assessment meant "fair," as opposed to good or excellent, and the analyst said that his judgment was three to one against success.[41] The CIA incorrectly expected that when the chips were down, and the invading exiles got in trouble, that Kennedy would allow U.S. military support. The expectation that there would be a popular uprising against Castro was unrealistic.

Part of this can be explained by the pressures of transition. The administration was a new team of people who did not yet know each other. They were involved with so many other pressing actions in taking control of the government that they were unable to devote sustained attention to this case. They were reluctant to challenge the expertise of the CIA, who had been working on the plan for a year. They did not want to seem weak by being afraid to take strong military action, and they did not want to be accused of blowing a chance to dethrone Castro. They were also affected by a hubris that often comes with new administrations that gives them the confidence that they are on a roll and can do nothing wrong.

The decision-making process was marked by a number of flaws. Experts who should have been heard from were not apprised of the plans. There was not a full military analysis. The same people who developed the plan in the CIA were trusted to evaluate it objectively. The assumptions underlying the plan were not fully explored and the planners were not pushed.

Kennedy let the CIA advocates of the plan dominate NSC meetings. The Kennedy advisers also suffered from what Irving Janis calls "groupthink." When a small group meets under high pressure, there is a tendency for them to develop a defensive attitude about their rectitude and wisdom. They tend to stereotype their adversaries as immoral and stupid, and suffer from the illusion of invulnerability. They develop a shared illusion of unanimity because any differences of opinion are not pursued and are seen as a threat to the good of the group.[42]

The implications of the Bay of Pigs invasion were far-reaching. Castro was pushed into further dependence on the Soviets and felt very insecure about a possible future invasion. Khrushchev saw the invasion simultaneously as a sign of weakness, because Kennedy did not ensure a U.S. victory, and as a sign of the reckless adventurism of an aggressive U.S. policy against communism. But Kennedy also learned lessons in crisis management that may have saved the world from nuclear war the next year.

Cuba II: Missile Crisis, 1962   On October 16, 1962, President Kennedy was shown reconnaissance photographs of Soviet ballistic missiles that might have contained nuclear warheads being assembled in Cuba. This was the kind of a Russian threat that the U.S. political system would not accept, and Kennedy decided immediately that he had to act. He called together a group of advisers as an Executive Committee (ExCom) of the National Security Council to consider the U.S. response.

The immediate consensus of the group, and Kennedy's first inclination, was that the U.S. should take out the missiles with a quick air strike.[43] But before acting, Kennedy led the group through a series of high-tension meetings over the next thirteen days to decide what to do. The debate considered a range of options, from ignoring the action to a full-scale invasion. In contrast to the earlier Cuban crisis, Kennedy and his civilian advisers did not hesitate to press the military people on recommended options. They discovered that a "surgical air strike" would not do the job. Even a full air attack, which would kill many Cubans and Russians, and perhaps provoke Russian retaliation, would not ensure the full destruction of the missiles and might leave some with nuclear warheads that could still be launched against the United States.

Kennedy finally decided that a naval blockade would be a way to confront Khrushchev, yet not close off as many options as an air attack would. It would also give Khrushchev time to reconsider his actions and possibly withdraw the missiles. Kennedy was careful not to fall into the groupthink syndrome this time. He deliberately did not attend some sessions of the ExCom so that his presence would not inhibit some of the junior members from speaking their minds. His brother Robert, the attorney general, played the role of inquisitor by carefully questioning the assumptions behind each proposal. Kennedy tried to put himself psychologically into Khrushchev's position and to understand the situation from his perspective. While he thought Khrushchev was duplicitous, he did not think that he was stupid. Despite the need for secrecy in the beginning, outside experts on the Soviet Union were brought into meetings to get their best advice. Weaknesses of each proposed course of action were carefully plumbed, and contingency plans were carefully formulated. The group was not forced into an early and false consensus, which was sometimes frustrating, but instead kept open minds, demonstrated by the fact that each member changed his mind at least once during the course of the deliberations.[44]

Kennedy was sensitive to Khrushchev's political and psychological need to save face and not appear to be backing down. So communications were carefully worded, and Kennedy deliberately refrained from attacking Khrushchev personally. He tried not to back Khrushchev into any corner that would make him feel so trapped that his only option would be to launch a nuclear strike against the United States.

After thirteen days of tension, the crisis ended when Russian ships carrying more missiles turned around rather than confront the American blockade. Khrushchev announced that he would disassemble the missiles already in place in return for a U.S. promise not to invade Cuba. Robert Kennedy also made secret assurances to the Soviet ambassador that U.S. missiles in Turkey would be withdrawn, but this was not acknowledged as part of the deal.

These contrasting cases from the Kennedy administration illustrate several dimensions of presidential decision making. From Cuba I, we learn the importance of presidential advisory structures. In 1961, the Kennedy administration was new in office, the White House team was not yet fully seasoned, and the president accepted uncritically the advice of the CIA, which was both planner and evaluator of the proposed invasion. The possible consequences of the invasion were not realistically evaluated or fully explored.

In 1963, a more experienced Kennedy paid much more attention to structuring the decision-making process, and he took pains to ensure that a range of options was fully explored. The United States was sensitive to the psychological dimensions of the Soviet leader and was careful not to close off his options prematurely. The failure at the Bay of Pigs had clearly taught Kennedy lessons that led to the peaceful resolution of the 1962 Cuban missile crisis.

Two Decisions on Iran: Carter and Reagan

Both the Carter and Reagan administrations had serious problems with U.S. hostages held by Iran or its allies. President Carter managed to get the U.S. hostages home alive, but his hopes for reelection were seriously damaged by the hostage situation. President Reagan compromised his principles in an attempt to free several other hostages, and the subsequent Iran-Contra affair seriously damaged his presidency.

Iran I: Carter and Hostages Taken The fate of Jimmy Carter's presidency became tangled with Iran when rioting Iranian "students" surrounded and occupied the U.S. embassy in Tehran in November 1979. It had been U.S. policy since the 1950s to support the regime of the Shah, and the U.S. continued to supply him with arms into the 1970s. Thus, when the revolutionary forces led by Ayatollah Khomeini drove the Shah from the country and took over, they saw the United States as their enemy. While U.S. diplomats were trying to establish relations with the new regime, the embassy was taken over and fifty-three U.S. diplomatic personnel were captured as hostages.

Carter's reaction was to put the White House in a crisis mode to deal with the situation. The problem was that, given the intransigence of the Iranian government and its claimed inability to control the "students" occupying the U.S. embassy and holding the U.S. diplomats hostage, there was not much that Carter could do.

Iranian assets in the United States were frozen and diplomatic pressures were applied, but to no avail. Carter made the release of the hostages his highest priority and cut back on public appearances to work on their release. The news media helped focus public attention on the hostage crisis, and the nightly TV news shows reminded viewers how many days had elapsed since the hostages were captured.

Although Carter's public approval ratings initially went up when the hostages were taken, the longer-term effect of the situation was corrosive. The situation seemed to symbolize the helplessness of the U.S. superpower in the face of a small band of terrorists. Carter's personal political popularity declined and left him vulnerable to a challenge in his own party in the 1980 Democratic primaries and to defeat by Ronald Reagan later in the year.

Though the hostages were Carter's highest priority during his last year in office, there was little he could realistically do to solve the problem. While a military attack would initially have been a popular move with the American public, the hostages would probably have been killed. So Carter seemed helpless in the situation. In April 1980, after months of frustration, Carter ordered a commando raid to attempt to rescue the hostages. The mission was launched by ninety U.S. military personnel. But in a nighttime rendezvous in the desert, a helicopter collided with a plane, killing eight men, and the mission had to be aborted. The probability for success of the mission was always minimal because the rescuers would have had to travel to urban Tehran undetected, neutralize all of the guards at the embassy, and extract more than fifty hostages safely.

After the rescue-mission failure, Carter continued to use diplomatic means to try to free the hostages. During the 1980 presidential campaign, the hostage situation made Carter seem weak and ineffectual and was a major factor in his defeat by Ronald Reagan. Although progress in obtaining the release of the hostages was made in the fall of 1980, final agreement was not reached until the last hours of the Carter administration. The hostages were finally released minutes after Ronald Reagan was sworn in as president.[45]

IRAN II: REAGAN HOSTAGE RELEASE ATTEMPTS   The fate of the Reagan administration was also to become entwined with hostages in the Middle East. In 1984 and 1985, seven Americans were kidnapped in Lebanon by Shiite Muslims closely connected to the Iranian leadership. Iran and Iraq were at war, and Iran had a desperate need for military equipment and spare parts to fix its weapons, many of which had come from the United States during the period it supported the Shah. Several intermediaries proposed a deal that would include the release of the hostages in exchange for the United States supplying spare airplane parts and missiles to Iran.

Through news accounts and appeals from families of the hostages, President Reagan had become extremely concerned with the plight of the hostages, one of whom was a CIA station chief. His concern was reflected by NSC staffers, who made arrangements to exchange U.S. arms and spare parts for Iranian intervention to have the hostages in Lebanon released. NSC staffers also argued that it was important to try to reestablish U.S. ties to Iran, so that when Ayatollah Khomeini died, the United States would have some influence in Iran. Iran had been a Cold War ally of the United States, and the Reagan White House did not want it to fall under Soviet influence. Thus, the hostages deal was intended to strengthen U.S. ties to "moderates" in Iran. Israel also wanted to open ties to Iran and to support it in its war with Iraq. So Israel agreed to ship arms to Iran, which would then be replaced by the United States. Later, the United States shipped arms directly to Iran.[46]

Reagan's decision to trade arms for hostages can be questioned on several grounds, from its wisdom to its legality. First of all, although the NSC staffers believed they were negotiating with moderates in the Iranian government, there is some doubt that there were any "moderates" in positions of influence in Iran at the time. Khomeini held tight control of the government, and it is doubtful that he would have allowed any officials not controlled by him to negotiate U.S. arms shipments or the release of the hostages held in Lebanon.

Second, the United States had a firm policy of not negotiating with terrorists for the sound reason that it would merely encourage them to continue their terrorist tactics. President Reagan called Iran part of "Murder Inc." and promised never to make concessions to terrorists. The Carter administration had imposed an embargo on arms shipments to Iran, and the Reagan administration initiated "Operation Staunch," a diplomatic effort to stop U.S. allies from sending arms to Iran. For these reasons, in meetings on the hostage deal, Secretary of State George Shultz and Secretary of Defense Caspar Weinberger vigorously opposed sending arms to Iran. Trading arms in hopes of freeing hostages contradicted long-standing U.S. policies and public statements of President Reagan.

In addition, there was the legal problem of the Arms Export Control Act of 1976, which prohibited the sale of U.S. arms to nations designated as sponsors of terrorism. Iran had been so designated since 1984. Presidential approval of the transfer of U.S. arms from Israel and, later, direct U.S. sales of arms to Iran, appeared to violate this law. In addition, the National Security Act governing covert actions specified that they were to be taken only after an official "finding" by the president that the covert action is important to national security. National Security Adviser John Poindexter testified before Congress that President Reagan had signed such a finding for the earlier approaches to Iran but that Poindexter had later destroyed it to save the president from possible embarrassment. President Reagan also signed a finding on January 17, 1986, authorizing U.S. direct arms sales to Iran. Public law provides that Congress is to be notified before covert actions are undertaken, or if that is impossible, "in a timely fashion."[47] Congress did not learn of the arms-for-hostages initiatives until they were disclosed by a Mideast newspaper months later.

The Reagan administration's actions to gain the release of the hostages over the course of several shipments of arms turned out to be futile. Three hostages were released, but three more hostages were captured shortly thereafter. The courting of "moderates" in Iran was also unsuccessful because some of the missiles were inferior equipment and the Iranians were overcharged for the missiles. How would inferior goods at artificially high prices induce the Iranian "moderates" to undertake a rapprochement with the United States?

These problems deepened when it was disclosed that Oliver North, a Marine lieutenant colonel on the National Security Council staff who had done much of the negotiating with Iran, undertook to use the surplus funds from the sales of arms to Iran to support the Contras in Nicaragua during a period when such support was prohibited by law. The constitutional crisis provoked by North's actions are analyzed in Chapter 8.

The two episodes with Iran illustrate several aspects of the presidency, one international and one personal. Presidents must now deal with a modern world where the United States is vulnerable to terrorism of several types for which the U.S. military cannot be effectively used. Despite the most powerful military establishment in the world, the United States could not use that power to save a relatively small number of U.S. citizens held hostage.

The second insight is that U.S. presidents are personally vulnerable to emotional pleas from the families of U.S. citizens in trouble in foreign lands. The plight of the hostages in Iran led President Carter to undertake a high-risk military operation that failed to save the hostages. The plight of the hostages in Lebanon led President Reagan to act contrary to his own principles, counter to declared U.S. policy, and against the advice of his secretaries of state and defense, in a futile attempt to gain the release of the hostages.

President Bush: Two Wars in Two Years

George W. Bush fought two wars in his first twenty-eight months in office, one in Afghanistan and one in Iraq. Though both grew out of the attacks of 9/11, they were quite different wars. The war in Afghanistan was fought to pursue al-Qaeda and Osama bin Laden, who had planned the attacks of September 2001. Only several hundred U.S. ground troops were involved before victory was achieved. The war in Iraq was waged to depose Saddam Hussein in accord with the Bush doctrine of preempting threats to the United States before they could be carried out. About 150,000 ground troops were engaged, with several hundred thousand additional support personnel active in the region. After the successful war came a difficult occupation of Iraq by U.S. troops in order to lay the groundwork for a democratic government. But questions were also raised about the arguments that President Bush made in arguing for the war in Iraq.

THE WAR IN AFGHANISTAN   Immediately after the terrorist attacks of 9/11, President Bush assembled his "War Cabinet," which included Vice President Cheney, National Security Adviser Rice, Secretary of State Powell, Secretary of Defense Rumsfeld, Chief of Staff Card, and Director of Central Intelligence, George Tenet. The War Cabinet considered several options for the U.S. pursuit of al-Qaeda in Afghanistan. A strike with cruise missiles could have been implemented quickly, but the targets might have been abandoned by the terrorists, and that option seemed too much like President Clinton's strike in 1998 that achieved nothing. Another option was cruise missiles along with bomber attacks, and a third was a combination of the first two along with "boots on the ground," that is U.S. soldiers in Afghanistan.[48] The president decided that it was important to have U.S. soldiers committed to battle in order to demonstrate U.S. resolve and commitment. The problem was that there were no existing military plans, and it would take time to set up staging areas and rescue teams before U.S. personnel could be placed in the country.

The administration asked for and got sweeping authority to pursue an international war on terrorism. On September 14, 2001, Congress passed a joint resolution giving President Bush broad discretion in his direction of the military response to the terrorist attacks. Section 2(a) of the resolution provided

> that the President is authorized to use all necessary and appropriate force against those nations, organizations, or persons he determines planned, authorized, committed, or aided the terrorist attacks that occurred on September 11, 2001, or harbored such organizations or persons, in order to prevent any future acts of international terrorism against the United States by such nations, organizations or persons.

The grant of power was sweeping, even broader than the Gulf of Tonkin Resolution of 1964, in that it allowed the president to decide as "he determines" which "nations, organizations, or persons" United States forces may attack.

The president was impatient to get U.S. troops into Afghanistan, but by September 26 only the CIA had any personnel in Afghanistan, a covert team of about ten men.[49] The U.S. bombing attack on Taliban targets began on October 7; although some hard Taliban targets were hit (e.g., buildings and airfields), the major early challenge was the lack of targets to bomb. The Taliban did not mass their troops, and there were no U.S. personnel on the ground in position to call in air strikes on the enemy.[50]

Later in October, the Army had placed several Special Forces units on the ground, but the lack of targets was still a problem. Bush had made a key decision not to introduce significant numbers of American troops to fight the war. Instead, the United States would depend on the "tribals" in Afghanistan, including the loose "Northern Alliance," to confront the Taliban and do the ground fighting. While not as well-equipped or well-trained as the professional U.S. troops, the local ethnic groups had the advantage of knowing the territory and language, as well as having scores to settle with the Taliban, which they had been fighting for years. But the United States, despite spending millions of dollars supplying and "renting" the tribals, could not make them engage the enemy before they felt they were ready.

In early November, the United States had four CIA paramilitary and three military Special Forces teams in Afghanistan that were assisting the local warlords and preparing to call in airstrikes when the battle was engaged.[51] The president and his advisers were getting frustrated at the delay by the anti-Taliban tribes in engaging Taliban forces, and contingency plans were made to send in significant numbers of U.S. troops. Despite the doubts and contingency planning by the president and his advisers, by mid-November the whole picture had turned around. The Northern Alliance began to attack the Taliban, which had begun to mass its troops.

One of the indicators of the type of war being conducted was a cavalry charge of 600 Afghan men on horses attacking Taliban forces at the same time these forces were being hit by massive and accurate bombing support by U.S. planes using the most sophisticated guidance systems in the world.[52] Once the tribal warriors began to attack in the north and the south, the tide quickly turned against the Taliban, and within several weeks, Kabul had been taken in the north (November 12) and Kandahar in the south of Afghanistan (December 7). Even the president expressed his surprise, "It's amazing how fast the situation has changed. It is a stunner, isn't it?"[53]

The total number of U.S. personnel in Afghanistan during the war were 110 CIA paramilitary troops and 316 Special Forces soldiers, and the defeat of the Taliban had taken only 102 days, with very few U.S. casualties (26 dead and 121 wounded as of January 25, 2003).[54] The new president, Hamid Karzai, took his oath of office in Kabul on December 22. The key to the U.S. victory was the desire of the Afghanistan tribal leaders to rid Afghanistan of the Taliban, which had oppressed the country for years. But the key to getting the active support of the tribal leaders was the strategic dispersion of $70 million in cash by the CIA to the various leaders in Afghanistan to gain their support and supply their troops. United States air power was decisive, but victory could not have been achieved without the Afghan warriors on the ground. Indigenous troops were probably more effective than would have been the better-equipped and more professional U.S. soldiers in the mountains and valleys of Afghanistan.

After Afghanistan had been liberated from its Taliban rulers, U.S. forces were introduced in large numbers to ensure the peace and begin rebuilding the country. They engaged Taliban forces, with mixed success, in the mountains near Tora Bora, adjacent to Pakistan. Their mission was to destroy remnants of the Taliban and their supplies and to block their escape across the border into Pakistan. During this period, Osama bin Laden apparently slipped out of the country while an aide took his cell phone on a different route to mislead U.S. forces.

Although President Bush rejected the idea of U.S. troops as nation builders, there was little choice but to try to establish stability so that the country could rebuild itself. After the Soviets withdrew their forces in defeat in 1989, warring factions led to chaos and anarchy and paved the way for takeover by the oppressive Taliban regime. By the fall of 2002, there were 10,000 U.S. troops in Afghanistan, though the new government did not fully control the country outside the capital of Kabul. U.S. troops were training a new Afghan army, but the government had trouble raising the money to pay the new recruits. Although the U.S. was spending billions of dollars on maintaining the U.S. military in Afghanistan, spending on reconstruction projects was relatively small. "Abject poverty, malnutrition and starvation still haunt each section of the country," according to one account in the fall of 2002.[55] In 2006, the Taliban was trying to make a comeback, and the future of the Afghan government was uncertain.

THE WAR IN IRAQ Although the public campaign for war with Iraq did not begin until 2002, President Bush and part of his administration began considering it immediately after September 11, 2001.[56] On September 17, 2001, when President Bush signed a top-secret plan for the war in Afghanistan, he also directed that the Defense Department to plan for a war with Iraq.[57] In 2003, White House officials said that Bush decided soon after the terrorist attacks that Iraq had to be confronted, but that he did not make his decision public because "he didn't think the country could handle the shock of 9/11 and a lot of talk about dealing with states that had weapons of mass destruction."[58]

Detailed planning for war in Iraq began in November 2001, but President Bush did not make public his decision to pursue Iraq until the State of the Union message on January 29, 2002. His decision was somewhat obscure and stated at a high level of generality because of his inclusion of Iran and North Korea along with Iraq in what he called an "axis of evil." In the speech Bush declared: "The United States of America will not permit the world's most dangerous regimes to threaten us with the world's most destructive weapons. . . . History has called America and our allies to action. . . ."[59] The administration started talking publicly about "regime change" in Iraq during the spring of 2002. The next major public pronouncement by the president on national security and Iraq came in the 2002 commencement address he gave at the U.S. Military Academy at West Point, where he argued that the United States had to "take the battle to the enemy, disrupt his plans, and confront the worst threats before they emerge."[60]

During the summer of 2002, some of the professional military began to voice reservations about U.S. plans to attack Iraq. It is not unusual for the professional military to not see eye-to-eye with the White House, but it is very unusual for their concerns to be voiced so openly to the press. *Washington Post* articles cited "senior U.S. military officers" and "some top generals and admirals in the military establishment, including members of the Joint Chiefs of Staff," who argued for a cautious approach to Iraq. They were not convinced that Iraq had any connection to the 9/11 terrorist attacks; they felt that containment had worked up until then; they thought a military invasion would be costly; and they thought that a likely U.S. victory would entail a lengthy occupation of Iraq.[61] In August, members of President Bush's father's administration Brent Scowcroft and James A. Baker came out publicly against war with Iraq.[62] Some combat veterans and retired generals also expressed reservations about the wisdom of war with Iraq.[63]

On August 5, 2002, at Colin Powell's initiative, Condoleezza Rice arranged for him to spend two hours with the president in order to explain his own reservations about war with Iraq. He argued that it would destabilize the whole Middle East, that an American occupation would be seen as hostile by the Muslim world, and that it could not be done unilaterally. He argued that if the president wanted to pursue a military attack, then the U.S. had to recruit allies, preferably through the United Nations.[64] Although Bush was not persuaded by Powell's reservations about war with Iraq, by mid-August the administration decided that the president should make his scheduled speech to the United Nations on September 12 about Iraq.

The Bush administration believed that opposition to war with Iraq was building and had to be countered, so Vice President Cheney took the occasion of an address to the Veterans of Foreign Wars convention on August 26, 2002 to lay out the administration's case in blunt terms:

> Deliverable weapons of mass destruction in the hands of a terror network or a murderous dictator, or the two working together, constitutes as grave a threat as can be imagined. . . . Saddam Hussein could . . . subject the United States or any other nation to nuclear blackmail.[65]

President Bush had carefully gone over the speech with Cheney before it was delivered, but that fact was not immediately released to the public.

The administration had planned to begin an intensive political campaign in September to convince Congress and the country that war with Iraq was necessary. Plans had been made in the summer of 2002, but as Chief of Staff Andrew Card explained, "From a marketing point of view you don't introduce new products in August."[66] In his speech to the United Nations on September 12, the president framed the issue as one of credibility for the UN and the need for its many resolutions to be enforced. He urged the UN to pass a resolution demanding that Saddam disarm. Shortly after Bush's UN speech, the administration released a new national security doctrine for the United States that justified preemptive military strikes by the United States.[67] It concluded that the danger of inaction while enemies build their forces was greater than the danger of attacking enemies preemptively.

In August 2002, the Bush administration argued that the 1991 resolution authorizing President George H. W. Bush's decision to initiate the Gulf War extended to his son's initiating a war with Iraq in 2002 or 2003. A senior administration official said, "We don't want, in getting a resolution, to have conceded that one was constitutionally necessary."[68] The president, however, changed his mind and decided to ask Congress for a resolution giving him the discretion to take the country to war in Iraq.

In anticipation of the congressional vote on a resolution authorizing war with Iraq, the president made a speech to the nation from Cincinnati on October 7, 2002, in which he explained the need for the authorization to take military action:

> We have experienced the horror of September the 11th. . . . Our enemies would be no less willing, in fact they would be eager, to use biological or chemical or a nuclear weapon. Knowing these realities, America must not ignore the threat gathering against us. Facing clear evidence of peril, we cannot wait for the final proof, the smoking gun that could come in the form of a mushroom cloud.[69]

The final resolution, which was passed by the House on October 10 and by the Senate on October 11, was very similar to the draft resolution proposed by the White House. After detailing Iraq's refusal to comply with UN resolutions on weapons inspections and noting that members of al-Qaeda were in Iraq, the resolution stated:

> The president is authorized to use the armed forces of the United States as he determines to be necessary and appropriate, in order to: (1) defend the national

security of the United States against the continuing threat posed by Iraq; and (2) enforce all relevant United Nations Security Council resolutions regarding Iraq.

Although there was a debate in Congress and statements by those supporting and opposing the resolution, the debate lacked the drama of the deliberation in 1991 over the Gulf War resolution. There was never much doubt about the outcome. A number of Democrats voted for the resolution out of fear that a negative vote could be used against them in the upcoming 2002 congressional elections.

After the administration convinced Congress to give the president authority to attack Iraq, Colin Powell and U.S. diplomats went to work building a coalition to convince the UN Security Council to pass a new resolution on Iraq. While the United States did not get everything that it sought in the resolution, it was a major victory for the administration. United Nations Resolution 1441 put Saddam Hussein on notice that he had to comply with UN orders to get rid of his weapons of mass destruction, and if he did not, there would be widespread international support for U.S. military action against Iraq.

Pursuant to Resolution 1441, UN weapons inspectors searched Iraq with seeming carte blanche and made surprise visits to sites of possible weapons manufacture; but by late January, they had found no "smoking gun." Chief UN Inspector Hans Blix said that he needed more time to do a thorough job. But the United States began to deploy troops to the Middle East in preparation for war with Iraq, and the buildup was expected to exceed 150,000 troops in the region by late February.[70] When it became clear that a vote in favor of war with Iraq by the U.N. Security Council could not be won by the United States (particularly with objections by France and Germany), President Bush decided not to ask for one formally and to proceed with the planned invasion.

In his State of the Union address on January 28, 2003, President Bush said that the UN had given Saddam Hussein his "final chance to disarm," but "he has shown instead utter contempt for the United Nations and for the opinion of the world." Bush declared: "If Saddam Hussein does not fully disarm for the safety of our people, and for the peace of the world, we will lead a coalition to disarm him."[71] As one of the supporting arguments for war with Iraq, the president said, "The British government has learned that Saddam Hussein recently sought significant quantities of uranium from Africa." It was later disclosed that this statement was based, at least in part, upon forged documents, and critics argued that the president had misled the public in his arguments for war with Iraq by exaggerating the nuclear threat from Saddam.

Throughout February and early March, the United States and Britain continued to build up troop strength and military supplies in the region to prepare for war. As various last-minute peace attempts failed, President Bush decided to attack. At 8 PM on March 17 President Bush declared that "Saddam Hussein and his sons must leave Iraq within 48 hours" or the United States would commence military action against them.[72] As the deadline approached, U.S. intelligence sources obtained information that Saddam was in a bunker, and so the president ordered a focused bombing of that location on the evening of March 19, along with other bombing preparation for ground troops. The bombing did not appear to kill Saddam, and two days later 130,000 U.S. and British troops began a land invasion of Iraq and a rush to Baghdad. At the beginning of the war, U.S. forces totaled 90,000 in combat and more than 100,000 in the theater.[73]

Within two weeks U.S. forces were at the outskirts of Baghdad, but supply lines were overextended and had to be secured. After another week of combat and several days of intensive bombing, however, American troops over-whelmed the Iraqi Republican Guard. With only limited street fighting and relatively few American deaths (fewer than 150 to that point, about half from hostile fire), U.S. forces were successful in occupying Baghdad. U.S. forces continued to mop up remaining resistance in Baghdad, and Iraqis began to realize that Saddam's rule was over. The end of his reign was marked by jubilation on the part of many, but also looting and general disorder and the destruction of government buildings.

As U.S. forces began to restore order throughout the country and sought to assist the Iraqis in establishing an interim government, President Bush declared the end of combat on May 1, 2003. In a nationally televised address from the deck of an aircraft carrier off the coast of California, the president proclaimed: "In the battle of Iraq, the United States and our allies have prevailed."[74]

Throughout the summer and fall of 2003, however, resistance to the U.S. occupation increased, and U.S. soldiers were killed in ambushes and other irregular attacks. By the end of the summer, as many U.S. troops had died as had been killed during the weeks of combat. General John P. Abizaid, the new head of U.S. Central Command, described the situation as "a classical guerilla-type campaign against us."[75] Resistance to the U.S. occupation grew internally and attracted foreign fighters. By November of 2006, more than 2,800 U.S. soldiers had been killed and the country was slipping toward civil war.

DID PRESIDENT BUSH MISLEAD THE COUNTRY IN HIS ARGUMENTS FOR WAR WITH IRAQ?

After the initial combat phase of the war and the failure of U.S. troops to find any weapons of mass destruction (WMD) in Iraq, the CIA sent in a search force of 1,200 experts under the leadership of David Kay to locate the weapons. Kay's mission was to scour the country for weapons of mass destruction and report back to the president. As his search continued without success, critics of the administration began to charge that the president had misled the country about the presence of WMD in Iraq and thus the imminence of threat to the United States. Three aspects of the president's claims will be examined: first, the implied connection between Saddam Hussein and the atrocities of 9/11; second, the implications that Iraq had nuclear weapons; and finally, claims about Saddam's chemical and biological weapons.

Two days after the terrorist attacks of September 11, 2001, a Time/CNN poll found that 78 percent of respondents thought that Saddam Hussein was involved with the attacks on the twin trade towers in New York and the Pentagon in Washington.[76] From that time to the beginning of the war and into the summer of 2003, the President Bush and his administration strongly implied that there was a link between Saddam and the al-Qaeda hijackers, despite Osama bin Laden's contempt for Saddam as the head of a secular state.[77]

In early October 2002, President Bush was trying to convince Congress to pass a resolution to give him unilateral authority to go to war with Iraq. In a major address to the nation on October 7, he stated, "We know that Iraq and al-Qaeda have had high-level contacts that go back a decade. . . . We've learned that Iraq has trained al-Qaeda members in bomb-making and poisons and deadly gasses." In the same speech, the president closely connected the need to attack Iraq with the 9/11 attacks: "Some citizens wonder, 'after eleven years of living with this [Saddam Hussein] problem, why do we need to confront it now?' And there's a reason. We have experienced the horror of September the 11th." Thus the terrorist attacks of 9/11 were a major reason for attacking Iraq. Vice President Cheney, National Security Adviser Condoleezza Rice, and Secretary of Defense Donald Rumsfeld echoed the president's statements in their own public pronouncements.

The problem was that evidence for a connection between Saddam and al-Qaeda was not very solid. Neither the FBI nor the CIA was able to establish that the 9/11 terrorist Mohamed Atta had been in Prague to meet with an Iraqi official, as the Bush administration had asserted.[78] And a UN terrorism committee could find no link between al-Qaeda and Saddam.[79] Despite the lack of solid evidence, President Bush continued to connect the war in Iraq with al-Qaeda and 9/11. In his victory speech on May 1, 2003 on an aircraft carrier off the coast of California, he said: "The battle of Iraq is one victory in a war on terror that began on September the 11, 2001. . . . We've removed an ally of al-Qaeda, and cut off a source of terrorist funding. . . . With those attacks [of 9/11], the terrorists and their supporters declared war on the United States. And war is what they got."[80]

But on September 18, 2003, President Bush conceded: "No, we've had no evidence that Saddam Hussein was involved with September the 11th."[81] He gave no explanation as to why the previously implied connection was abandoned.

In 2002 President Bush and his administration also made a number of assertions about Saddam Hussein's potential nuclear capacity. The claim was that Saddam Hussein had reconstituted his nuclear weapons program and was potentially less than a year away from possessing nuclear weapons. This was a powerful argument that deposing Saddam Hussein was important for U.S. national security. Even those who thought that Saddam could be deterred from using chemical and biological weapons (as he had been in 1991) might be persuaded that an attack was necessary if they were convinced that Saddam was closing in on a nuclear weapons capability. Thus the claim of Saddam's nuclear capacity was one of the strongest arguments that President Bush could make for war with Iraq.

Before the president's campaign to convince Congress of the necessity of war with Iraq, the White House asked the CIA to prepare a National Intelligence Estimate on Iraq. According to the CIA, "A National Intelligence Estimate (NIE) is the most authoritative written judgment concerning a national security issue prepared by the Director of Central Intelligence. . . . NIEs are addressed to the highest level of policy making—up to and including the President."[82] The NIE stated: "If Baghdad acquires sufficient fissile material from abroad it could made a nuclear weapon within several months to a year."[83]

This NIE was used as a basis for President Bush's speech in Cincinnati on October 7, 2002, to convince Congress to give him the authority to go to war with Iraq and convince the nation of the immediacy of the threat from Saddam Hussein. In his speech, President Bush said:

> We agree that the Iraqi dictator must not be permitted to threaten America and the world with horrible poisons and diseases and gasses and atomic weapons. . . . The evidence indicates that Iraq is reconstituting its nuclear weapons program . . . he could have a nuclear weapon in less than a year. . . . Facing clear evidence of peril, we cannot wait for the final proof, the smoking gun that could come in the form of a mushroom cloud.

Then, in his State of the Union Speech on January 28, 2003, President Bush said the sixteen words that would become the center of controversy: "The British Government has learned that Saddam Hussein recently sought significant quantities of uranium from Africa." The African country in question was Niger.

The problem with this series of statements was that the evidence upon which the president's claims were based turned out to be questionable. Two claims of evidence for Saddam's nuclear capacity that the administration relied upon were of dubious authenticity: the claim that Iraq sought uranium oxide, "yellowcake," from Niger and that aluminum tubes shipped to Iraq were intended to be used as centrifuges to create the fissile material necessary for a nuclear bomb. Each of these claims will be examined separately.

CIA Director George Tenet had warned the British that the Niger claim published in their September 24 dossier was probably not true, but they used it anyway. Before the president's Cincinnati speech, Deputy National Security Adviser Stephen Hadley received two memoranda (on October 5 and 6) from the CIA expressing the CIA's reservations about the Niger claim. In addition, Tenet personally called Hadley and told him that the claim was not sound. Tenet was successful in convincing the White House to delete the claim from the president's October 7 speech in Cincinnati (though the claim was included in the State of the Union Speech three months later).[84] The CIA was suspicious because the evidence for the claim was based in part on forged documents. Although knowledge of the forged letters was made public in February 2003, the sentence did not arouse public controversy until, in the wake of the U.S. war with Iraq, little evidence of weapons of mass destruction, much less nuclear weapons, could be found.

After intensive press inquiry in the summer of 2003 about how the sentence got into the State of the Union address, CIA Director George Tenet took responsibility for the inclusion of the inaccurate sentence on July 13, stating: "I am responsible for the approval process in my agency. And . . . the President had every reason to believe that the text presented to him was sound. These sixteen words should never have been included in the text written for the President."[85] Later, on July 21, Rice's deputy, Stephen Hadley, said that he was at fault for the reference to uranium.[86] Finally, on July 30 the president said, "I take personal responsibility for everything I say, of course. I also take responsibility for making decisions on war and peace. And I analyzed a thorough body of intelligence, got solid, sound intelligence that led me to come to the conclusion that it was necessary to remove Saddam Hussein from power."[87]

In addition to the Niger yellowcake claim, the administration also adduced as evidence for Iraq's reconstituting its nuclear program reports of large numbers of aluminum tubes purchased by Iraq. President Bush said in his September 12 speech to the United Nations: "Iraq has made several attempts to buy high-strength aluminum tubes used to enrich uranium for a nuclear weapon. Should Iraq acquire fissile material, it would be able to build a nuclear weapon within a year."[88]

The evidence of the aluminum tubes was also featured in the National Intelligence Estimate issued in early October, which played an important role in convincing members of Congress to vote for the resolution giving the President the authority to take the United States to war with Iraq. The State Department's Bureau of Intelligence and Research (INR), however, dissented from the argument of the rest of the National Intelligence Estimate:

> In INR's view Iraq's efforts to acquire aluminum tubes is central to the argument that Baghdad is reconstituting its nuclear weapons program, but INR is not persuaded that the tubes in question are intended for use as centrifuge rotors. INR accepts the judgment of technical experts at the U.S. Department of Energy (DOE) who have concluded that the tubes Iraq seeks to acquire are poorly suited for use in gas centrifuges to be used for uranium enrichment and finds unpersuasive the arguments advanced by others to make the case that they are intended for that purpose. INR considers it far more likely that the tubes are intended for another purpose, most likely the production of artillery rockets.[89]

The physical characteristics of the tubes—diameter, length, composition, coating—matched closely the dimensions of aluminum tubes used in Medusa Rockets but did not track as closely with the dimensions of centrifuge rotors.[90]

There is no doubt that Iraq sought nuclear weapons in the 1970s and 1980s. In 1976 Iraq bought a nuclear reactor from France that it assembled at Osiraq, but just before it was to come on line in 1981, the Israelis launched an air attack that destroyed it. And at the end of the 1991 Gulf War, it was discovered that Saddam was very close to achieving a nuclear capacity. But that capacity was destroyed by UN inspectors in the 1990s. Nevertheless, in spite of the lack of more recent evidence, some U.S. intelligence agencies concluded that Saddam's nuclear program had been reconstituted.

The alternative view of the State Department assistant secretary for INR was included in the NIE. It stated:

> The activities we have detected do not, however, add up to a compelling case that Iraq is currently pursuing what INR would consider to be an integrated and comprehensive approach to acquire nuclear weapons. . . . INR is unwilling to speculate that such an effort began soon after the departure of UN inspectors or to project a timeline for the completion of activities it does not now see happening.[91]

In his interim report to Congress in the fall of 2003, David Kay told Congress that Iraq's nuclear program was in "the very most rudimentary" state. "It clearly does not look like a massive, resurgent program, based on what we discovered."[92] According to Kay's report, Iraqi scientists said that Hussein "remained firmly committed to acquiring nuclear weapons" and "would have resumed nuclear weapons development at some future point." But "to date we have not uncovered evidence that Iraq undertook significant post-1998 steps to actually build nuclear weapons or produce fissile material."[93]

The Bush administration also claimed with some certainty that Iraq possessed chemical and biological weapons. President Bush said on September 26, 2002, that "the Iraqi regime possesses biological and chemical weapons. The Iraqi regime is building the facilities necessary to make more biological and chemical weapons."[94]

That Iraq had chemical and biological weapons in the 1980s is certain, in part because some of the materials came from the United States and because Saddam used chemical weapons against Iran and against the Kurds in northern Iraq. But serious questions about the administration's claims were raised when U.S. forces were not able to find evidence of Iraq's chemical and biological weapons after the war, despite the diligent searching of U.S. military forces and the 1,200 member Iraq Survey Group headed by David Kay.[95] Kay reported that with respect to chemical weapons, " . . . Iraq's large-scale capability to develop, produce, and fill new CW munitions was reduced—if not entirely destroyed—during Operations Desert Storm and Desert Fox, thirteen years of UN sanctions and UN inspections." With respect to biological weapons, the Iraq Survey Group found evidence of various "biological warfare activities" and one "vial of live C. botulinum Okra B," from which "a biological agent can be produced."[96] But they found no biological weapons.

Possible justifications for war with Iraq ranged from the idealistic goal of bringing democracy to Iraqis and the humanitarian desire to rid them of a tyrant to geostrategic concerns about the future of the Middle East. That Saddam was a vicious tyrant who tortured his political enemies, gassed his own people, and invaded other countries was known long before the Bush administration decided to go to war to depose him. But the most compelling arguments to the American people were the arguments that the national security of the United States was at risk. For this reason, the claims that Saddam's

WMD posed a direct threat were most effective in sustaining political support for war.

The administration's inference that Saddam Hussein was continuing his previous weapons programs was not an unreasonable conclusion. The problem was that there was little evidence to support their conclusion, and they used claims of dubious validity to make their case to the American people. There is no doubt that Saddam Hussein had significant conventional warfare capacity and was developing missiles and other weapons systems that violated UN resolutions, but the administration's main argument for war was that Saddam's WMD presented an imminent threat to the United States.

President Bush's critics had a point in arguing that his administration misleadingly implied that there was a connection between Saddam and the attacks of 9/11. Similarly, the implication that Iraq had reconstituted its nuclear capability was not supported by the evidence the administration presented. However, the assumption that Iraq had chemical and biological weapons was accepted widely by foreign intelligence services as well as by the United States. So President Bush cannot be faulted for his prewar claims about chemical and biological weapons, even though U.S. inspectors were not able to find such weapons in the first six months after the war.

As the U.S. search for weapons of mass destruction in Iraq looked more and more futile, the administration shifted its justification for the war to the brutality of Saddam and the importance of democracy for the people of Iraq. The ultimate judgment about the success of the war with Iraq, therefore, will depend upon whether a viable democracy is established in that country and whether the war increased or decreased the likelihood of terrorist attacks against the United States.

PRESIDENT BUSH AND THE COMMANDER IN CHIEF AUTHORITY

The atrocities of 9/11 gave President Bush the opportunity to act according to his expansive interpretation of presidential power. The nation was traumatized by the events of 9/11, and neither Congress nor the public was willing to stop the president from doing what he deemed necessary to protect the nation. In addition, many of the initial legal justifications and executive orders expanding presidential power were carried out in secret, even excluding members of the executive branch who normally would have participated in deliberations about the issues (e.g., in the Justice, State, and Defense Departments).[97] The "state secrets" claim was also used by the Bush administration not only to exclude certain information from being made public in court proceedings but also to stop entire cases from being heard by the judiciary.[98]

The assertions of power of the Bush administration involved basic issues of constitutional rights and the rule of law. Several issues will be considered here: the legality of presidential commissions to try suspected terrorists, the right of President Bush to suspend the Geneva Conventions regarding treatment of detainees, and the right of the president to wiretap citizens without first obtaining a judicial warrant.

One of the challenges stemming from 9/11 concerned how to deal with suspected terrorists or allies of al-Qaeda. The administration felt that normal trials would afford too many legal protections to terrorists, and so President Bush ordered that military commissions be established entirely within the executive branch to try them. In a Military Order issued on November 13, 2001, President Bush instructed that any noncitizen "whom I determine" was a terrorist or abetted one could be "detained at an appropriate place" by the Secretary of Defense and tried by military tribunal.[99] The military tribunals (or commissions) did not require the usual elements of due process; for instance, they could use coerced testimony and deny the defendant the right to see the evidence used against him.[100] Congress later passed a law, the Military Commissions Act of 2006, that gave the president much of the authority that he had previously claimed.

In dealing with suspected terrorists, the administration also practiced "extraordinary rendition," in which suspects would be handed over to governments that were likely to torture the suspects in order to obtain information about terrorism. In addition, the CIA kidnapped terrorist suspects and secretly took them to "black sites" in European countries for interrogation, though nothing about the operation or activities of these secret black sites was publicly revealed by the Bush administration.[101]

Regarding the treatment of detainees in captivity, President Bush issued an executive order on February 7, 2002, that announced that the Geneva Conventions would not apply to members of al-Qaeda.[102] The order was issued over the objections of Secretary of State Colin Powell and many career Judge Advocate General lawyers in the Department of Defense, who warned that it would undermine the traditional standards of treatment of detainees, endanger captured U.S. soldiers, and hurt the United States' image abroad. These warnings turned out to be prescient when the abuses at Abu Ghraib were revealed in 2004. It was further revealed that U.S. personnel had tortured detainees, some of them to death, at Abu Ghraib and bases in Afghanistan.[103] President Bush also asserted that U.S. citizens, if he determined they were "enemy combatants," could be detained indefinitely.

Shortly after 9/11, President Bush ordered the National Security Agency (NSA) to listen in on conversations between al-Qaeda suspects in foreign countries and people within the United States. Public law permits NSA to monitor calls and other transmissions in foreign countries, but the Foreign Intelligence Surveillance Act of 1977 (FISA) requires that all domestic wiretapping or surveillance be undertaken pursuant to a warrant, and it set up a special court for that purpose. President Bush asserted that he had the inherent authority as commander in chief to disregard the law and order surveillance in the domestic United States without obtaining a warrant issued by the special FISA judges.[104]

This was problematical because the Fourth Amendment protects citizens against unreasonable searches and seizures without a warrant, and the Foreign

Intelligence Surveillance Act forbids electronic surveillance of U.S. citizens within the United States without a warrant, as provided in that statute. President Bush's claim that he had the constitutional authority to undertake such surveillance amounts to a claim that the executive has the authority to ignore the law if he determines that it is in the interest of national security to do so.

It is not as if President Bush did not have the means to undertake the NSA spying within the law. He could have sought warrants by the special FISA courts set up for that very purpose. If speed was of importance, NSA could have carried out the surveillance and come back to the FISA court within 72 hours for retrospective authorization, as provided for by the law. Or if the law, as written, was too narrow to allow the kind of surveillance deemed necessary (e.g., data mining or call tagging), the president could have asked Congress to change the law. But President Bush did none of these things; instead, he secretly ordered NSA to conduct the surveillance, and when his actions were disclosed, he asserted that he had the constitutional authority to ignore the law.

This brings us to the fundamental issue of constitutionalism itself, which is at stake here. In our system of limited government, the Constitution sets limits on what the government can do, and it lays out procedures for making laws and amending the Constitution. Article I provides that "All legislative Powers herein granted shall be vested in a Congress of the United States. . . ." Article II provides that the president "shall take Care that the Laws be faithfully executed. . . ." In making the claim to the constitutional authority to ignore the FISA law the president argued that his constitutional commander-in-chief powers overrode his duty to faithfully execute the laws. As in other cases, the administration argued that its actions were unreviewable by the courts.

The problem in each these cases was that President Bush was asserting that he was not bound by the law. Congressman David Obey's (D-Wisc.) exaggerated in making his rhetorical point: "This administration thinks that Article I of the Constitution was a fundamental mistake."[105] The rule of law is fundamental to a free society and to democracy, because neither can exist without it. As Thomas Paine argued in *Common Sense*, "in America THE LAW IS KING. For as in absolute governments the King is law, and so in free countries the law *ought* to be King; and there ought to be no other." (Emphasis in original.)[106] James Madison put it this way in Federalist 47: "The accumulation of all powers, legislative, executive, and judiciary, in the same hands, whether of one, a few, or many, and whether hereditary, self-appointed, or elective, may justly be pronounced the very definition of tyranny."

In the cases where President Bush asserted inherent presidential power to ignore the law, he was claiming that the checks and balances in the Constitution were not binding on him. In the case of military tribunals, the president would act as lawmaker in creating the commissions himself and not in accord with enacted laws. He would act as executive in detaining suspects in prisons. And he would act as judge in conducting the trials, imposing sentences, and serving as the final appeal. In the case of the Geneva Conventions and torture, President Bush would act as lawmaker in suspending the treaty, which according to the Constitution is "the supreme Law of the Land." He would act as executive in carrying out the policy by interrogating prisoners with harsh interrogation practices. And he would act as judge by keeping the proceedings secret and arguing that federal courts did not have jurisdiction to consider appeals of detainees. In the case of the NSA warrantless wiretapping of people in the United States, President Bush would act as lawmaker by determining that he could ignore the regularly enacted law in order to conduct surveillance in the United States. He would act as executive in ordering NSA to carry out his policies. And he would act as judge by arguing that it was his inherent right as president to do it in secret and prevent any review by the courts.

The Supreme Court delivered several setbacks to President Bush's claims to executive power. Yaser Hamdi was an American citizen who was captured in Afghanistan; when he was being held at the U.S. military detainment camp at Guantanamo Bay, Cuba, he filed for a writ of habeas corpus in order to challenge the right of the government to continue to hold him prisoner. In *Hamdi v. Rumsfeld* (159 L.Ed. 2d 578 [2004]), the Court ruled that Congress had authorized the war against al-Qaeda and thus the president had the authority to detain enemy combatants to prevent them from returning to the battlefield, but that "indefinite detention for the purpose of interrogation is not authorized."

The Court declared that "the most elemental of liberty interests" is "the interest in being free from physical detention by one's own government [without due process of law]," arguing that "history and common sense teach us that an unchecked system of detention carries the potential to become a means for oppression and abuse of others who do not present that sort of threat." The Court thus reaffirmed "the fundamental nature of a citizen's right to be free from involuntary confinement by his own government without due process of law." The Court stated that this requirement of due process does not apply to "initial captures on the battle field" but "is due only when the determination is made to *continue* to hold those who have been seized."[107]

In making these judgments, the Court asserted that it had jurisdiction over executive branch imprisonments and that it was willing to enforce constitutional rights even during a time of war. In *Rasul v. Bush* (159 L. Ed. 2d 548 [2004]), the Court held that noncitizens also had the right to challenge their imprisonment through a habeas corpus petition.[108]

On the issue of whether the United States is permitted to try noncitizen enemy combatants by military commission, the Supreme Court in *Hamden v. Rumsfeld* ruled in the negative, overturning a Court of Appeals decision.[109] Hamden was a Yemeni national who was captured in Afghanistan in November 2001 and turned over to U.S. forces. He was transported to Guantanamo, where he was charged with conspiracy to aid al-Qaeda (as Osama bin Laden's driver) and was going to be tried by a military commission established by President Bush.[110]

Hamden filed a habeas corpus petition, arguing that he was entitled to be tried under the requirements of Common Article 3 of the Third Geneva Convention and that the charge of conspiracy was not a violation of the law of war. Justice Stevens, writing for the Court, after ruling on standing and justiciability, concluded that the military commissions and procedures established by President Bush were not authorized by the Constitution or any U.S. law (not the Authorization to use Military Force or the Detainee Treatment Act, nor the Uniform Code of Military Justice (UCMJ), and thus the president had to comply with existing U.S. laws. He explained that the "structures and procedures violate both the UCMJ and the four Geneva Conventions signed in 1949."[111] Part of the problem with the commissions was that the accused could be excluded from being present and could be tried without being told of the evidence used against him. Also, the commissions could use any evidence that the presiding officer thought "would have probative value to a reasonable person," and thus might include evidence coerced through torture. The commissions also violated the Geneva Convention Common Article 3, which provides that detainees, "as a minimum," are entitled to be tried "by a regularly constituted court affording all the judicial guarantees . . . recognized as an indispensable by civilized peoples."[112] The Court did not say that Hamdan could not be detained for the duration of the hostilities, but if the government wanted to try him for a crime, it had to use regularly constituted courts that comply with minimal requirements of procedural due process to do so. The Court finally concluded: "Even assuming that Hamden is a dangerous individual who would cause great harm or death to innocent civilians given the opportunity, the Executive nevertheless must comply with the prevailing rule of law in undertaking to try him and subject him to criminal punishment."[113] The Military Commissions Act of 2006 later gave the president the authority to constitute military tribunals and try detainees with them.

Perhaps the most important principle established in these Supreme Court cases was Justice Sandra Day O'Conner's statement in the majority opinion of the Hamdi case: "We have long since made clear that a state of war is not a blank check for the President when it comes to the rights of the Nation's citizens."[114]

CONCLUSION

This chapter has examined some of the most far-reaching and important powers that U.S. presidents wield. The struggle between the president and Congress over the war powers, divided in the Constitution between the two branches, has tilted toward the president in the twentieth century. On the other hand, since the "imperial presidencies" of Johnson and Nixon, Congress has played a more active role in the details of national security and foreign policy. Executive branch national security policy development has been centralized and institutionalized in the White House since 1960, as national security issues have become more complex. Presidential crisis decision making, however, is still highly dependent on personality and context.

An understandable irony of American politics is that presidents who deal successfully with crises—especially via military confrontations—are treated as heroes by the American public. Danger and the possibility for disaster is high, and Americans rightly give credit to presidents who are effective military leaders. But the irony of leadership is that the same adulation is not given to those who *prevent* situations from becoming crises in the first place.

For instance, John Kennedy is justly given credit for his effective leadership in the Cuban missile crisis of 1962. His restraint and sensitivity in confronting Khrushchev brought the world back from the brink of nuclear war. Yet, some historians argue that if Kennedy had sent clear early signals to Khrushchev that Soviet missiles in Cuba would be seen as a direct threat by the United States, Khrushchev might not have put the missiles there in the first place.

Similarly, George H. W. Bush is justly praised for his leadership as commander in chief of U.S. forces during the Persian Gulf War of 1991. But it is also clear that U.S. policies toward Iraq during the 1980s—helping to build up its military power as a counterbalance to Iran—encouraged Saddam Hussein and made possible his formidable military capacity. U.S. actions up to the months before the war continued to support and encourage Saddam Hussein.

Both of these observations are made with the benefit of hindsight, which President Eisenhower used to say is usually more accurate, but much less useful, than foresight. The principle still holds, however, that military leadership is an important dimension of our evaluation of presidents.

NOTES

1. Theodore C. Sorensen, *Kennedy* (New York: Bantam, 1965), p. 573.

2. Gaillard Hunt, ed., *The Writings of Jams Madison* (NY: G.P. Putnam's Sons, 1906), p. 152; quoted in David Gray Adler, "The President as King: The Usurpation of War and Foreign Affairs Powers in the Modern Age," in Michael Genovese and Lori Cox Han eds., *The Presidency and the Challenges of Democracy* (NY: Palgrave, 2007).

3. John Jay, Federalist No. 4, in Alexander Hamilton, James Madison, and John Jay, *The Federalist* (London: Everyman's Library, 1992), p. 13.

4. Max Farrand, ed., *The Records of the Federal Convention of 1787*, vol. II (New Haven, CT: Yale University Press, 1911, 1966), p. 318.

5. Max Farrand ed., *The Records of the Federal Convention of 1787*, vol. II (New Haven, CT: Yale University Press, 1911, 1966), p. 318–319.

6. Gaillard Hunt, ed., "Letters of Helvidius, No. 1," in *The Writings of James Madison*, vol. 6 (New York: Putnam, 1900–10), p. 174; quoted by Robert A. Katzman, "War Powers: Toward a New Accommodation," in Thomas E. Mann, ed., *A Question of Balance* (Washington, DC: Brookings, 1990), p. 38.

7. *The Federalist Papers* (New York: Mentor Books, 1961), p. 418.

8. Michael J. Glennon, "The Gulf War and the Constitution," *Foreign Affairs* 70:2 (Spring 1991), p. 88.

9. Arthur Schlesinger, Jr., *The Imperial Presidency* (Boston: Houghton Mifflin, 1989), p. 443.

10. Nelson, *Congressional Quarterly Guide to the Presidency* (Washington, DC: Congressional Quarterly, 1989), p. 542.

11. Ellen C. Collier, "The War Powers Resolution: Eighteen Years of Experience," *Congressional Research Service Report No. 92–133F* (Washington, DC: Library of Congress, February 4, 1992).

12. Louis Fisher, *Presidential War Power* (Lawrence, KS: University Press of Kansas, 1995), pp. 194–197.

13. For an analysis of these issues, see James P. Pfiffner, "Presidential Policy Making and the Gulf War," in Marcia Whicker, Raymond Moore, and James Pfiffner, eds., *The Presidency and the Persian Gulf War* (New York: Praeger, 1993).

14. Statement of Tom Foley at a luncheon for the 75th anniversary of the Brookings Institution, Capital Hilton, Washington, DC (May 6, 1991). The author was present.

15. "Remarks by the President at Building Dedication of the Social Sciences Complex," Princeton University (May 10, 1991), p. 2 of White House press release.

16. *Ex Parte Milligan,* 71 U.S. 2 (4 Wall.) (1866), 246, 249.

17. Nelson, *Congressional Quarterly Guide to the Presidency,* p. 1100.

18. Cecil Crabb, *Presidents and Foreign Policy Making* (Baton Rouge, LA: Louisiana State University Press), p. 27. Lock Johnson and James M. McCormick, "Foreign Policy by Executive Fiat," *Foreign Policy* 28 (Fall 1977), p. 117.

19. Nelson, *Congressional Quarterly Guide to the Presidency,* p. 513.

20. Barry Blechman, *The Politics of National Defense* (New York: Oxford University Press, 1990), p. 31.

21. Blechman, *The Politics of National Defense,* p. 41.

22. See James P. Pfiffner, "Congressional Oversight of Defense Management," George Mason University, The Institute of Public Policy, Working Paper 92:12 (April 1992); "The President and the Postreform Congress," in Roger Davidson, ed., *The Postreform Congress* (New York: St. Martin's Press, 1992).

23. See the analysis of John Hart, *The Presidential Branch* (New York: Pergamon Press, 1987), p. 65.

24. Hart, *The Presidential Branch,* p. 65.

25. *United States Government Manual, 1996/1997* (Washington, DC: Government Printing Office, 1996.)

26. Hart, *The Presidential Branch,* p. 67.

27. John Prados, *Keepers of the Keys* (New York: William Morrow, 1991), pp. 57–96.

28. Anna Kasten Nelson, "National Security I: Inventing a Process 1945–1960," in Hugh Heclo and Lester Salamon, eds., *The Illusion of Presidential Government* (Boulder, CO: Westview Press, 1981), p. 250.

29. Hart, *The Presidential Branch,* p. 70.

30. I. M. Destler, "National Security II: the Rise of the Assistant," in Heclo and Salamon, *The Illusion of Presidential Government,* pp. 263–264.

31. For an insightful analysis of Condoleezza Rice's role as national security advisor, see John P. Burke, "Condoleezza Rice as NSC Advisor," *Presidential Studies Quarterly,* vol. 35, no. 3 (September 2005), pp. 554–565.

32. Fred I. Greenstein and John P. Burke, "Dynamics of Presidential Reality Testing: Evidence from Two Vietnam Decisions," *Political Science Quarterly* (Winter 1989–1990), pp. 557–580.

33. John P. Burke and Fred I. Greenstein, *How Presidents Test Reality* (New York: Russell Sage Foundation, 1990), p. 54.

34. Greenstein and Burke, "Dynamics of Presidential Reality Testing," p. 564.

35. Greenstein and Burke, "Dynamics of Presidential Reality Testing," p. 565.

36. Chester Cooper described the atmosphere of NSC meetings: "During the process I would frequently fall into a Walter Mitty-like fantasy: when my turn came I would rise to my feet slowly, look around the room and then directly look at the president and say, very quietly and emphatically, 'Mr. President, gentlemen, I most definitely do *not* agree.' But I was removed from my trance when I heard the president's voice saying, 'Mr. Cooper, do you agree?' And out would come a 'Yes, Mr. President, I agree.' " Quoted in Larry Berman, *Planning The Tragedy: The Americanization of the War in Vietnam* (New York: Norton, 1982), p. 3.

37. Greenstein and Burke, "Dynamics of Presidential Reality Testing," p. 571.

38. Greenstein and Burke, "Dynamics of Presidential Reality Testing," p. 575.

39. Alexander L. George, *Presidential Decisionmaking in Foreign Policy* (Boulder, CO: Westview Press, 1980).

40. Irving Janis, *Victims of Groupthink* (Boston: Houghton Mifflin, 1982), p. 139.

41. Richard Neustadt and Ernest May, *Thinking in Time* (New York: Free Press, 1986), p. 142.

42. Janis, *Victims of Groupthink*, pp. 1–13.

43. Janis, *Victims of Groupthink*, p. 143.

44. Janis, *Victims of Groupthink*, p. 152.

45. For a compelling personal account of the hostage crisis, see the book by Ambassador L. Bruce Laingen, charge' d'affaires of the U.S. embassy in Tehran when he was taken with the rest of the hostages: *Yellow Ribbon* (Washington, DC: Brassey's, 1992).

46. For a vivid account of the futile attempts of Secretary of State George Shultz to stop President Reagan from continuing to try to trade arms for hostages (and even to admit that he was in fact doing so), see George Shultz, *Turmoil and Triumph: My Years As Secretary of State* (New York: Charles Scribner's Sons, 1993).

47. See George Shultz, *Turmoil and Triumph: My Years as Secretary of State* (New York: Charles Scribner's Sons, 1993).

48. Woodward, *Bush at War*, pp. 79–80.

49. Woodward, *Bush at War*, p. 147.

50. Woodward, *Bush at War*, p. 312.

51. Woodward, *Bush at War*, pp. 293–294.

52. Woodward, *Bush at War*, p. 301.

53. Woodward, *Bush at War*, p. 306.

54. Woodward, *Bush at War*, pp. 212–213. Casualty figures from Marc Kaufman, "On Afghan Border, War Drags On," *Washington Post* (January 25, 2003), pp. 1, A14.

55. Peter Tomsen, "A Rebuilding Plan That Already Needs Repair," *Washington Post* (October 27, 2002), p. B3. See also Margaret Coker, "Afghan War Over, But Nation-Building Battle Continues," Cox News Service (October 6, 2002) [no page number]; Carlotta Gall, "Half a Million Are Left Homeless in Afghan Cities as Winter Bites," *New York Times* (January 2, 2003), pp. 1, A8. For an upbeat analysis that calls for more U.S. aid to Afghanistan, see Robert Oakley, "The New Afghanistan: Year 2," *Washington Post* (January 3, 2003), p. A19.

56. Woodward, *Bush at War*, pp. 84–91.

57. Glenn Kessler, "U.S. Decision On Iraq Has Puzzling Past," *Washington Post* (January 12, 2003), pp. 1, A20.

58. Kessler, "U.S. Decision on Iraq," p. A20.

59. Weekly Compilation of Presidential Documents, *Administration of George W. Bush, 2002* (January 29, 2002), pp. 133–139.

60. Weekly Compilation of Presidential Documents, *Administration of George W. Bush, 2002*, "Commencement Address at the United States Military Academy in West Point, New York" (June 1, 2002), pp. 944–948.

61. Thomas E. Ricks, "Some Top Military Brass Favor Status Quo in Iraq," *Washington Post* (July 28, 2002), pp. 1, A23. Also, Thomas E. Ricks, "Generals, Officials Are Split Over Iraq," *Washington Post* (August 1, 2002), pp. 1, A24, in which he says, "Much of the senior uniformed military, with the notable exception of some top Air Force and marine generals, opposes going to war anytime soon, a stance that is provoking frustration among civilian officials in the Pentagon and in the White House."

62. Brent Scowcroft, "Don't Attack Saddam," *Wall Street Journal* (August 15, 2002), p. A12. James A. Baker III, "The Right Way to Change a Regime," *New York Times* (August 25, 2002), p. WK9.

63. Senator Chuck Hagel of Nebraska, *Newsweek* (September 2, 2002), p. 28. See also Associated Press story in the *New York Times* (August 26, 2002), p. 1. Retired General Anthony Zinni, former head of Central Command, *Washington Post*, "Powell Aide Disputes Views on Iraq." (August 28, 2002) p. A16; James Webb, Vietnam veteran and former Secretary of the Navy, James Webb, "Heading for Trouble," *Washington Post* (September 4, 2002), p. A21. General Wesley Clark, former NATO Supreme Allied Commander, Tara Tuckwiller, "Don't invade yet, ex-NATO chief says," *Charleston Gazette* (October 15, 2002), p. 1A; General Norman Schwartzkopf, commander of U.S. forces in the 1991 Gulf War, Thomas E. Ricks, "Desert Caution," *Washington Post* (January 28, 2003), p. C1.

64. Woodward, *Bush at War*, pp. 333–334.

65. Dana Milbank, "Cheney Says Iraqi Strike Is Justified," *Washington Post* (August 27, 2002), p. 1, A8.

66. Elizabeth Bumiller, "President to Seek Congress's Assent over Iraq Action," *New York Times* (September 5, 2002), p. 1, A10.

67. George W. Bush, 2002b. *The National Security Strategy of the United States of America*, The White House, (available from http://www.whitehouse.gov/nsc/print/nssall.html).

68. Mike Allen and Juliet Eilperin, 2002, "Bush Aides Say Iraq War Needs No Hill Vote," *Washington Post* (August 26, 2002), pp. 1, A12.

69. The address was printed in the *Washington Post* (October 8, 2002), p. A20.

70. Erick Schmitt, "U.S. Force in Gulf Is Said to be Rising to 150,000 Troops," *New York Times* (January 12, 2003), p. 1.

71. State of the Union address (January 28, 2003), *Washington Post* (January 29, 2003), pp. A10–A11.

72. "President Says Saddam Hussein Must Leave Iraq Within 48 House, Remarks by the President in Address to the Nation," transcript on White House Web site at http://www.whitehouse.gov.

73. Peter J. Boyer, "The New War Machine," *The New Yorker* (June 30, 2003), p. 61.

74. The speech was printed in the *New York Times* (May 2, 2003), p. A14.

75. Vernon Loeb, "'Guerilla' War Acknowledged," *Washington Post* (July 17, 2003), p. A1.

76. Dana Milbank and Claudia Deane, "Hussein Link to 9/11 Lingers in Many Minds," *Washington Post* (September 6, 2003), p. 1.

77. In a tape urging Muslims to fight against the United States, Osama bin Laden said that the fighting should be for God, not for "pagan regimes in all the Arab countries, including Iraq. . . . Socialists are infidels wherever they are, either in Baghdad or Aden." Transcript posted on Web site: www.indybay.org. Accessed April 10, 2003.

78. Dana Milbank and Walter Pincus, "Cheney Defends U.S. Actions in Bid to Revive Public Support," *Washington Post* (September 15, 2003), p. 1, A19. Dana Milbank and Claudia Deane, "Hussein Link to 9/11 Lingers in Many Minds," *Washington Post* (September 6, 2003), p. 1.

79. Associated Press, "U.N. Panel Finds No Evidence to Link Iraq, Al-Qaeda," online version 6/26/03; TruthOut.org.

80. Quoted in Milbank and Deane, "Hussein Link to 9/11 Lingers," p. 1.

81. Dana Milbank, "Bush Disavows Hussein-Sept. 11 Link," *Washington Post* (September 18, 2003), p. A18; David E. Sanger, "Bush Reports No Evidence of Hussein Tie to 9/11," *New York Times* (September 18, 2003), p. A18.

82. Steven Mufson, "Forget WMD. What's an NIE?" *Washington Post* (July 20, 2003), p. B3.

83. Central Intelligence Agency. 2003. Key Judgments [from October 2002 NIE] Iraq's continuing Programs for Weapons of Mass Destruction. Declassified excerpts published on the CIA Web site: www.odci.gov/nic/pubs/research. Accessed October 10, 2003, pp. 5–6.

84. Associated Press, "White House Official Apologizes for Role in Uranium Claim," *New York Times* (July 22, 2003), nytimes.com (accessed July 22, 2003).

85. Michael Duffy and James Carney, "A Question of Trust," *Time* (July 21, 2003), pp. 23–26.

86. Associated Press, "White House Official Apologizes for Role in Uranium Claim," *New York Times* (July 22, 2003), *New York Times* Web site, no page number, accessed July 2, 2003.

87. Richard W. Stevenson, "Bush Denies Claim He Oversold Case for War," *New York Times* (July 31, 2003), *New York Times* Web site, no page number, accessed July 31, 2003.

88. President Bush's Address to U.N., printed in the *New York Times* (September 13, 2003), p. A31.

89. Central Intelligence Agency. 2003. Key Judgments [from October 2002 NIE] Iraq's continuing Programs for Weapons of Mass Destruction. Declassified excerpts published on the CIA Web site: www.odci.gov/nic/pubs/research. Accessed October 10, 2003, p. 9.

90. Barton Gellman and Walter Pincus, "Depiction of Threat Outgrew Supporting Evidence," *Washington Post* (August 10, 2003), pp. 1, A9.

91. Central Intelligence Agency. 2003. Key Judgments [from October 2002 NIE]. Iraq's Continuing Programs for Weapons of Mass Destruction. Declassified excerpts published on the CIA Web site: www.odci.gov/nic/pubs/research. Accessed October 10, 2003, pp. 8–9.

92. Dana Priest and Walter Pincus, "Search in Iraq Finds No Banned Weapons," *Washington Post* (October 3, 2003), p. 1.

93. David Kay, "Report on the Activities of the Iraq Survey Group to the House Permanent Select Committee on Intelligence and the House Committee on Appropriations, Subcommittee on Defense and the Senate Select Committee on Intelligence," p. 7. The page references are to the unclassified report published on the CNN Web site, www.cnn.allpolitics (accessed October 10, 2003).

94. Dana Priest and Walter Pincus, "Bush Certainty on Iraq Arms Went Beyond Analyst's Views," *Washington Post* (June 7, 2003), pp. 1, A17.

95. Walter Pincus and Dana Priest, "Iraq Weapons Report Won't Be Conclusive," *Washington Post* (September 25, 2003), pp. 1, A24.

96. Kay Report on the Activities of the Iraq Survey Group, p. 6.

97. Jane Mayer, "The Hidden Power," *The New Yorker* (June 6, 2006), Web site: www.newyorker.com.

98. Mark Follman, "The Bush Code of Secrecy," Salon.com (June 23, 2006), p. 1 of 4.

99. Military Order: "Detention, Treatment, and Trial of Certain Non-Citizens in the War Against Terrorism," Federal Register, vol. 66, no. 222, p. 57, 833 (November 16, 2001). Military Commission No. 1, March 21, 2002

100. Department of Defense, Military Commission No. 1, March 21, 2002, "Procedures for Trials by Military Commissions of Certain Non-United States Citizens in the War Against Terrorism."

101. Though rendition had in the past been a useful device to return suspects to their country of origin, in some of the Bush cases, detainees were sent to countries, such as Egypt, that were likely to torture them. For instance a Canadian, Maher Arar, was seized by U.S. agents in New York and sent to Syria where he was tortured. After ten months of imprisonment, he was released because they could discover no connection between him and terrorism. Jim Hightower, "Bush's Imperial Presidency," Truthout.org, accessed on May 2, 2006, p. 4 of 6.

102. Memorandum TO: Counsel to the President and Assistant to the President for National Security Affairs, FROM: Colin L. Powell (26 January 2002) SUBJECT: Draft Decision Memorandum for the President on the Applicability of the Geneva Convention to the Conflict in Afghanistan."

103. For details, see: James P. Pfiffner, "Torture and Public Policy," *Public Integrity* vol. 7, no. 4 (Fall 2005), pp. 313–330.

104. When the Office of Professional Responsibility of the Department of Justice began an investigation of the NSA unwarranted surveillance of people in the United States, it had to stop the investigation because its investigative lawyers could not get necessary clearances to examine some of the classified documents. When asked why, Attorney General Alberto Gonzales told the Senate Judiciary Committee, "The president of the United States makes decisions about who is ultimately given access." Neil A. Lewis, "Bush Blocked Ethics Inquiry, Gonzales Says," *New York Times* (July 19, 2006) Web site: www.nytimes.com.

105. Quoted by Andrew Rudalevige, *The New Imperial Presidency* (Ann Arbor: University of Michigan Press, 2005), p. 212.

106. Thomas Paine, *Rights of Man and Common Sense and Other Political Writings*, ed. by Mark Philp (NY: Oxford University Press, 1995), p. 34.

107. *Hamdi et al. v. Rumsfeld, Secretary of Defense* 159 Lawyers Edition 2d 578 (2004).

108. *Rasul v. Bush* 159 L. Ed. 2d 548 (2004).

109. *Hamdan v. Rumsfeld*, No. 05-184 (decided June 29, 2006), Slip Opinion, Supreme Court Web site.

110. The commissions were established by Military Order of November 13, 2001, "Detention, Treatment, and Trial of Certain Non-Citizens in the War Against Terrorism," Federal Register, vol. 66. no. 222 (November 16, 2001), pp. 57831–57836.

111. Slip Opinion, p. 4.

112. Slip Opinion, pp. 4, 6.

113. Slip Opinion, p. 7.

114. *Hamdi et al. v. Rumsfeld, Secretary of Defense* 159 Lawyers Edition 2d 578 (2004). In remarks after she had retired from the Supreme Court, Justice O'Conner said about the intimidation of federal judges, "We must be ever-vigilant against those who would strong-arm the judiciary into adopting their preferred policies. It takes a lot of degeneration before a country falls into dictatorship, but we should avoid these ends by avoiding these beginnings." Her remarks were reported by Nina Totenberg of National Public Radio according to Raw Story, "Retired Supreme Court Justice hits attacks on courts and warns of dictatorship," (March 10, 2006), Web site: rawstory.com.

ABUSE OF POWER AND PRESIDENTIAL REPUTATION

The previous chapters have explored the growing capacity and resources of the presidency. The modern presidency has seen the presidential staff grow in numbers, organizational resources, and power. The need for managerial oversight and limits to that staff power is one of the lessons of the modern presidency. Chapters 1 and 2 explored the relationship of the president with the American public. Chapter 3, 4, and 5 analyzed the growth in importance of the White House staff vis-à-vis the rest of the executive branch, the departments, and agencies. Much of this centralization of control and concentration of power has been inevitable, and parts of it are desirable.

Insofar as centralization enables the president to direct the executive branch and be held accountable for his actions, it is justified. But the executive branch is far too vast and complex to be run from the White House. To be effective, presidential interventions at the programmatic level must be selective. The theme of Chapters 3, 4, and 5 is that central direction from the White House should be balanced with policy advice and implementation in the departments. Presidents should use, and not let atrophy, the talents of the line officers they appoint and the career executives who run the programs of the government.

Chapters 6 and 7 emphasized the role that Congress plays in the making of public policy and the struggle between the president and Congress over the national agenda. This chapter once again takes up these themes. First we analyze the two most serious and dangerous cases of corruption in the presidency—Watergate and Iran-Contra—most serious because they were carried out at high levels in the White House, and most dangerous because the goals of the actions were the subversion of the legal and constitutional order in the polity. These two scandals were made possible by a large and highly centralized White House staff. Then we examine the scandals of the Clinton administration and put them into historical perspective.

But the danger of these scandals was mitigated by the operation of the constitutionally designed separation-of-powers system. According to scholar Hugh Heclo:

> The first and, historically speaking, most astonishing answer to the question of what has happened to the separation of powers system is, it has survived.... The Founders' mixed view of human nature seems to have gotten it about right: people are bad enough not to be trusted with power but virtuous enough to govern themselves within properly designed constitutional institutions for allocating power.[1]

Despite the frustrations of modern presidents, the Framers never intended that presidents would be able to dominate the political system. Congress has, at times, overstepped its bounds and interfered with legitimate executive functions. More often, it has abdicated its right and duty to take a clear stand on public-policy issues. It has often not asserted itself in confronting budget deficits or presenting coherent foreign policy alternatives to the nation. But whatever the faults and weaknesses of Congress as an institution, we ought not to ignore Article I of the Constitution, as some advocates of executive power would have us do. Congress may not always be wise, but it is an essential balance and check on the executive. This theme of balance is illustrated in the role that Congress played in the Watergate and Iran-Contra scandals. We will also examine the impeachment of President Clinton by the House in 1998 and his trial in the Senate in 1999.

In evaluating the presidency in the constitutional system, the few cases of corruption and abuse of power raise broad, normative issues. So, also, do questions of the historical reputations of presidents. Presidents sometimes take on mythic qualities after sufficient time has passed, and modern presidents always seem to suffer in comparison to great presidents of the past. This chapter examines some of the vagaries of presidential reputation and the relationship between short-term popularity and longer-term reputations of modern presidents. Finally, it examines the problem of the unrealistic expectations we have of our presidents.

CORRUPTION AND ABUSE OF POWER

Corruption is no stranger to the American political system, and the presidency is no exception. There are plenty of examples of presidential advisers and cabinet secretaries who have succumbed to temptations to enrich themselves at the public's expense. Some of the larger scandals have involved bribery and illegal gain by presidential aides, and even vice presidents. The Credit Mobilier scandal of the 1870s involved the acceptance by public officials of stock in the Transcontinental Railroad Building Company in order to stop an investigation of profit skimming. President Ulysses S. Grant's vice president, Schuyler Colfax, had accepted some of the railroad stock when he was a member of Congress. Grant's second-term vice president, Henry Wilson, was also implicated in the scheme, and other Grant administration officials were involved in corruption, although Grant himself was cleared of any wrongdoing.[2]

During the Harding administration in the early 1920s, corruption reached the cabinet when Secretary of the Interior Albert Fall secretly leased U.S. oil reserves at Teapot Dome, Wyoming, and Elk Hills, California, to oil companies and received $400,000 in "loans" and a $100,000 gift. Fall was eventually fined $100,000 and went to jail.[3] Several White House aides in the Truman administration were convicted of taking bribes and other unethical advantages of their official positions.[4] Sherman Adams was forced to resign after accepting a vicuña coat and other favors from a businessman who was under regulatory investigation. In the 1960s, Democratic campaign contributor Billy Sol Estes engaged in fraud concerning federal subsidy programs and used his influence in the Department of Agriculture to help his business. Lyndon Johnson protégé Bobby Baker, secretary to the Senate majority, used his influence to obtain a government contract for a friend and was involved in questionable campaign contributions to the Democratic Party.[5]

Financial corruption reached the vice-presidential level again when President Nixon's vice president, Spiro Agnew, was forced to resign in October 1973. In a plea bargain, Agnew was allowed to plead nolo contendere to one count of income-tax evasion and was fined $10,000 and given three years of unsupervised probation. If he had not made the deal with prosecutors, the Justice Department was ready to charge him with accepting payoffs from engineering firms that had received contracts when Agnew was county executive of Baltimore County and governor of Maryland. Even as vice president, Agnew continued to receive money (from the firms) from men who came into his office and residence with envelopes containing thousands of dollars in cash. Agnew also received payments for a contract by the General Services Administration when he was vice president.[6]

All of these examples, and there are more of them, involve money and the pursuit of personal gain by government officials. While these are illegal, morally wrong, reprehensible, and undermine the public trust in government, they are also mundane forms of petty corruption, in the sense that the primary motivation was *personal* greed. When such instances of corruption are discovered, the guilty can be punished and their actions condemned. As bad as these types of crimes are, they are not as corrupting of the public trust as some broader political crimes of abuse of power. These crimes undermine the very fabric of limited and constitutional government by using the power of government not merely for personal gain but for the more insidious ends of staying in power or undermining the political process.

The Watergate and Iran-Contra scandals stand out in American history as being in a category by themselves. Watergate involved, among other things, the use of the power of the presidency to illegally undermine political opposition, obstruct justice, and avoid accountability. The term "Watergate," in a narrow sense, refers to the break-in at the Democratic National Headquarters in the Watergate Building in 1972 and the subsequent White House cover-up of the crime. But more loosely, the term is used to also include a number of other abuses of power and campaign "dirty tricks" engaged in by the Nixon White House. Iran-Contra involved the concerted effort by White House staffers to avoid the constitutional limits of public law by carrying out, in secret, a policy that the Reagan administration had not been able to accomplish through constitutional political and legislative processes.

WATERGATE

The seeds of Watergate were contained in the character of Richard Nixon. He was a tragic figure, in the classical sense, because he was capable of greatness, which he showed in some of his foreign-affairs actions. But Nixon believed that his political enemies were out to get him and that he had to use every means at his disposal to fight them. He felt that his election in 1968 gave him a mandate to accomplish his policy goals regardless of the checks and balances in the constitutional system. Three aspects of Nixon's actions stand out: (1) the pursuit of personal gain, (2) undermining his political opponents, and (3) the Watergate cover-up.

Nixon, as president, was not immune from the first type of petty corruption for personal gain. He had his personal residences at San Clemente, California, and Key Biscayne, Florida, improved at taxpayer expense. These included not merely legitimate security measures but also clearly personal improvements, such as a shuffleboard court and a gazebo.[7] Nixon also made unallowable claims concerning the donation of his vice-presidential papers to the National Archives. The Internal Revenue Service ruled that the claimed deductions were not allowed and forced him to pay back taxes plus interest for the illegitimate claims. The most damning aspect of this set of actions was the back dating of papers relating to the donation in order to make him eligible for the deductions that he wrongly claimed.[8]

The second and more important aspect of Nixon's abuse of power involved using the powers of his office to undermine the political opposition and stay in office. Nixon's staffers compiled lists of "enemies" that included a wide variety of persons in the media and entertainment business as well as in political life. The list included ten U.S. senators, African American congressmen, the Brookings Institution, Common Cause, labor organizations, celebrities, businessmen and corporations, and scholars.[9] The main criterion for being on the enemies list seemed to be political opposition to some aspect of Nixon's political agenda. A constitutional, democratic polity depends, in essence, on the ability of the people to change rulers. This implies tolerating political opposition and treating opponents as the "loyal opposition." That is, political opponents are considered loyal to the country and the Constitution even though they want to replace the current rulers by means of democratic elections. The distinction between a loyal opposition and enemies of the state was often lost on the Nixon White House.

The administration attempted to use the IRS to harass some of their "enemies" by having their tax returns audited, and they intended to use other governmental power to, as John Dean put it, "screw our political enemies."[10] Part of the attempt to ensure Nixon's reelection involved "dirty tricks" to undermine the opposition candidates. Donald Segretti, the person in charge of dirty tricks, drew a $50,000 salary from Nixon's lawyer, Herbert Kalmbach. These tricks were sometimes petty and humorous, as when Segretti once dropped white mice on the floor at a Muskie press conference. The mice had blue ribbons tied to their tails that had "Muskie is a rat fink" printed on them.[11]

The intent of these systematic efforts was to subvert the democratic process by not giving voters a chance to vote for candidates on the merits of their positions but to undermine their standing with the voters by sabotaging their campaigns. The most notorious of these dirty tricks was the sabotage of Edmund Muskie's primary campaign for president in 1972. The Nixon White House considered Muskie the most serious potential Democratic presidential candidate, and so they set out to undermine his campaign. In addition to a number of minor harassments, the Nixon operatives stole Muskie-for-President campaign stationery from his headquarters and sent a letter to Democrats, supposedly from Muskie, accusing his Democratic primary opponents of scurrilous behavior.[12] But the final blow came when the ultraconservative New Hampshire newspaper, the *Manchester Union-Leader,* printed a letter accusing Muskie of insulting Canadian Americans (calling them "Canucks") and accusing his wife of being an alcoholic. The author of the letter could never be found. In defending his wife at a press conference, Muskie shed some tears, and his candidacy was essentially finished because of the implication that he was not "tough enough" to be president. Muskie's withdrawal set the stage for George McGovern's nomination, the preferred outcome of the Nixon White House.

The Nixon campaign operation, The Committee to Reelect the President (CREEP), raised record amounts of campaign contributions for the reelection effort. The problem was that not all of it was legal. Some of the contributions were not reported as required by law; some of the money was collected illegally from corporations; and some of the funds were illegally "laundered," that is, shifted among various bank accounts to hide their origin.[13] The administration also raised money by "selling" ambassadorships. While many presidents have rewarded big contributors to their campaigns with ambassadorial appointments, the reward is usually not part of an explicit quid pro quo. In the Nixon administration, among other ambassadorial appointments, Nixon fund-raiser Herb Kalmbach pled guilty to a charge of promising a federal job in exchange for a campaign contribution.[14]

These actions were part of a pattern in the Nixon administration to thwart the democratic process by using the power of the government to undermine the political opposition and stay in power, not giving voters a fair choice in the election. As Nixon said in September 1972: "I want the most comprehensive notes on all those who tried to do us in. . . . We have not used the power for this first four years. . . . We have never used it. We haven't used the Bureau and we haven't used the Justice Department, but things are going to change now. . . . They're going to get it right."[15]

White House operatives organized a secret team of "plumbers" to plug "leaks" of inside information from the White House. Among other things, the plumbers broke into the office of Daniel Ellsberg's psychiatrist. Ellsberg had given a copy of the Pentagon Papers—an internal Department of Defense account of the decision making about the Vietnam War—to the *New York Times,* which published the account. Although the Supreme Court decided that the analysis of past decision making did not threaten U.S. security, the Nixon administration evidently felt that discrediting Ellsberg would affect the public's perception of the account in the Pentagon Papers.[16]

The third category of corruption was the series of actions to cover up Watergate, that is, using the powers of office to impede a criminal investigation. The initial incident from which this whole series of scandals received its name was the break-in by the plumbers into the Democratic National Headquarters, which was located in the Watergate complex on the Potomac River in Washington, DC. The break-in on June 17, 1972, by burglars who had been paid by campaign funds controlled by White House officials, was for the purpose of fixing a bug (listening device) that had been placed on Democratic National Committee Chairman Larry O'Brien's phone.

The break-in was part of a larger plan formulated by G. Gordon Liddy and presented to John Mitchell, close friend of President Nixon and attorney general of the United States. The illegal entry was discovered when the burglars were caught in the building, but the whole scheme began to unravel when it was discovered that the jailed burglars had connections to CREEP and the White House. Nevertheless, for the remainder of 1972 the connection of the burglars to the White House was successfully covered up, and Nixon was reelected by a landslide. After congressional hearings and a criminal investigation by a special prosecutor were begun in 1973, the extent of White House involvement was gradually disclosed.

Richard Nixon denied that he had any knowledge of the White House connection to the Watergate break-in, but Nixon aide Jeb Stuart Magruder disclosed in 2003 that he had personally heard Nixon in a phone call with John Mitchell tell Mitchell to give money to Liddy for the Watergate break-in.[17] In any case, Nixon was in fact closely involved with the cover-up from the beginning. Five days after the burglars were caught, H. R. Haldeman told the president that FBI investigators were tracing the money carried by the Watergate burglars and were about to discover that it had come from CREEP and White House safes. On June 23, 1972, Haldeman suggested that the way to stop the FBI investigation would be to have the CIA tell the FBI that further investigations would jeopardize CIA operations and that they should drop the money trail: "That the way to handle this now is for us to have Walters [of the CIA] call Pat Gray [director of the FBI] and just say, 'Stay the hell out of this . . . this is ah, business here we don't want you to go any further on it.' That's not an unusual development." After this suggestion, Nixon told Haldeman to tell

CIA director Richard Helms that "the president believes that it is going to open the whole Bay of Pigs thing up again. And . . . that they [the CIA] should call the FBI in and [unintelligible] don't go any further into this case period!"[18] This exchange was the "smoking gun" that convinced the House Judiciary Committee, in 1974, to vote articles of impeachment. It clearly showed incontrovertible evidence in Nixon's own words that he wanted to use his powers as president to interfere with a criminal investigation. This was an obstruction of justice and a felony.

Nixon tried to impede the investigation in other criminal ways. The burglars who broke into the Watergate were in jail and threatened to disclose their connections to the White House unless they were paid money. Under threat of this blackmail and with the approval of the president, the burglars were given more than $500,000.[19] The president also urged his aides to commit perjury before the grand jury that was investigating the Watergate crimes in order to maintain the cover-up. On March 21, 1973, Nixon told John Dean and Haldeman: "Perjury is a tough rap to prove. . . . [J]ust be damned sure you say, 'I don't remember, I can't recall.'"[20] Suborning of perjury is also a criminal felony.

When it was disclosed in congressional hearings that Nixon had a taping system in the Oval Office, the special prosecutor who was investigating the Watergate case subpoenaed the tapes as evidence. Nixon refused to give up the tapes on the grounds of executive privilege—that such records were confidential to the executive branch. Under pressure, Nixon agreed to release transcripts of the tapes. But at the appeal of the special prosecutor, the Supreme Court decided unanimously to compel the release of the original tapes, and it was discovered that some of the transcripts had been altered in key places to cover up presidential involvement. It was also discovered that there was an eighteen-and-one-half-minute gap in the recording of a meeting on June 20, 1972, between Nixon and his top aides about the Watergate break-in. Experts concluded that the tape had been erased.

The release of the tapes and their damning evidence provided the final impetus for the House Judiciary Committee to vote on articles of impeachment. Once passed by the committee, the articles would go to the full House for a vote, and if passed, then go to the Senate, which would try the case and decide whether to convict the president on the charges and remove him from office. Impeachment Article I charged the president with failure to fulfill his oath of office and obstruction of justice. It mentioned specifically the break-in of Ellsberg's psychiatrist's office, misuse of the CIA to obstruct the Justice Department investigation, withholding evidence, and counseling perjury, among other things. Article II charged the president with failing to faithfully execute the laws by using the IRS to harass his political opponents, by using the FBI to place unlawful wiretaps on citizens, by maintaining a secret investigative unit in the White House paid for by campaign funds, and by impeding criminal investigations, among other things. Article III charged the president with refusing to honor congressional subpoenas lawfully issued by the House Judiciary Committee and impeding the Congress from constitutionally exercising its impeachment powers.[21]

Two other articles were debated by the committee but rejected. One of the articles would have charged the president with the secret bombing of Cambodia during the Vietnam War, undermining the constitutional powers of Congress. The other article would have charged the president with income tax evasion. But before the articles could be presented to the full House for action, President Nixon resigned and left office on August 9, 1974.

Former President Nixon and others have minimized Watergate as a "third-rate burglary" and merely one in a series of a long line of presidential abuses of power. But as William Ruckelshaus, deputy attorney general for Nixon, said: "The break-in was trivial but what happened afterwards was not trivial. It was profound."[22]

The argument made by Nixon that "everybody does it" is also not convincing. In the first place, other crimes do not justify further crimes. But in the second place, the Watergate crimes were in important ways unprecedented in American history. According to historian C. Vann Woodward:

> Heretofore, no president has been proved to be the chief coordinator of the crime and misdemeanor charged against his own administration as a deliberate course of conduct or plan. Heretofore, no president has been held to be the chief personal beneficiary of misconduct in his administration or of measures taken to destroy or cover up evidence of it. Heretofore, the malfeasance and misdemeanor have had no confessed ideological purpose, no constitutionally subversive ends. Heretofore, no president has been accused of extensively subverting and secretly using established government agencies to defame or discredit political opponents and critics, to obstruct justice, to conceal misconduct and protect criminals, or to deprive citizens of their rights and liberties. Heretofore, no president has been accused of creating secret investigative units to engage in covert and unlawful activities against private citizens and their rights.[23]

Regardless of the domestic and foreign policy accomplishments of the Nixon administration, Watergate must stand as a cautionary lesson in American constitutional history.

IRAN-CONTRA

The Iran part of the Iran-Contra scandal, as described in Chapter 7, involved the sale of U.S. arms to Iran in hopes of freeing U.S. hostages held in Lebanon. The violation of declared U.S. policy and the reversal of U.S. posture toward Iran over the objections of the secretaries of state and defense may have been unwise, but they were not illegal. On the other hand, the possible violations of the Arms Export Control Act and the refusal of the administration to inform Congress of the covert operations were more serious matters. But these infractions, serious as they were, do not approach in constitutional magnitude the diversion of funds from the Iran arms sales to support the Contras in Nicaragua.

From the beginning of the 1980s, the Reagan administration felt the leftist Sandinista government of Nicaragua posed a serious threat to the United States. The administration therefore helped to create an armed rebel opposition to the regime called the Contras. Support of the Contras was a high priority throughout the Reagan administration. Financial and operational aid was provided to the Contras by the administration, but military aid was subject to a series of limitations written into public law between 1982 and 1986. Despite the best arguments of the Reagan administration, Congress was dubious of the wisdom and efficacy of continuing to arm the Contras. In November 1984, Congress passed, and President Reagan signed, a law providing continuing appropriations for fiscal year 1985. The law contained language, known as the Boland Amendment, prohibiting the United States from giving aid to the Contras during fiscal year 1985:

> During fiscal year 1985, no funds available to the Central Intelligence Agency, the Department of Defense, or any other agency or entity of the United States involved in intelligence activities may be obligated or expended for the purpose or which would have the effect of supporting, directly or indirectly, military or paramilitary operations in Nicaragua by any nation, group, organization, movement, or individual. [Public Law 98–473, 98 STAT 1935–37, sec. 8066][24]

Despite the law, the administration was committed to continuing support of the Contras. It was at this time that National Security staffer Lt. Col. Oliver North had the "neat idea" to use money received from the sale of arms to Iran to support the Contras. To carry this out, North and his colleagues set up secret accounts in Switzerland and funneled the money through them.

In addition to the funds obtained from selling U.S. arms to Iran (and thus the legal property of the U.S. government), the administration also raised funds by requesting money from Middle East nations. Some of these nations were the recipients of U.S. military aid. North and other White House aides also solicited donations from private U.S. citizens for the purpose of aiding the Contras. North later testified that CIA Director William Casey hoped to set up an entity (the "Enterprise") to conduct covert operations entirely independent of congressional appropriations.

This secret attempt to fund the Contras was in direct violation of public law and a serious threat to the Constitution. The president's aides decided that what they could not achieve through the public constitutional process (continuing aid to the Contras) they would accomplish through secret means. There was no doubt about what the law prohibited; there had been a high-level public debate over aid to the Contras throughout the 1980s, and the administration had not been able to convince a majority of the Congress that continued military aid to the Contras in 1985 was essential to U.S. security. But the White House aides decided that aid to the Contras ought to continue, and some argued that the White House was not covered by language in the Boland Amendment. There is no doubt that President Reagan strongly supported aid to the Contras and that he communicated this directly to his staff. Reagan, however, denied any knowledge of the diversion of funds to the Contras, a denial that was later disputed by Oliver North.

It was fairly clear that a majority of the U.S. public did not favor U.S. military action in Nicaragua. Public opinion polls demonstrated this, and the refusal of the Reagan reelection campaign in 1984 to highlight the issue, in hopes of getting a mandate to support the Contras during a second term, also attests to public attitudes. But public opinion is beside the constitutional point—the way authoritative public policy is determined is through the constitutional process. The results of that process seemed clear to many in 1985: no funds for the Contras.

Some members of the administration thought that raising funds from other nations and private citizens could get around the legal and constitutional problems. But others pointed out that with a public law prohibiting the United States from giving funds to the Contras, the funds were solicited from Third World nations who were dependent on the United States for military aid, and who had reasonable expectations (explicit or not) that, in the future, the United States would make up for any funds they sent to the Contras. From the perspective of critics of the administration, the power and authority of the presidency were being used to raise money for purposes forbidden by public law. Similarly, according to this interpretation, funds were solicited from wealthy individuals, not by private-citizen Oliver North but by an official of the U.S. government, a lieutenant colonel in the Marines, who clearly represented the president and who intended to handle the funds through the White House. North brought President Reagan in to thank groups of people who donated money for their patriotism. These donors were giving money because they were assured by government officials that their money was being used to counter a threat to the United States.

Defenders of the Reagan administration and the signers of the minority report of the congressional investigating committees argued that the administration was guilty only of "mistakes in judgment, and nothing more." The minority report continued: "We grant that the diversion does raise some legal questions. . . ." But that the fundamental issues had to do "with the policy decisions themselves, and with the political judgments. . . ." and that treating the issues as legal questions was a sign of "interbranch intimidation."[25]

To critics of the diversion of funds, however, accountability is the key concept. The president and Congress are accountable to voters, and executive branch officials are accountable to the law. In the terms of the Constitution: "The President shall take care that the Laws be faithfully executed." The majority report of the congressional committee investigating the Iran-Contra affair concluded:

> In the Iran-Contra Affair, officials viewed the law not as setting boundaries for their actions, but raising impediments to their goals. When the goals and the law collided, the law gave way. . . . [T]he ultimate responsibility for the events in the Iran–Contra Affair must rest with the President. If the President did not know what his National Security Advisers were doing, he should have. . . . It was the President's policy—not an isolated decision by North or Poindexter—to sell arms secretly to Iran and to maintain the Contras "body and soul," the Boland Amendment notwithstanding. To the NSC staff, implementation of these policies became the overriding concern.[26]

At the bottom of both the Watergate and the Iran-Contra scandals is the principle that the United States is a constitutional republic of limited government. U.S. constitutional principle rejects Nixon's justification: "When the president does it, that means that it is not illegal."[27] In the United States, even the president is not above the law. As Supreme Court Justice Louis Brandeis put it: "Crime is contagious. If the Government becomes a law-breaker, it breeds contempt for law, it invites every man to become a law unto himself, it invites anarchy."[28]

Both scandals also displayed a marked lack of respect for the balance between the two branches established in the Constitution. Members of both administrations sometimes failed to distinguish disagreement with the policy preferences of the members of the opposition party in Congress and contempt for the Congress itself. President Nixon decided to accomplish by administrative means what he could not get Congress to agree to by impounding funds, keeping secret his bombing of Cambodia, and refusing to release evidence vital to the Watergate investigation. The Reagan administration refused to comply with laws in continuing to send aid to the Contras. Some members of each administration interpreted the opposition of political opponents as disloyalty to the United States.

Both scandals are marked by ironies. The scandals that forced Nixon to resign and constituted the greatest threat to Reagan's presidency were not due to attacks by their political enemies but to actions by White House loyalists. The lessons of each scandal are that presidents must pay attention to White House management and ensure that their lower-level subordinates are kept on a tight leash. In the Watergate case, G. Gordon Liddy, Charles Colson, and others should not have been allowed to go forward with their illegal and unethical attacks on Nixon's political opponents. In the Iran-Contra affair, the chief of staff and the president should have been aware of what White House staffers were doing in the president's name.

After disclosures of corruption in his administration, President Harding said in an interview with journalist William Allen White, "My God, this is a hell of a job! I have no trouble with my enemies, I can take care of my enemies all right. But my damn friends ... my God-damn friends, White, they're the ones that keep me walking the floor nights!"[29] In the cases of Watergate and Iran-Contra, the atmosphere engendered in the White House discouraged any dissent and tended to view it as disloyalty. And, as with the corrupt officials in the Harding administration, presidential loyalists were the ones who endangered their presidents.

The final irony is that neither set of actions accomplished what was intended. Richard Nixon did not need all the extra money and extra legal help in the 1972 campaign. He would have won the election in any case. If he had acknowledged the initial Watergate break-in and denounced the aides who perpetrated it, there would have been a brief scandal, but the obstruction of justice would not have happened, and Nixon would probably have served out his full second term. In Reagan's case, only a small percentage of the funds ($3.8 of $16.1 million) that were diverted to the Contras actually got to their alleged destination; the bulk of the money went to pay middlemen and into secret Swiss bank accounts for those involved.[30]

Both of these incidents demonstrate that the constitutional system in the United States is vulnerable to those who do not respect the rule of law and feel that their own policy ends justify extralegal and extraconstitutional means to achieve them. According to Justice Brandeis, "The greatest dangers to liberty lurk in insidious encroachment by men of zeal, well-meaning but without understanding."[31] In Watergate, the "men of zeal" believed that the reelection of the president was more important than the law. In Iran-Contra, the "men of zeal" believed they could judge the national security interests of the country by themselves and did not need to bother with the constitutional process.[32]

The Framers were right: Power must be checked, and ambition must be made to counteract ambition. The balance among the branches is crucial to liberty and constitutional government. Justice Brandeis wrote:

> The doctrine of the separation of powers was adopted by the Convention of 1787, not to promote efficiency but to preclude the exercise of arbitrary power. The purpose was, not to avoid friction, but, by means of the inevitable friction incident to the distribution of the governmental powers among three departments, to save the people from autocracy.[33]

Watergate and Iran-Contra, insofar as the country treats them as aberrations to be deplored, will not be basic threats to the Republic. The system of checks and balances will have worked. But insofar as they are treated as precedents to justify further abuses, or to justify toleration of further abuses ("everybody does it"), they will have contributed to the undermining of the American system of government.

President Clinton's Impeachment and Senate Trial

The Clinton administration was dogged by scandal and allegations of wrong-doing from its first year in office. But despite the potential seriousness of other administration scandals (Whitewater finances, Travel Office firings, White House use of FBI files, or campaign finance abuses—all alleged but not proven), what brought about the impeachment of President Clinton was his sexual affair with a young White House intern, Monica Lewinsky. The president denied his actions to a grand jury in a deposition in a civil case that was later thrown out of court, but his alleged attempt to get Ms. Lewinsky to lie was sufficient justification for Independent Counsel Kenneth Starr to open an investigation and present impeachment charges to the House of Representatives. This section examines how the president got into this situation, the constitutional issues presented by impeachment, and the actions of the House and Senate in the impeachment and trial of President Clinton.

THE MONICA LEWINSKY AFFAIR   The most politically threatening of the scandals in the Clinton administration involved an alleged affair between the president and a young White House intern, Monica Lewinsky. Shortly after graduating from college, Lewinsky came to work in the White House in June 1995 as one of many interns. According to her account, she and the president began having an affair in November of that year, and she received a salaried position in the Office of Legislative Affairs. By April 1996, some White House staffers felt she was seeing the president too often, and they had her transferred to a public-affairs job in the Pentagon. Over the next 21 months, White House logs recorded that she was cleared to enter the White House thirty-seven times.[34] While at the Pentagon, Lewinsky made friends with a former White House secretary, Linda Tripp, who also worked in the Pentagon. Tripp had been the source for a news story about an encounter between President Clinton and Kathleen Willey in the White House, and when her credibility was questioned by the president's lawyer in the fall of 1997, she began to tape her phone conversations with Lewinsky. The tapes contained assertions by Lewinsky about her relationship with the president and her frustration because he was not calling her.

In the meantime, a suit brought against the president by Paula Jones had been under way for several years. Jones alleged that in an encounter in a Little Rock hotel room, then-Governor Clinton had crudely propositioned her and that she had turned him down. The suit was a civil action alleging sexual harassment. In the course of building their case, Jones's lawyers were gathering evidence about other women with whom Clinton might have had relationships over the years in order to demonstrate a pattern of sexual harassment.

On January 12, 1998, Linda Tripp gave the tapes of her conversations with Lewinsky to Kenneth Starr. After this, Starr asked for and received permission from the Justice Department to investigate Clinton for possible obstruction of justice. The president was scheduled to give a deposition in the Paula Jones case on January 17. With knowledge of the Tripp-Lewinsky tapes, the lawyers for Paula Jones asked Clinton if he had had sex with Lewinsky. When asked about an affair, Clinton denied a sexual relationship, providing the grounds for charges of perjury and eventual impeachment if Starr could prove that they had in fact had a sexual relationship. Having sex with an intern is not illegal (however wrong it might be), but intentionally lying about it in a civil deposition could constitute perjury. Thus, the question by Jones's lawyers about Lewinsky set Clinton up for a possible perjury charge. Based on the tapes, Starr also suspected that Clinton might have tried to illegally cover up their affair.

On January 21, 1998, the story of the tapes and Lewinsky's conversations with Tripp became public, and the media began a feeding frenzy about all aspects of the scandal. In a strong statement President Clinton publicly denied that he had had a sexual relationship with Lewinsky: "I want you to listen to me. I'm going to say this again. I did not have sexual relations with that woman, Miss Lewinsky. I never told anybody to lie—not a single time, never. These allegations are false. And I need to go back to work for the American people."[35] In addition to the President's denials, the First Lady was an effective advocate for her husband, as she had been in the past, and she attacked his enemies, charging that there was a "vast right-wing conspiracy" that was trying to bring down her husband.

The series of revelations raised two levels of problems for the president. At the public, political level, Clinton was vulnerable to public disapproval of his alleged affair with a young White House intern. But the president's problem with the public and its trust were only part of his vulnerability. He was also subject to the legal investigations of Independent Counsel Kenneth Starr, who had expanded his investigations from the Whitewater financial dealings in Arkansas during Clinton's governorship to actions in the White House that might lead to indictment or impeachment. The justification for Starr's jurisdiction to investigate was not Clinton's alleged sexual affair with Lewinsky, which might have been foolish and reckless, but was not illegal. It was instead the possible obstruction of justice in efforts to get Lewinsky a job in order to buy her silence about the affair. The main focus of the Starr investigation became the possible charge of perjury because Clinton had denied an affair with Lewinsky in his deposition in the Paula Jones case. In addition, Lewinsky reportedly implied to Tripp that Clinton suggested that she lie about their relationship, which would amount to suborning perjury (one of the impeachment charges against Nixon). If Starr were able to prove that the president lied under oath, suborned perjury, or attempted to obstruct justice, the House of Representatives might consider impeachment charges. Thus, the stakes for Clinton were high in 1998.

Starr's investigation of Clinton continued through the spring and summer of 1998. In July, Starr came to an immunity agreement with Monica Lewinsky, assuring her that she would not be prosecuted based on her testimony about her relationship with Clinton. Lewinsky testified in detail about their relationship and provided evidence that convinced the grand jury that she and Clinton had had a sexual relationship. Based on evidence from the Lewinsky testimony, Starr sought to subpoena the president to testify before a grand jury; Clinton agreed and was interrogated on August 17, 1998.

THE STARR REPORT TO THE HOUSE   On September 9, Kenneth Starr sent his report to Congress concerning possible impeachable offenses by President Clinton. The report was not merely a presentation of evidence but an elaborately constructed case for the impeachment of the president. The report stated that the independent counsel was submitting "substantial and credible information that President William Jefferson Clinton committed acts that may constitute grounds for an impeachment."[36] The report cited eleven instances in which, Starr asserted, the president had committed impeachable offenses. The list of charges boiled down to allegations that the president had lied under oath in his deposition in the Paula Jones sexual harassment case and in his testimony on August 17, that he had urged Lewinsky and his secretary to lie under oath, that he tried to obstruct justice by having his secretary hide evidence, and that he had tried to get Ms. Lewinsky a job to discourage her from revealing their relationship.

The 445-page Starr Report contained detailed evidence about Clinton's relationship with Lewinsky, and it was accompanied by a 2,500-page appendix and seventeen boxes of other materials with thousands of pages of documents. The House voted to release the videotape of the president's testimony from August 17, and it was shown on national television. The House then debated whether to open impeachment hearings by the Judiciary Committee.

On October 5, the Judiciary Committee of the House voted 21–16 along party lines to recommend impeachment hearings. Three days later, on October 8, the full House voted 258–176 (with thirty-one Democrats voting in favor and no Republican against) to open an impeachment inquiry. This was only the third time in the history of the country that the House had taken such a step.

President Andrew Johnson was impeached by the House in 1868, but survived in office when the Senate failed to convict by a margin of one vote. President Nixon resigned in 1974 before the Judiciary Committee reported articles of impeachment to the full House.

THE CONSTITUTIONAL ISSUES FACING THE HOUSE IN THE FALL OF 1998 Much of the debate over the possible impeachment and removal of President Clinton was marked by partisan rancor and cynicism. As Alexander Hamilton predicted in Federalist No. 65, impeachment proceedings against the president "will seldom fail to agitate the passions of the whole community, and to divide it into parties more or less friendly or inimical to the accused. In many cases it will connect itself with the preexisting factions, and will enlist all their animosities, partialities, influence, and interest on one side or on the other; and in such cases there will always be the greatest danger that the decision will be regulated more by the comparative strength of parties, than by the real demonstrations of innocence or guilt."

When the Framers deliberated the impeachment clauses of the Constitution, they adopted a formula that was intended to enable Congress to remove the president for treason, bribery, or "other high crimes and misdemeanors." The implication of the word *other* is that actions meriting impeachment would be comparable to treason and bribery. The Framers also made it clear that impeachment is primarily a political process rather than a narrow legal exercise. According to Hamilton in Federalist No. 65, impeachments "are of a nature which may with peculiar propriety be denominated POLITICAL, as they relate chiefly to injuries done immediately to the society itself." The political nature of impeachment is why "Judgment in Cases of Impeachment shall not extend further than to removal from Office, and disqualification ... but the Party convicted shall nevertheless be liable and subject to Indictment, Trial, Judgment, and Punishment, according to Law" (Article I, Section 3).

It can be reasonably inferred from this provision that the primary purpose of impeachment is to remove a president who has used his office in such a way as to undermine the Constitution or whose continuance in office poses a threat to the citizenry. Punishing a president for misbehavior is secondary and can be accomplished by prosecution after removal from office. Thus from a constitutional perspective, impeachment should be less concerned with justice for an individual president than about the future of the polity. According to nineteenth-century legal scholar Joseph Story, impeachment is "a proceeding purely of a political nature. It is not so much designed to punish an offender as to secure the state against gross official misdemeanors. It touches neither this person nor his property, but simply divests him of his political capacity."[37]

According to James Madison's account of the debates over the Constitution, George Mason wanted to broaden impeachment offenses from treason and bribery by adding the offense of "maladministration." But James Madison objected that "so vague a term will be equivalent to a tenure during pleasure of the Senate." Thus, Mason withdrew maladministration and substituted "other high crimes & misdemeanors against the State." Shortly thereafter the word *State* was replaced with (according to Madison) "the words 'United States' inserted unanimously, in order to remove ambiguity." The Committee on Style and Arrangement, which was authorized to make no substantive changes, later removed the words "against the United States."[38] These proceedings from the Constitutional Convention make it clear that the Framers thought that impeachable offenses would be only high matters of state rather than petty crimes.

In the case of President Clinton in 1998, the principled—rather than partisan—argument for impeachment (and removal) was that he had violated his oath of office and undermined the judicial system when he lied under oath and denied that he had had sex with Monica Lewinsky. According to David P. Schippers, the counsel for the House Republican majority, in his statement recommending that the full House conduct an impeachment inquiry, "The sanctity of the oath taken by a witness is the most essential bulwark of the truth-seeking function. ... The subject matter of the underlying case, whether civil or criminal, and the circumstances under which the testimony is given, are of no significance whatever. It is the oath itself that is sacred and must be enforced." According to Schippers, the president's misconduct constituted "an ongoing series of deliberate and direct assaults by Mr. Clinton upon the justice system of the United States and upon the judicial branch of our government."[39]

Republicans also argued in accord with Kenneth Starr's allegations that in a discussion with his secretary, Betty Currie, Clinton obstructed justice by coaching her as a witness and that he conspired with her to hide evidence (presents that Clinton had given to Lewinsky). It was also alleged that Vernon Jordan's attempts to get Lewinsky a job were intended to get her to deny her relationship with Clinton.

The principled argument against impeachment held that the president may have lied to the grand jury under oath and to the country, but his motive was to prevent personal embarrassment, not to undermine the Constitution. While his actions were wrong and he may have deserved some level of reprimand, Clinton's actions did not rise to the level of impeachable offenses against the Constitution or polity that the Framers had contemplated. His actions were sordid rather than sinister. On the other charges, the evidence that Clinton coached Currie to lie was ambiguous; it is just as plausible to assume that his intention was to refresh his own memory rather than to suborn perjury. Nor was there evidence that Clinton told Currie to retrieve the gifts from Lewinsky. The attempts to get Lewinsky a job had begun before she was subpoenaed and were not credibly connected to any attempt to get her to lie about her relationship with Clinton.

These concerns prompted the proposals for censure by Congress that were made by former Attorney General Elliot Richardson and others, and the proposal by former President Gerald Ford for an official "rebuke" of President Clinton by Congress rather than impeachment.[40] Despite the lack of constitutional provision for a rebuke or sanction, the intention was to solve the dilemma that failure to impeach might seem to imply that the Congress condoned unacceptable behavior by a president.

THE HOUSE OF REPRESENTATIVES IMPEACHES PRESIDENT CLINTON   After the House voted on October 8, 1998, to open impeachment deliberations, members of Congress returned to their districts to campaign for reelection. Although impeachment was the backdrop of every election race, Republicans did not make it the focus of the campaign, because clear majorities of the public opposed impeachment. The congressional elections of November 3 resulted in the Democratic addition of five seats, the first time since 1934 that the president's party picked up seats; elections forecasts had predicted that the Democrats would probably lose up to twenty seats. At the public level, it seemed that the impeachment drive by the Republicans was losing steam because of the election outcome. But the public perception did not take into account the determination of the conservative Republicans, particularly Henry Hyde and Tom Delay, to impeach the president.

In the impeachment hearings, the Republicans decided not to call any witnesses except Kenneth Starr, who presented his case against the president on November 19. On December 11 and 12, the Judiciary Committee voted along party lines in favor of four articles of impeachment. A Democratic motion to censure the president was easily defeated by the Republicans, and the articles were reported out to the full House.

The House of Representatives met on December 19, 1998, to vote on impeachment articles. The four articles reported out from the Judiciary Committee were voted upon; two were approved and two were rejected by the full House.[41] The approved impeachment articles were Article I and Article III:

> Article I charged that President Clinton "willfully provided perjurious, false, and misleading testimony to the grand jury" on August 17, 1998, concerning his relationship with Monica Lewinsky and his attempts to cover it up. The vote was 228–206 in favor (five Democrats in favor, five Republicans against).

> Article III charged that President Clinton "prevented, obstructed, and impeded the administration of justice" in order to "delay, impede, cover up, and conceal the existence of evidence and testimony" in the Paula Jones case by encouraging a witness to lie, by concealing evidence, and by trying to prevent truthful testimony by finding a job for Monica Lewinsky. The vote was 221–212 in favor (five Democrats in favor, twelve Republicans against).

Each of these articles concluded that "William Jefferson Clinton has undermined the integrity of his office, has brought disrepute on the Presidency, has betrayed his trust as President, and has acted in a manner subversive of the rule of law and justice, to the manifest injury of the people of the United States." The House rejected two other articles asserting that Clinton committed perjury in the Paula Jones deposition of January 17, 1998, and that he refused to cooperate with the House impeachment process.[42]

The House then voted to appoint thirteen managers to prosecute the trial in the Senate. Democrats questioned the legitimacy of a partisan impeachment vote by a lame-duck session of Congress, and President Clinton declared on the day of impeachment that he would serve in office "until the last hour of the last day of my term."[43]

THE IMPEACHMENT TRIAL IN THE SENATE   The trial in the Senate opened on Wednesday, January 13, 1999. The House impeachment brief argued that the president had indeed committed the crimes charged in the two articles—that he lied under oath before the grand jury investigating him on August 17, 1998 (Article I), and that he attempted to obstruct justice by encouraging Lewinsky to lie about their relationship, concealing evidence, and getting Lewinsky a job (Article II).

The House brief concluded:

> This is a defining moment for the Presidency as an institution, because if the President is not convicted as a consequence of the conduct that has been portrayed, then no House of Representatives will ever be able to impeach again and no Senate will ever convict. The bar will be so high that only a convicted felon or a traitor will need to be concerned. ... If this is not enough, what is? How far can the standard be lowered without completely compromising the credibility of the office for all time?[44]

The White House impeachment memorandum emphasized that the president had been reelected to office and that the Senate had an obligation not to overturn a popular election except in the most serious of circumstances. It argued that the president had admitted that he had a "wrongful relationship" with Monica Lewinsky and that he tried to keep it secret. But in refuting Article I, the memorandum denied that the president made any false statements, and in denying the charges in Article II (voted on in the House as Article III) that he had obstructed justice to hide his improper relationship. The White House concluded that the charges, even if proven, did not rise to the level of offenses considered by the Framers to be impeachable and that removal from office would upset the balance of power among the branches:

> Removing this president on these facts would substantially alter the delicate constitutional balance, and move us closer to a quasi-parliamentary system, in which the President is elected to office by the choice of the people, but continues in office only at the pleasure of Congress.[45]

In his presentation, Charles Ruff stated, "We are not here to defend William Clinton the man." But he argued that impeachment and removal from office are ultimate acts and that "removal from office is an act of extraordinary proportions to be taken only when no other response is adequate to preserve the integrity and viability of our democracy."[46]

On February 12, 1999, the final vote was taken, and both articles failed to receive the two-thirds majority necessary for conviction and removal from office. Article I, charging perjury, was defeated 55–45; and Article II, charging obstruction of justice, was defeated 50–50. Chief Justice William Rehnquist then declared: "It is, therefore, ordered and adjudged that the said William Jefferson Clinton be, and he hereby is, acquitted of the charges in the said articles."

Clinton's Impeachment in Perspective   The Clinton scandals are not in the same class as Watergate and Iran-Contra, each of which involved the abuse of power by an administration for political purposes rather than personal gain. Congressional Republicans argued that Clinton's lying under oath and alleged attempts to influence witnesses amounted to an assault on the judicial system and that his actions went far beyond lying to cover up an embarrassing affair, but undermined the rule of law. However, they were not successful in convincing a majority of the American public or congressional Democrats that his actions warranted removal from office.

Watergate, in addition to the break-in and cover-up, involved a range of illegitimate actions to undermine President Nixon's political opposition in the 1972 campaign. Iran-Contra involved a systematic and coordinated attempt to accomplish the Reagan administration's policy goals of aiding the Contras, despite public law that forbade it. These actions undermined constitutional provisions that give Congress law-making authority and order the president to take care that the laws be faithfully executed. President Nixon was directly involved with the Watergate crimes and would have likely been impeached and removed from office if he had not resigned. President Reagan asserted that he was not aware of the diversion of funds to the Contras, though Oliver North disputed his denial. The Democratic Congress did not think that the country was ready for an attempt to impeach the popular President Reagan and thus did not pursue an impeachment inquiry.

Even if the actions that led to President Clinton's impeachment and trial are not comparable to the Watergate or Iran-Contra incidents, his breach of trust with the American people should not be minimized. In his affair with an intern, Clinton manifested an arrogance that made him willing to put at risk his whole policy agenda, the respect of his allies and aides, and the privacy of his family. When he lied about his affair in public and under oath, he demonstrated a willingness to rupture the ties of trust between himself and the American people. A Democratic proposal for a congressional censure resolution read in part: "Whereas William Jefferson Clinton['s behavior] ... was shameless, reckless, and indefensible ... [and he] deliberately misled and deceived the American people ... [he did] demean the Office of the President ... [therefore] President Clinton fully deserves censure for engaging in such behavior."[47]

In the longer term, Clinton's refusal to provide answers to questions about his affair and Independent Counsel Kenneth Starr's single-minded pursuit of evidence led to some important precedents. Presidential conduct will now be subject to civil litigation. Future claims of executive privilege may be harder for presidents to make successfully. White House aides and lawyers will be easier to subpoena for testimony. Even the Secret Service will not be able to resist testimony. Thus, future presidents will be potentially vulnerable to frivolous or politically motivated law suits. While Clinton's political and policy legacy will be debated for a long time, the legal precedents set during the Starr investigation have disturbing implications for future presidents.

PRESIDENTIAL POPULARITY AND REPUTATION

Presidential reputations fluctuate over the years depending on current political issues, differing perspectives on historical eras, and historical scholarship.[48] Historical reputation should not be confused with presidential popularity as measured by current public opinion polls, because the two can often diverge dramatically. The degree of agreement in the historical ranking of our greatest presidents is striking.[49] In each of the major polls over the past half century, the top president has consistently been Abraham Lincoln and the next two have been George Washington and Franklin Roosevelt, with Washington generally ranking number two until the 1980s, after which he is replaced by Franklin Roosevelt.[50] There was also general consensus on the other "great" presidents, with Jefferson, Jackson, Theodore Roosevelt, Wilson, and sometimes Truman sharing the next places. Harding, Grant, and Nixon were consistently in the "failure" category. Despite this consistency at the top and bottom over the past half century, there are interesting changes and discrepancies among the mid-level ranks, particularly Truman and Eisenhower, which will be addressed below.

Franklin Roosevelt is consistently seen as one of the great presidents, primarily because of his moral leadership and vision in leading the country through the traumas of the Great Depression and World War II. When he was in office, however, he was opposed by a significant portion of the political system because his policies were seen as hostile to business interests and as giving too much economic power to the federal government. His conviction that the United States had to enter World War II on the side of the allies encountered serious opposition in the Congress and in isolationist attitudes in the population. Only the Japanese attack on Pearl Harbor galvanized the country for war. In the negotiations at the end of World War II, many believed that Roosevelt conceded too much influence to the Soviet Union.

Yet, in retrospect, there is a consensus across the political spectrum that FDR was a great president. That consensus is so widespread that even Ronald Reagan would invoke FDR in his speeches and champion the Social Security system that conservatives of the 1930s denounced as creeping socialism. With Reagan's blessing, FDR is firmly set in the pantheon of great presidents for the indefinite future.

Harry Truman inherited the presidency quite unprepared for it; he said that he thought a million men were more qualified for the office than he was. During his years as president, many politicians on both sides of the political spectrum agreed with that assessment. The Republican Speaker of the House said that Truman was "the worst president in history," and liberals felt that he was such

TABLE 8.1 | PRESIDENTIAL APPROVAL RATINGS, 1953–2002

President	Average	High	Low
Eisenhower	65%	79%	48%
Kennedy	70	83	56
Johnson	55	79	35
Nixon	49	67	24
Ford	47	71	37
Carter	45	74	28
Reagan	53	65	35
Bush	61	89	29
Clinton	55	73	37
Bush	n/a	90	31*

*George W. Bush: as of July 2006.
Source: Gallup Poll data from Gallup Web site at http://www.gallup.com, February 7, 1999; updated by author.

an unworthy heir to their hero FDR that they tried to draft Eisenhower to run as the Democratic nominee in 1948.[51] Yet, in 1948, Truman became the patron saint of presidents who are down in the polls and running for reelection when he came back from what was assumed to be Thomas Dewey's insurmountable lead to win election in his own right.[52] (See Table 8.1.)

Truman's approval rating in the public opinion polls dropped from a high of nearly 90 percent at the close of World War II to a low of 23 percent in November 1951, tying him with Richard Nixon in the midst of Watergate in January 1974.[53] His attempt to extend the New Deal with his own liberal legislative program, known as the Fair Deal, was generally unsuccessful. He proposed national medical insurance and civil rights legislation but was unable to win passage of the proposals in Congress. Many of his proposals were not to become public policy until the Johnson presidency.

The reversal of Truman's reputation from incompetent to feisty and firm arose out of a broad consensus that Truman "grew into the office" and provided firm leadership in the early years of the Cold War with the Soviet Union. Truman brought World War II to a close in Europe and the Pacific. He began the rebuilding of Europe with the Marshall Plan and helped to create the North Atlantic Treaty Organization (NATO). He committed the United States to countering aggression in Korea, but when General Douglas MacArthur maneuvered to extend the war north into China, Truman fired the war hero for insubordination. Since the early 1960s, Truman has consistently ranked in the top eight presidents in the estimation of presidency scholars.[54]

In contrast to Truman, President Eisenhower was quite popular during his eight years in office. His public approval rating ranged from a high in the high-seventies to a low in the high-forties, with the average at the higher end of this range. The opinion of scholars and historians in the first decade after his presidency, however, did not coincide with public opinion in the 1950s. In a 1970 ranking of presidents, Eisenhower was placed at number twenty, right behind Herbert Hoover. In popular presidency textbooks, he was often faulted for seeming not engaged in his own presidency, preferring to play golf while Sherman Adams ran the government.

Scholarly opinion of that era was no doubt affected by the dashing figure of John Kennedy, who advocated an activist presidency and proposed a number of legislative initiatives. But by the 1980s, polls of presidential reputation placed Eisenhower in the top ten or eleven, and a number of scholarly reassessments of Eisenhower came out in the 1980s. Some of these were based on the release of documents from the Eisenhower presidency, which were not available earlier, that showed a president much more engaged in the politics of his administration than had been evident at the time. Eisenhower was seen as consciously projecting an image of not being familiar with the details of policies and relying on the presidential role as symbolic chief of state rather than as political head of government. Eisenhower's was, in Fred Greenstein's phrase, a "hiddenhand" presidency.[55]

In later years, after Vietnam, Watergate, and Iran-Contra, the orderly and deliberative procedures of the Eisenhower administration were seen much more as assets than as the liabilities that many perceived in the 1950s, when it seemed that bureaucratic procedures were stifling the policy process. Policy development through an Eisenhower-style national security council system would likely not have allowed an Iran-Contra scandal to occur.[56] After the ensuing three decades, there is also a greater appreciation of Eisenhower's ability to keep the United States out of any major military confrontation after his conclusion of the Korean War. Orderly cabinet deliberations led to Eisenhower's refusal to commit the United States to a land war in Indochina.[57] Eisenhower also demonstrated a respect for Congress as a coequal branch of government that was sometimes lacking in future Republican Presidents Nixon, Reagan, and Bush.

John Kennedy's popularity and reputation were strongly affected by his assassination and the perception of him as a fallen hero. He won election, however, in one of the closest races in American history and did not have a mandate to deal from a position of strength with the Congress. He won a few victories, but he was not able to get Congress to enact a significant legislative program. His moral leadership, however, was buttressed by his stirring rhetoric and ability to perform well at live press conferences and in the international sphere (after the Bay of Pigs). A number of future leaders of both political parties, including President Clinton, said that they had been drawn to elected office and public service by Kennedy's inspiring leadership and the charge in his inaugural address, "Ask not what your country can do for you, but rather ask what you can do for your country."

Perhaps because of Kennedy's ability to inspire with his rhetoric and polished style, there is a disjuncture between evaluations of him by historians, who rank him twelfth or thirteenth among presidents, and his popularity with the American public in general. In surveys by the Gallup polling organization, people rank Kennedy first when asked, "What three presidents do you regard as the greatest?" and "Of all the presidents we have ever had, who do you wish were president today?"[58] More recent revelations about Kennedy's promiscuous sex life and his dependence on drugs to relieve his constant pain seem not to have affected his popular reputation.[59]

What Kennedy would have accomplished had he lived, and whether he would have withdrawn the 16,000 troops he had sent to Vietnam, will never be known. But it seems likely that he will continue to be seen as a hero by liberals, as the respected Cold War confronter of Khrushchev by conservatives, and that his rhetoric will continue to be quoted by politicians of both political parties in the future. Three decades after Kennedy's election, several biographies were published that were as one-sidedly negative in their evaluation as early biographies were enthusiastically positive.[60]

Lyndon Johnson won by a landslide, beating the conservative Barry Goldwater in 1964. Johnson will continue to be respected for his ability to put through Congress the large liberal agenda of 1965. Many of these programs still exist and are popular with Americans. Even though Ronald Reagan denounced Great Society programs as part of the governmental problem, he included some of them in his "social safety net" of programs not to be touched in the 1981 budget cuts (e.g., Medicare, Medicaid, and Head Start). Johnson's wiles as a politician have been viewed with awe but also with distaste. According to White House aide Joseph Califano, Johnson was "brave and brutal, compassionate and cruel, incredibly intelligent and infuriatingly insensitive, with a shrewd and uncanny instinct for the jugular of his allies and adversaries. He could be altruistic and petty, caring and crude, generous and petulant, bluntly honest and calculatingly devious—all within the same few minutes."[61] While most historians see Johnson from this dual perspective, one influential biography has interpreted Johnson's life primarily in terms of ambition, power, and greed.[62]

Regardless of future evaluations of Johnson's political style and domestic programs, his historical reputation will be heavily shadowed by the war in Vietnam. The war was widely seen as the first major military defeat for the United States. Those who were against the war believed that the United States had no business trying to impose its will in a civil war in Southeast Asia. Those who favored the war believed that Johnson imposed his own tactical judgment in what should have been strictly military decisions and that Johnson did not commit the United States firmly enough to win. The unpopularity of the war led Johnson, as it did Truman before him in another Asian war, to decide not to run for reelection in the face of almost certain defeat.

Richard Nixon will always be remembered as the president who resigned his office rather than submit to probable impeachment for his Watergate offenses. In the short run, Watergate dominated Nixon's reputation, but his foreign policy triumphs were significant. The opening to China was a historic opportunity that probably only Nixon, with his unimpeachable anticommunist

President Richard M. Nixon waves goodbye at the White House on August 9, 1974, the day that he resigned the presidency. (AP Images)

reputation, could have accomplished, given domestic political fears of communism. Similarly, the Strategic Arms Limitation Talks and détente with the Soviet Union were trusted only because of Nixon's legendary distrust of the Soviet Union. The domestic programs enacted during the Nixon administration were also significant (National Environmental Policy Act, Clean Air Act, Water Quality Improvement Act, Occupational Safety and Health Act, Equal Employment Opportunity Act, etc.), though some of these were forced on Nixon by the Democratic Congress. But it is likely that these programs will be overshadowed by the story of Nixon's battles with Congress and Watergate.

In the two decades after his resignation, Nixon undertook a determined effort to rehabilitate himself by meeting with foreign leaders, conferring with Republican presidents, and writing a series of books on political and international affairs. In his writings and public appearances, Nixon consistently downplayed Watergate as a minor incident and emphasized the role of his political enemies in bringing him down. In the end, however, it is doubtful if his reinterpretations will dispel the ghost of Watergate, regardless of the credit he may be given for his domestic and foreign policies.[63]

Jimmy Carter was defeated in his run for reelection under the cloud of hostages in Iran and runaway inflation. While it can be argued that there was no easy solution to the hostage crisis and that OPEC (Organization of Petroleum Exporting Countries) had much to do with inflation in the economy, Carter was not able to escape blame. (Though he appointed Paul A. Volcker to head the Federal Reserve Board, which did deal with inflation.) He was seen as an ineffectual president, rejected by the voters and ridiculed by the Reagan administration. His foreign policy successes stand out—particularly the Panama Canal Treaties and the Camp David Peace Accords, which brought Sadat of Egypt and Begin of Israel together to negotiate the first such peace agreement between Israel and Arab neighbor. But they do not dominate his popular image.

It is still too early to judge what historians will conclude about the Carter administration, but there is little doubt that he will be seen as an admirable ex-president. After returning to Georgia, Carter undertook a number of good works throughout the world. He set up programs to eradicate specific debilitating diseases in many Third World countries. He set up peace-making conferences for wars that were internal to countries rather than international. He promoted and worked for Habitat for Humanity, which built housing for poor people throughout the country. In addition, he wrote a number of books, including nonfiction, memoirs, poetry, and fiction. In the late 1980s and early 1990s, there was some reevaluation of Carter's presidency in a positive direction, but his presidency is still too close in history for a balanced view.

There is no doubt that Ronald Reagan will go down as one of the most conservative of the modern presidents. He led a major change in public opinion over the role of government in the United States. He led the country through a large tax cut, large domestic cuts in spending, and the largest peacetime military buildup in history. On the other hand, he presided over unprecedented budget deficits and a tripling of the national debt. He directed his staff to trade arms with Iran, and his management style allowed funds from the arms sales to be illegally diverted to the Contras in Nicaragua. It is too early to speculate about Reagan's place in history, but it is likely that he will be given credit for the conservative direction of the country in the 1980s and will be blamed for the Iran-Contra affair. Reagan will be given credit by conservatives for hastening the fall of the Soviet Union with his aggressive spending on defense and will be given credit by most scholars for his encouragement of Premier Gorbachev's transitory leadership. History's judgment of Reagan's fiscal policies may be influenced by the state of the U.S. economy in the early decades of the twenty-first century.

The public evaluation of President George H.W. Bush's performance reflects the ambivalence and volatility of U.S. public opinion toward presidents. In the first year of his presidency, he enjoyed approval ratings between 60 and 78 percent, and in 1990 his approval ratings dropped from the high seventies to below 50 percent as the U.S. military buildup in the Persian Gulf expanded. With the U.S. victory in the Gulf War, Bush's public approval shot up to a peak of 90 percent. But from that record high, his public-approval ratings dropped steadily in the longest sustained drop in history (57 percentage points) to

33 percent in August of 1992.[64] While the economy was still performing sluggishly and the president had not reacted decisively to racial disturbances in Los Angeles, there were no major blunders or changes that explained the huge drop in popularity. Bush was the same man, with all of the assets and liabilities evident throughout his presidency and public career. The precipitous drop must be explained as much by exaggerated public expectations as by presidential performance.[65]

In historical perspective, as vice president for Reagan, George Bush will share some of the credit or blame for the 1980s. As president, he will be credited with firm leadership in the Persian Gulf War, though it is still too early to know how much the United States contributed to Saddam Hussein's tyranny by U.S. aid to him in the 1980s. And it is too early to gauge the longer-term effects of the war on the Middle East or world peace. Despite his failure to win reelection, Bush may have a reasonably good chance for a positive historical ranking. In domestic policy, he finally confronted the savings-and-loan debacle that had been created and ignored during the Reagan administration. The costs to the budget and the economy were significant, but the Bush administration dealt with the problem successfully. Ironically, Bush may have suffered politically most for what was one of his most courageous political acts—the breaking of his "no new taxes" pledge in 1990. The deficit reduction package that he negotiated with the Democratic 102nd Congress reduced the deficit by about $500 billion over five years and established spending caps in the budget. Along with Clinton's 1993 deficit-reduction package, this must be given partial credit for the huge economic expansion of the late 1990s. In foreign policy, Bush handled the demise of the Soviet Union and the reunification of Germany within NATO with great subtlety and restraint.[66]

Bill Clinton will be remembered as the first elected president to be impeached and the first in 130 years to be tried in the Senate. The recklessness of his behavior in engaging in a sexual affair while in office and his lying under oath to the country about it will be important in any account of his presidency.

But Clinton will also be remembered for the prosperity of the 1990s and his role in the first balanced budgets since 1969. He also was the first president of the information age, after the Cold War and fall of the Berlin Wall. Clinton was a Democrat who favored free trade and integrating the United States into the new globalized economy of the world. His broader political legacy may center on his role as a "new Democrat" in bringing the Democratic Party toward the center of the political spectrum and getting it to accept the 1970s and 1980s conservative reaction against the governmental activism of the Great Society. In his State of the Union address of 1996, he declared that "the era of big government is over."

But in embracing the conservative rhetoric, Clinton also helped establish limits to how far that conservative reaction could go in trying to roll back the governmental programs of the New Deal and Great Society. His battle with the conservative Republicans of the 104th Congress was based on protecting Medicare, Medicaid, education, and the environment, and it was largely successful. In his own view of the role he played, Clinton told one of his

In the nineteenth century, British Scholar James Bryce observed in his classic study of American government and politics: "Impeachment ... is the heaviest piece of artillery in the congressional arsenal, but because it is so heavy it is unfit for ordinary use. It is like a hundred-ton gun which needs complex machinery to bring it into position, an enormous charge of powder to fire it, and a large mark to aim at. ... but ill adapted for the punishment of small transgressions." From James Bryce, *The American Commonwealth*, vol. I (London: Macmillan, 1892), p. 208. (AUTH © 1998 The Philadelphia Inquirer. Reprinted with permission of Universal Press Syndicate. All rights reserved.)

speechwriters: "FDR's mission was to save capitalism from its excesses. Our mission has been to save government from its own excesses so it can again be a progressive force."[67] Thus, Clinton disgraced himself in his personal behavior but played an important role in the public-policy battles of the 1990s; he helped adjust the United States to the post–Cold War era and the Democratic Party to a more conservative America.

Even before the end of President George W. Bush's first several years in office, it was possible to see the outlines of an important part of his historical legacy. The 2000 election was one of the most controversial in American history, with its outcome delayed thirty-six days and then only settled by a controversial 5–4 decision by the Supreme Court. The election will not soon be forgotten by his supporters or by his adversaries. President Bush will also be remembered as the nation's leader when the World Trade Center's twin towers in New York were downed and the Pentagon was attacked by terrorists on September 11, 2001. Bush will receive credit for reassuring the nation after the attacks and expressing U.S. determination to fight a war on terrorism.

The quick military victory in Afghanistan will be seen as thwarting al-Qaeda in the short run and liberating the country from the repressive Taliban regime. But the longer-term consequences of the war will depend on the ability of the Afghans to establish a stable society and whether al-Qaeda can reestablish itself as an international terrorist threat. In 2006 the outcome was not clear. Although the war in Afghanistan was a necessary response to al-Qaeda in the war on terrorism, the war in Iraq was the first preemptive (or preventive) war that was advocated by the Bush administration's new national security doctrine. In his political campaign for the war, President Bush was able to prevail against significant domestic doubts and over the broad opposition of the international community, including some long-time U.S. allies.

Military victory in Iraq was never in doubt, and U.S. forces were victorious within three weeks. But the aftermath of the war was more problematic. President Bush would have received credit if Iraq had been transformed into a thriving democracy in a stabilized Middle East. But the U.S. occupation was long and bitter, and rival religious and ethnic factions plunged the country into civil war. The U.S. occupying forces were not able to quell the internecine warfare and suffered many casualties trying to establish order in the country. The outcomes of the 2006 elections were interpreted as a referendum on the war and saddled President Bush with Democratic opposition in Congress for his final two years in office.

President Bush is also likely to be remembered for his extraordinary claims of executive war power. He asserted a constitutional prerogative to ignore the law against wiretapping without a warrant, to imprison enemy combatants indefinitely without trial, to establish unilaterally military tribunals, to suspend the Geneva Conventions and authorize harsh interrogation policies, and to establish secret prisons in Europe for suspected terrorists. He also used signing statements systematically to assert his right to ignore provisions of laws that he deemed unconstitutional infringements on his executive power.

Regardless of whatever else President Bush accomplished during his presidency, his disputed election, his response to the 9/11 attacks, and the two wars in his first several years in office will figure prominently in historical evaluations of his presidency.

CONCLUSION: PUBLIC EXPECTATIONS AND THE PRESIDENCY

The very rating of presidents by historical reputation is an indicator of the importance that Americans attach to their presidents, an importance usually out of proportion to the power that presidents wield or their abilities to deliver on the expectations of them. The high level of power people assume presidents have—either for good or for evil—is the result of several factors. One is the combination of the roles of symbolic chief of state with the more mundane role of head of government in the United States. The combination of the two roles in one office creates the opportunity for U.S. presidents to call on their symbolic role to shore up their political standing. But this combination also creates high expectations in the electorate that the president will be above petty politics and will always act in the best long-term interests of the country.

Because U.S. presidents serve a psychological function as symbols of the nation and vehicles for patriotic feelings, the expectations of the public are magnified. Schoolchildren are taught stories about early presidents, who come to symbolize historical periods for them. And the public tends to use the image of the president to reduce the complexity of American government and public policy.[68]

Despite the hagiography of presidents from the Federalist era through Lincoln, historical experience in the nineteenth century did not create the high expectations that presidents would control the political agenda and deliver the country from all of its troubles. But early in the twentieth century, the Progressives raised expectations by advocating an activist central government led by a president who represented the national interest and who would counter the legislature, which was dominated by narrow sectional interests.[69]

Public expectations were further raised by Franklin Roosevelt and the birth of the modern presidency. Roosevelt was the symbol of U.S. resolve that got the country through the Great Depression and the determination that won World War II. For the rest of the twentieth century, public expectations would force presidents to live "in the shadow of FDR."[70] In national security making, presidents would henceforth be aided by a centralized NSC staff. In the economic sphere, presidents would be aided by a Council of Economic Advisers and the national government would be responsible for full employment and the health of the economy.

After the Eisenhower hiatus from the activist presidency, public expectations were raised by John Kennedy's promise to "get the country moving again." The image of the presidency in contemporary textbooks was that of a powerful, benevolent, and forceful leader; often a liberal pitted against the conservative and regressive forces in Congress.

Public expectations were soon dashed by race riots in the cities of the 1960s, the quagmire of Vietnam, and the horrors of Watergate. But the post-imperial presidencies of Ford and Carter did not suit U.S. tastes. It was Reagan, in 1981, who restored grandeur to the office, and his impressive early policy victories eased public fears of an imperiled presidency. He seemed to end the string of truncated presidencies after Eisenhower: Kennedy assassinated, Johnson forced not to run again, Nixon's resignation, and Ford and Carter each defeated as incumbents.

But the lesson of the Reagan presidency is that even large electoral victories cannot ensure sustained policy performance. After the whirlwind performance of 1981, Reagan's legislative success steadily declined and he was not able to accomplish much of the rest of his conservative agenda. His second term brought the impressive 1986 Tax Reform Act but was marred by the Iran-Contra scandal.

President Bush's record-high popularity after the Gulf War of 1991 dissolved as the economy began to weaken, and voters rejected him for Bill

Clinton. The initial optimistic expectations of Democrats because of the return of unified government in 1993 were not fulfilled when Clinton's far-reaching health-care reform proposal foundered. And it was only through Clinton's firm opposition to the conservative 104th Congress and the weak challenge from Robert Dole that he managed to achieve reelection. George W. Bush did not make extravagant promises in his 2000 campaign, but his national security policy in the wake of 9/11 significantly changed the premises of U.S. national security policy to include preemptive war. His vision of establishing a stable, democratic government in Iraq proved to be wildly optimistic, and in 2006 public opinion began to reflect skepticism about the Iraq war as well as President Bush.

Americans have high expectations of their presidents and tend to attribute more credit and blame than a realistic assessment of actual presidential power would justify. This is in part because presidential candidates make sweeping promises when they are running for office. But it is also because many Americans are not sensitive to the fact that presidential powers are limited in our separation-of-powers system. Social trends (such as crime, drug use, or educational performance) in a country of 300 million people cannot be controlled by any one person or agency, and neither can a $10 trillion capitalist economy.

If presidential candidates would not overpromise, and citizens would lower their policy expectations of presidents, people might become less cynical and more realistic about U.S. politics. But in the United States, high public expectations of presidents will continue to prevail and present both opportunity and danger to U.S. presidents.

NOTES

1. Hugh Heclo, "What Has Happened to the Separation of Powers?" in James P. Pfiffner, ed., *Governance and American Politics* (Fort Worth, TX: Harcourt Brace, 1995), p. 297.

2. Michael Nelson, ed., *Congressional Quarterly Guide to the Presidency* (Washington, DC: CQ Press, 1989), p. 1280.

3. For details of corruption in the Harding administration, see Francis Russell, *The Shadow of Blooming Grove* (New York: McGraw-Hill, 1968), pp. 495–525.

4. Richard T. Johnson, *Managing the White House* (New York: Harper & Row, 1974), p. 58.

5. For details on these and other aspects of political corruption, see Suzanne Garment, *Scandal: The Culture of Mistrust in American Politics* (New York: Times Books, 1991).

6. Nelson, *Congressional Quarterly Guide to the Presidency*, pp. 1386–1387.

7. Stanley Kutler, *The Wars of Watergate* (New York: Knopf, 1990), p. 433.

8. Michael Genovese, *The Nixon Presidency* (New York: Greenwood Press, 1990), p. 223.

9. The list is reproduced in Larry Berman, *The New American Presidency* (Boston: Houghton Mifflin, 1987), p. 279.

10. On August 16, 1971, John Dean sent a memo to H. R. Haldeman entitled: "How We Can Use the Available Political Machinery to Screw Our Political Enemies," Berman, *The New American Presidency*, p. 174.

11. Berman, *The New American Presidency*, p. 276.

12. See the analysis in Genovese, *The Nixon Presidency*, p. 182.

13. For details, see Genovese, *The Nixon Presidency*, pp. 178–180.

14. Genovese, *The Nixon Presidency*, p. 180.

15. From the White House transcripts, in Berman, *The New American Presidency*, p. 286.

16. Berman, *The New American Presidency*, p. 285.

17. According to Magruder, Nixon said to Mitchell, "John, we need to—we need to get the information on Larry O'Brien. And the only way we can do that is through Liddy's plan. And you need to do that." David Von Drehle, "30 Years Later, a Watergate Allegation," *Washington Post* (July 27, 2003), p. A5.

18. White House Transcripts, in Berman, *The New American Presidency*, p. 287; and in Genovese, *The Nixon Presidency*, p. 189.

19. Genovese, *The Nixon Presidency*, p. 190.

20. Berman, *The New American Presidency*, p. 287.

21. The full texts of the impeachment articles are reprinted in Nelson, *Congressional Quarterly Guide to the Presidency*, pp. 1387–1388.

22. Kutler, *The Wars of Watergate*, p. 226.

23. C. Vann Woodward, "The Conscience of the White House," in Woodward, ed., *Responses of the President to Charges of Misconduct* (New York: Dell, 1974), p. xxvi; quoted in Genovese, *The Nixon Presidency*, p. 226.

24. Robert J. Spitzer, *President and Congress* (Philadelphia: Temple University Press, 1993), p. 223.

25. Report of the Congressional Committees Investigating the Iran-Contra Affair, S. Rept. No. 100–216, H. Rept. No. 100–433 (November 1987), pp. 18–21.

26. *Iran-Contra Affair*, pp. 437, 442.

27. Kutler, *Wars of Watergate*, p. 614.

28. *Iran-Contra Affair*, p. 22.

29. Russell, *The Shadow of Blooming Grove*, p. 560.

30. *Iran-Contra Affair*, p. 274.

31. Dissenting opinion in *Olmstead v. U.S.*, 277 U.S. 438 (1928), p. 479.

32. See William S. Cohen and George J. Mitchell, *Men of Zeal* (New York: Viking, 1988).

33. Quoted in Theodore Draper, *A Very Thin Line* (New York: Hill and Wang, 1991), p. 598.

34. *Washington Post* (February 8, 1998), p. A20.

35. Jeffrey Toobin, "Circling the Wagons," *The New Yorker* (July 6, 1998), p. 29.

36. *The Findings of Independent Counsel Kenneth W. Starr on President Clinton and the Lewinsky Affair, Referral to the U.S. House of Representatives Pursuant to Title 28, U.S. Code, Par. 595 (c) Released by Congress on September 11, 1998* (New York: Public Affairs, 1998).

37. Raoul Berger, *Impeachment: The Constitutional Problems* (Cambridge, MA: Harvard University Press, 1973), p. 79.

38. James Madison, *Notes on Debates in the Federal Convention of 1787* (New York: W. W. Norton, 1969), pp. 605–606.

39. From the statement reprinted in the *Washington Post* (October 6, 1998), p. A9.

40. See the op-ed piece by Elliot L. Richardson in the *New York Times* (September 18, 1998), p. A27; Gerald R. Ford, "The Path Back to Dignity," *New York Times* (October 4, 1998), p. WK15.

41. On December 16, the debate had been postponed for a day because the U.S. launched air strikes against Saddam Hussein for his refusal to cooperate with UN weapons inspectors. In addition, House Speaker–designate Robert Livingston announced on the day of impeachment that he had been unfaithful in his marriage and would not run for Speaker of the 106th Congress and would step down from Congress in six months.

42. The votes are reported in *Congressional Quarterly Weekly*, p. 3372.

43. *Congressional Quarterly Weekly*, p. 3321.

44. "House of Representatives Impeachment Brief," *New York Times* (January 12, 1999), p. A16.

45. "White House Impeachment Trial Memo," *New York Times* (January 14, 1998), pp. A14–15.

46. Opening statement by Charles Ruff, pp. A26–28.

47. "Text of a Proposed Censure Resolution Prepared by Senator Dianne Feinstein" (D-Calif.), *New York Times* (February 6, 1999), p. A8.

48. For an analysis of the methodology, validity, and value of presidential ranking by scholars, see James P. Pfiffner, "Rating the Presidents: Continuity and Volatility," *White House Studies* vol. 3. no. 1 (2003), pp. 23–34.

49. These include the Schlesinger, Sr., Poll (1948) [N=55 "experts"], Schlesinger, Sr. (1962) [N=75]; Maranell (1970) [N=571]; U.S. Historical Society (1977) [N=85]; *Chicago Tribute* (1982) [N=49]; Murray-Blessing (1982) [N=846]; Porter (1982) [N=41]; Schlesinger, Jr. (1996) [N=32]; and C-SPAN (2000) [N=58]. The rankings along with citations can be found in James P. Pfiffner, *The Modern Presidency*, 3rd ed. (New York: St. Martin's Press, 2000), pp. 233–235; and Robert K. Murray and Tim H. Blessing, *Greatness in the White House* (University Park: Pennsylvania State University Press, 1994), pp. 16–17. The 1996 Schlesinger poll is in the *New York Times Magazine* (December 15, 1996), pp. 46–51. The C-SPAN poll is from www.americanpresidents.org (February 24, 2000); it was also reported in *Washingtonian Magazine* (April 2000), pp. 53–55. Note that the C-SPAN poll ranked presidents by compiling their scores on ten separate leadership categories rather than by asking respondents to make an overall judgment about presidential greatness. This may explain in part why Nixon, who was quite a skillful president, despite his character failings, was ranked number 25, much higher than in most other expert polls.

50. Arthur B. Murphy, "Evaluating the Presidents of the United States," in David C. Kozak and Kenneth N. Ciboski, eds. *The American Presidency* (Chicago: Nelson-Hall, 1985), pp. 438–448.

51. Alan Brinkley, "Work Hard, Trust in God, Have No Fear," *New York Times Book Review* (June 21, 1992), p. 1.

52. Harry Truman's daughter, Margaret, wrote an article taking exception to George H. W. Bush's invocation of her father's name in his acceptance speech at the Republican National Convention in 1992. She believed that New Dealer Truman would feel uncomfortable being invoked by conservative Republican Bush. *Washington Post* (August 27, 1992), p. A31.

53. *Washington Post* (August 17, 1992), p. A11.

54. See Arthur B. Murphy, "Evaluating the Presidents of the United States," in David C. Kozak and Kenneth N.Ciboski, eds., *The American Presidency* (Chicago: Nelson-Hall, 1985), pp. 437–448.

55. Fred I. Greenstein, *The Hidden-Hand Presidency* (New York: Basic Books, 1982).

56. Philip G. Henderson, *Managing the Presidency* (Boulder, CO: Westview Press, 1988).

57. John P. Burke and Fred I. Greenstein, *How Presidents Test Reality: Decisions on Vietnam, 1954 and 1965* (New York: Russell Sage, 1989).

58. James M. Burns, J. W. Peltason, Thomas Cronin, and David B. Magleby, *Government by the People* (Englewood Cliffs, NJ: Prentice Hall, 1993), p. 442.

59. For an analysis of sexual probity and presidential character, see James P. Pfiffner, *The Character Factor: How We Judge America's Presidents* (College Station, TX: Texas A&M University Press, 2004), chap. 4.

60. Positive accounts of the Kennedy administration include memoirs by Theodore Sorensen, *Kennedy* (New York: Bantam, 1965); and Arthur Schlesinger, Jr., *A Thousand Days* (New York: Fawcett Publications, 1965). The negative biographies include Nigel Hamilton, *JFK, Reckless Youth* (New York: Random House, 1992); Thomas C. Reeves, *A Question of Character: A Life of John F. Kennedy* (New York: Free Press, 1991); and Seymour Hersh, *The Dark Side of Camelot* (New York: Little, Brown, 1997). Balanced perspectives include Herbert Parmet, *JFK: The Presidency of John F. Kennedy* (New York: Penguin Books, 1984); Richard Reeves, *President Kennedy: Profile of Power* (New York: Simon and Schuster, 1993) and Robert Dallek, *An Unfinished Life: John F. Kennedy, 1917–1963* (Boston: Little Brown, 2003).

61. Joseph Califano, *The Triumph and Tragedy of Lyndon Johnson* (College Station, TX: Texas A&M University Press, 1999).

62. Robert Caro, *The Path to Power* (New York: Knopf, 1982), and *Means of Ascent* (New York: Knopf, 1990). His third volume, *Master of the Senate* (New York: Knopf, 2002), gave Johnson credit for more of a mixture in his motives.

63. See Kutler, *The Wars of Watergate.*

64. *Washington Post* (August 17, 1992), p. A11.

65. See the insightful article by Marjorie Williams, "What We Know about George," *Washington Post Magazine* (August 16, 1992), p. 7.

66. See the argument by Jonathan Rauch, "Father Superior: Our Greatest Modern President," *The New Republic* (May 22, 2000), pp. 22–25.

67. Jacob Weisberg, "The Governor-President," *New York Times Magazine* (January 17, 1999), p. 33.

68. Thomas Cronin, "The Textbook and Prime-Time Presidency," *The State of the Presidency* (Boston: Little, Brown, 1980).

69. Lester G. Seligman and Cary R. Covington, *The Coalitional Presidency* (Chicago: Dorsey Press, 1989), chap. 2.

70. William E. Leuchtenburg, *In the Shadow of FDR* (Ithaca, NY: Cornell University Press, 1983).

PRESIDENTS OF THE UNITED STATES

1.	George Washington (F)	(1789–1797)
2.	John Adams (F)	(1797–1801)
3.	Thomas Jefferson (DR)	(1801–1809)
4.	James Madison (DR)	(1809–1817)
5.	James Monroe (DR)	(1817–1825)
6.	John Quincy Adams (DR)	(1825–1829)
7.	Andrew Jackson (D)	(1829–1837)
8.	Martin Van Buren (D)	(1837–1841)
9.	William Henry Harrison (W)	(1841)*
10.	John Tyler (W)	(1841–1845)
11.	James K. Polk (D)	(1845–1849)
12.	Zachary Taylor (W)	(1849–1850)*
13.	Millard Fillmore (W)	(1850–1853)
14.	Franklin Pierce (D)	(1853–1857)
15.	James Buchanan (D)	(1857–1861)
16.	Abraham Lincoln (R)	(1861–1865)[†]
17.	Andrew Johnson (R)	(1865–1869)
18.	Ulysses S. Grant (R)	(1869–1877)
19.	Rutherford B. Hayes (R)	(1877–1881)
20.	James A. Garfield (R)	(1881)[†]
21.	Chester A. Arthur (R)	(1881–1885)
22.	Grover Cleveland (D)	(1885–1889)
23.	Benjamin Harrison (R)	(1889–1893)

(continued)

24.	Grover Cleveland (D)	(1893–1897)
25.	William McKinley (R)	(1897–1901)[†]
26.	Theodore Roosevelt (R)	(1901–1909)
27.	William H. Taft (R)	(1909–1913)
28.	Woodrow Wilson (D)	(1913–1921)
29.	Warren G. Harding (R)	(1921–1923)[*]
30.	Calvin Coolidge (R)	(1923–1929)
31.	Herbert C. Hoover (R)	(1929–1933)
32.	Franklin D. Roosevelt (D)	(1933–1945)[*]
33.	Harry S Truman (D)	(1945–1953)
34.	Dwight D. Eisenhower (R)	(1953–1961)
35.	John F. Kennedy (D)	(1961–1963)[†]
36.	Lyndon B. Johnson (D)	(1963–1969)
37.	Richard M. Nixon (R)	(1969–1974)[‡]
38.	Gerald R. Ford (R)	(1974–1977)[§]
39.	Jimmy Carter (D)	(1977–1981)
40.	Ronald Reagan (R)	(1981–1989)
41.	George H. W. Bush (R)	(1989–1993)
42.	Bill Clinton (D)	(1993–2001)
43.	George W. Bush (R)	(2001–)

F = Federalist. DR = Democratic Republican. R = Republican. D = Democratic. W = Whig.
[*]Died in office of natural causes.
[†]Assassinated.
[‡]Resigned August 9, 1974.
[§]Appointed Vice President in 1973.

THE CONSTITUTION OF THE UNITED STATES OF AMERICA: ARTICLES I AND II

We the People of the United States, in Order to form a more perfect Union, establish Justice, insure domestic Tranquillity, provide for the common defence, promote the general Welfare, and secure the Blessings of Liberty to ourselves and our Posterity, do ordain and establish this Constitution for the United States of America.

ARTICLE I

SECTION 1. All legislative Powers herein granted shall be vested in a Congress of the United States, which shall consist of a Senate and House of Representatives.

SECTION 2. The House of Representatives shall be composed of Members chosen every second Year by the People of the several States, and the Electors in each State shall have the Qualifications requisite for Electors of the most numerous Branch of the State Legislature.

No Person shall be a Representative who shall not have attained to the age of twenty five Years, and been seven Years a Citizen of the United States, and who shall not, when elected, be an Inhabitant of that State in which he shall be chosen.

Representatives and direct Taxes shall be apportioned among the several States which may be included within this Union, according to their respective Numbers, which shall be determined by adding to the whole Number of free Persons, including those bound to Service for a Term of Years, and excluding

Indians not taxed, three fifths of all other Persons. The actual Enumeration shall be made within three Years after the first Meeting of the Congress of the United States, and within every subsequent Term of ten Years, in such Manner as they shall by Law direct. The Number of Representatives shall not exceed one for every thirty Thousand, but each State shall have at Least one Representative and until such enumeration shall be made, the State of New Hampshire shall be entitled to chuse three, Massachusetts eight, Rhode-Island and Providence Plantations one, Connecticut five, New-York six, New Jersey four, Pennsylvania eight, Delaware one, Maryland six, Virginia ten, North Carolina five, South Carolina five, and Georgia three.

When vacancies happen in the Representation from any State, the Executive Authority thereof shall issue Writs of Election to fill such Vacancies.

The House of Representatives shall chuse their Speaker and other Officers; and shall have the sole Power of Impeachment.

SECTION 3. The Senate of the United States shall be composed of two Senators from each State, chosen by the Legislature thereof, for six Years; and each Senator shall have one Vote.

Immediately after they shall be assembled in Consequence of the first Election, they shall be divided as equally as may be into three Classes. The Seats of the Senators of the first Class shall be vacated at the Expiration of the second Year, of the second Class at the Expiration of the fourth Year, and of the third Class at the Expiration of the sixth Year, so that one third may be chosen every second Year; and if Vacancies happen by Resignation, or otherwise, during the Recess of the Legislature of any State, the Executive thereof may make temporary Appointments until the next Meeting of the Legislature, which shall then fill such Vacancies.

No Person shall be a Senator who shall not have attained to the Age of thirty Years, and been nine Years a Citizen of the United States, and who shall not, when elected, be an Inhabitant of that State for which he shall be chosen.

The Vice President of the United States shall be President of the Senate, but shall have no Vote, unless they be equally divided.

The Senate shall chuse their other Officers, and also a President pro tempore, in the Absence of the Vice President, or when he shall exercise the Office of President of the United States.

The Senate shall have the sole Power to try all Impeachments. When sitting for that Purpose, they shall be on Oath or Affirmation. When the President of the United States is tried the Chief Justice shall preside: And no Person shall be convicted without the Concurrence of two thirds of the Members present.

Judgment in Cases of Impeachment shall not extend further than to removal from Office, and disqualification to hold and enjoy any Office of honor, Trust or Profit under the United States: but the Party convicted shall nevertheless be liable and subject to Indictment, Trial, Judgment and Punishment, according to Law.

SECTION 4. The Times, Places and Manner of holding Elections for Senators and Representatives, shall be prescribed in each State by the Legislature thereof; but the Congress may at any time by Law make or alter such Regulations, except as to the Places of chusing Senators.

The Congress shall assemble at least once in every Year, and such Meeting shall be on the first Monday in December, unless they shall by Law appoint a different Day.

SECTION 5. Each House shall be the Judge of the Elections, Returns and Qualifications of its own Members, and a Majority of each shall constitute a Quorum to do Business; but a smaller Number may adjourn from day to day, and may be authorized to compel the Attendance of absent Members, in such Manner, and under such Penalties as each House may provide.

Each House may determine the Rules of its Proceedings, punish its Members for disorderly Behaviour, and, with the Concurrence of two thirds, expel a Member.

Each House shall keep a Journal of its Proceedings, and from time to time publish the same, excepting such Parts as may in their Judgment require Secrecy; and the Yeas and Nays of the Members of either House on any question shall, at the Desire of one fifth of those Present, be entered on the Journal.

Neither House, during the Session of Congress, shall, without the Consent of the other, adjourn for more than three days, nor to any other Place than that in which the two Houses shall be sitting.

SECTION 6. The Senators and Representatives shall receive a Compensation for their Services, to be ascertained by Law, and paid out of the Treasury of the United States. They shall in all Cases, except Treason, Felony and Breach of the Peace, be privileged from Arrest during their Attendance at the Session of their respective Houses, and in going to and returning from the same; and for any Speech or Debate in either House, they shall not be questioned in any other Place.

No Senator or Representative shall, during the Time for which he was elected, be appointed to any civil Office under the Authority of the United States, which shall have been created, or the Emoluments whereof shall have been encreased during such time; and no Person holding any Office under the United States, shall be a Member of either House during his Continuance in Office.

SECTION 7. All Bills for raising Revenue shall originate in the House of Representatives; but the Senate may propose or concur with amendments as on other Bills.

Every Bill which shall have passed the House of Representatives and the Senate, shall, before it become a Law, be presented to the President of the United States; If he approve he shall sign it, but if not he shall return it, with his Objections to that House in which it shall have originated, who shall enter the Objections at large on their Journal, and proceed to reconsider it. If after such Reconsideration two thirds of that House shall agree to pass the Bill, it shall be sent, together with the Objections, to the other House, by which it shall likewise be reconsidered, and if approved by two thirds of that House, it shall become a Law. But in all such Cases the Votes of both Houses shall be determined by Yeas and Nays, and the Names of the Persons voting for and against the Bill shall be entered on the Journal of each House respectively. If any Bill shall not be returned by the President within ten Days (Sunday excepted) after it shall have been presented to him, the Same shall be a Law, in like Manner as if he had signed it, unless the Congress by their Adjournment prevent its Return, in which Case it shall not be a Law.

Every Order, Resolution, or Vote to which the Concurrence of the Senate and House of Representatives may be necessary (except on a question of Adjournment) shall be presented to the President of the United States; and before the Same shall take Effect, shall be approved by him, or being disapproved by him, shall be repassed by two thirds of the Senate and House of Representatives, according to the Rules and Limitations prescribed in the Case of a Bill.

SECTION 8. The Congress shall have Power To lay and collect Taxes, Duties, Imposts and Excises, to pay the Debts and provide for the common Defence and general Welfare of the United States; but all Duties, Imposts and Excises shall be uniform throughout the United States;

To borrow Money on the credit of the United States;

To regulate Commerce with foreign Nations, and among the several States, and with the Indian Tribes;

To establish an uniform Rule of Naturalization, and uniform Laws on the subject of Bankruptcies throughout the United States;

To coin Money, regulate the Value thereof, and of foreign Coin, and fix the Standard of Weights and Measures;

To provide for the Punishment of counterfeiting the Securities and current Coin of the United States;

To establish Post Offices and post Roads;

To promote the Progress of Science and useful Arts, by securing for limited Times to Authors and Inventors the exclusive Right to their respective Writings and Discoveries;

To constitute Tribunals inferior to the supreme Court;

To define and punish Piracies and Felonies committed on the high Seas, and Offenses against the Law of Nations;

To declare War, grant Letters of Marque and Reprisal, and make Rules concerning Captures on Land and Water;

To raise and support Armies, but no Appropriation of Money to that Use shall be for a longer Term than two Years;

To provide and maintain a Navy;

To make Rules for the Government and Regulation of the land and naval Forces;

To provide for calling forth the Militia to execute the Laws of the Union, suppress Insurrections and repel Invasions;

To provide for organizing, arming, and disciplining, the Militia, and for governing such Part of them as may be employed in the Service of the United

States, reserving to the States respectively, the Appointment of the Officers, and the Authority of training the Militia according to the discipline prescribed by Congress;

To exercise exclusive Legislation in all Cases whatsoever, over such District (not exceeding ten Miles square) as may, by Cession of Particular States, and the Acceptance of Congress, become the Seat of the Government of the United States, and to exercise like Authority over all Places purchased by the Consent of the Legislature of the State in which the Same shall be, for the Erection of Forts, Magazines, Arsenals, dock-Yards, and other needful Buildings;—And

To make all Laws which shall be necessary and proper for carrying into Execution the foregoing Powers, and all other Powers vested by this Constitution in the Government of the United States, or in any Department or Officer thereof.

SECTION 9. The Migration or Importation of such Persons as any of the States now existing shall think proper to admit, shall not be prohibited by the Congress prior to the Year one thousand eight hundred and eight, but a Tax or duty may be imposed on such Importation, not exceeding ten dollars for each Person.

The Privilege of the Writ of Habeas Corpus shall not be suspended, unless when in Cases of Rebellion or Invasion the public Safety may require it.

No Bill of Attainder or ex post facto Law shall be passed.

No Capitation, or other direct, Tax shall be laid, unless in Proportion to the Census of Enumeration herein before directed to be taken.

No Tax or Duty shall be laid on Articles exported from any State.

No Preference shall be given by any Regulation of Commerce or Revenue to the Ports of one State over those of another; nor shall Vessels bound to, or from, one State, be obliged to enter, clear or pay Duties in another.

No Money shall be drawn from the Treasury, but in Consequence of Appropriations made by Law; and a regular Statement and Account of the Receipts and Expenditures of all public Money shall be published from time to time.

No Title of Nobility shall be granted by the United States; And no Person holding any Office of Profit or Trust under them, shall, without the Consent of the Congress, accept of any present, Emolument, Office, or Title, of any kind whatever, from any King, Prince or foreign State.

SECTION 10. No State shall enter into any Treaty, Alliance, or Confederation; grant Letters of Marque and Reprisal; coin Money; emit Bills of Credit; make any Thing but gold and silver Coin a Tender in Payment of Debts; pass any Bill of Attainder, ex post facto Law, or Law impairing the Obligation of Contracts, or grant and Title of Nobility.

No State shall, without the Consent of the Congress, lay any Imposts or Duties on Imports or Exports, except what may be absolutely necessary for executing its inspection Laws; and the net Produce of all Duties and Imposts, laid by any State on Imports or Exports, shall be for the Use of the Treasury of the United States; and all such Laws shall be subject to the Revision and Control of the Congress.

No State shall, without the Consent of Congress, lay any Duty of Tonnage, keep Troops, or Ships of War in time of Peace, enter into any Agreement or Compact with another State, or with a foreign Power, or engage in War, unless actually invaded, or in such imminent Danger as will not admit of delay.

ARTICLE II

SECTION 1. The executive Power shall be vested in a President of the United States of America. He shall hold his Office during the Term of four Years, and, together with the Vice President, chosen for the same Term, be elected, as follows

Each State shall appoint, in such Manner as the Legislature thereof may direct, a Number of Electors, equal to the whole Number of Senators and Representatives to which the State may be entitled in the Congress; but no Senator or Representative, or Person holding an Office of Trust or Profit under the United States, shall be appointed an Elector.

The Electors shall meet in their respective States, and vote by Ballot for two Persons, of whom one at least shall not be an Inhabitant of the same State with themselves. And they shall make a List of all the Persons voted for, and of the Number of Votes for each; which List they shall sign and certify, and transmit sealed to the Seat of the Government of the United States, directed to the President of the Senate. The President of the Senate shall, in the Presence of the Senate and House of Representatives, open all the Certificates, and the Votes shall then be counted. The Person having the greatest Number of Votes shall be the President, if such Number be a Majority of the whole Number of Electors appointed; and if there be more than one who have such Majority, and have an equal Number of Votes, then the House of Representatives shall immediately chuse by Ballot one of them for President; and if no Person have a Majority, then from the five highest on the List the said House shall in like Manner chuse the President. But in chusing the President, the Votes shall be taken by States, the Representation from each State having one Vote; a quorum for this Purpose shall consist of a Member or Members from two thirds of the States, and a Majority of all the States shall be necessary to a Choice. In every Case, after the Choice of the President, the Person having the greatest Number of Votes of the Electors shall be the Vice President. But if there should remain two or more who have equal Votes, the Senate shall chuse from them by Ballot the Vice President.

The Congress may determine the Time of chusing the Electors, and the Day on which they shall give their votes; which Day shall be the same throughout the United States.

No Person except a natural born Citizen, or a Citizen of the United States, at the time of the Adoption of this Constitution, shall be eligible to the Office of President; neither shall any person be eligible to that Office who shall not have attained to the Age of thirty five Years, and been fourteen Years a Resident within the United States.

In Case of the Removal of the President from Office, or of his Death, Resignation, or Inability to discharge the Powers and Duties of the said Office, the Same shall devolve on the Vice President, and the Congress may by Law provide for the Case of Removal, Death, Resignation or Inability, both of the President and Vice President, declaring what Officer shall then act as President, and such Officer shall act accordingly, until the Disability be removed, or a President shall be elected.

The President shall, at stated Times, receive for his Services, a Compensation, which shall neither be encreased nor diminished during the Period for which he shall have been elected, and he shall not receive within that Period any other Emolument from the United States, or any of them.

Before he enter on the Execution of his Office, he shall take the following Oath or Affirmation: "I do solemnly swear (or affirm) that I will faithfully execute the Office of President of the United States, and will to the best of my Ability, preserve, protect and defend the Constitution of the United States."

SECTION 2. The President shall be Commander in Chief of the Army and Navy of the United States, and of the Militia of the several States, when called into the actual Service of the United States; he may require the Opinion, in writing, of the principal Officer in each of the executive Departments, upon any Subject relating to the Duties of their respective Offices, and he shall have Power to grant Reprieves and Pardons for Offenses against the United States, except in Cases of Impeachment.

He shall have Power, by and with the Advice and Consent of the Senate, to make Treaties, provided two thirds of the Senators present concur; and he shall nominate, and by and with the Advice and Consent of the Senate, shall appoint Ambassadors, other public Ministers and Consuls, Judges of the supreme Court, and all other Officers of the United States, whose Appointments are not herein otherwise provided for, and which shall be established by Law; but the Congress may by Law vest the Appointment of such inferior Officers, as they think proper, in the President alone, in the Courts of Law, or in the Heads of Departments.

The President shall have Power to fill up all Vacancies that may happen during the Recess of the Senate, by granting Commissions which shall expire at the End of their next Session.

SECTION 3. He shall from time to time give to the Congress Information of the State of the Union, and recommend to their Consideration such Measures as he shall judge necessary and expedient; he may, on extraordinary Occasions, convene both Houses, or either of them, and in Case of Disagreement between them, with Respect to the Time of Adjournment, he may adjourn them to such Time as he shall think proper; he shall receive Ambassadors and other public Ministers; he shall take Care that the Laws be faithfully executed, and shall Commission all the Officers of the United States.

SECTION 4. The President, Vice President and all Civil Officers of the United States, shall be removed from Office on Impeachment for, and Conviction of, Treason, Bribery, or other high Crimes and Misdemeanors.

C APPENDIX | CONSTITUTIONAL AMENDMENTS THAT AFFECT THE PRESIDENCY: AMENDMENTS XII, XX, XXII, AND XXV

AMENDMENT XII (1804)

The Electors shall meet in their respective states, and vote by ballot for President and Vice President, one of whom, at least shall not be an inhabitant of the same state with themselves; they shall name in their ballots the person voted for as President, and in distinct ballots the person voted for as Vice-President, and they shall make distinct lists of all persons voted for as President, and of all persons voted for as Vice-President, and of the number of votes for each, which lists they shall sign and certify, and transmit sealed to the seat of the government of the United States, directed to the President of the Senate;—The President of the Senate shall, in the presence of the Senate and House of Representatives, open all the certificates and the votes shall then be counted;— The person having the greatest number of votes for President, shall be the President, if such number be a majority of the whole number of Electors appointed; and if no person have such majority, then from the persons having the highest numbers not exceeding three on the list of those voted for as President, the House of Representatives shall choose immediately, by ballot, the President. But in choosing the President, the votes shall be taken by states, the representation from each state having one vote; a quorum for this purpose shall consist of a member or members from two-thirds of the states, and a majority of all the states shall be necessary to a choice. [And if the House of Representatives shall not choose a President whenever the right of choice shall devolve upon them, before the fourth day of March next following, then the Vice-President shall act as President, as in the case of the death or other constitutional disability of the President—] The person having the greatest number of votes as Vice-President, shall be the Vice-President, if such number be a majority of the whole number of Electors appointed, and if no person have a majority, then from the two highest numbers on the list, the Senate shall choose the Vice-President; a quorum for the purpose shall consist of two-thirds of the whole number of Senators, and a majority of the whole number shall be necessary to a choice. But no person constitutionally ineligible to the office of President shall be eligible to that of Vice-President of the United States.

AMENDMENT XX (1933)

SECTION 1. The terms of the President and Vice President shall end at noon on the 20th day of January, and the terms of Senators and Representatives at noon on the 3d day of January, of the years in which such terms would have ended if this article had not been ratified; and the terms of their successors shall then begin.

SECTION 2. The Congress shall assemble at least once every year, and such meeting shall begin at noon on the 3d day of January, unless they shall by law appoint a different day.

SECTION 3. If, at the time fixed for the beginning of the term of the President, the President elect shall have died; the Vice President elect shall become President. If a President shall not have been chosen before the time fixed for the beginning of his term, or if the President elect shall have failed to qualify, then the Vice President elect shall act as President until a President shall have qualified; and the Congress may by law provide for the case wherein neither a President elect nor a Vice President elect shall have qualified, declaring who shall then act as President, or the manner in which one who is to act shall be selected, and such person shall act accordingly until a President or Vice President shall have qualified.

SECTION 4. The Congress may by law provide for the case of the death of any of the persons from whom the House of Representatives may choose a President whenever the right of choice shall have devolved upon them, and for the case of the death of any of the persons from whom the Senate may choose a Vice President whenever the right of choice shall have devolved upon them.

SECTION 5. Sections 1 and 2 shall take effect on the 15th day of October following the ratification of this article.

SECTION 6. This article shall be inoperative unless it shall have been ratified as an amendment to the Constitution by the legislatures of three-fourths of the several States within seven years from the date of its submission.

Amendment XXII (1951)

SECTION 1. No person shall be elected to the office of the President more than twice, and no person who has held the office of President, or acted as President, for more than two years of a term to which some other person was elected President shall be elected to the office of President more than once. But this Article shall not apply to any person holding the office of President when this Article was proposed by the Congress, and shall not prevent any person who may be holding the office of President, or acting as President, during the term within which this Article becomes operative from holding the office of President or acting as President during the remainder of such term.

SECTION 2. This article shall be inoperative unless it shall have been ratified as an amendment to the Constitution by the legislatures of three-fourths of the several States within seven years from the date of its submission to the States by the Congress.

Amendment XXV (1967)

SECTION 1. In the case of the removal of the President from office or of his death or resignation, the Vice President shall become President.

SECTION 2. Whenever there is a vacancy in the office of the Vice President, the President shall nominate a Vice President who shall take office upon confirmation by a majority vote of both Houses of Congress.

SECTION 3. Whenever the President transmits to the President pro tempore of the Senate and the Speaker of the House of Representatives his written declaration that he is unable to discharge the power and duties of his office, and until he transmits to them a written declaration to the contrary, such powers and duties shall be discharged by the Vice President as Acting President.

SECTION 4. Whenever the Vice President and a majority of either the principal officers of the executive departments or of such a body as Congress may by law provide, transmit to the President pro tempore of the Senate and the Speaker of the House of Representatives their written declaration that the President is unable to discharge the powers and duties of his office, the Vice President shall immediately assume the powers and duties of the office as Acting President.

Thereafter, when the President transmits to the President pro tempore of the Senate and the Speaker of the House of Representatives his written declaration that no inability exists, he shall resume the powers and duties of his office unless the Vice President and a majority of either the principal officers of the executive department or of such other body as Congress may by law provide, transmit within four days to the President pro tempore of the Senate and the Speaker of the House of Representatives their written declaration that the President is unable to discharge the powers and duties of his office. Thereupon Congress shall decide the issue, assembling within forty-eight hours for that purpose if not in session. If the Congress, within twenty-one days after receipt of the latter written declaration, or, if Congress is not in session, within twenty-one days after Congress is required to assemble, determines by two-thirds vote of both Houses that the President is unable to discharge the powers and duties of his office, the Vice President shall continue to discharge the same as Acting President; otherwise, the President shall resume the powers and duties of his office.

Index